HISTORICAL DICTIONARIES OF RELIGIONS, PHILOSOPHIES, AND MOVEMENTS
Edited by Jon Woronoff

1. *Buddhism,* by Charles S. Prebish, 1993
2. *Mormonism,* by Davis Bitton, 1994. *Out of print. See No. 32.*
3. *Ecumenical Christianity,* by Ans Joachim van der Bent, 1994
4. *Terrorism,* by Sean Anderson and Stephen Sloan, 1995. *Out of Print. See No. 41.*
5. *Sikhism,* by W. H. McLeod, 1995
6. *Feminism,* by Janet K. Boles and Diane Long Hoeveler, 1995
7. *Olympic Movement,* by Ian Buchanan and Bill Mallon, 1995. *Out of print. See No. 39.*
8. *Methodism,* by Charles Yrigoyen Jr. and Susan E. Warrick, 1996
9. *Orthodox Church,* by Michael Prokurat, Alexander Golitzin, and Michael D. Peterson, 1996
10. *Organized Labor,* by James C. Docherty, 1996
11. *Civil Rights Movement,* by Ralph E. Luker, 1997
12. *Catholicism,* by William J. Collinge, 1997
13. *Hinduism,* by Bruce M. Sullivan, 1997
14. *North American Environmentalism,* by Edward R. Wells and Alan M. Schwartz, 1997
15. *Welfare State,* by Bent Greve, 1998
16. *Socialism,* by James C. Docherty, 1997
17. *Bahá'í Faith,* by Hugh C. Adamson and Philip Hainsworth, 1998
18. *Taoism,* by Julian F. Pas in cooperation with Man Kam Leung, 1998
19. *Judaism,* by Norman Solomon, 1998
20. *Green Movement*, by Elim Papadakis, 1998
21. *Nietzscheanism,* by Carol Diethe, 1999
22. *Gay Liberation Movement,* by Ronald J. Hunt, 1999
23. *Islamic Fundamentalist Movements in the Arab World, Iran, and Turkey,* by Ahmad S. Moussalli, 1999
24. *Reformed Churches,* by Robert Benedetto, Darrell L. Guder, and Donald K. McKim, 1999
25. *Baptists*, by William H. Brackney, 1999
26. *Cooperative Movement*, by Jack Shaffer, 1999
27. *Reformation and Counter-Reformation*, by Hans J. Hillerbrand, 2000

28. *Shakers,* by Holley Gene Duffield, 2000
29. *United States Political Parties,* by Harold F. Bass Jr., 2000
30. *Heidegger's Philosophy,* by Alfred Denker, 2000
31. *Zionism,* by Rafael Medoff and Chaim I. Waxman, 2000
32. *Mormonism,* 2nd ed., by Davis Bitton, 2000
33. *Kierkegaard's Philosophy,* by Julia Watkin, 2001
34. *Hegelian Philosophy*, by John W. Burbidge, 2001
35. *Lutheranism*, by Günther Gassmann in cooperation with Duane H. Larson and Mark W. Oldenburg, 2001
36. *Holiness Movement*, by William Kostlevy, 2001
37. *Islam,* by Ludwig W. Adamec, 2001
38. *Shinto,* by Stuart D. B. Picken, 2002
39. *Olympic Movement,* 2nd ed., by Ian Buchanan and Bill Mallon, 2001
40. *Slavery and Abolition,* by Martin A. Klein, 2002
41. *Terrorism,* 2nd ed., by Sean Anderson and Stephen Sloan, 2002
42. *New Religious Movements,* by George D. Chryssides, 2001
43. *Prophets in Islam and Judaism,* by Scott B. Noegel and Brannon M. Wheeler, 2002
44. *The Friends (Quakers)*, by Margery Post Abbott, Mary Ellen Chijioke, Pink Dandelion, and John William Oliver Jr., 2003
45. *Lesbian Liberation Movement,* by JoAnne Myers, 2003

Historical Dictionary of the Friends (Quakers)

Margery Post Abbott
Mary Ellen Chijioke
Pink Dandelion
John William Oliver Jr.

Historical Dictionaries of Religions, Philosophies, and Movements, No. 44

The Scarecrow Press, Inc.
Lanham, Maryland, and Oxford
2003

SCARECROW PRESS, INC.

Published in the United States of America
by Scarecrow Press, Inc.
A Member of the Rowman & Littlefield Publishing Group
4501 Forbes Boulevard, Suite 200
Lanham, Maryland 20706
www.scarecrowpress.com

PO Box 317
Oxford
OX2 9RU, UK

British Library Cataloguing in Publication Information Available

Library of Congress Cataloging-in-Publication Data

Abbott, Margery Post.
Historical dictionary of the Friends (Quakers) / Margery Post Abbott, Mary Ellen Chijioke, Pink Dandelion
p. cm. — (Historical dictionaries of religions, philosophies, and movements; no. 44)
Includes bibliographical references.
ISBN 0-8108-4483-4 (hardcover : alk. paper)
1. Society of Friends—History—Dictionaries. I. Chijioke, Mary Ellen, 1944– II. Dandelion, Pink. III. Title. IV. Series.
BX7611 .A3 2003
289.6'03—dc21

2002012989

∞™ The paper used in this publication meets the minimum requirements of American National Standard for Information Sciences—Permanence of Paper for Printed Library Materials, ANSI/NISO Z39.48-1992.
Manufactured in the United States of America.

Contents

Editor's Foreword

When it comes to religions, there is little correlation between size and influence, and even less the degree of piety or closeness to the truth. Quakerism (or the Religious Society of Friends) only numbers a few hundred thousand members at most. This certainly makes it one of the smaller denominations. Yet it is known around the world and, increasingly, has members almost worldwide. From its origins in Great Britain, it has spread to North America, and more recently Latin America, Africa, and Asia. Such basic concepts as the "inward light" and "friendly persuasion" are widely known and admired. The call for cooperation, joint decision making, and peaceful resolution of problems has even been heeded by politicians, definitely to the good of all. Yet, the Quakers have not been immune to divisions and differences amongst themselves, few as they are. Nor have they remained so rooted to the past that they could not grow with the times and adapt to varied cultures, climates, and social contexts.

This *Historical Dictionary of the Friends (Quakers)* is very welcome, not only because it tells us more about this small denomination, which remains rather poorly known despite its popular appeal and sometimes romantic images in the general literature. Indeed, by focusing on facts, which are presented in a straightforward manner without unnecessary flourishes, it helps us to escape appealing but misleading stereotypes and come closer to realities. It makes it easier to grasp why the Quakers' influence has reached far beyond their own circle and also why that circle has remained relatively tight. The bulk of the information appears in the dictionary entries on persons, places, events, institutions and associations, and economic, social, cultural, and religious activities. The introduction integrates these many facets, and the chronology shows the progression over time. But there will always be more to learn, and the seeker can find further sources in the comprehensive bibliography.

This volume was edited by four persons who know the Religious Society of Friends very well, although they would probably not want to be called "experts." They are all or have been Quakers and, most fortunately, they have a varied background with direct exposure to Quakerism in Great Britain, the United States, and Africa. The three Friends are active in their local and broader meetings. Most of them are, at least partly, academics, which means they have lectured on Quakerism to students, and they have also written on the subject for a broader audience, whether in articles or books. One is also a librarian, most useful for the bibliography. The details of their combined qualifications can be found at the end of the book. Here at the beginning it is merely necessary to note that Margery Post Abbott, Mary Ellen Chijioke, Pink Dandelion, and John William Oliver Jr. have made a precious contribution to understanding Quakerism, something that will benefit Quakers and outsiders alike.

Jon Woronoff
Series Editor

Preface

This volume attempts to describe the scope and history of the Religious Society of Friends (Quakers) worldwide and the modern diversity of its theology and practice. In many ways Friends are a microcosm of the multiple perspectives and resultant tensions within western Christianity today. Some Friends are active participants in the Christian evangelical movement, others are focused on interfaith work or are influenced by non-Christian writings and experience. Friends' belief in peace and justice leads some people to radical political witness, while others work within the governments of their respective countries. Their form of worship differs among the various branches, and no central governing or coordinating body speaks for all Friends.

We have sought to provide a balanced view of the many varieties of Quaker faith and practice. To do this, we address theological questions by offering first the perspective of the founding members of the Society, then indicating the evolution that has produced a wide range of belief and practice in succeeding centuries.

Various Friends have long wanted a dictionary or encyclopedia that might serve as a widely accepted reference for distinctive Quaker language and practices as well as an easily accessible guide for the general reader who knows little about the Religious Society of Friends. We are thankful to Scarecrow Press for providing the impetus and funding for such a volume.

Most biblical quotations are from the New Revised Standard Version. Words in bold or in all capitals refer to other entries in this dictionary. "Britain" refers to England, Scotland, Wales, the Isle of Man, and the Channel Islands. Dates before 1752, when England adopted the Gregorian calendar, are given in both Old Style and New Style, where applicable. For example, January 1660 under the Julian calendar would be considered January 1661 today and is cited in this volume as January 1660/61.

A sampling of living persons is included among the biographies, but it should be noted that, as Friends have no bishops and little hierarchical structure, there are many more equally important people who have been omitted for lack of space. In part, this reflects the absence of any central governing body among Friends, which leaves no easy measure for indicating which contemporary individuals should be identified. This decision also reflects the fact that the number of Friends deserving mention is much too large for incorporation in this slim volume. A separate group of scholars based at Swarthmore and Haverford Colleges in the United States and at the library at Friends House (Britain) are in the process of compiling a Dictionary of Quaker Biography.

Length of the entry sometimes reflects the complexity of a particular topic rather than its relative importance. Added emphasis is also given to topics where Quaker usage differs significantly from standard terminology and to those not covered by other standard reference works.

The *Historical Dictionary of the Friends (Quakers)* is the combined work of Friends from Europe, North America, Africa, South America, and Asia with experience in every branch of Friends. A full list of the contributors is included as an appendix. When more than one name is listed after an entry, the names are in alphabetical order. Brief biographical information about the members of our Advisory Committee is also appended. We wish to offer special thanks to members of our Advisory Committee who not only wrote many entries for the dictionary, but also read the manuscript and offered much insight on this volume.

We have sought to present a perspective that affirms the common heritage shared by all Friends and to describe, with respect, the wide variation among Friends today. We intend this work to give the general reader a sense of who Friends are and the sources of today's range of beliefs and practices. We also hope this volume might provide a useful tool for Friends to see themselves as a whole and to consider anew how each might fit into this complex gathering of individuals.

Please note that boldface terms throughout the chronology, introduction, and dictionary refer to main entries in the dictionary.

Acronyms and Abbreviations

AEC	Associated Executive Committee on Indian Affairs
AFSC	American Friends Service Committee
AV	Authorized Version of the Bible (King James Version)
CO	Conscientious Objectors
CPS	Civilian Public Service Camps
CSAYM	Central and South Africa Yearly Meeting
EAYM	East Africa Yearly Meeting
EFI	Evangelical Friends International
EFM	Evangelical Friends Mission
ESR	Earlham School of Religion
FAM	Friends Africa Industrial Mission
FCNL	Friends Committee on National Legislation
FGC	Friends General Conference
FOR	Fellowship of Reconciliation
FUM	Friends United Meeting
FWCC	Friends World Committee for Consultation
INELA	Iglesia Nacional Evangélica "Los Amigos"
MM	Monthly Meeting
NGO	Nongovernmental Organization
QMI	Quaker Men International
UN	United Nations
UNESCO	United Nations Economic and Social Council
USFWI	United Society of Friends Women International
WCTU	Woman's Christian Temperance Union
WILPF	Women's International League for Peace and Freedom
YM	Yearly Meeting
YMCA	Young Men's Christian Association
YWCA	Young Women's Christian Association

Chronology

1624 Birth date of **George Fox**.

1647 George Fox has opening that "there is one, even, **Christ** Jesus, who can speak to thy condition."

1652 George Fox's vision on **Pendle Hill**, **England**, of a great people to be gathered. Considered the beginning of the **Quaker** movement.

1656 First Friends arrive in **North America**. **James Nayler**'s entry into Bristol and trial by Parliament.

1659–1660/1661 Four Quakers hanged on Boston Common; anti-Quaker laws enacted in Virginia.

1660/1661 Declaration of **Peace Testimony** to Charles II of England.

1661 First **General Meeting** held in Newport, Rhode Island; start of New England **Yearly Meeting**, the oldest such body in the world.

1668 First Quaker schools in England.

1670 Trial of **William Penn** and **William Meade** establishing rights of juries.

1675 Quakers acquire West New Jersey.

1676 **Robert Barclay**'s *Apology* published; **Meeting for Sufferings** organized in London.

1681 William Penn obtains charter for Pennsylvania.

1683 First Friends' school in North America.

1688 Germantown Meeting in Pennsylvania protests against slavery.

1691 Death of George Fox.

1694 Publication of George Fox's *Journal*.

1694 **John Archdale** appointed governor of Carolina colony.

1727 **James Logan** demonstrates function of pollen in fertilizing Indian corn.

1756 Quakers relinquish control of Pennsylvania legislature.

1758 Philadelphia Yearly Meeting condemns slaveholding by Friends.

1774 Publication of **John Woolman**'s *Journal*. Seventeen Philadelphia Quakers exiled to Virginia for refusing to take oath of allegiance.

1787 Northwest Ordinance opened the area north of the Ohio River for settlement as free territory and **migration**.

1790 **Moses Brown** applies power-driven machinery to spinning of cotton yarn in Rhode Island.

1796 York Retreat, the first modern mental hospital, is founded by Friends in England.

1808 **John Dalton** states atomic theory.

1813 **Elizabeth Fry** begins **prison** reform work at Newgate prison in England.

1816 First **Peace** Society in England founded by **William Allen** and Joseph T. Price.

1817 Friends Asylum, the first modern mental hospital in the United States, founded in Frankford, Pennsylvania.

1821 Benjamin Lundy begins publication of *The Genius of Universal Emancipation*, an antislavery periodical.

1825 **Edward Pease** opens the Stockton and Darlington Railway, the first passenger railway in England.

1827–1828 The Great Separation in North America into **Hicksite** and **Orthodox** branches.

1833 Joseph Pease elected to the British Parliament; **John Greenleaf Whittier** published *Justice and Expediency*.

1835 Isaac Pidgeon and family become first Quakers to settle west of the Mississippi River.

1843 **John Bright** enters British Parliament.

1843 Indiana Yearly Meeting of Anti-Slavery Friends separates from Indiana Yearly Meeting.

1845 The **Gurneyite-Wilburite** separation in New England.

1846 **Levi Coffin** settles in Cincinnati, Ohio, and becomes known as "president" of the **underground railroad**.

1846–1847 Quaker famine relief in Ireland.

1848 **Lucretia Mott** initiates organization of the first **women**'s rights convention in Seneca Falls, New York.

1854 Gurneyite-Wilburite separation in Ohio.

1860 Conference held at Ackworth, England, for active consideration of new forms of foreign **missionary** work by Friends.

1862 Quakers undertake **relief** and **educational** work for freed slaves.

1865 Provisional Committee of Foreign Gospel Service established in England.

1866 **Rachel Metcalf** sent by British Friends to undertake missionary work in India; Home Mission Association established by the women of Indiana Yearly Meeting.

1869 American Friends undertake supervision of Indian agencies in Nebraska, Kansas, and Indian Territories; **Sybil** and **Eli Jones** sent by New York Yearly Meeting as missionaries to Ramallah, Palestine, and help establish school for girls there.

1870–1871 British Quaker relief work in Franco-Prussian War; Indiana Yearly Meeting Foreign Missionary Association established.

1871–1895 Gulielma M. H. Purdie of North Carolina and Samuel A. Purdie of New York sent as missionaries to **Mexico**, initially by Indiana Yearly Meeting.

Ca. 1875 **Pastoral Movement** takes hold among American Friends.

1882 John Bright resigns from British cabinet in protest against bombardment of Alexandria, Egypt; Theophilus Waldmeier establishes Girls School in Brummanha, Lebanon, then Lebanon Hospital for Mental Diseases.

1885 Joseph and Sarah Cosand of Kansas sent by Philadelphia Yearly Meeting (Orthodox) to open a mission in Japan.

1886 Iowa Yearly Meeting is first to formally accept pastoral system.

1887 **Richmond Declaration of Faith** adopted by most Gurneyite North American Yearly Meetings.

1891 Women's Foreign Missionary Society of Western Yearly Meeting established.

1892 **Lenna M. Stanley** sent by Ohio Yearly Meeting to China. **Walter and Emma Malone** open a Christian Workers Training School in Cleveland, Ohio.

1892–1938 **Esther Baird** sent by Ohio Yearly Meeting as missionary to India.

1895 **Manchester Conference** held in England.

1897 Robert and Carry Sams sent by California Yearly Meeting to Alaska.

1900 **Friends General Conference** (FGC) established.

1902 Five Years Meeting (renamed **Friends United Meeting** [FUM] in 1965) established.

1903 **Willis R. Hotchkiss**, **Arthur B. Chilson**, and Edgar Hole sent by Five Years Meeting to **East Africa**.

1914 War Victim's Relief Committee established by British Friends. Friends Ambulance Unit created to provide care for soldiers and civilians injured in World War I.

1917 **American Friends Service Committee** (AFSC) established.

1919–1924 Friends undertake feeding program for German children at request of **Herbert Hoover**; program then expands into Poland, Russia, and other European countries.

1920 First "All Friends Conference" held in London and publishes *Friends and War*.

1921 Emma Morrow and Walter Lanstom sent by Central Yearly Meeting to Bolivia.

1924 Central Yearly Meeting, Westfield, Indiana, withdraws from Five Years Meeting.

1926 Oregon Yearly Meeting withdraws from Five Years Meeting.

1928 Herbert Hoover elected president of the United States. British Friends Service Council formed.

1933 AFSC begins work camp programs for youth.

1937–1939 Nonpartisan relief work in Spanish Civil War.

1937 Second World Conference of Friends held in Swarthmore, Pennsylvania. **Friends World Committee for Consultation** (FWCC) founded.

1939–1946 Quaker war relief in Europe and Asia.

1940 **Civilian Public Service** camps for **conscientious objectors** to war established by U.S. government and administered by AFSC.

1945 Reunion of yearly meetings separated in 1845 to form the modern New England Yearly Meeting.

1943 **Friends Committee on National Legislation** (FCNL) established.

1946 **East Africa** Yearly Meeting formed, the first such body in Africa.

1947 Nobel Peace Prize awarded to AFSC and Friends Service Council (**Britain**) on behalf of the **Religious Society of Friends**.

1947–1970 Association of Evangelical Friends meets regularly.

1952 Third World Conference of Friends held in Oxford, England.

1955 Meetings divided by 1827 separation rejoin, forming united yearly meetings in New York, Canada, and Philadelphia.

1960 Opening of **Earlham School of Religion**.

1963–1965 Establishment of Evangelical Friends Alliance (becoming **Evangelical Friends International** [EFI] in 1990).

1967 Fourth World Conference of Friends held in Greensboro, North Carolina.

1968 Separated yearly meetings in the Middle Atlantic states form the **consolidated** Baltimore Yearly Meeting. **Richard Nixon** elected president of the United States.

1970 St. Louis Conference on The Future of Friends sponsored by Committee of Concerned Friends for Renewal initiates "Faith and Life Movement"; Evangelical Friends Church in Guatemala established as an independent body.

1973 Committee on Concern formed; becoming Friends Committee for Lesbian and Gay Concerns in 1978.

1974 Bolivian Friends Yearly Meeting established; **Friends Disaster Service** (U.S.) formed.

1975 First "Youthquake" held in Southern California, gathering young Friends, particularly from the **programmed meeting** traditions; establishment of the **Alternatives to Violence Program** in New York state prisons; New Call to Peacemaking Program begins series of conferences including Mennonites and the Church of the Brethren.

1976 First National Friends' Ministers' Conference held in Dallas, Texas; **New Foundation Fellowship** formed.

1985 First World Gathering of Young Friends held at Guilford College, North Carolina.

1990 First International Theological Conference of Quaker Women held at **Woodbrooke Quaker Study Centre** in England.

1991 Fifth World Conference of Friends on Three Sites held at venues in Kenya, the Netherlands, and Honduras.

1993 Fellowship of Quakers in the Arts formed. Formation of a new **Conservative** yearly meeting, "Friends in Christ." Opening of the *Iglesia de los Amigos Evangelicos* (Evangelical Friends Church) in the metropolitan area of Mexico City. Some Friends' groups cosponsor the Parliament of the World's Religions.

1994 Friends Church Southwest Yearly Meeting brought its entire organization and missions program under the umbrella of EFI.

1996 Sixth Consultation on Mission and Service held in Uganda.

1998 FGC establishes its Traveling Ministries Program.

1999 EFI-Africa Region opened the **Great Lakes School of Theology** at Bujumbura, Burundi. Right Sharing of World Resources is set off from FWCC as an independent organization.

2001 Great Lakes Initiative begun to promote reconciliation in Rwanda and Burundi.

Introduction

The modern reputation of Friends is grounded in the **relief work** they have conducted in the presence and aftermath of war. Friends (also known as **Quakers**) have coordinated the feeding and evacuation of children from war zones around the world. They have helped displaced persons without regard to politics. They have engaged in the relief of suffering in places as far-flung as Ireland, France, Germany, Ethiopia, Egypt, China, and India. Their work was acknowledged with the award of the Nobel Peace Prize in 1947 to the **American Friends Service Committee** (AFSC) and the Friends Service Council of Great **Britain**. More often, however, Quakers live, worship, and work quietly, without seeking public attention for themselves.

Formally known as the **Religious Society of Friends** or the **Friends Church**, Quakers are not an easy group to categorize. The Quaker movement began in Europe in the 17th century and rapidly spread to **North America**. In the 20th century, Friends developed vibrant and growing churches in **East Africa** and among the Aymara people of Bolivia and Peru. Most Friends are ardent believers in the saving work of **Christ** Jesus. Some Friends draw sustenance from Buddhism or Judaism as well as Christianity and see the **Light** working in people of every faith as well as in people without any religious affiliation. Some Friends gather together for worship in silent, expectant waiting without appointed **ministers** or formal sermons. Others have professionally educated **pastors** who preach each week and lead worship in a way familiar to most Protestants. Friends are a complex group, embodying many contradictions and tensions, yet they still have managed to make an impact well beyond their numbers.

Distinctive Quaker teachings are affirmed in all branches of their Society. Essential to these doctrines is the very real possibility of an individual, direct, and experiential relationship with **God** and the potential of a transformed life that bears witness to that relationship. Friends' worship and business practices reflect their belief in Christ present, guiding the congregation as well as individuals. Their witness, which Friends speak of as "**testimonies**," connects faith with daily living. Most modern Friends affirm a particular **peace testimony** as well as testimonies for personal integrity, the **equality** of all people, and **simplicity**. Friends also believe in the importance of listening for divine guidance; the potential for the presence of the Spirit during **worship** without the use of the traditional outward **sacraments**; the conduct of church **business** in a **meeting for worship**; and the possibility that all members may see themselves as having a call to some form of **ministry**.

As part of living out their faith, most Friends hold a corporate testimony for peace, which is experienced in many ways, based on individual consciences. They have established peace institutes in several countries and are engaged in nonviolent conflict resolution in places as diverse as Northern Ireland, eastern Europe, and South Africa. During the 20th century, Friends in the United States and Britain helped establish the right to refuse to serve in the armed forces for reasons of conscience. During **World War II**, some joined the military, believing this was the best way to stop Hitler's atrocities and bring peace, but others worked in the Friends Ambulance Units, helped Jews and other threatened peoples escape Europe, or worked in **Civilian Public Service** camps. More recently, Friends risked their livelihoods and lives as they sought to reconcile their neighbors in Burundi and Rwanda.

BEGINNINGS

Friends once saw themselves as having special insights to **Truth**. Their roots are in the turmoil of 17th-century England, which was marked by the execution of King Charles I in the wake of the **Puritan** victory in the Civil War. **George Fox** was a young man at the time and like so many others, intensely religious. At age 19, he left home to continue his search to know God. He wandered England, reading the Bible, facing temptations and asking questions of everyone he met who professed to be Christian. In 1647, he had a great revelation, which he reports in his ***Journal***, saying, "And when all my hopes in [the priests] and in all men were gone, . . . Oh then, I heard a voice which said, 'There is one, even

Christ Jesus, that can speak to thy condition,' and when I heard it, my heart did leap for joy." Fox also had a vision of the ocean of light which overcomes the ocean of darkness he saw within the human condition. Then, after a period of depression, he "was come up in spirit through the flaming sword" into the "state of Adam which he was in before he fell." Fox then saw in spirit "a state in Christ Jesus, that should never fall." This series of visions articulates a long process whereby Fox faced the darkness within his own soul with the help of Christ. By knowing the **truth** of human nature and the Truth and Love that is Christ Jesus, Fox came to know what early Friends spoke of as "**perfection**": whereby all humanity might live in the perfect love of God. This experiential knowledge of the living presence of Christ, which offered freedom from **sin** for all people who turned "to the grace of God, and to the Truth in the heart, which came by Jesus," ignited Fox and so many others.

In 1652, George Fox had a vision on **Pendle Hill**, **England**, of a "great people to be gathered." Fox quickly attracted many like-minded **Seekers** as he traveled through northern England. His success in convincing hearers in the following weeks is generally acknowledged as the founding of the Quaker movement. A number of individuals calling themselves the **Children of the Light** and known more recently as the **Valiant Sixty** soon spread across England in pairs, setting up and nurturing meetings for worship. Several of these "publishers of Truth" spread their message to England's American colonies. A few also carried their message across Europe to Africa and Asia. Individuals such as **James Nayler**, **Edward Burrough**, **Francis Howgill**, **Elizabeth Hooten**, and **William Dewsbury** were among the leaders of the growing movement. **Women** preached regularly, and **Margaret Fell** became widely known for her extensive work in supporting those traveling in the ministry or in prison, lobbying the king and Parliament, and in helping **meetings** to organize. They became known pejoratively as Quakers because of the way they trembled at the power of God as they worshipped, and gradually came to also call themselves Friends of Truth in reference to John 15, when Jesus named his disciples as his friends.

The first generation of Friends knew Christ as the Light or the Seed present to every person and as the present Guide to those who responded to the inward Light. They saw that the Light was present in women, children, and people of all races as well as men. This was a radical and upsetting doctrine in an age when Calvinists taught that **salvation** was only for the chosen few. Friends sought to bring every detail of their lives and words into conformance with the Light of Christ. Integrity was central. They refused to take oaths, seeing them as implying a double standard of truth and in contradiction to the words of Jesus in Matthew 5:37: "Let your word be 'Yes, Yes' or 'No, No'; anything more than this comes from the evil one." They insisted on holding public **meetings for worship** even after the passage of the Quaker Act in 1662 made such gatherings illegal and grounds for imprisonment. Simplicity in living, dress, and speech was another aspect of their faith. Calling all people to equal humility before God, they refused to tip their hats in deference to anyone, even the king. The individualism of their **theology** was balanced by a commitment to unity in church government and mutual support in a loving community.

Friends saw themselves as living in the "end times," believing that the **Day of the Lord** had come. Their response was to call on people to open their hearts to Christ and to end all dishonest dealings, hatred, and greed. They were convinced that Christ had washed away all past sin and the Light of Christ would lead them away from present sin. In this, they were called to be perfect, even as God is perfect (Matthew 5:48). The **Lamb's War** was part of their theology, a war against evil with Christ at its head. The Lamb's War was an unusual war that turned all human expectations upside down. The only weapons were spiritual. Wealth and possessions were not the goal. This was a war won in the human heart and soul with victory evidenced by humility, simplicity, and the equality of all people before the perfection of God's love. As all persons are sanctified in that love, they are freed from the power of sin and their lives will become more like that of Christ.

EVOLUTION OF A PECULIAR PEOPLE

The first generation of Friends burst out upon the world with immense vigor and, as a consequence, experienced substantial persecution. The 1660s, which saw the restoration of a Stuart king, Charles II, to the throne, also saw the immediacy of victory in the Lamb's War receding and increased pressure on Friends and other dissenting groups. Leaders like Fox and Fell felt the need for a more formal network of meetings that could keep track of those who suffered because of their faith so as to give them physical and spiritual support. Friends also began to articulate a **discipline** for individuals who called themselves Quakers and moderated their radical theology. They also developed a process based on Matthew, Chapter 18, for laboring with "disorderly walkers" (2 Thess. 3:6) who did not behave in a manner Friends saw as consistent with the Truth.

In 1689, the passage of the Act of Toleration remitted the severe penalties on dissent from the Church of England and allowed Quakers in England to practice their faith for the first time without fear of imprisonment. They gradually came to see themselves as a "**peculiar** people," not in the sense of "strange" but rather as "select," a "holy nation, God's own people" (Titus 2:14). In their own eyes, they became a "precious remnant" keeping Truth alive until the world was ready to hear it.

The 18th century was a complex time, as Friends sought to define a way of life founded on living out the Kingdom of God without the evangelical and expressive fervor of the Lamb's War. Great energy went into the creation of the "**Holy Experiment**"—the colony of Pennsylvania established by **William Penn** that attracted many Friends from England and Wales. Pennsylvania was governed by Quakers until 1756, when the crisis caused by the French and Indian War led most Friends to leave the government rather than support the war effort. Friends came to boast about their respect for civil liberties and religious freedom. They claimed that their policy of respect for the rights of **Native Americans** brought peace without the necessity of taxes to support the military. Many Friends prospered as their frugal, careful ways brought substantial wealth. In the early colonial period, Friends were also active in governing other colonies, particularly in Rhode Island, West New Jersey, and the Carolinas, where Quaker **John Archdale** was governor for two terms.

As Friends moved away from the Lamb's War, they focused increasingly on **family** life and the continuation of a system of traveling ministers, who knit together the now far-flung and sometimes isolated groupings of Quakers. Individual Friends with a gift for ministry often felt the call to travel for weeks and months on end through all kinds of physical conditions in order to share what they knew of Christ in their lives and to nurture Friends' testimonies. They worshipped with Friends wherever they went and met with each family, teaching and reinforcing the discipline of the Society.

Friends became known for their skill as merchants, prospered as farmers, and were leaders in the Nantucket whaling industry. In Britain, the law prevented Friends from attending universities or participating in politics. They continued to experience other restrictions, largely because of their refusal to take oaths. Instead, they found outlets for inventiveness in **business**, industry, and the growing field of **science**.

The Great Awakening (1726–1756) among Protestants on both sides of the Atlantic grew up around men such as George Whitefield, an Anglican priest, and the American Jonathan Edwards. It found echoes among Friends concerned about spiritual renewal within their own Society, which was struggling to maintain a distinctive culture against the pressures of increasing worldliness and wealth. **Samuel Fothergill**, a British Friend, was one of many who traveled widely both in his home country and in the colonies calling for a restoration of the primitive Christianity of the first generation of Friends. The reformers sought to persuade Friends to strengthen the discipline, maintain distinctive patterns of **plain dress and speech**, and end all ownership of slaves. The tireless work of individuals like **John Woolman** and **Anthony Benezet** led, by the end of the century, to a strong stance by all Friends against owning or trading human beings as slaves and laid the groundwork for the **abolitionists** of the following century.

Often referred to as the **Quietist** period, the 18th century, however, was both a period of significant activism and a time when Friends affirmed "The **Hedge**" between themselves and the world through adherence to the testimonies and restrictions against **marriage** to non-Quakers. Quietism—the emphasis on subduing self-will in both daily life and meeting for worship—always had been a central aspect of Friends' faith from the start. Friends had long sought to shelter their children and raise them in the Truth. They continued to strengthen the close-knit networks among families. These networks provided support throughout **continental Europe** and North America and also gave welcome hospitality to ministers traveling to distant Quaker meetings. They also offered opportunities for Quaker businessmen and industrialists to meet other like-minded individuals. **Overseers** from each meeting supported and nurtured members yet also worked to change the habits of those who got into debt, drank excessively, or otherwise violated Quaker perceptions of the Christian life. The distinctive plain dress and speech of Friends clearly identified them as different from their neighbors. Wanting to ensure that children were brought up in the faith and adults lived a life consistent with Truth, meetings enforced rules under which Friends were **disowned** for such varied reasons as marrying contrary to discipline (i.e., by a judge or a clergyman), playing cards, or cheating in business. By the end of the century, Friends were disowned if they fought in any war, including the American Revolutionary War, owned slaves, or otherwise refused to comply with the discipline.

SEPARATION AND REVIVAL

The late Quietist period was a time when some meetings lost members and felt a lack of vibrant ministry. In addition, the strict discipline drove many young people out of the Society. The second Great Awakening (ca. 1795–1830) stirred up new interest in biblical literacy and conformity of belief. In Britain, where **New Lights** had already been disowned, most Friends embraced evangelical theology, and no major schisms occurred. The Society opened to the wider world while retaining the traditional **unprogrammed** form of meeting for worship. The start of the 19th century was filled with the energy of the successful industrialists, the work of Friends like **Elizabeth Fry** in initiating **prison** reform, and a new wave of Friends such as **James Backhouse**, who traveled overseas and started meetings in **Australia** in 1832.

On the other side of the Atlantic, the opening of the American continent following the Revolution attracted Friends into the Ohio Valley and points west. Migrants were also attracted by the passage of the Northwest Ordinance, which prevented slavery in the Northwest Territories. Once all Friends were free of slave holding, many individual Friends turned their attention to ending that institution in the United States and **Caribbean** Islands.

The varied pressures of the new nation, however, combined to stretch Friends' meetings in North America to the breaking point. In 1827 disagreements over theology and church governance and differences between urban and rural perspectives, combined with strong personalities among Quakers in Philadelphia, culminated in what is known as the **Great Separation**. Two groups emerged, the **Hicksites** and the **Orthodox**. Each claimed to be *the* Philadelphia Yearly Meeting.

Elias Hicks, whose name became associated with one group, was a charismatic minister from New York. A farmer and surveyor and an ardent opponent of slavery, Hicks preached of the Inward Light of Christ as more central to faith than the authority of Scripture and rejected the orthodox Christian doctrine of **atonement**. While Hicks was singled out, the Hicksites were in fact united only in their opposition to the Orthodox, not in matters of theology. The Orthodox body drew Friends who had formed close ties with non-Quaker evangelicals in philanthropic and reform work. These Friends valued a more orthodox Christian theology, strongly asserting the authority of the Bible over that of the Inward Light and emphasizing **salvation** through the atoning death of Christ. They distrusted the Hicksites as coming too close to **Unitarianism**.

During the following year, separations occurred among Friends in Baltimore, Indiana, New York, and Ohio yearly meetings. The tendency for disagreements to lead to separations continued throughout the 1840s and 1850s as **Progressive Friends** (who later died out) split off from the Hicksites. Both were spiritual ancestors of modern **liberal Friends**. The Orthodox branch split into **Gurneyites** and **Wilburites** in a series of divisions beginning in New England in 1845. **Friends United Meeting** and **Evangelical Friends International** are the heirs of Gurneyite Quakerism. Wilburites are included in the group now known as **Conservative** Friends.

After the American Civil War (1861–1865) Orthodox Friends experienced rapid and radical change. Now known as "Gurneyites," because of the influence of the evangelical writings of the British Friend **Joseph John Gurney**, this group came increasingly under the influence of the Wesleyan **holiness movement** associated with the **revivals** of the later 19th century. This had two major outward consequences. First, they began to employ **pastors** and to substitute a **programmed** worship service for the traditional silent waiting, and second, they rediscovered the missionary enthusiasm of the early period of Quakerism and opened **mission** fields around the world.

The end of the century also initiated great changes toward **modernism** which affected both Hicksites and those Orthodox Friends who were not caught up in the holiness movement. An American Friend with many close ties to British modernists, **Rufus Jones** is the best known of the ministers and scholars who embraced modernist biblical scholarship and saw **mysticism** as central to understanding early Friends. **Mysticism** became the core of a new vision that shaped liberal Friends in the 20th century. In England, the 1895 **Manchester Conference** symbolized the shift of British Quakerism from **evangelicalism** to liberalism.

Despite the sadness, disruption, and pain caused by these divisions and transitions, Friends seemed to generate new energy, which found outlet in many directions. Individual Friends from all branches, to varying degrees, provided leadership in advocating the abolition of slavery and assisting the **underground railroad** before the Civil War, in the movement for women's rights (the organizers of the 1848 Woman's Rights Convention at Seneca Falls were predominantly Quakers), and in providing education and other opportunities for freed slaves. They were active in the **temperance** movement and in advocacy for Native Americans. Friends were also visible in the relief work and peace advocacy which eventually took new shape in the creation of the **American Friends Service Committee** and many other similar organizations.

THE SEPARATE BRANCHES OF MODERN QUAKERS

Early Friends combined in creative tension many of the apparently contradictory aspects of faith and life that now are visible in the different branches of Quakerism. Each modern branch takes on some of the characteristics of what was once a unified whole and has added new aspects. By the late 20th century, there were three primary branches of Friends and one distinctive smaller group.

The two largest groups, Friends United Meeting (FUM) and Evangelical Friends International (EFI), developed out of the Gurneyite branch and have much in common. While affirming the ministry of all believers, their worship is frequently led by a pastor, often with a prepared message, designated hymns, **Bible** readings, and appointed time for vocal **prayers**. They strongly endorse the **Great Commission** as stated in Matthew 28:16–20 and Mark 16:15–18 to proclaim the good news of Jesus Christ to the world and thus have active missionary programs that draw many new **members** into the Society. For the most part, they continue Friends' traditional practices such as conducting the business of the meeting by seeking unity in the Spirit and the affirmation of the exclusively inward and spiritual nature of the **sacraments**.

Today, in North and **South America**, Africa, and parts of Asia, the majority of Friends are in meetings that belong to either FUM or EFI. The differences between the two groups started in the United States in the late 19th century. In 1887, Gurneyite Quakers gathered in Richmond, Indiana, to consider and reject some of the more radical doctrines of the holiness movement and the new forms being introduced, such as use of the outward sacraments, particularly water **baptism**. FUM, then called Five Years Meeting, had its origins in this gathering, which also developed the **Richmond Declaration of Faith**, a uniform statement of faith still found in most books of discipline in both FUM and EFI.

The Gurneyite Ohio **Yearly Meeting**, which was the center of the efforts to introduce water baptism, never joined FUM. In 1925, Oregon was the first member yearly meeting to split off from FUM as an increasingly fundamentalist approach to the Bible conflicted with the growing **modernism** among the Orthodox Friends of FUM. Some Holiness Friends also were not at ease with the focus of the American Friends Service Committee on war relief and other work without a clear recognition that true peace and social justice began with the transforming work of Jesus Christ in the soul. In 1965, four independent yearly meetings—Oregon, Kansas, Ohio, and Rocky Mountain—decided to form an Evangelical Friends Alliance (EFA) for cooperative programs. Other yearly meetings soon joined and EFA was renamed Evangelical Friends International (EFI) in 1990 as their ties expanded worldwide.

Over the course of the century, many EFI meetings have strengthened their ties with other holiness churches such as the Nazarenes. Decisions by vote, use of water baptism, and the low priority of the **peace testimony** are some of the most visible changes in practice adopted by some EFI meetings. FUM meetings are generally more supportive of the peace testimony and conscious of a distinctive Friends' interpretation of the Gospel. FUM meetings are also more varied in their worship and theology, as a significant number of meetings continue to worship in expectant silence and also belong to **Friends General Conference (FGC)**.

FGC represents the third major grouping of Friends. While primarily a North American organization, members of most European meetings and many small Friends meetings around the world would feel most at home with FGC Quakers. In the 20th century, Hicksites and other Friends from **independent meetings** started to call themselves "**liberal Friends**." Their political stance intended to reflect the "**social**

gospel" of aid to the poor and displaced, as expressed in Matthew 25:40, and was a major draw for new members. The term also expressed their acceptance of modernism in theology, openness to biblical criticism and evolutionary **science**, and faith in responding to **continuing revelation** by the **Holy Spirit**.

Liberal Friends are extremely conscious of calling themselves Quaker, but are less unified about whether they are Christian, a fact symbolized when Britain Yearly Meeting, which had been evangelical a century before, changed the name of its book of church discipline from *Christian Faith and Practice* to *Quaker Faith and Practice* in 1994. In these meetings the focus is on how people live and maintain Quaker practice rather than on formal beliefs. Thus, many meetings include members who find much value in, and occasionally belong to, other denominations and faiths, from Anglican to Hindu to Jewish. Liberal Quakers strongly believe that early Friends set an important example for the world in the unique forms they established for worship, for the conduct of business, and for daily living grounded in integrity, peace, equality, community, and simplicity, even as they adapt these practices to modern thought.

One now much smaller grouping of Friends has had an importance well beyond their numbers. Conservative Friends perhaps come nearest to continuing both the faith and the practice of 18th-century Friends. They speak of themselves as "conservative" in the sense of conserving Quaker tradition. They worship and conduct their business in the traditional manner of waiting upon the Spirit of Christ. They are also clear that Jesus Christ is their present Teacher, Guide, and Lord and that knowledge of the Bible is essential to the formation of faith and practice. A few adopt the plain dress with bonnets and broad-brimmed hats—and plain speech, using "thee" and "thou" instead of "you," which were part of general Friends' practice for two and a half centuries. Conservative Friends still meet in Ohio, North Carolina, Iowa, and Britain, with a few scattered members elsewhere.

A few yearly meetings such as Central and Alaska, which have evangelical roots, and the three independent liberal bodies in western United States remain unaffiliated and in some cases have separated themselves from other Friends.

In 20th-century North America, Friends such as Rufus Jones worked toward the creation of institutions that might bring Friends of different branches together. The AFSC, **Friends Committee on National**

Legislation (FCNL), and **Friends World Committee for Consultation** (FWCC) are the main bodies that were created by this hope. By mid-century, **reunification** of several separated yearly meetings became a reality. As the century wore on, however, new alignments occurred among what had been the more centrist yearly meetings, and increasingly, different practices and theology pushed the edges further apart. In this, the Religious Society of Friends reflects the pressures that face many churches.

While Friends' congregations and schools were established in places like Jamaica, Cuba, India, and China by 1905, the rapid expansion and evangelical zeal of Friends churches in **East** and **Central Africa**, and South America and new churches being formed in Asia, is another facet of modern Quakerism. Around the world, bodies that were subordinate to British or North American yearly meetings at the start of the 20th century came into their own as self-governing institutions with many responsibilities. For instance, by the time East Africa Yearly Meeting was set up as a body independent of American control in 1946, Friends had created over 250 schools, a Bible college, and two hospitals in Kenya. Australian Friends became independent of Britain in 1964. In Bolivia, the Quaker *Iglesia Nacional Evangélica Los Amigos* was incorporated in 1956 but only recognized by North American Friends in 1974. The church has done much to bring literacy and new skills as well as a new faith to the Aymara people in the Andean mountains.

Many small groups of liberal Friends exist in Europe, Australia, New Zealand, and elsewhere. They are extremely active in many areas, including efforts to end the use of nuclear weapons, training children in nonviolent conflict resolution, and working with the homeless. Schools established by Orthodox Friends during the previous century in places like Ramallah, Palestine, provided new challenges for Friends who sought to maintain a witness for peace.

The beginning of the 21st century finds Friends in a state of transition. Some liberal Friends ask themselves whether they have been too lax about teaching their faith to their children and newcomers in their meetings. They look for better ways to articulate their faith that affirm their Quaker heritage and yet accept that Christianity is not the only path to Truth. Some Friends in EFI and FUM also look at their numbers in North America and ask what messages Quakers have for the modern world or whether their future lies with other nondenominational Christian churches. [Margery Post Abbott]

The Dictionary

–A–

ABOLITION. The Religious Society of Friends has a long, if uneven, history of grappling with the relationship between slavery and religious conviction. Like many activities of modern society, slavery, as practiced in the North American and Caribbean English colonies, violated the **testimonies** of **equality** and nonviolence (*see* PEACE) in the minds of increasing numbers of Friends.

As traveling Quaker **ministers** first encountered chattel slavery in America, their reactions ranged from silence to **George Fox**'s direction that slave holders ensure the religious instruction of their servants to **William Edmundson**'s total rejection of the institution. By 1700, several North American **monthly meetings**, including Germantown and Darby meetings, petitioned Philadelphia **Yearly Meeting** to prohibit slavery among its members. In addition, a number of individuals attempted to alert their monthly meetings to the danger that slaveholding posed to the spiritual health of Quaker individuals and **meetings**. American reformer **Benjamin Lay** stood barefoot in the snow outside a meetinghouse, in order to dramatize the vulnerability of underclothed slaves. Others, such as **John Woolman** and **Anthony Benezet**, provided reading instruction to **African Americans**, in an attempt both to demonstrate black people's mental capacities, and to prepare them to take up their lives as free people.

In a series of decisions between the 1750s and the 1770s, the American yearly meetings concluded that members must either relinquish slaveholding, or relinquish their membership as Friends. Though some people chose to leave Friends rather than give up their slaves, many Quakers took this opportunity to free their slaves. Between 1770 and 1820, many individuals and meetings in Pennsylvania, Virginia,

Maryland, and North Carolina even purchased other people's slaves in order to free them. The Missouri Compromise of 1821, which legitimized the expansion of slavery, compelled many Friends to take a more vigorous stand. Taking their cue from British Friends who had helped effect the abolition of slavery in the West Indies, American Quakers joined with such British reformers as **Elizabeth Fry** and **Joseph John Gurney** to shape antislavery sentiment into an international movement.

Across North America, Quakers worked individually, and in concert with other reformers, to take a stand against slavery. Friends helped found the first antislavery society in 1775 in Pennsylvania. Quakers supported the "Free Produce" committees that refused to purchase slave-produced goods. Many individuals, and two entire meetings from North Carolina and South Carolina, relocated to western states in order to distance themselves from the social pollution of the slave system. From these vantage points they assisted slaves in their flight to freedom.

Crusader Benjamin Lundy (1789–1839) published and distributed his newspaper, *The Genius of Universal Emancipation*, from various locations in Maryland, Ohio, Illinois, and Tennessee. A Free Produce storekeeper, he encouraged fellow Quakers, who had already cleansed their own communities of the stain of slavery, to put their efforts into ending the system altogether. **Levi Coffin** and **Thomas Garrett** were two of many Quakers and hundreds of often-nameless black people who "operated" the **underground railroad** and helped fugitive slaves find refuge in **Canada**.

United in their goals, antislavery Friends were not always united in their methods. In 1843, Indiana Yearly Meeting (**Orthodox**) divided when Friends who favored immediate emancipation and were willing to work with non-Friends to achieve it were disciplined by the leaders in some meetings who believed that it was important to move gradually, obey the laws of the land, and avoid the "contamination" of non-Quaker practices. Radical antislavery Friends like Levi Coffin formed the separate "Indiana Yearly Meeting of Anti-Slavery Friends." Aggressive in recruiting and aiding fugitive slaves and in challenging slave owners and slave catchers, and more willing to accept the possibility that ending slavery might involve violence (*see* PEACE TESTIMONY), this group quickly grew to include Quakers as far away as Ohio and Iowa. Within a few years, however, most Indiana Friends came to this more militant antislavery position, and Friends quietly reunited.

By the 1850s there were Quakers—Orthodox and **Hicksite**, east and west—who aided fugitive slaves, formed "Free Produce" stores and intentional communities, supported schools, orphanages, and other social service agencies for African Americans, and researched new areas (e.g., **Canada**, **Mexico**, and West Africa) where slaves might relocate. Two Iowa Quakers even accompanied John Brown (1800–1859) in his attempt to spark a definitive slave revolt by seizing arms from the federal arsenal in Harpers Ferry, West Virginia.

A few American Quakers folded African Americans into their social circles, but most did not. Instead, they focused their efforts on the injustice of legal inequality rather than on the more subtle questions of social equality. The American Civil War eventually ended slavery, but threw American Quakers into a dilemma: was it better to avoid the violence of war or to join with an army that would effect an end to slavery? Meetings—and families within meetings—split over this question, but once slavery was ended, meetings redirected their energies to the relief and education of freedmen. [Emma Jones Lapsansky]

ADDAMS, JANE (1860–1935). American **peace** activist, social reformer, and friend of Friends. Originator of the settlement house movement, she won the Nobel Peace Prize for her role in cofounding and leading the **Women's International League for Peace and Freedom**. *See also* BALCH, EMILY; LEWIS, LUCY.

ADVANCEMENT. In 1902, **Friends General Conference (FGC)** established the Committee for the Advancement of Friends Principles to nurture the spiritual health of small meetings, in particular, and isolated individuals through visitation and correspondence. Always suspicious of proselytization, **liberal Friends** in North America use the term also to denote **outreach** to non-Friends. In the early 20th century, some Friends institutions called their fund-raising or development activities *institutional advancement*. *See also* MISSIONS: MODERN MISSIONARY MOVEMENT. [Mary Ellen Chijioke]

ADVICES. *See* QUERIES AND ADVICES.

AFRICA. *See* CENTRAL AFRICA; EAST AFRICA; SOUTHERN AFRICA; WEST AFRICA.

AFRICAN AMERICANS. Believing in the universality of the **light** of **Christ** within every human being, early Friends did not question that men and women of African descent had souls. During his visit to Barbados in 1671, **George Fox** urged slave owners to provide religious instruction and opportunities for worship for their slaves (*see* ABOLITION). Similar provisions for religious instruction for slaves were made in Jamaica; in the American colonies masters were urged to bring their slaves with them to **meeting**, and later, to appoint special **meetings for worship** for them.

The question of admitting blacks to **membership** in the Religious Society of Friends did not formally arise until 1796 when a Cynthia Myers, "a Mulatto woman," applied for membership in Rahway, New Jersey, **monthly meeting**. The case was referred to the Philadelphia **Yearly Meeting**, and it was agreed that there should be no distinction on the basis of color. Cynthia was then accepted. In 1799 David (d.1835) and Grace Mapps (1764–1836) joined Little Egg Harbor Meeting. Isaac Linagar, "a mixed colored man," became a member of Deep River Monthly Meeting in 1801. **Paul Cuffe**, a black sea captain, was admitted to membership in Westport Monthly Meeting in 1808.

Generally, however, these were exceptions. There has been no definitive study of black membership in the Society of Friends since **Henry J. Cadbury**'s "Negro Membership in the Society of Friends," which was anecdotal, but most historians agree that such membership has been sparse, particularly on the East Coast of the United States. Friends continued to ask black members to sit in separate benches at the back of the **meetinghouse**, a custom generally prevalent in other denominations, and this offended many blacks who might otherwise have joined. In 1841 **Sarah Mapps Douglass** made a protest against this form of discrimination, which became a cause célèbre in both the United States and England. Sarah was the granddaughter of Cyrus Bustill, a prominent attender of North Meeting, who was at one point the baker who supplied the American Revolutionary army with bread. The entire Bustill family attended meeting, regularly, but none was ever invited to join.

Similarly, Eastern Friends generally did not invite black children into Quaker schools until well into the 20th century, though there were a few exceptions (*see* EDUCATION). Instead, they developed separate schools for blacks. In Philadelphia this began with a school opened by **Anthony Benezet** in Philadelphia 1770, followed by Clarkson Hall, established by the largely Quaker Pennsylvania Abolition Society in 1790, and the Institute for Colored Youth (now Cheyney University), opened in 1837 (*see* RICHARD HUMPHREYS FOUNDATION). There was also a Quaker-based African School in New York. Many individual meetings ran separate schools for blacks.

In the Midwest, Friends also developed separate schools for blacks, but were also on occasion willing to admit black students to Friends schools. In Grant County, Indiana, local Quakers played a role in establishing a public integrated secondary school.

Friends' finest hour in black education came at the end of the American Civil War. Moved by the plight of the newly freed slaves, Friends of all persuasions became active in reconstruction work throughout the South (*see* FRIENDS FREEDMEN'S ASSOCIATION). Following an immediate period of **relief work**, they began setting up schools for the blacks who were eager for instruction. At one time there were perhaps 150 such schools under Quaker auspices. Some of these became permanent institutions, including the Penn School on St. Helena Island, the Laing School in Mt. Pleasant, and the Schofield School, all in South Carolina, and the Christiansburg Institute in Virginia. In addition, Hampton Institute was given initial Quaker support.

The most famous of these schools was the one established at **Southland**, Arkansas, by Indiana Yearly Meeting A regiment of black soldiers stationed nearby bought 30 acres and built the first buildings, presenting them to the Yearly Meeting in 1866. The school and a teacher training institute, called Southland College, continued to operate until 1925. A Quaker meeting was established, becoming a monthly meeting in 1873 and subsequently establishing several preparative meetings. A number of **ministers** recorded at Southland became active in the Five Years Meeting.

In the first half of the 20th century Friends began to welcome African Americans into membership. As a result, such outstanding persons as Dr. Ira Reid (1901–1968), a professor at **Haverford College**, novelist and poet Jean Toomer (1894–1967), **Bayard Rustin**, and Barrington Dunbar (1901–1978), author and activist, became

Friends. Friends schools also began to accept African American students, in small numbers at first, later in much larger numbers. Today, Friends' meetings of all branches actively seek African American members, though some are more successful than others in this effort, and most Quaker schools, **colleges**, and institutions are thoroughly integrated. *See also* URBAN MINISTRIES. [Margaret Hope Bacon]

ALANGUIA, TEODORO (ca. 1930–). A **pastor** and educator, he served in 1998 and 1999 as one of the first **missionaries** named by Peru **Yearly Meeting** (*see* SOUTH AMERICA). An Aymara, Alanguia has played an important role in developing and encouraging leadership in the yearly meeting. Since the early 1970s, he taught at the Instituto Biblico Los Amigos (Friends Bible Institute), an extension learning program, then was director of this institute in 1996 and 1997. He has been recording **clerk** of Peru Yearly Meeting, as well as of his **monthly** and **quarterly meetings**. Currently, Alanguia is pastor of the Suancata Friends Church near Lake Titicaca, Peru. [Dan Cammack]

ALDANA, JOSÉ MARÍA DURÉN. Early 20th-century teacher at the Friends School in Guatemala. *See also* CENTRAL AMERICA.

ALEXANDER, HORACE GRUNDY (1889–1989). British Friend who worked closely with **Mahatma Gandhi**. *See also* SOUTH ASIA.

ALLEN, WILLIAM (1770–1843). British Friend, leading chemist of his day and a Fellow of the Royal Society (*see* SCIENCE AND TECHNOLOGY), also a determined **philanthropist** who began the journal *The Philanthropist*. Allen was very active in **ecumenical** campaigns for the **abolition** of slavery, also in the British and Foreign **Bible** Society, and with **relief** for London's poor. His main work was in the **education** of the children of the poor, and he helped set up a school in London, part of a movement that later became the British and Foreign Schools Society. This was for many years the mainstay of nondenominational educational provision until a government bill in 1870 provided some form of schooling for all. [Pink Dandelion]

AMERICA. *See* CARIBBEAN; MEXICO; CENTRAL AMERICA; NORTH AMERICA.

AMERICAN FRIENDS SERVICE COMMITTEE (AFSC). In 1917 a diverse coalition of **North American** Friends created AFSC as an independent Quaker organization to provide alternative service opportunities for **conscientious objectors (COs)** to war and to offer services to victims of war, without regard to politics, religion, or nationality. Since then, AFSC has worked through programs that witness against war, confront injustice, and express concern for those who are disenfranchised and oppressed, both domestically and internationally.

Rufus Jones and **Henry Cadbury** did much to shape the organization. During World War I, volunteers provided wartime care and medical services for civilians in France. Beginning in 1919, AFSC undertook feeding programs in Europe, reaching over a million children in Germany, Austria, and Poland, and distributing food and medicine for famine **relief** in Russia. In the United States, AFSC staff worked in settlement houses, reform schools, and schools for **Native Americans** and **African Americans**. During the Depression, AFSC fed children of unemployed coal miners in Appalachia, organized volunteer work camps, and helped form homestead projects and cooperatives.

The devastation of World War I established **peace** education work as an ongoing priority of AFSC. Peace caravans and Institutes of International Relations; active resistance to the Vietnam and Gulf wars; support for demilitarization and the end of nuclear weapons; concern about the expansion of Junior Reserve Officers Training Corps programs in U.S. schools and the issue of "child soldiers" are all part of this program.

Heading up to **World War II**, under the leadership of **Clarence Pickett**, executive secretary from 1929 to 1950, AFSC supported the work of the Friends Centre in Berlin, which aided concentration camp inmates and helped Jewish and other threatened peoples flee from Germany. In the United States, AFSC administered **Civilian Public Service** units for COs and aided Japanese-American victims of the forced relocation and internment. In 1947, AFSC and the British Friends Service Council received the Nobel Peace Prize on behalf of the Religious Society of Friends for humanitarian service, work for reconciliation—including relief and reconstruction work following the war—and the spirit in which these were carried out.

During the U.S. Civil Rights Movement, AFSC worked on housing, voter registration, and school desegregation projects (*see* EQUALITY). Ongoing programs work for the rights of Native Americans and indigenous peoples, people of color, poor people, sexual minorities, youth, and immigrants. Regarding no one as an enemy, AFSC sent medical aid to civilian victims of war in Vietnam, continues to operate a rehabilitation center in Cambodia providing prostheses to war victims, and seeks openings for reconciliation with Cuba, Iraq, and North Korea, and for peacemaking in the **Middle East**.

AFSC is active today in 22 countries and nine U.S. regions with staff in 43 locations. It is governed by a corporation of 120–180 Friends, half of whom are named by U.S. **yearly meetings**, the other half by the AFSC Corporation. Most policy decisions are made by a 50-member Board of Directors.

Throughout its history, there have been differing discernments between AFSC and some yearly meetings. Some yearly meetings do not participate because of the absence of a clear Christian message. In the 1950s and 1960s, some Friends felt that AFSC was "too political" or "too left-leaning." In the late 1970s, AFSC adopted an affirmative action plan, based on the Quaker belief in the worth of every person and with the intent of more fully reflecting American society. Implementation of this plan caused tensions within AFSC and between the Corporation and Friends, and some yearly meetings withdrew their support. AFSC maintains that it is possible to be diverse in composition, true to Quaker values, and divinely led. [Karen Cromley, Jack Sutter]

AMIGITSI, RABEKA (1889–1971). Early Friends leader in Kenya and wife of Yohana Amugune (1878–1960), who was also active in Quaker **leadership**. Amigitsi was one of the founders of the **women**'s meetings in **East Africa** and leader of the first Women's **Yearly Meeting**, which was formed in 1951, five years after the establishment of East Africa Yearly Meeting.

ANABAPTISM. Anabaptist (which means rebaptizer) was the nickname given in the 16th century to groups in what is now called the "Radical Reformation," which extended but also challenged the work of Martin Luther and John Calvin. Anabaptists limited church membership, and hence **baptism**, to totally committed adults. Their roots were in wider reactions against the wealth, power, and worldliness of the inclusive Roman Catholic Church that had worked to include, infuse, and educate whole nations in the Middle Ages.

Anabaptists preached and identified dates for the Apocalypse and started popular movements which were violently repressed in 1527. But the surviving Mennonite communities in Holland exchanged ideas with both the earliest English Baptists and early Friends, whom they claim as heirs. With the German Baptist "Church of the Brethren," they became "the quiet in the land" in early Pennsylvania, and are still recognized as fellow "**peace** churches" with Friends.

Early Friends were labeled Anabaptists by their **Puritan** enemies, and are still claimed as an offshoot by Mennonite historians, but Anabaptist influence upon **George Fox**, **James Nayler**, and the "**Valiant Sixty**" was mainly transmitted through English Baptists. *See also* PERFECTION; SEPARATISTS. [Hugh Barbour]

ANDUGU, JOSEPH (1943–). A **pastor** and an educator, Andugu is a member of Central **Yearly Meeting** in Kenya (*see* EAST AFRICA). After serving as a pastor in Nakuru and the Central Rift Valley in 1966–1967, he became tutor and deputy principal at what is now **Friends Theological College** in Kaimosi in 1971 and served until 1978, then again from 1982 until 1985. After a decade as western regional coordinator for the National Council of Churches of Kenya, he became executive secretary for **Friends World Committee for Consultation**, Africa Section, starting in 1998 and is **clerk** of the General **Superintendents** and Pastors Fellowship.

ANGELL, STEPHEN LEROY (1919–). A member of New York **Yearly Meeting**, Angell is a leader in development of the Alternatives to Violence (AVP) program in prisons, which began in 1975 with Lawrence S. (Larry) Apsey (1902–1997), Bernard LaFayette (1940–), Paul Tillquist, Peter Matusewitch, and Steven F. (Steve) Stalonas as facilitators. Angell became a coordinator of the AVP program at Fishkill penitentiary in New York (*see* PENAL REFORM). Over the years he has traveled widely, with a minute of support from his **monthly meeting** endorsed by New York Yearly Meeting, helping spread the AVP program to all parts of North America and to Britain, Australia, and New Zealand. He has also been active in **Friends World Committee for Consultation.** [Margery Post Abbott]

ANTHONY, SUSAN BROWNELL (1820–1906). North American **women**'s rights leader. Born and raised in North Adams, Massachusetts, Susan B. Anthony spent most of her adult life in Rochester, New York, where her family moved in 1845. She taught until 1849, then devoted herself to family enterprises and political activities. After their meeting in 1851, she and **Elizabeth Cady Stanton** formed a life-long friendship and political alliance. For many years Stanton, who raised a large family, was the chief writer and strategist of the pair; the unmarried Anthony was the public traveler and speaker. They formed the American Equal Rights Association in 1866, their major objective being women's suffrage. In 1872, Anthony was arrested for attempting to vote in Rochester. From 1892 to 1900 she was president of the National Woman Suffrage Association, which she and Stanton had helped found in 1869. [Mary Ellen Chijioke]

AP JOHN, JOHN (1625?–1697). Leading Welsh **minister** in the 1650s. He traveled with **George Fox** in Wales and built up Quakerism there before it largely disappeared for a time through **migration** to **North America**.

APOCALYPSE. Derived from the Greek *apokalypsis*, the word literally means "unveiling," or "revelation." In New Testament usage, the word relates to the end times, as in the Book of Revelation, the "Apocalypse of John." As a form of **eschatology** (doctrine of "last things"), Christian apocalyptic emphasizes a divine revelation (such as the Quaker Inward **Light**) that manifests end-time realities here and now and empowers humans to live according to them. Early Friends saw themselves as participating in the victory of the **Lamb's War** and living out the Kingdom of God on earth. [Douglas Gwyn]

APOLOGY. A volume in the tradition of "apologies" or written defenses of doctrine which began with Plato. **Robert Barclay**'s *Apology for the True Christian Divinity*, published in Latin in 1676 and English in 1678, became the standard theological authority for Quakerism for several generations. It remains in print as *Barclay's Apology in Modern English* and in a Spanish version. [Dean Freiday]

ARCHDALE, JOHN (1642–1717). Colonial governor of Carolina in 1685–86 and again in 1695–1696 (*see* CIVIL GOVERNMENT), Archdale was known for promoting religious toleration and **peace** with the **Native Americans**.

ARTS. Positive Quaker contributions to the arts include the wealth of Quaker **journals**; a fine craftsmanship of an austere style in practical arts such as architecture, carpentry, quilting, and embroidery; and arts related to natural history, such as garden design and botanical drawing. In addition to Quaker journals and tracts, Friends also wrote poetry from the beginning. British Quaker poets of the past include **Thomas Ellwood**, John Scott of Amwell (1730–1783), and Bernard Barton (1784–1839).

In 17th-century **Britain**, the high arts were perceived by Friends as serving the purposes of either the apostate church or the decadent aristocracy. Early Friends also saw them as carnal and self-intoxicating. Indulgence in sensory gratification, "vain imaginings," and useless ornamentation were distractions from attending to the pure Life. It was untruthful to tell a story that never happened, paint an imaginary scene, play a role on the stage, or sing songs (including psalms) expressing what one did not feel (*see* TRUTH). Music and the theater were regarded as particularly corrupting.

The taboo on most high arts continued throughout the **Quietist** period. Painter Benjamin West (1738–1820) left the Society, as did Charles Brockton Brown (1771–1810), the first American novelist. As the **revivals** took hold in the 19th century, music became a regular part of **worship** among **Gurneyite** Friends. Today, church choirs are common in Friends' churches in **North America**. The Kakamega and other Quaker church choirs are widely renowned in Kenya (*see* EAST AFRICA). An increasing number of hymns have been written by Quakers or incorporate Quaker themes. Friends who hold to **unprogrammed worship** have produced hymnals and songbooks.

Among these latter Friends the arts began to gain acceptance in the 19th century and have played an increasing role in the 20th. In

Britain, a Quaker arts network was formed in the 1950s and disbanded in 2002. The **Leaveners** are active in performing and commissioning new musical and dramatic work on Quaker themes. In **North America**, the arts have proliferated since **Hicksite** Friends held the first Quaker conference on the arts in 1915. The Fellowship of Quakers in the Arts, founded in 1993, fosters communication among artists in the United States and **Canada**.

Quaker artists widely feel the creative process as akin to waiting on the **Holy Spirit** in Quaker worship; many are struggling to uncover a deeper synergy between art and Quaker **spirituality**. The paintings of **Edward Hicks** are well known, as are the poems of **John Greenleaf Whittier**. The Swedish novelist Elin Wägner (1882–1949) was influential as a forerunner of ecofeminism. The sculpture of Sylvia Shaw Judson (1897–1978) incorporated a vision of **simplicity**. Printmaker **Fritz Eichenberg** integrated the intellectual, spiritual, and political in his works. Among contemporary artists, James Turrell, of **Wilburite** background, is noted for his imageless installations using light as a medium. [Esther Greenleaf Mürer]

ASERO, MARIANNO (d. 1997). A Bolivian, Asero converted to Quakerism as a boy. He became a **pastor** and evangelist, facing much persecution during his life. He was a key figure in Iglesia Nacional Evangelica "Los Amigos'" (INELA). *See* SOUTH AMERICA.

ASHBRIDGE, ELIZABETH (later SAMPSON SULLIVAN) (1713–1755). Prominent Quaker **minister** of 18th-century Philadelphia. Moving from England to **North America** as an indentured servant at age 19, Elizabeth became a **convinced** Friend after visiting Quaker relatives. Although she wrote only one piece of literature—her spiritual autobiography—that text is now considered to be a staple of the early American literary canon. Her autobiography tracks the experiences and spiritual reflections of a **woman** who has moved from being a widow, an immigrant, and an indentured servant, to being a Quaker convert, an abused wife (by her non-Quaker husband), and, ultimately, a respected and cherished minister of the Religious Society of Friends. She was a contemporary of **John Woolman**, and some scholars believe her **journal** inspired Woolman to begin writing his own. Hers is a narrative of fascinating individual development fused with the corporate identity of Quakers; it was published in 1774, and was circulated widely among Friends to inspire others on their spiritual journeys. *See also* WOMEN. [Michele Lise Tarter]

ASIA. *See* EAST ASIA; INDIA; JAPAN; SOUTHEAST ASIA.

ATIAMUGA, MARIA (1903–1981). Early Kenyan Quaker leader and key figure in the development of the **Women**'s **Yearly Meeting** in 1951. In 1946 Atiamuga became a member of the preachers' board. *See also* EAST AFRICA.

ATONEMENT. In Christian and Quaker thought, and experience, atonement is the healing of broken relationships between **God** and humankind. Atonement presupposes human **sin** as the reason for this. Early Friends insisted that **salvation** depends on **sanctification** as well as the atonement and was one with it. In the Hebrew scriptures the shedding of blood accompanying the sacrifice of animals was believed to effect reconciliation with God. In the Christian tradition the sacrifice of Jesus **Christ** on the **Cross** has been interpreted as necessary for reconciliation with God. In the history of Christian thought there have been several theories of atonement.

George Fox and other early Friends differed from most theories of atonement in their day by insisting that salvation depends on sanctification and response to the saving **Light** of Christ as well as atonement. On page 34 of his *Journal*, George Fox wrote: "For I saw that Christ died for all men, and was propitiation for all, and had enlightened all men [and women] with his divine and saving Light and that none could be true believers but who believed in it." Likewise **Robert Barclay**'s *Apology* claimed that the saving Light of Christ presupposed his atoning death.

Atonement emerged as a divisive issue among Friends in the late 18th century. In the 19th century, Friends became identified as **Hicksites** and **Gurneyites**. **Elias Hicks** placed little emphasis on innate human sin and the need for the redemptive work of Christ. He held that humanity's fall was altogether an act of choice. Insofar as Hicks believed in atonement, he spiritualized it. **Joseph John Gurney** adopted an evangelical definition of atonement when he asserted in *A Peculiar People*: "It is only through the precious blood of Jesus

Christ, shed for us on the cross," that our "iniquity is forgiven" and our "sin covered."

Twentieth-century Friends held an increasingly wide range of views on atonement. Many Friends have great difficulty with the concept that salvation was won or bought by the death of one man 2,000 years ago. They more often affirm that humanity was made in God's image, but there is an ongoing need for personal atonement and forgiveness. Other Friends largely concur with Gurney and affirm atonement through Jesus Christ by which persons are reconciled to God. Today, some hold strongly to the necessity of the atonement for salvation, while others consider it unnecessary to their spiritual well-being. [Wilmer A. Cooper]

AUDLAND, JOHN (1630–1663/64). Preacher from Westmoreland, in northern England, former leader of a separated congregation, Audland joined with **George Fox** in 1652, and was the leader with **John Camm** of the successful Bristol **mission** (1654–1655) and also a mission to London. He died young, in **prison**.

Audland's wife Anne (d.1705) was one of the **Valiant Sixty**. After his death she married Camm's son Thomas.

AUSTRALIA. The first Friends to migrate to Australia did so for personal reasons rather than any conscious desire to establish Quakerism. Then in 1832, **James Backhouse**, a Friend from Yorkshire, England, began a six-year religious visit to Australia, meeting with Quakers as well as documenting the situation of convicts who had been deported from England and of the Aborigines. During this time, **meetings** were established in Hobart Town, Sydney, and Adelaide. About 45 meetings existed by the late 20th century. A **general meeting** (attached to London Yearly Meeting) was established in 1901, becoming an autonomous **yearly meeting** in 1964.

A Friends School, established in Hobart in 1887, had an enrollment of over 1,000 students in the year 2000. Friends organized widespread anticonscription campaigns prior to World War I. Quaker Service Australia developed aid programs, largely in Cambodia and Vietnam, in the 1960s (*see* PEACE AND SERVICE AGENCIES). The yearly meeting is an active member of the National Council of Churches. [David Purnell]

AYDELOTT, PHOEBE S. (ca. 1840–1911). American supporter of **missionary** activities and first president of the Woman's Foreign Missionary Society of Friends in America, now **United Society of Friends Women International**. *See also* MISSIONS.

AYDELOTTE, FRANK (1880–1956). Aydelotte was president of **Swarthmore College** from 1922 until 1940 and created Swarthmore's signature Honors Program. He was director of the Institute for Advanced Studies at Princeton University from 1940 until 1953.

AYLLÓN, JUAN (ca. 1900–). South American missionary. Aymara grandson of a Catholic priest, Ayllón was educated in a prestigious Methodist School in La Paz, Bolivia. From a very early age he had been inclined toward Christianity, enjoying and helping at open-air street meetings. He was deeply moved by the Gospel witness of William Abel, a **North American** Indian missionary who passed away from smallpox at the age of 47 soon after the 1919 street meeting where they met.

Feeling a **prophetic** call, but needing training, Ayllón went to the Berea Bible College (later Seminary) in Chiquimula, Guatemala. After an extended journey from Peru via New York, he reached Chiquimula on March 9, 1921. There he met Tomasa Valle, and they were married. After graduation in 1924, Juan and Tomasa returned to Bolivia to start the **ministry**. With the help of California Friends **Mission** in Guatemala, the Ayllóns very soon opened up a new church in La Paz City. They started a school, distributed tracts, preached the **Word** of **God** and prayed. They are the founders of the **Friends Church** in Bolivia (*see also* CENTRAL AMERICA).

Ayllón did not get along with Northwest Yearly Meeting's missionaries who came to work in Bolivia. Their ideas of doing **mission** work differed from his own. In the mid-1940s, Juan Ayllón and his family finally left the Friends Church, which was under Northwest Yearly Meeting, to start a new National Friends Church led totally by the nationals. Though small, this church still exists today. [Diego Chuyma]

AYUBA, KIFA. East African Quaker leader, Ayuba founded the Church of the Holy Spirit which split off from Friends in Kenya. *See also* PENTACOSTALISM.

AZUSA PACIFIC UNIVERSITY. Founded in Southern California as Huntington Park Training School for Christian Workers in 1899, later Azusa College, it merged with Los Angeles Pacific College in 1965, becoming Azusa Pacific College. They were joined in 1968 by Arlington College of Long Beach and became a university in 1981. Currently affiliated with six denominations, including **Evangelical Friends International**, it maintains a Friends Center.

–B–

BACKHOUSE, JAMES (1794–1869). British botanist, **minister**, and **temperance** advocate. Backhouse operated a plant nursery in York (*see* SCIENCE AND TECHNOLOGY) when he felt called to visit **Australia**. He sailed from England in 1831 with George Washington Walker as companion. By 1838 they had visited all the then-inhabited parts of the country, mainly on foot, documenting the situations of transported prisoners, settlers, soldiers, and Aborigines. In addition to his 1843 *Narrative* on the social and natural history of Australia, he published notes on South Africa where he and Walker sojourned from 1838 to 1840. Backhouse later traveled in the **ministry** in Norway in 1853 and **Ireland** in 1854 and 1861. The annual lecture of Australia **Yearly Meeting** is named after Backhouse who started the first Quaker **meeting** in Australia, at Hobart in 1833. [Sabron R. Newton]

BACON, MARGARET HOPE (1921–) and SAMUEL ALLEN (1919–). On June 28, 1942, Margaret Hope married Allen Bacon, a **conscientious objector** who was soon assigned to a mental hospital in Maryland where Margaret also worked during **World War II**. The Bacons are members of Philadelphia **Yearly Meeting**. Margaret served for 22 years as assistant secretary for information and interpretation for the **American Friends Service Committee (AFSC)**. She has written 13 books, making Quaker history accessible to the general public through her works on **Lucretia Mott**, **Isaac Hopper**, Abbey Kelley Foster (1810–1887), **Henry J. Cadbury**, and numerous other topics. Allen graduated from Antioch College in Ohio and Harvard University School of Education before becoming a teacher.

He then became a social worker in the inner city of Philadelphia, and later, director of the Greater Philadelphia Federation of Settlements (*see* URBAN MINISTRIES). He also served as director of the AFSC nationwide work camp program.

BAILEY, HANNAH CLARK JOHNSON (1839–1923). Suffragist and promoter of **peace**, **temperance**, and **missions**. Bailey helped shape and was head of the Peace and Arbitration Departments of the Woman's Christian Temperance Union (WCTU) in the United States from 1887 to 1916 and at the world level starting in 1891. Through these positions and as editor of two monthlies, she advocated arbitration and disarmament, opposed war toys, military training in schools, capital punishment, and lynching. She served on the boards of two Friends schools and represented New England **Yearly Meeting** at the 1887 Richmond Conference and the subsequent Five Years Meetings (*see* FRIENDS UNITED MEETING; RICHMOND DECLARATION). She served as president of the Maine Suffrage Association from 1891 to 1897 and was a life member of two peace societies. [Sabron Reynolds Newton]

BAIRD, ESTHER (1861–1950). Author of *Adventurying with God* (1932), graduate nurse, and leader of the American Friends **mission** to Bundelkhand, India, from 1896 to 1937. She cofounded the Friends mission with two **ministers**, Delia Fistler and Martha (Matti) Barber, after working with the Methodists for some years. *See also* CATTELL, CATHERINE and EVERETT; SOUTH ASIA.

BALBY, EPISTLE OF THE ELDERS OF. First of many disciplinary documents and the probable model for later ones, it covered all aspects of a Quaker's life. Produced by a conference of Yorkshire and North Midland **meetings** in October 1656, its most important signatories were **William Dewsbury** and **Richard Farnworth**.

This epistle became widely known in the 20th century, as most liberal **yearly meetings** included the postscript to the letter in their books of **discipline**. This postscript, referencing 2 Corinthians 3:6, reads: "Dearly beloved Friends, these things we do not lay upon you as a rule or form to walk by, but that all, with the measure of light which is pure and holy, may be guided: and so in the light walking and abiding, these may be fulfilled in the Spirit, not from the letter, for the letter killeth, but the Spirit giveth life." [Rosemary Anne Moore]

BALCH, EMILY GREENE (1867–1961). American **peace** activist, educator, scholar, and social reformer. Raised in a Unitarian family, Balch was first introduced to Friends at **Bryn Mawr College**, graduating in 1889. While undertaking graduate work, she was inspired by the example of **Jane Addams** to work with poor Italian children in Boston as she prepared a handbook on laws and institutions related to juvenile delinquency. She helped start Denison Settlement House in Boston in 1892. Two years later, she joined the American Federation of Labor and helped found the Women's Trade Union League, as she became involved in the plight of **women** in the tobacco industry and telephone operators. In 1918, Wellesley College fired her from her post as chairperson of the Department of Economics and Sociology for "her outspoken views on pacifism and economics."

Balch cofounded the **Women's International League for Peace and Freedom (WILPF)**, a largely Quaker-inspired and -led organization, and was an officer or president from 1919 to 1961. Balch also wrote important studies. A 1926 study, requested by Haitian women, resulted in the book *Occupied Haiti* and contributed to the eventual withdrawal of U.S. troops from that country.

While in Geneva, Switzerland, in 1921, she joined the Religious Society of Friends as a member of London **Yearly Meeting** to avoid the American separations. Never an absolute pacifist, she reluctantly supported American participation in **World War II**. In 1946 she was awarded the Nobel Peace Prize for her work with WILPF. [Margery Post Abbott]

BAPTISM. Friends consider the **sacraments** to be inward and spiritual, as indicated in Galatians 3:27, without the necessity of physical expression with water or bread and wine. This is rooted in the conviction that **God** "communicates" the divine presence directly and immediately to human beings and initiates a sacramental encounter each time men and women gather to **worship** God in Spirit. **Christ**'s baptism is seen to be the inward receiving of the **Holy Spirit** for all those who wait on God and not dependent on outward baptism with water for either adults or infants. A few Friends have practiced water baptism since the controversy involving **David Updegraff** in the late 19th century.

BARCLAY, ROBERT (1648–1690). A Scottish Friend, known primarily for his theological writings, especially the ***Apology***. Barclay also engaged in a **mission** to continental Europe with **George Fox**, **George Keith**, and **William Penn** in 1677, and had the major role in converting the Proprietary Colony of East New Jersey (1682–1702) into a haven for persecuted Scots of all denominations.

"The Apologist" was the son of Col. David Barclay (1610–1686), an officer under Cromwell, and Catherine Gordon, daughter of Sir Robert Gordon of Gordonstown and a cousin of James VI of Scotland (James I of England). As a boarder at the Scots College in Paris, Robert Barclay—already a Latin and French scholar—learned Greek and Hebrew. Later, Barclay taught himself **theology**, **church** history, and patristics.

Robert Barclay was **convinced** in 1666 after worshipping with Friends, when he "felt a secret power among them" and "found the **evil** weakening in me and the good raised up." In 1670, his **marriage** to Christian Molleson "after the manner of Friends," by the mutual exchange of vows, created quite a furor because of the lack of officiating clergy. Barclay died at the age of 42 of a violent fever contracted on a religious visit to the north of Scotland.

In contrast to many Friends, Barclay and **William Penn** were well-educated gentlemen. Their writings were aimed at a well-educated audience and provided intellectual models for articulating the Quaker witness. In this process, they helped create broader toleration of Friends, but also aided in redefining the movement as it became more respectable. Barclay's first publications were a series of defensive dialogues (1670 to 1672). His *Catechism and Confession of Faith* came out in 1673. In 1676, he published *The Anarchy of the Ranters*, which defended **gospel order** against both anarchists and those who believed in church hierarchy. In Barclay, the theme of the **Lamb's War** subsided and restoration of New Testament Christianity became central.

Barclay's most important work, the *Apology*, grew out of an earlier publication, the *Theses Theologicae* directed at Nicholas Arnoldus, a Dutch Reformed theologian. Barclay's 14 theses, renamed propositions, became the basis of the *Apology*. To these Barclay added a 15th thesis "concerning salutations and recreations." This was the first systematic formulation of what later became known as the **testimonies** of **peace**, integrity (*see* TRUTH), **simplicity**, **equality**, and community (*see* CHURCH) that are still the basis of much Quaker practice.

While using the sequence of the *Westminster Shorter Catechism*, the *Apology* only addresses some of the topics of that document. Barclay's 15 Theological Theses ran counter to the then-predominant Calvinist doctrine by arguing the Quaker perspective on the work of the **Holy Spirit** over a literalist approach to the **Bible**; universal redemption, which is available even to those who have not heard of Jesus Christ; and **perfection** in the "reborn man" who knows "**Christ**, living, reigning, and ruling in him and revealing the law of the Spirit of life in him" [*Apology*, Proposition 8, II].

Used by some Friends today to defend **unprogrammed worship**, Quaker testimonies, and **universalism**, and by others to support central Christian doctrines, the *Apology* remains a living document. [Dean Freiday]

BARCLAY, ROBERT (OF REIGATE) (1833–1876). The British Friend whose book *The Inner Life of the Religious Societies of the Commonwealth* was published in 1876. It was an extensive work detailing early Friends and their antecedents, from an evangelical perspective. It has been claimed that this book set the template for consequent Quaker historical studies. [Pink Dandelion]

BARCLAY COLLEGE. Barclay College was founded in 1892 in Haviland, Kansas, as the Friends Haviland Academy. In 1917, under the leadership of Scott T. Clark, it became Kansas Central Bible Training School. The name was changed to Friends Bible College in 1925 and to Barclay College in 1990 after the 17th-century Scottish Friend, **Robert Barclay**.

BARNARD, HANNAH JENKINS (1754?–1825). Born to Baptist parents, Hannah Jenkins became a Quaker by **convincement** in 1773 through the Oblong **Monthly Meeting** in New York State, which her father had joined some years before.

In 1779, Jenkins married Peter Barnard, a carter by trade, under the care of the Oblong Meeting. Five years later they removed to the city of Hudson, New York. Hannah Barnard became increasingly active in the business of the Hudson Monthly Meeting. By the mid-1790s she was recognized as a **minister**, traveling extensively in New England and New York State. Her meeting granted her a certificate to pursue her ministry in the British Isles, and in July 1798 she arrived in England with a companion, **Elizabeth Coggeshall**.

While in **Ireland** (1799–1800), she came under the influence of Abraham Shackleton and the "**New Lights**," who opposed the literal reading of the **Bible** and the emphasis on correct doctrine then dominant in British and Irish Quakerism. With her independent thinking reinforced, Barnard openly questioned scriptural passages that she regarded of dubious origin or authority. When she returned to England in the spring of 1800, she was denied permission to accompany Coggeshall to the Continent. She was directed to cease **preaching** and to leave for the United States "by the first convenient opportunity." After exhausting all appeals, she rejected the offer of London **Yearly Meeting** to pay her passage home.

London Yearly Meeting sent two messages to ensure that this record of **discipline** would be received by the Hudson Monthly Meeting. Upon her return, Barnard found charges already pending against her. She was **disowned** in June 1802, partly in ratification of her censure abroad and partly because of "a Caviling, Contentious disposition of mind" that the **elders** of her meeting attributed to her during her spirited defense of these charges. A guarded admirer of **Elias Hicks**, who visited her in Hudson towards the end of her life, Barnard's challenge to orthodoxy foreshadowed the **Great Separation** of 1827. Later, she was attracted to **Unitarianism**, but it is unlikely that she formally joined that church. She remained an outspoken opponent of armed conflict, condemning especially the War of 1812. [David W. Maxey]

BARTRAM, JOHN (1699–1777). North American naturalist. Born in Darby, Pennsylvania, John Bartram educated himself in the classics, modern languages, history, philosophy, and **science**. Continuing to maintain himself as a farmer, he became the father of American botany. Journeying through Maryland, New Jersey, New York, Virginia, the Carolinas, and Florida with his son William (1739–1823), they described the flora they found. Bartram's Garden remains a mecca for horticulturists. **Disowned** in 1758 for refusing to acknowledge the divinity of **Christ**, he was officially reinstated by Darby **Monthly Meeting** in 1993. [Mary Ellen Chijioke]

BATHURST, ELIZABETH (1655–1685). Author of *Truth's Vindication* (1695), one of the few Quaker works of systematic **theology**, she became a convinced Friend in 1678. Despite being sickly most of her life, Bathurst was imprisoned for her faith (*see* PRISON) soon after her **convincement** and later traveled extensively in the **ministry** throughout Britain.

BAXTER, RICHARD (1615–1691). Noted Independent (Congregationalist) religious leader, who disputed with **James Nayler** and other Quakers. The Richard Baxter Society in Kidderminster, England, promotes interest in his life and work. *See also* PERFECTION.

BEACONITES. The group of about 400 Friends, mainly from Manchester and Kendal, England, led out of **London Yearly Meeting** by Isaac Crewdson (1780–1844) in 1835. These were **evangelical** Friends who believed the inward **Light** to be a delusive notion. They set up their own chapel with a revised system of **church** government and **leadership**. After Crewdson's death a few years later, the group dwindled. Their position would have been more acceptable within the Yearly Meeting 20 years later. [Pink Dandelion]

BEAN, HANNAH (ELLIOTT) SHIPLEY (1830–1909) and JOEL (1825–1914). Influential yet controversial leaders who favored older Quaker traditions at a time when **revivalism** and **holiness** theology were gaining support among many Friends.

Joel was born in New Hampshire to Quaker parents. Educated in public schools and a Quaker boarding school, he moved to Iowa in 1853 to begin his primary profession of teaching. Joel was recorded as a **minister** in 1858 and married Hannah Elliott Shipley the following year. Raised in a prominent **Orthodox** Philadelphia Quaker family, Hannah shared many interests with Joel, including their occupation as school teachers and their service among Friends. In 1861 they became the first Quaker **missionaries** to visit Hawaii. Upon their return, they helped to form Iowa **Yearly Meeting**, with Joel becoming the presiding **clerk** in 1867. That same year, they began to serve as the teachers of a new Friends Academy in West Branch.

Following an extended visit with Friends in England and a teaching position in Rhode Island, Joel resumed his role as Iowa Yearly Meeting's presiding clerk in 1877. Reacting to what they perceived as excesses of the revival movement and the loss of Quaker traditions, a concerned group separated from the main body to form the Iowa Yearly Meeting of Friends (**Conservative**). The Beans, liberal and tolerant in spirit, sympathized with the separatists and many of their views, yet remained loyal to the **Gurneyite** Yearly Meeting. However, this centrist position proved difficult to maintain. After **David Updegraff** held evangelistic meetings in their home town of West Branch in 1880, Joel published a pivotal critique of the revival, entitled *The Issue*. He was saddened by the new methods brought by the revivalists and disagreed with various holiness teachings on topics such as the emphasis on **sanctification** and a literal interpretation of the **Bible**.

The Beans attempted to avoid the growing tensions by relocating in 1882 to San Jose, California, but the controversy followed them. The San Jose **Monthly Meeting** was subordinate to Iowa Friends, and it split within a few months over revival-related issues, with the Beans leading one of the factions. Eventually, revival-influenced Friends in Iowa discontinued the San Jose Meeting, and the Beans were **disowned**, forfeiting their recording as ministers. These highly publicized actions helped to shape opinions and forge alliances among Friends on both sides of the Atlantic. Over 400 British Friends decried Iowa's "inquisitional proceedings" in a widely circulated letter. Generally, those who favored revivalism opposed the Beans while moderates and conservatives supported them. Although they remained traditionalists who lamented change, the Beans' legacy includes an innovation: the development of the College Park Association of Friends in 1889, the model for the **independent meetings movement**. [James Le Shana]

BEANITES. A 20th-century term used to designate followers of **Hannah and Joel Bean** and members of liberal, **independent meetings**.

BEARD, ELKANAH (1833–1905) and IRENA (1835–1920). American **missionaries** who left to go to India in the fall of 1869. *See also* SOUTH ASIA.

BELLERS, JOHN (1654–1725). Author, visionary, and social reformer. Bellers was a second-generation British Friend, much involved in the **relief** of the poor and the **education** of children. Many later thinkers, including Robert Owen and Karl Marx, who cited him in *Das Kapital*, were influenced by his thinking. Bellers drew much from biblical sources in articulating patterns of moral authority, particularly Luke 16:19–31, Matthew 25:31–46, and Acts 17:23–28. Bellers's wide-ranging interests led him to write works regarding world government, vocational training, cooperative communities, and health. [Margery Post Abbott]

BENEZET, ANTHONY (1713–1784). American schoolteacher and **abolitionist**. Born in St. Quentin, France, Anthony Benezet emigrated with his Huguenot family in 1715. In 1731, he reached Philadelphia, where he joined the Religious Society of Friends, marrying Joyce Marriot, a **minister**, in 1736. He spent most of his adult life teaching in Philadelphia Friends schools, taught **African Americans** for 20 years in his home, evenings, and persuaded Friends to build the first school for African Americans in 1770.

Benezet was part of the group of younger Philadelphia Friends in the 1750s who set out to reform **North American** Quakerism and the wider world. He was active in causes including **Native American** rights, war **relief** to the Acadians, **temperance**, **peace**, and **education**. While **John Woolman** was persuading Friends to clear themselves of the taint of **slavery**, Benezet spoke to Friends and the outside world. He had unparalleled impact on two major antislavery activists, Granville Sharp (1735–1813) and **Thomas Clarkson**, as well as the Methodist John Wesley (1703–1791) and the entire Quaker community. Sharp utilized Benezet's *A Short Account of that Part of Africa Inhabited by the Negroes* (1762) in his first legal battle in 1767. Clarkson credited Benezet's *Some Historical Account of Guinea* (1771) as the factor that drew him into the antislavery cause. The same tract was used by Wesley as the first half of his own antislavery tract in 1774. A committed antiracist, Benezet testified to his experience of the natural **equality** of all people. [Irv A. Brendlinger]

BENITO, JOAQUIN (ca. 1915–). A traveling **minister** and evangelist, Benito has been involved personally in starting numerous **meetings** in Peru. An Aymara, Benito made his decision to follow Jesus **Christ** in 1961 and became one of the first Quakers in Peru. He is recognized as a prayer warrior and presently carries on a **ministry** of encouragement to existing meetings despite his old age. He has held various leadership positions in Peru **Yearly Meeting** throughout the years. *See* SOUTH AMERICA. [Dan Cammack]

BENNETT, ASIA ALDERSON (1933–). Born in Washington, D.C., Asia Alderson was educated in Quaker schools, attended **Bryn Mawr College** from 1951 to 1953, when she married Lee C. Bennett Jr., then earned her bachelor's degree in psychology from the University of Pennsylvania in 1973. The Bennetts have three children; Brooks, Bruce, and Miriam. After teaching young children for almost two decades, she joined the community relations staff of **American Friends Service Committee** (AFSC) starting in 1971, and served as executive secretary for AFSC from 1980 until 1992. She then became executive secretary of **Friends World Committee for Consultation**, Section of the Americas, serving until her retirement in 1998. She was the first woman regularly appointed to either position. Over the years she has served on numerous Quaker **committees** and various boards for **Haverford College** and is a **Guilford College** trustee. The Bennetts now live in Washington State and are members of North Pacific **Yearly Meeting**.

BENSON, LEWIS (1906–1986). Leader of a **prophetic**, **Christ**-centered Quaker movement started among **liberal Friends** in the second half of the 20th century. Lewis Benson was born in Manusquan, New Jersey, to Quaker parents. Formal education bored him, and he never completed high school, so he began working early. After a disillusioning experience as a follower of the metaphysical leader George Gurdjieff, Benson found himself, at the age of 24, empty and despairing. Asked to examine a group of old Quaker books in the Manusquan meetinghouse to determine if they were worthy of retention, he instead began to read them. He was deeply affected by the ***Journal*** of **George Fox**, especially Fox's account of being rescued from the depths of despair by the voice of the Lord. Studying Fox and the early Friends and spreading their message became his life work. Benson joined the **Young Friends Movement** and there met Sarah Potts, whom he married in 1937. She became his life-long partner in his work. His studies, in part at **Woodbrooke** (Birmingham, England) and **Pendle Hill** (Pennsylvania), led him to emphasize the centrality of Christ as the unifying force of Quaker **worship**. Beginning with the American publication of his book, *Catholic Quakerism*, in 1968, a small group of supporters grew, encouraged by the Bensons' extensive travels in both **North America** and **Britain**. The **New Foundation Fellowship** continues to spread Lewis Benson's message of prophetic Quakerism throughout the world. [Peter Curtis]

BEREA BIBLE SEMINARY. Founded on February 10, 1921 in Chiquimula, Guatemala, as Berea Bible College with 16 students in the first class. It is operated by the Evangelical National **Friends Church** in Guatemala for training pastors. *See* CENTRAL AMERICA.

BIBLE. In 1649 **George Fox** was imprisoned the first time following his outburst in the Nottingham church, where he interrupted the preacher and called out, "Oh no, it is not the scriptures" but the "**Holy Spirit**, by which the holy men of **God** gave forth the Scriptures, whereby opinions, religions and judgments" are to be tried (Fox, *Journal*, Nickalls, p. 40). From this and other criticisms of wooden uses of Scripture, it has often been assumed early Quakers devalued the place and authority of the Bible. However, this is not the case. In challenging the Nottingham preacher, Fox was actually correcting his interpretation of 2 Peter 1:19–21, a passage Fox knew by heart. Here and elsewhere, Friends sought to uphold the biblical emphasis upon the revelatory work of God.

Through most of its development, Quakerism has been rooted firmly in the beliefs that the Scriptures are inspired by God and that their regular and prayerful reading provides a unique and irreplaceable source of spiritual direction, challenge, and nurture. At the same time, Friends have taken seriously the conviction that the Holy Spirit who inspired the writing of the Scriptures is also at work in the world, leading people into the **truth** of **Christ**. Therefore, Friends have emphasized the ongoing work of revelation, rather than seeing it confined to a written text or a conciliar body; a conviction rooted in Scripture (John 14–16).

In **Robert Barclay**'s formulation, while the Scriptures are a full and adequate account of all of the chief principles of the doctrine of Christ, they are only a declaration of the source, and not the source itself. Therefore, according to the Scriptures, the Spirit is the first and principal leader (Romans 8:14). Barclay highlights the importance of reading the Scriptures with an openness to the illuminating work of God. This process also takes place through reading, interpretation, and application of Scripture. **Samuel Fisher** described this approach as getting into the marrow of the text and drawing from a deeper well than literalistic approaches can avail.

Fox was sharply critical of ways the Scriptures were used by religious authorities of his day, as were other Quaker leaders. "I saw also how people read the Scriptures without a right sense of them, and without duly applying them to their own states," wrote Fox (*Journal*, Nickalls, p. 31). Further, those who "make a trade on chapter and verse" (*Journal*, p. 109), but fail to be transformed spiritually and morally, do not really know the Scriptures. They are akin to the Scribes and Pharisees of Jesus's day, and Fox even calls "antichrists" those who "profess the Scripture's spirit and live not in the life and power of them" (*Journal*, p. 135). Samuel Fisher in his *Rusticus ad Academicos* (From the Rustic to the Academics, 1660) likewise criticized the Puritans' dogmatic use of Scripture in favor of considering readings of the text in its original language. Friends thus contributed significantly to historical/critical approaches to Bible study—over and against traditionalist approaches—emerging in the modern era.

While the reading of Scripture and other religious books has been a long-standing emphasis of Friends, programmatic approaches to **religious education** and the assimilation of Scripture have been troubling to some. In the early 19th century, tensions between emphasis on the inward **Light** and **continuing revelation** and emphasis on the authority of Scripture came to a head in the **Great Separation** of 1827. In the early 1830s, the Bible Association of Friends in America was organized among **Orthodox** Friends in Philadelphia for the purpose of providing Bibles to Friends and others who needed them. Many other biblical-literacy concerns have also been furthered by Friends, and this can be seen in many of the later Quaker **revivalistic** and **missionary** ventures. By the end of the century, tensions arose as different groups of Friends turned toward either **fundamentalist** or **modernist** readings of Scripture, eventually leading to further divisions.

For the past two centuries, Friends have often been divided on the use and authority of Scripture. Some Friends diminish the appeal to

Scripture, or any external source of authority, advocating instead the ongoing possibility of divine revelation and the importance of being open to it, regardless of the source. Conversely, most Friends have felt it important to develop one's **spirituality** and social concern around the central teachings of Scripture. They also stress the importance of familiarity with Scripture as an objective referent by which to check subjective leadings.

Quaker biblical scholars of note include **J. Rendell Harris** and **Henry J. Cadbury**. Quaker contributions to the meaningful interpretation of Scripture also have been considerable in popular devotional readings. [Paul N. Anderson]

BIDDLE, ESTHER (1629–1696). British traveling **minister**. Biddle became a Quaker in 1654, preached publicly for 39 years, traveling and ministering to people in Ireland, Scotland, Newfoundland, Barbados, Holland, and France. She was incarcerated at least 14 times for being a Quaker minister and writer, and it is believed that she gave birth to a son during one of these imprisonments. At the age of 65, Biddle was spiritually moved to visit Queen Mary, and subsequently King Louis XIV in France; granted an audience by the two rulers, she spoke to each of them about wartime mediation and **peace**. This Spiritual Mother wrote eight Quaker tracts, some of them from **prison** cells. [Michele Lise Tarter]

BISHOP, GEORGE (d. 1688). Leading organizer and publicist of the early Quaker movement in Bristol, England.

BLACKBURN, ELISHA (1873–1958). American medical **missionary** to Kenya from 1903 to 1906. *See also* EAST AFRICA; LUNG'AHO, DAUDI.

BOLLING, LANDRUM (1928–). President of **Earlham College** in Indiana from 1958 to 1973, Bolling was a founder of the **Earlham School of Religion**. Bolling then served as the president and chairman of the board of the Lilly Foundation and later as chairman of the National Council on Foundations before becoming director of Mercy Corps International, a nonprofit organization that works to build secure, productive, and just communities. Bolling has served as an international mediator, becoming a link between the U.S. government and Palestinian leaders and also helping build an interfaith dialogue among Muslims, Jews, and Christians there (*see* PEACE TESTIMONY). He has also helped in negotiations and in sustaining communications between the U.S. government and the emerging national leaders in the Balkans, as well as assisting in economic and redevelopment projects. He is a founding member of Harvard University's Conflict Management Group in Massachusetts and is a senior fellow at the Center for International Policy in Washington, D.C.

BOSTON MARTYRS. Name given to four Quakers who were hanged on Boston Common by the **Puritan** authorities for attempting to reenter the Massachusetts Bay Colony in order to preach after being banished. **Mary Dyer**, Marmaduke Stephenson, and William Robinson were hanged in 1659/60, William Leddra (b. 1596) in 1660/61.

BOULDING, ELISE (1920–) and KENNETH EWART (1910–1993). Mystic, poet, economist, and **peace** activist, Kenneth Boulding was a leader in studying the economic basis of imperialism, war, peace, and disarmament. His work also addressed the economic issues in social systems, pollution, and ecology and, as in *The Organizational Revolution* (1953), was explicitly rooted in Christian ethical assumptions. Raised in Liverpool, England, Kenneth Boulding's teaching career started at the University of Edinburgh before he moved to the United States in 1937.

In the late 1950s, Boulding became part of a gathering of scientists concerned with peace who created the *Journal of Conflict Resolution* and the Center for Research on Conflict Resolution at the University of Michigan, two crucial steps in the founding of the movement for peace research. Boulding published many scholarly books on economics as well as devotional works such as *Sonnets From the Inner Life* (1954). His personal witness to peace resulted in an epistle (cosigned by his wife, Elise) which cost him a position at the League of Nations; a multi-year struggle to gain U.S. citizenship without promising to bear arms; participation in many vigils; and a refusal to sign a loyalty oath in 1961, which led to the loss of a teaching post.

Elise Bjørn-Hansen Boulding taught for many years at Dartmouth College and is known for her groundbreaking sociological studies of women and her international work for peace. She served as president of the **Women's International League for Peace and Freedom** and has written extensively on the **family** as a small society and as the way for creating a peaceful future. [Margery Post Abbott]

BOWLES, GILBERT (1869–1960) and MINNIE PICKETT (1868–1958). North American **missionaries** to Japan. Born to Iowa Quaker farmers, Gilbert Bowles attended Friends Academy, Kansas, received his B.A. and M.A. from **William Penn College**, Iowa, and his Ph.D. from the University of Chicago. In 1898, he married Minnie Pickett, sister of **Clarence Pickett**, who had just completed five years teaching at Tokyo Friends School. Gilbert absorbed Minnie's interest in Japan, and between 1901 and 1941 the Bowleses, and their growing family, served six terms in Japan under the auspices of the Philadelphia **Yearly Meeting** (**Orthodox**). They managed the Friends School and established the Tokyo Friends Center. In 1941, the Bowleses moved to Hawaii, where Gilbert worked to aid Japanese Americans. After **World War II**, they helped plan Japanese **relief work** for the **American Friends Service Committee** and the **Friends World Committee for Consultation**. *See also* EAST ASIA. [Mary Ellen Chijioke]

BOWLY, SAMUEL (1802–1884). English business leader and chairman of the Birmingham and Gloucester Banking Company, Bowly's first public cause was the **abolition** of slavery. A founder (1852) and longtime president of the Friends **Temperance** Union, he also served as cochair of the first World's Temperance Convention in 1846, and was the first president of the National Temperance League (1862–1884).

BRAITHWAITE, JOSEPH BEVAN (1818–1905). Evangelical British **minister**. Braithwaite married Martha Gillett in 1851. He also traveled extensively in the United States and was one of six delegates sent to the conference of **Orthodox** Friends in Indiana in 1887 and led in the drafting of the **Richmond Declaration of Faith**. Braithwaite was a leading figure in British Quakerism for decades but failed to convince **London Yearly Meeting** to adopt the Richmond Declaration. From the late 1880s, he watched in increasing distress as

Friends in **Britain** adopted **liberal** theology. His death, in the same year as **J. W. Rowntree**, symbolized the final demise of evangelical Quakerism in **Britain**. [Pink Dandelion]

BRAITHWAITE, WILLIAM CHARLES (1862–1922). British banker, lawyer, historian, and son of **Joseph Bevan Braithwaite**. A leading **liberal** thinker, he coauthored the Rowntree series in Quaker history with **Rufus Jones**. *See also* SCIENCE AND TECHNOLOGY.

BRIGHT, JOHN (1811–1889). English statesman and orator. Born in Rochdale, Lancashire, Bright developed skill in speaking in early 1830s through the Rochdale Juvenile **Temperance** Band and became president of the British Temperance League from 1842 to 1844. Upon his marriage in 1839, he set a policy of having no intoxicating beverages in his home.

Following the repeal of the Test Act in the 1830s, which had excluded nonconformists such as Quakers from public office (*see* POLITICS), Bright became the second Quaker Member of Parliament in 1843 and held a seat during most of the next 45 years. Bright joined with Richard Cobden in a successful campaign for the 1846 repeal of the Corn Laws, which were keeping food prices high during an Irish famine. Bright led the **Peace** Society and lost his seat in Parliament in the 1850s for opposing the Crimean War, but was later reelected. During the American Civil War, he helped keep Britain from breaking the Union blockade of Confederate ports by force. Bright became the first Quaker cabinet member at William E. Gladstone's invitation in 1868, but resigned from a second cabinet appointment in 1882 over British military intervention in Egypt. [Margery Post Abbott, Sabron Newton]

BRINTON, ANNA (SHIPLEY) COX (1887–1969) and HOWARD HAINES (1884–1973). North American scholars, educators, and administrators. The early story of **Pendle Hill**, the Quaker adult study center founded near Philadelphia in 1930, "is essentially the story of Howard and Anna Brinton." She was director of administration from 1936 to 1949 and he acting director in 1934 to 1935 and director of studies from 1936 to 1952. Their skills were complementary: Howard Brinton as philosopher and mystic and Anna Brinton as activist and organizer; she as fundraiser and organizer; he as gardener and a carpenter who could fix almost anything.

A granddaughter of **Hannah and Joel Bean**, Anna Cox grew up in California, and joined Philadelphia **Yearly Meeting (Orthodox)** while at Westtown boarding school. She majored in Classics at Leland Stanford University in California, and received her doctorate in 1917. She taught Classics at Mills College until 1920.

Howard Brinton, born in Chester County, Pennsylvania, was descended from generations of Quaker farmers and merchants. He earned both bachelor's and master's degrees from **Haverford College**, where he was a student of **Rufus Jones**. He earned another master's degree from Harvard University and in 1925 received his Ph.D. from the University of California. He taught in Quaker schools, for several years headed the Mathematics Department at **Guilford College**, and in 1917–1918 was acting president of that college. He and Anna Cox met while they were doing postwar **relief work** in Europe with the **American Friends Service Committee (AFSC)**.

The Brintons taught at **Earlham College** from 1921 to 1928 and then moved to California where Anna served as dean of the Mills College faculty. In 1931, the Brintons called together Friends from California, Oregon, and Washington to found the Pacific Coast Association of Friends, later Pacific Yearly Meeting, from which two other **independent yearly meetings**—North Pacific and Intermountain—have grown.

In 1936, they accepted the joint directorship of Pendle Hill, an institution near extinction, with only six students. They recruited 25 students for the following year. In Pendle Hill the Brintons saw an opportunity to apply Quaker principles to both method and content of adult education. The Brintons brought 1,500 AFSC trainees and students to Pendle Hill, and linked the center with graduate work in religion at Haverford College.

Howard published numerous pamphlets and eight books on **mysticism**, Quaker **journals**, **education**, **worship**, and Quaker religious philosophy. Anna published scholarly works on Virgil's *Aeneid* and such significant Pendle Hill pamphlets as "Toward Undiscovered Ends" and "Wide Horizon." After 1949, Anna Brinton served as AFSC Commissioner for Asia and later as director of the International Relations Program. In postwar Japan she set up two relief centers, while Howard joined her as Quaker international affairs representative. *See also* MENTAL HEALTH REFORM. [Paul Lacey]

BRITAIN. The Religious Society of Friends began in Britain in the 1650s. The imperative to publish the **Truth** throughout the world quickly led to temporary and permanent **migration**, and it is possible to identify a distinctive British Quakerism, discrete from Quakerism elsewhere, from the early 1660s.

Although Quakerism was the most successful of the sects of the period, early hopes of divinely ordered global transformation through the **Lamb's War** had dimmed with the restoration of the monarchy in 1660. What followed was a more pragmatic approach. The Quaker Act of 1662 and Conventicle Acts of 1664 and 1670 led to the imprisonment of thousands of Friends (*see* PRISON). While Quakers in some **North American** colonies early enjoyed religious toleration and political power, British Friends remained a persecuted group and only gradually won toleration under the law. In 1689, Quaker **worship** was legalized, but it was not until 1870 that Friends could be full citizens in Britain while retaining their **testimonies** against oaths (*see* RESTORATION) and **tithes**.

In the late 17th century, religious toleration and the death of **George Fox**, **Robert Barclay**, and later of **Margaret Fell** and **William Penn**, combined with the usual challenges facing second and third generations of believers to create an increasingly institutionalized church that included hereditary **membership** after 1737, the establishment of **elders**, and the regulation of behavior. **Disownment** became more frequent, for offenses such as debt, drunkenness, and other unacceptable behaviors, and, in particular, for **marriage** by a priest. These **Quietist** Friends believed they were "His People"; thus, maintenance of purity became the primary concern. Less effort was put into **convincement** and, by 1860, membership was at its lowest. From a possible 80,000 in 1660, the number of Friends in Britain had fallen to around 13,000.

Friends experienced increasing prosperity in the 18th and 19th centuries. Families such as that of **Abraham Darby** (*see* SCIENCE AND TECHNOLOGY) were central in the Industrial Revolution. Later, the family of **George Cadbury** was one of several involved in the growing chocolate **business**. After the British Reform Bill of

1832, Friends such as **John Bright** were able to run for public office (*see* CIVIL GOVERNMENT).

Influenced by evangelical **revivals** outside the **Yearly Meeting**, British Friends' beliefs began to shift after the 1820s. The emphasis on the inward **Light** was replaced by the primacy of scriptural authority and book learning was no longer deemed too worldly. At this stage, Friends ceased to see themselves as the gathered remnant but rather as part of the wider Christian church. The "**hedge**" between themselves and "the world" (*see* PECULIARITY) was felt to be anachronistic, and in the 1850s and 1860s reforms were introduced to open the Yearly Meeting to new ideas and new converts. By 1910, membership had risen to 20,000 aided by the relaxation of the number of disownable offenses and the work of **Home Mission** Meetings and the Adult School Movement.

Paradoxically, this new freedom undermined the **evangelical** enterprise. However, British Friends never adopted pastors as **North American** Friends did, and resisted water **baptism**. The next revival, that of **liberal** Quakerism, began in the 19th century with new biblical scholarship and was heralded by the 1895 **Manchester Conference**. Starting in the 20th century, the Yearly Meeting focused on what it viewed as the 17th-century Quaker **distinctives**, e.g., **unprogrammed** worship and a lack of outward forms, in an attempt to place experience, not the **Bible**, at the heart of Quaker religiosity. In Britain, during this period, the doctrine of **continuing revelation** allowed Friends to define themselves as a seeking church.

The second half of the century ushered in a period of liberal influence, which has allowed the **membership** of non-Christian Friends and a general increase in diversity of beliefs. In 1993, a new **Conservative** yearly meeting, "Friends in Christ," was set up as a reaction to this pluralism. In a fashion which can be traced back to Quietist days and even before to the 1656 *Epistle of the Elders of Balby* (*see* BALBY, EPISTLE OF THE ELDERS OF), the majority of British Quakerism is united in its manner of silent **worship** rather than by doctrinal assent. In Britain Yearly Meeting in 2000, 16,000 members plus 9,000 attenders populate close to 500 local **meetings**. As has always been the case, the vast majority of British Friends live in England. *See also* VALIANT SIXTY. [Pink Dandelion]

BROKEN. Early Friends spoke with satisfaction of "tender broken **meetings**" when the love of **God** had broken the hearts of worshippers and opened them to the **leadings** of **Christ**. Some Friends today speak of "breaking meeting," meaning closing worship with the shaking of hands.

BROWN, MOSES (1738–1836). Rhode Island Quaker **elder**, reformer, and **philanthropist**. A successful merchant and director of the first bank in Rhode Island, he became active as a leader among Friends and in the **abolition** movement after his wife Anna died in 1773.

BRYN MAWR COLLEGE. Bryn Mawr College in Bryn Mawr, Pennsylvania, was founded in 1885 by provisions of the will of Joseph Wright Taylor (1810–1880), an **Orthodox** Friend. It has never been affiliated with any **yearly meeting** although many Friends attended the college.

BURNELL, JOCELYN SUSAN BELL (1943–). British astrophysicist who was instrumental in the discovery of pulsars, Burnell is dean of science at the University of Bath and president of the Rogal Astronomical Society (*see* SCIENCE AND TECHNOLOGY). Born into a Irish Quaker family, she is active among Friends, with particular interests in the **ministry** of the wounded, which she addressed in her 1989 Swarthmore Lecture at Britain **Yearly Meeting**, and in **ecumenical** relationships. She was the Quaker representative to the British Council of Churches assembly from 1978 until 1990 and served as **clerk** of Britain Yearly Meeting from 1995 until 1998.

BURROUGH, EDWARD (1634–1662/63). Born in Kendal, Westmoreland, Burrough was an English **minister** who joined with **George Fox** in 1652 and was one of the **Valiant Sixty** and leader of Quaker London **mission** 1654–1656 with **Francis Howgill**. He was a major political and theological pamphleteer. He was arrested in 1661 and died in Newgate **prison** 1662/63 in London. [Rosemary Anne Moore]

BUSINESS AND ECONOMICS. On both sides of the Atlantic, generations of Quakers have been highly successful innovators in the development of products and processes as well as commercial and financial practices.

In **Britain**, Quaker families were associated with many of the technological innovations of the Industrial Revolution, including the use of coke as a fuel, the smelting and fabrication of iron, processing of precious metals, and building of the first railways (*see* SCIENCE AND TECHNOLOGY). **Abraham Darby** and his descendants built Coalbrookdale into a leading iron-making center, with one crowning achievement being the Iron Bridge at Coalbrookdale, the first cast-iron bridge. Many of the Quaker names found in British economic history of this period are recognizable to this day: Wilkinson in metals, Cadbury (*see* CADBURY, GEORGE) and **Rowntree** in cocoa and chocolates, as well as Barclay and Lloyd in banking and finance. In **North America** as well, the Quaker merchants of Philadelphia achieved legendary success and wealth. Macy's and Strawbridge and Clothier department stores and Bethlehem Steel Company are among the notable establishments with Quaker beginnings.

One reason this small group spawned such a disproportionately large and accomplished business sector is that, particularly in England, the radical beliefs and behavior of the Quakers excluded them from doing much else. Barred from the universities, most of the professions, and much of public life, this excluded religious minority sought to be productive in one of the few spheres remaining: the marketplace.

For Friends engaged in commerce, their religious attitudes and testimonies led to highly profitable business practices. Insisting on **truth** in all matters and convinced that the honest price could not vary from customer to customer, Quakers created the successful innovation of **fixed-price** retailing. The expectation that individuals would work hard and live simply (*see* SIMPLICITY) assisted the accumulation of significant capital. The international social and religious network among Friends provided a ready set of commercial contacts for Quaker merchants and manufacturers. Friends were also required by their **meetings** to live within their means and avoid speculative enterprise. This created an unusually stable economic base for their community. Such factors could not guarantee commercial success, but they certainly helped.

While **Kenneth E. Boulding**'s work has gained prominence, no single school of thought exists among Friends with regard to economic affairs in the 20th century. Disillusionment with the ethical standards of large corporations has turned many Friends away from business to nonprofit activities, especially education and medicine. A shared core of values continues with a high degree of consistency, but debates about comparative economic systems, labor practices, government policies, the limits to growth, and the right sharing of resources in a global economy clearly illustrate that there is no single Quaker view of the economy. [Thomas Head]

BUSINESS MEETINGS. Business meetings, or **meetings** for **worship** for **church** affairs, are at the very heart of the Quaker self-understanding of what it means to be a church. Business meetings are structured to a conscious **discipline** which reflects a profound **theology** sometimes described as **gospel order**.

Business meetings reflect the faith that the primary authority is that of **God**: as the God whose will is sought; as **Christ** who presides; and as the **Holy Spirit** who inspires and empowers. Thus the task of the meeting is to listen in worship under that authority, to discern (*see* DISCERNMENT, SPIRITUAL) the right way forward on any piece of business. Some meetings expect each person only to speak once to any item of business and that there should be no attempt to persuade or sway a meeting, but that a trust that God will find the speakers to say what needs to be said. Another aspect of the discipline is that those who cannot attend a meeting accept the decisions of those who were there, trusting that those present sought the will of God.

A **gathered** body under the authority of God may find unity in actions that only become apparent during the course of the business meeting. Unity in the Spirit is not synonymous with unanimity and is generally referred to as the "sense of the meeting." Friends seek to follow God's way in their work, not simply human understanding or consensus. Though the process may take some time, at the end it can find a united meeting able to act swiftly because the action has been widely agreed.

Clerks facilitate the process and record the business, especially the decisions, in **minutes.** The minutes are discussed and agreed within the meeting, becoming authoritative for the meeting concerned. The process differs somewhat in **Britain** and in **North America**. Americans tend to have one clerk to preside and a second to record the minutes. Their minutes are relatively detailed and are sometimes presented all together at the close of a business session. A British clerk presides and prepares the minutes with an assistant to help. The minutes tend to focus on the main points considered, and each minute is presented as part of its own item.

Until the late 19th century, **women** held separate business meetings, which were limited in the range of business addressed. Women's meetings are still held in parts of Africa. [Janet Scott]

BUTLER, ESTHER HETTIE (1851–1921). American **missionary**. A recorded **minister**, Esther Butler was the first American Quaker missionary to China, arriving in 1887 (*see* EAST ASIA) and the first missionary sent abroad under the auspices of Ohio **Yearly Meeting** (**Gurneyite**). During her 30-year tenure as superintendent of the mission, Butler organized the Friends Hospital for Woman and Children, Nanjing (Nanking) Memorial Hospital, Peace Hospital in Luho, a training school for women, Union Nurse School, an orphanage, day and boarding schools for children, numerous street chapels, and the Nanjing and Luho Friends churches.

Butler was born in Mahoning County, Ohio, to Benjamin and Hannah Stanley Butler, members of prominent Quaker families in the region. She taught school near her home in Ohio, in North Carolina, and, briefly in 1873, at the Pottowatomie Indian school in Kansas.

In 1884, Butler was spiritually transformed under the ministry of Mary Moon Meredith (1845–1924), a **holiness** Quaker who conducted interdenominational **revival** meetings in North Carolina and Iowa. Thereafter, Butler felt divinely called to serve as a missionary evangelist. Even though there were no signs or visions, Butler later recalled, there was a "conviction that never allowed one question. I knew the country was China, the place Nankin." Butler remained in China as a mission superintendent until her death in Guling (Kuling). [Jacalynn Stuckey Baker]

–C–

CADBURY, GEORGE (1839–1922). One of the owners of the Cadbury Cocoa works, George Cadbury was instrumental in moving it to the country site of Bournville, England, in the 1880s, where he began to build a model village for his workers. Shrewd in **business**, he made Cadburys the main chocolate manufacturer throughout the British Empire. An immensely wealthy **philanthropist** and industrialist, he later owned three newspapers. A supporter of **mission** work but also part of the group of Friends keen to encourage **liberal** Quakerism in **Britain** at the start of the 20th century, his home at **Woodbrooke** became a Quaker study center in 1902. He married twice: first to Mary Tyler, and, after her death in 1877, to Elizabeth Mary Taylor. [Pink Dandelion]

CADBURY, HENRY JOEL (1883–1974). Biblical scholar, and **peace** activist. Henry Cadbury was born into an **Orthodox** Philadelphia Quaker family and married Lydia Caroline Brown in 1916. He joined the **Haverford College** faculty in 1910, then was suspended in 1918 for writing a letter to the *Public Ledger* urging peace. In 1919 he was appointed to the faculty of Andover Theological Seminary; he later taught at **Bryn Mawr College** and Harvard University.

A member of the committee that developed the *Revised Standard Version* of the **Bible** between 1929 and 1952, Cadbury published widely as a biblical scholar and a Quaker historian. He was also an active participant in peace conferences, and chaired the **American Friends Service Committee** from 1928 to 1934. Within Philadelphia **Yearly Meeting** he participated in the **Young Friends Movement** and was active in efforts to reunite the **Hicksite** and Orthodox branches. [Margery Post Abbott]

CALDERONE, MARY STEICHEN (1904–1998). North American physician and pioneer of sex education.

CALVERT, GILES (1612–1663). Noted London printer of radical books, the first regular Quaker printer, and a brother of **Martha Simmons**.

CAMM, JOHN (1605–1656/57). A preacher from Westmoreland in northern England, possibly a former Grindletonian preacher, Camm joined with **George Fox** in 1652. He interviewed Oliver Cromwell on behalf of Friends in 1654. Camm and **John Audland** led the successful Bristol **mission** of 1654–1655.

CAMMACK, DOROTHY NORTHCROSS and IRVIN HORN (1850–1929). Pioneer **missionaries** in Tegucigalpa, Honduras, sent by California **Yearly Meeting** to **Central America** from 1909 to 1914.

CAMP, KATHERINE LINSAY (KAY) (1918–) and WILLIAM (1917–1999). American peace and social reformers. He was a leader in **mental health reform** and a founder of Physicians for Social Responsibility. Kay was international president of **Women's International League for Peace and Freedom** from 1974 to 1980.

CANADA. Friends moved into Upper Canada (Ontario) in enough numbers to organize a monthly meeting in the Niagara district by 1797. Most had moved north, unwilling to fight for either side in the American War of Independence (1775–1783) (*see* PEACE), but others came because of their opposition to slavery (*see* ABOLITION) or desire to open up the frontier (*see* MIGRATIONS). The division of New York **Yearly Meeting** in 1828 entangled its Canadian members. As a result, Canada Yearly Meeting (**Orthodox**) formed in 1828. Genesee Yearly Meeting (**Hicksite**) was created in 1834 by both Canadian and New York Friends. Canada Yearly Meeting (**Conservative**) was established in 1885 as a reaction to revivalism. Canadian young Friends participated in the Friends Ambulance Unit and other Quaker **relief work** units during World War I and **World War II**. Canadian Friends Service Committee (*see* PEACE AND SERVICE AGENCIES; NATIVE AMERICANS) was formed jointly by all three yearly meetings in 1931. The Hicksite and Orthodox yearly meetings began holding concurrent sessions beginning in 1928 and all three yearly meetings formally reunited in 1955. Canada Yearly Meeting belongs to **Friends General Conference** and **Friends United Meeting**. Also, new churches are being founded outside Canada Yearly Meeting with connections to **Evangelical Friends International**. *See also* NORTH AMERICA. [Margery Post Abbott]

CARIBBEAN. In the 16th century, many Friends visited the Caribbean, and some settled there, forming meetings and schools in Barbados and elsewhere. Many of those Friends voiced strong concerns about the conditions of prisons and other aspects of life they found there (*see* PENAL REFORM). **George Fox** urged better treatment and education of slaves, and **William Edmundson** was one of the earliest voices against the institution of slavery (*see* ABOLITION) as a result of his visit to Barbados. Few of these communities of Friends survived to the present day.

Jamaica has long Quaker connections, including a visit by Fox in 1671. Admiral William Penn, father of **William Penn** the founder of Pennsylvania, had won Jamaica from Spanish control for the British crown in 1655. By 1740, a **meeting** and a Friends school had been established, but little remained a century later. In 1881, Evi Sharpless (ca. 1844–1913) was sent by Iowa **Yearly Meeting** to establish a **mission** in Jamaica and began the work that is the basis of the modern Yearly Meeting founded in 1941. **Education** continued as a major concern with the creation of the Continuation School in Highgate, and the Happy Grove School. Friends also support the Lyndale Home for Girls and the Swift Purcell Home for Boys.

Iglesia de los Amigos (Cuaqueros) en Cuba (Cuba Yearly Meeting), formed in 1927, has its modern roots in the mission work initiated by Benjamin F. Trueblood (1847–1916) and other Friends in Iowa Yearly Meeting in 1900. A number of schools were established, which were then taken over by the government in 1961 after Fidel Castro came to power. Fortunately, Cuba has had a long tradition of strong local pastors, such as **Juan Guzman**, who nurtured many congregations in the 1940s and 1950s, and Cuban Quakerism survived its isolation in good health. Five **monthly meetings** exist in Holguin and Las Tunas Provinces. [Margery Post Abbott]

CASTILLO, MARIA LUZ (d. 1976). Mexican educator and **minister** of Matehuala, San Luis Potosi Friends Church. During the post-revolutionary years (1920–1930s) she kept open the Friends school in her town until her death. She was recognized as a leader in private **education** in her native state San Luis Potosi. *See also* MEXICO.

CASTRO, ÁNGEL (1900–1957). Early Friends physician in Chiquimula, Guatemala. *See* CENTRAL AMERICA.

CATTELL, CATHERINE ISABELLA DeVOL (1906–1986) and EVERETT LEWIS (1905–1981). Everett and Catherine spent 21 years as **missionaries** in Bundelkhand, India (*see* SOUTH ASIA).

They married in 1927 and arrived in India in 1936, soon after five young staff members resigned over disagreements with **Esther Baird**. The staff had wanted to replace the schools she started with a mass movement of evangelism to the "untouchables."

The Cattells returned to the United States in 1957 when he was called as **superintendent** of Ohio **Yearly Meeting** (later Evangelical Friends Church, Eastern Region). Everett served as president of **Malone College** in Canton, Ohio, from 1960 to 1972, and as president of the World Evangelical Fellowship. The daughter of missionaries to China (*see* DeVOL FAMILY), Catherine DeVol Cattell wrote many books for children drawn from her missionary experience.

One of the leading Quaker voices articulating the tradition of the **holiness movement** in the mid-20th century, Everett Cattell was influential in opening Evangelical Friends Alliance (later **Evangelical Friends International** [**EFI**]) to interactions with other Friends. During a 1969 Conference on Evangelism directed by Billy Graham, he persuaded leaders from EFI and **Friends United Meeting** to invite all American Friends, including members of **Friends General Conference**, to gather in St. Louis in 1970 on the theme "The Future of Friends." Everett gave the keynote address. This gathering of 131 Friends opened opportunities for dialogue among all Friends. Its work was continued as the Faith and Life Movement sponsored by **Friends World Committee for Consultation**. The national meeting in 1973 was the first occasion when official representatives of every **North American** yearly meeting met together. In 1977, a bilingual Friends' conference included delegates from **Bolivia**, **Mexico**, and **Central America**, one of several gatherings sparked by the work of the Faith and Life Movement. *See also* ECUMENISM; SANCTIFICATION. [Margery Post Abbott]

CELESTIAL FLESH. A modern term used to describe the earliest Friends' immanent **theology** of **Christ** present within. Gathered in **meetings**, **Quaker** men and women waited for the currents of **God** to move through their bodies, leading them to divine revelation and **prophecy**; when spirit poured onto flesh, they became "the living Christ," and their bodies were perceived to be perfect and in a prelapsarian state (i.e., restored to **perfection** as before the fall from the Garden of Eden). This doctrine of celestial inhabitation was manifested in the thousands of hands-on healings **George Fox** conducted throughout his **ministry**, all ushering in a movement of primitive Christianity and profound **convincements**. The act of quaking (*see* QUAKER) was ultimately a testament to the divine savior inhabiting every particle of Friends' bodies and souls. [Michele Lise Tarter]

CENTRAL AFRICA (BURUNDI, CONGO, RWANDA). Quakerism was brought to the French-speaking countries of central Africa by **North American** Friends from the **evangelical** branch. In 1934 Mid-America **Yearly Meeting** started Friends Africa Gospel Mission in Burundi. For 50 years the **mission** engaged in evangelizing and church planting, while serving physical needs through medicine, **education**, technical aid, agriculture, and community development. In 1984, Burundi **Friends Church** became a full **yearly meeting**. Church leaders, led by **David Niyonzima**, are deeply involved in **peace** and reconciliation efforts throughout central Africa.

Work in Congo began in 1984 as an outreach of Burundi Yearly Meeting and the Friends Church in Rwanda was begun by **Evangelical Friends Mission**. In February 1986, a missionary team arrived in Rwanda, and Friends' worship services started in May 1987. Legal recognition followed in October. In 1993 there were 24 Friends churches in Rwanda.

Central African Friends suffered greatly in the region's civil disturbances of the 1990s. Nevertheless, Friends' presence continued to grow. In 1997, Rwanda had over 50 worshipping groups; by 2001, Burundi had approximately 12,000 members in more than 70 congregations; and membership in Congo reached 1,300 in 2001. Friends' activities in the region are coordinated through **Evangelical Friends International (EFI)**–Africa Region. In April 1999, EFI-Africa Region opened the **Great Lakes School of Theology** at Bujumbura, Burundi.

Since 2001 Burundi Friends Church has cooperated with the Great Lakes Peace Initiative of Friends Peace Teams in operating a Reconciliation Center in Bujumbura. [James Morris]

CENTRAL AMERICA. The Quaker presence in Central America has grown from the early 20th-century **missionary** work of California Friends. In 1902, California **Yearly Meeting** of Friends Church, now

Friends Church Southwest Yearly Meeting, first sent missionaries to Guatemala.

Thomas J. Kelly (d.1903) and Clark Buckley (d.1905) left San Francisco, California, on January 2, 1902, for the Pacific coast of Guatemala. Undecided between Jalapa and Chiquimula, they knelt and waited before hearing God answer: "Chiquimula is the place." From Chiquimula, they traveled to Honduras, where Clark Buckley died in 1905. Kelly returned to California where he died in 1903. The missionary work in Guatemala was continued by two young women: Esther Bond and Alice Zimmer.

On November 22, 1906, **Ruth Esther Smith** arrived in Chiquimula and became the main pillar of missionary Quaker work in Central America. Under her leadership, many Friends' **meetings** formed in Guatemala and Honduras. The first yearly meeting was organized in 1946.

Friends' missionary work developed in Honduras, through the work of Smith and the national leader **Pedro Leiva**. By December 1909 they had established themselves in San Marcos, Ocotepeque. The first national preacher was **Magdaleno Hernandez**. Later on, Emilio Salgado (1909–1997), Pedro Oliva and others extended the work to Tegucigalpa, Honduras. Eventually, the meetings around the Tegucigalpa area were formally transferred to the **Holiness** Missionary Society, and new believers ceased to be Friends, but older ones maintained their Quaker beliefs.

The spread of Quakerism in Guatemala occurred mainly by establishing schools. The girls' school started in late 1908, and the boys' by June 1912. These schools united to become the Friends School. The Berea Bible College (now **Berea Bible Seminary**) opened on February 10, 1921. There, many new leaders were trained and, as the first group graduated in October 1923, they spread the Friends' Christian message, establishing many new meetings. Graduates included the Bolivian **Juan Ayllón,** and his Honduran wife, Tomasa Valle. They soon left for Bolivia (*see* SOUTH AMERICA) to start a Friends meeting with the support of Guatemalan Friends. Berea's first graduating class also included Lidy Asturias, from Guatemala City, and Juana Velásquez, Manuela Morales (1896–1967), and Victoria España (1896–1967), from Chiquimula, Guatemala, all of whom became national leaders in Guatemala, Honduras, and Bolivia. Other key local Friends included **Bernardino Ramírez**, Armando Peralta (1878–1942), and Emilio Salgado. Adolfo Marroquín (1898–1980), **José María Durán Aldana**, Pilar Álvarez, and Salomón Prado (d.1955) were among the teachers at the Friends School. American missionaries continued to provide important support for the work.

Growth continued from 1940 on and the number of believers reached 4,500. By the end of that decade, the death of two key leaders, national worker Bernardino Ramírez and the pioneer missionary Ruth Esther Smith, forced changes in leadership, but the church remained vigorous. A General Congress, organized by young people in 1947, produced new vitality. In 1963, the Yearly Meeting began broadcasts over a local radio station. Soon broadcasts started over other stations, including *Volviendo a Jesús, Destellos de Luz*, and caused a notable increase in believers. The *Amigos* FM Radio Station was founded by the Friends National Church.

The Central America Yearly Meeting of Friends was, finally, set apart as an autonomous group by California Yearly Meeting of Friends in November 1970, taking on the name Guatemala National Friends Church. Later, other yearly meetings were set off by Guatemalan Friends: Honduras Yearly Meeting, El Salvador Yearly Meeting, and Amigos de Santidad (Holiness Friends Yearly Meeting), also in Guatemala. Holiness Friends founded the **Quaker Theological Seminary** in 1985 and, having supported the international *Volviendo a Jesús* Radio Broadcast for 34 years, expanded its radio work to the Educational and Evangelical Radio Truth, on short wave. The Berea Bible Training School under Guatemala National Friends Church became a college and, more recently, **Berea Bible Seminary**.

By 1999, **evangelical** Friends had expanded in Central America, with thousands of members in Guatemala, some in Honduras and El Salvador, and a few in Nicaragua. A few groups of Friends hold **unprogrammed worship** in Antigua and Guatemala City, as well as in Monte Verde and San José, Costa Rica.

In 1950, a group of **Conservative Friends** from Fairhope, Alabama, emigrated to Costa Rica as a protest against the burgeoning military economy and the military draft (*see* PEACE). This group founded the farming community of Monteverde in the mountains about 125 miles from San José, with its own store, **meetinghouse**, school, sugar mill, dairy, and cheese factory. Since then, they have developed the Monteverde Cloud Forest Preserve and the Monteverde Conservation Institute (*see* ENVIRONMENT) as well as aiding refugees throughout Central America. San José Meeting was begun in 1983 by Friends who established the Peace Center there. [Édgar Amílcar Madrid and Margery Post Abbott]

CÉRÉSOLE, PIERRE (1879–1945). Swiss Friend, **peace** activist, physicist, and leader in the International Work Camp Movement. After teaching for a number of years, Cérésole traveled around the world prior to World War I, returning to Switzerland with radical ideas about wealth and military service as contrary to the teachings of Jesus. He turned over his inheritance to the Swiss government because he had not earned it. Cérésole then refused to pay the compulsory military tax, an action that led to the first of many imprisonments.

In 1919, at a conference of the International Fellowship of Reconciliation (FOR), Cérésole and others developed the idea of volunteers from around the world cooperating to rebuild after the war. A French village become the site of the first international work camp of the *Service Civil International*. Cérésole served for many years as president of that organization. The creation of the U.S. Peace Corps was adapted from the international work camp model as was a similar United Nations program. Starting with the FOR conference, Cérésole worked with many Quakers, eventually joining London **Yearly Meeting** in 1934. He was a central figure in the creation of Switzerland Yearly Meeting a decade later. During **World War II**, he entered Germany illegally in order to address the plight of Jews and was imprisoned. Returning home, he again stood witness to the folly of war, spending his last Christmas in a Swiss prison. [Margery Post Abbott]

CERTIFICATE. Friends have historically used certificates not only to document **marriages** and similar events, but also to record a **meeting**'s approval of individuals. These latter include certificates of removal for transfer of **membership** and traveling certificates to introduce **ministers** or other valued members to Friends in other meetings.

CHALKLEY, THOMAS (1675–1741). London-born North American **minister**. Chalkley was a merchant, planter, and sea captain, who settled in Pennsylvania in 1701. He made many fresh **convincements**

during his travels, and his **journal** became a standard work among American Friends.

CHETSINGH, DORIS (ca. 1897–1977) and RANJIT (1902–1977). Indian Quaker pacifists, founders of Delhi Quaker Center (*see* SOUTH ASIA). Ranjit Chetsingh served as General Secretary for **Friends World Committee for Consultation** in 1954–1955. *See also* PEACE.

CHEYNEY UNIVERSITY. *See* RICHARD HUMPHREYS FOUNDATION.

CHILDREN OF THE LIGHT. This phrase derives from several New Testament texts, especially Ephesians 5:6–14, referring to the chosen people of **God,** and was in fairly common use in the mid-17th century. **Quakers**, in particular, frequently used it of themselves. Around 1655–1656, they heavily promoted it as a name for their movement as a whole, but had no long-term success as the general public knew them better by the nickname "Quakers." [Rosemary Anne Moore]

CHILSON, ARTHUR BENTON (1872–1939) and EDNA HILL. Founders, with **Willis Hotchkiss** and Edgar Hole of the Friends Africa Industrial Mission. Chilson also served as **Superintendent** of Kansas **Yearly Meeting** and pioneer of the Friends' **mission** to Kivimba in the then Belgian Congo. Edna Hill Chilson was a **minister** and a missionary who served in **East Africa** with her husband from 1907 to 1927. She wrote *Arthur B. Chilson, Ambassador of the King*. [John W. Oliver]

CHRIST. Early Quaker understanding of Christ may be summarized by Paul's sentence, "Christ in you, the hope of glory" (Colossians 1:27). These Friends claimed the indwelling, life-giving presence and **Light** of Christ Jesus in all human hearts and lives as their central faith experience. On the island of Barbados in 1671 **George Fox** encountered a Colonel Lyne who had heard that Quakers were "no Christians." When Fox finished explaining to him the centrality of Christ Jesus in Quaker faith and practice, Lyne exclaimed, "Now I perceive you exalt Christ in all his offices" (*Journal*, Nickalls, p. 598).

Early Friends stressed the offices, or saving work of Christ, more than his "divine-human nature." Rejecting creedal formulations about Christ's person, and inconsistent in such statements before 1658, Friends, nevertheless, fully accepted Jesus as The Christ, **God**'s eternal Son to whom all authority in **heaven** and on earth has been given. Fox variously described Christ as: Christ the Light who enlightens everyone in the world; savior from **sin**; priest who died for humanity; shepherd to feed humankind; and great prophet to open **truth** to all people. Consequently, with the Light of Christ, Christ is always present in the human heart, and each person can realize that Christ has come to teach his people himself. Drawing on the imagery of the Book of Revelation, **James Nayler** saw Jesus as conquering Lamb with the sword of the Spirit coming out of his mouth and leading his faithful troops to overcome evil through faithful witness and suffering love until the end of history (*see* LAMB'S WAR; PURITANISM).

Over the centuries, Friends' individual experience and understanding of Christ has coalesced into separate doctrines. In the **Great Separation** of 1827, those who had embraced a more orthodox Christian **theology** became part of the **Orthodox** bodies, while the **Hicksites** included Friends of a wide variety of views on Christ, from orthodox to **universalist**.

Contemporary Friends exhibit a spectrum of views toward Christ Jesus and his authority. Some Friends see in Jesus of Nazareth a great human spiritual and ethical teacher. Many of these Friends experience what they know as the Inward Christ, or Inward Teacher, as central to their religious life. They do not, by and large, accept claims that Jesus Christ is uniquely divine or God's preexistent and eternal son. The Inward Light is seen as the central authority, often without direct reference to the **Bible** or Christ. Some hold a concept of Christ without any reference to Jesus.

Other Friends claim Christ Jesus as personal savior and some stress also the authority of Scripture as "the **Word** of God." For these groups, the work of Christ is understood primarily as mediator, redeemer, and savior from sin who promises eternal life through personal faith in him. Their stress is on **evangelism** and personal **salvation**. [T. Canby Jones]

CHRISTIAN ENDEAVOR. A **North American** interdenominational **evangelical** youth movement founded in 1881 by Maine Congregational minister Francis E. Clark, the Christian Endeavor Society stressed bringing youth to **Christ**, active service of Christ Jesus as Lord, loyalty to one's own denomination, and Christian fellowship. Local societies helped revitalize Sunday Schools, train young people in leadership, and raise money for local and foreign **missions**.

Christian Endeavor Societies formed in many Friends' **meetings** and **churches** in the United States, principally in the **Gurneyite** branch, during the 1880s and 1890s. In 1892, the International Friends' Union of Christian Endeavor, with some 9,000 members, was recognized by the Conference of Friends in America. In 1907, the Union became a department of the Five Years' Meeting (later **Friends United Meeting**). It continued to cooperate with the interdenominational United Society of Christian Endeavor. Esfuerza Cristiana (Christian Endeavor Societies) were also established in the Friends' churches in Cuba (*see* CARIBBEAN). By 1945 the **yearly meetings** and Five Years' Meeting had largely dropped the name Christian Endeavor, although local societies continued in many communities. *See also* YOUNG FRIENDS. [Elizabeth Cazden]

CHURCH. In Proposition X of his *Apology,* **Robert Barclay** uses the word "church" in three ways. The church is all those called and gathered by **God** to walk in the **Light** and Life. This forms the invisible, catholic church of all those who do the will of God and are obedient to the Light in their hearts. It is also the visible church gathered by God's Spirit, of those who profess the Christian faith, meet together to wait upon God in **worship**, testify to the **Truth**, and care for one another. Finally, it is the "church of the apostasy," which is any church that has let the outward form triumph over the inward life.

The first usage forms a basis for Quaker Christian **universalism**, since Barclay is clear that this church is not limited by nation, language, or religion: "There may be members therefore of this catholick church both among heathens, Turks, Jews, and all the several sorts of Christians, men and women of integrity and simplicity of heart . . . [who] loving to follow righteousness, are by the secret touches of this Holy Light in their souls, enlivened and quickened, thereby secretly united to God" (*Apology,* Freiday, p. 173).

The second usage is a basis for calling the **Religious Society of Friends** a church. Such a church contains those who have the inward life, which makes them part of the invisible church, but is itself visible through its worship, its common life, and its lived **testimonies**. Thus **gospel order** is one of the signs of the Quaker way of being church, and **business meetings** are more properly seen as **meetings for worship** for church affairs. Since the latter part of the 19th century, when the **pastoral movement** and **programmed** worship started in **North America**, the use of the term "**Friends Church**" has become common for these congregations and has been spread by their missionaries.

Since the time of Barclay, the third usage has altered. Quakers no longer refer to other churches as being in apostasy. The **evangelical** movements among Friends in **Britain** and the United States in the 19th century brought Friends closer to other churches; in the 20th century, involvement in the **ecumenical** movement signaled a recognition that other churches are also part of the invisible church, and are a different way of being visible church. [Janet Scott]

CHURCHMAN, JOHN (1705–1775). North American farmer, surveyor, **abolitionist**, and **minister**. Born in Pennsylvania, John Churchman played a key role in the 18th-century movement for reform of **North American** Quakerism and in strengthening the bond between American and British Friends.

Long concerned about what he saw as growing worldliness among Friends, Churchman advocated a guarded **education** for Quaker children and strict enforcement of the **discipline**. A close friend of **John Woolman**, he urged Friends to free their slaves and supported abstinence from drinking alcohol (*see* TEMPERANCE).

From 1750 to 1754 Churchman traveled in the ministry to **Britain**, **Ireland**, and Holland, accompanied at different points by William Brown (d.1760), **John Pemberton**, and others, returning to America with British Friend **Samuel Fothergill**. The journey helped establish enduring ties between the American reformers and their English counterparts like Fothergill.

As deputy surveyor of Pennsylvania, Churchman was often the target of threats from those unhappy with his work. During the French and Indian War of the 1750s, he advocated withdrawal from the Pennsylvania Assembly and refused to pay his war taxes (*see* PEACE). He served only a brief time as magistrate before turning his attention fully to Quaker service.

In 1729, John Churchman married Margaret Brown (d. 1770). [Jack D. Marietta]

CIVIL GOVERNMENT. Friends have been actively concerned with government and politics since their beginnings, though their views and relationships have varied widely over time, always based on their belief in "that of **God** in everyone" (*see* LIGHT). In **John Woolman**'s words, **Christ**'s "spirit in the hearts of his people leads to an inward exercise for the **salvation** of [humanity]," and this meant that the inward Spirit should transform the outward world, including governments.

In 17th-century **Britain**, Friends related to the government mainly as petitioners (*see* POLITICS). The main Quaker experience in governance came in the **North American** colonies. Even before the founding of Pennsylvania, Friends exercised significant political power in Rhode Island, North Carolina, New Jersey, and Maryland. Friends elected governors and constituted a majority of the Rhode Island assembly during King Philip's War of 1675–1676. Quakers in government distinguished between their personal **peace** witness and their obligations as magistrates, a distinction that continued to characterize the role of Quakers in Rhode Island until the American Revolution. In North Carolina and Maryland, Quakers lost political power after 1700 when the authorities required all assembly members to take an oath of allegiance. Friends settled West Jersey and created the most democratic constitution in early America, but uncertainty over who had the right to govern resulted in a loss of Quaker political power in 1702, when New Jersey became a royal colony. Quakers still served in the assembly and governor's council, being allowed to affirm their loyalty.

Quakers are best known for their **Holy Experiment** in Pennsylvania. Friends created the colony and constituted an absolute majority in the assembly until 1755 and nearly 50 percent of the members until 1775. **William Penn**'s *Frames of Government* sought to reform government by providing for religious toleration, ending tithes, and instituting rule by laws consented to by the people in an assembly. Pennsylvania created no militia, and so Penn attempted to create peace by treating the **Native Americans** justly.

The reform movement of the 1750s within Philadelphia **Yearly Meeting** coincided with the growing conflict between Britain and

France over western Pennsylvania that led to the French and Indian War. In 1755, under pressure from the yearly meeting and a threat from the British government to tender an oath to all Assembly members, a sufficient number of Friends resigned office that the war could be prosecuted. Among themselves, Friends debated whether they could pay a tax for war. The yearly meeting embraced **abolition**, Native American rights, and a reinvigorated **peace testimony**. After the war ended, many Quakers returned to the Assembly. Quakers lost political power during the American Revolution. They had supported the protest against British taxation, but withdrew from politics when American boycotts of British goods threatened to become a war. In early 1776, American yearly meetings drafted a statement of principle declaring their neutrality. They rejected the older Rhode Island formula distinguishing between personal and official responsibilities and **disowned** not only men who served in the military or took loyalty oaths but also those who held any office requiring them to enforce loyalty oaths or militia laws.

After the British Reform Bill of 1832 repealed restrictions on dissenters serving in Parliament, a few Quakers became Members of Parliament. The most important of these, **John Bright**, gained fame as a defender of laissez-faire economics and anti-imperialism, and a critic of the Crimean War.

The main Quaker influence on government in the 20th century came through ostensibly nonpolitical service organizations like the **American Friends Service Committee (AFSC)**. AFSC's informal motto: "Speak Truth to Power" conveys the way Friends practiced politics through personal contacts. **Herbert Hoover** was a Quaker who kept close contacts with Friends during his tenure as secretary of commerce and president. **Clarence Pickett**, head of AFSC, was a friend of Eleanor Roosevelt and, through her, could gain access to the president. **D. Elton Trueblood** had strong contacts with President Dwight D. Eisenhower. President **Richard Nixon** was a Quaker who enjoyed support among **evangelical** Friends, but his war policies were opposed by many Friends. For all their present-day differences, there is a basic consistency from the 1650s to the 21st century in the Quaker view of civic responsibility. Friends do not believe in sectarian withdrawal; they find in the life and teachings of Jesus of Nazareth a morality that should be reflected in personal as well as political life. [J. William Frost, Lonnie Valentine]

CIVILIAN PUBLIC SERVICE (CPS). During **World War II**, the U.S. Congress established CPS camps as venues for **conscientious objectors (COs)** to find significant nonmilitary work yet remain isolated from the general population. In 1940–1941, **Thomas E. Jones** was the central figure in organizing the CPS camps on behalf of the **American Friends Service Committee (AFSC)**. Friends, through AFSC, were responsible for the camps, along with officials of the Mennonites and Church of the Brethren, despite disagreements with U.S. Army Selective Service System, which held ultimate authority over the camps. The three **peace** churches provided all financial support for the camps. The 12,000 COs in the camps received no pay for their work in mental hospitals, as volunteer subjects for medical research, in fighting fires, or other work. Many COs became a key part of the next generation of Quaker **leadership**. Their experience left many disillusioned with the idea of achieving peace through cooperation with **civil government**. [Margery Post Abbott]

CLARK, DOUGAN, JR. (1828–1896). Medical doctor, longtime member of the faculty of **Earlham College**, and a recorded **minister**. He was the most widely read writer on second-experience **sanctification** among Friends through books like his *The Offices of the* ***Holy Spirit*** (1878). His converts to instant sanctification include **J. Walter and Emma Brown Malone**.

CLARKSON, THOMAS (1760–1846). British (non-Quaker) **abolitionist** and author of *A Portraiture of Quakerism* (1805). *See also* BENEZET, ANTHONY.

CLEARNESS. Clearness has had a range of meanings in the course of Quaker history. Clearness **committees** for **marriage** and **membership** have been part of Quaker practice from the early days of organization when a primary purpose was to ensure that individuals were clear of other entanglements and able to live up to their commitments.

In more recent times, the **meeting**'s clearness committees often have multiple functions. They emphasize the **discernment** and clarity of committee members. By gathering pertinent facts, some committees also clear business to bring it into the discernment process of the meeting. "Clearance" as fact gathering differs from clearness. Clearness committees are also used to support individuals' discernment of **God**'s guidance in crises or new circumstances. Gathered in prayerful quiet, members listen for signs of the Spirit's movement as the individual speaks of his inward sense and outward circumstances. They listen within themselves for guidance in probing dimensions of the issue not illuminated.

In the 1960s, **Young Friends** of **North America** revived the practice of seeking clearness, which originated as early as **Robert Barclay**. The practice of holding Clearness Committees for personal as well as group decision making apparently spread through the Movement For A New Society in Philadelphia, then more widely among Friends. Here the word "clearness" referred to conscious intuitive or intellectual clarity about divine guidance. Quaker tradition includes a tacit sense that, by faithfulness to such clarity, we grow in awareness of, and harmony with, ever-present guidance by the **Holy Spirit** (*see* PERFECTION). Clearness about "what the Lord requires of us" is the result of spiritual discernment both in particular instances and cumulatively over a lifetime. [Patricia Loring]

CLERKS. Clerks preside over the **business meeting**; clarify, gather, and record the substantial unity or "sense of the **meeting**" when a decision has been made; maintain records and official correspondence for the meeting; and are often called on to speak officially for the meeting.

COFFIN, CATHERINE WHITE (d. 1909) and LEVI (1798–1877). Raised in Guilford County, North Carolina, Levi Coffin was deeply moved by the suffering of slaves he witnessed as a child. Coffin married Catherine White in 1826, and they settled north of Richmond, Indiana, near a community of free black people who came there with the aid of North Carolina Friends. Aiding the efforts of this community to assist fugitive slaves, the Coffins made their home a stop on the **underground railroad** for an estimated 2,000 escaped slaves during the years before the American Civil War.

In 1843, Friends in Indiana **Yearly Meeting** (**Orthodox**) separated over the issue of **abolition**. Work with non-Quakers, tensions over the testimony of integrity (*see* TRUTH), and a perception of "extremism" associated with the underground railroad activists all contributed to the separation. The Coffins were part of the new Indiana Yearly Meeting of Anti-Slavery Friends until it rejoined the older body 13 years later. After the American Civil War they worked to raise funds and create opportunities for freedmen to become self-supporting. [Margery Post Abbott]

COGGESHALL, ELIZABETH (1770–1851). Born Elizabeth Hinshaw, she married Caleb Coggeshall in New York City about 1800. She traveled in the **ministry** with **Hannah Barnard**.

COLEGIO JORGE FOX. Quaker Bible school established in 1980 at the San Marcos *Centro Evangélico de los Amigos*, Ocotepeque, Honduras, for the training of **pastors**.

COLLEGES. Although always committed to the **education** of their children, Quakers were slow to develop colleges, which had long been associated with training for the clergy. Until the mid-19th century, Friends regarded colleges and universities with considerable suspicion. Despite their clerical function, the moral atmosphere of traditional American and European colleges was often marked by rioting, drunkenness, dueling, and other behavior that consistent Friends found offensive.

As higher education expanded in the United States after 1830 and came to focus more on professional training and preparation and less on the preparation of clergy, many Friends, both **Orthodox** and **Hicksite**, became more open to it. First, a few Friends enrolled in such institutions as Harvard, Brown, Amherst, Bowdoin, Oberlin, and Antioch. As interest in higher education among Orthodox Friends grew, concerns also mounted that attendance at non-Quaker schools would draw Friends away from the Society, and they opened their own colleges. **Haverford** was the first in 1856, followed by **Earlham** in 1859, and by 1900 it was a given that almost every **Gurneyite yearly meeting** would have its own college. Hicksites collaborated in managing **Swarthmore College**, which opened in 1869. Union Bible College was founded in 1911 as a Seminary with close ties to Central Yearly Meeting.

With changes among Friends, the roles and functions of colleges changed. None was able to remain "select" for more than a few years; financial necessity quickly forced the admission of non-Quaker students. By 1900, in the colleges affiliated with Gurneyite yearly meetings, preparation of **pastors** had become an important function, reflecting other changes among Friends (*see* PASTORAL MOVEMENT).

Today, it is difficult to generalize about the functions of Quaker colleges. Some, like **Friends Theological College** in Kenya and **Barclay College** in Kansas, are tightly focused on the preparation of religious leaders. Others, like Haverford, Swarthmore, and **Bryn Mawr**, have become elite liberal arts institutions. Still others, such as **George Fox University**, William Penn College, and **Malone** College, have positioned themselves as part of the Christian college movement. Several have strong Quaker and **peace** studies programs. Others, most notably **Guilford** and Earlham, see themselves as national liberal arts colleges with identities and curriculum firmly grounded in their Quaker heritage.

In the United States today, 13 colleges belong to the Friends Association for Higher Education. Several graduate programs exist in conjunction with other universities. Elsewhere around the world, Friends have established institutions for Bible study such as **Friends Theological College**, **Colegio Jorge Fox**, and **Great Lakes Theological Center**. Two adult study centers exist: **Woodbrooke** in England and **Pendle Hill** outside Philadelphia.

A few colleges founded by Friends no longer exist. **Southland College** in Helena, Arkansas, was established by Indiana Yearly Meeting in 1866, the first black college west of the Mississippi. It closed in 1925. Miami Valley College in Springborough, Ohio, existed from 1870 to 1883 under the care of Indiana Yearly Meeting (Hicksite). Nebraska Central College in Central City, Nebraska, was opened in 1899 by Nebraska Yearly Meeting and closed in 1953.

Friends World College on Long Island, sponsored by New York Yearly Meeting, opened in 1965 and merged with Long Island University in 1991. **Azusa Pacific University** originated as Huntington Park Training School for Christian Workers in 1899 and still maintains a Quaker Center in southern California. It became Pacific Bible College, then eventually Azuza Pacific after relocation and merger with Los Angeles Pacific College in 1965. Cheyney University, in Pennsylvania, grew out of a school founded for **African American** students through the **Richard Humphreys Foundation**. [Thomas D. Hamm]

COLLINSON, PETER (1693–1768). Preeminent **British** botanist and Fellow of the Royal Society. A successful businessman, he was self-deprecating about his own scientific abilities, but enabled others to thrive in their chosen areas of expertise and to achieve greater public fame. He was a correspondent of Linnaeus and mentor to **John Bartram**. One observer commented that no other garden in all of Europe had so many rare and exotic plants as his. [Geoffrey Morries]

COMLY, JOHN (1773–1850). Teacher, **minister**, and leader of Philadelphia **Hicksites** before and after the **Great Separation** of 1827.

COMMITTEE. **Leadership** in Friends **meetings** has always been widely shared. Until the rise of the **pastoral movement** in the late 19th century among some Friends, Quakers had no separate clergy to make decisions and conduct the daily affairs of the group. Meetings therefore operate largely through committees, which derive their authority from and report to the **business meeting**. Their functions range from pastoral work and care for the spiritual health of the meeting to finance and hospitality. **Clearness** committees may be appointed for special occasions requiring **discernment**. Many wider Friends organizations also use the name "committee"—**American Friends Service Committee**, **Friends Committee on National Legislation**, **Friends World Committee for Consultation**—to indicate their consultative relationship with meetings and other groups of Friends. [Mary Ellen Chijioke]

COMMUNION. Friends consider the **sacraments** to be inward and spiritual, and most do not practice outward communion of bread and wine. Affirming that the divine reality is communicated not through particular visible signs, but rather immediately and directly into human hearts, many Friends speak of the communion experienced in the gathered **meeting for worship**.

COMSTOCK, ELIZABETH ROUS WRIGHT (1815–1891). Michigan Quaker antislavery activist (*see* ABOLITION) who worked with

Laura Smith Haviland to assist freed slaves during and after the American Civil War. She especially became known for visiting prisons and hospitals.

CONCERN. The name, dating from the earliest period of Friends, given to a **leading** from **God** "laid upon" an individual as a call to action. Testing the concern with the local **meeting** provides a check as to its validity. The meeting may also unite with the concern, that is, share the sense of rightness for action. The meeting may then act on its own behalf or take the concern to a wider constituency of Friends. Most new directions for Quaker work and witness have begun life as an individual concern. Some concerns remain with a single person but with meeting support of the individual witness. [Pink Dandelion]

CONGREGATIONAL FRIENDS. Groups of Friends who feel that final authority rests in the local worshipping group, not in a wider body. In the 1840s in **North America**, some meetings broke away from **Hicksite yearly meetings** on these grounds. In the 20th century, some North American yearly meetings adopted a congregational model, with authority centered in the **monthly meeting**, and claim no authority over these constituent meetings. Elsewhere, the tendency operates unofficially. *See also* PROGRESSIVE FRIENDS. [Pink Dandelion]

CONSCIENTIOUS OBJECTORS (COs). Conscientious objection to war emerged in Europe at least as early as the 16th century. A century later, by 1660, Quakers asserted the **peace testimony** as an essential part of their faith in declarations to King Charles II. Friends have frequently suffered for their testimony against taking up arms.

Prior to the American Civil War, when Friends recognized the dilemma of young men called to fight against slavery (*see* ABOLITION), Friends took an absolutist position on the peace testimony and **disowned** any individual who fought, undertook any alternative service, or in any way cooperated with the military even in a civilian capacity.

In the 20th century, Friends were in the forefront of efforts to establish the legal right to refuse military service. In World War I, **Britain** was the first, and at that time only, country to permit secular grounds for objection in principle to war as legally acceptable grounds for pacifism. Britain and the United States, among other countries, now legally recognize CO status. During **World War II**, the three historic peace churches in the United States—Quakers, Mennonites, and Church of the Brethren—formed the National Service Board for Religious Objectors along with others concerned about the status of COs. Quakers undertook the administration of some of the federal **Civilian Public Service** camps which provided alternative service for COs. Some Friends, in this as in other wars, refused all cooperation with the government in regard to military service and were imprisoned for this stance.

Over the centuries, individual Friends have also taken on other actions such as conscientious nonpayment of taxes used to support the military, but such action is not legally recognized as a right in the way CO status has been defined in a number of countries. [Margery Post Abbott]

CONSERVATIVE FRIENDS. Conservative Friends can be found in three small **North American** and one British **yearly meeting** as well as among individual Friends around the world. Their **meetings** of **unprogrammed**, waiting **worship** usually have a strong Christian orientation. These Friends also maintained traditional Quaker **testimonies**, especially a plainness or **simplicity** of dress, speech, and lifestyle, longer than most other Quaker groups.

Following the **Great Separation** of 1827, **Orthodox** Friends in North America were increasingly influenced by the **evangelical** ministry of **Joseph John Gurney**, whose ideas already predominated among Friends in **Britain**. As early as 1832, the Rhode Island minister **John Wilbur** prophesied that the elevation of the **Bible** above the **Holy Spirit** would result in changes to Quaker practice. His **disownment** by New England Yearly Meeting led to the creation of a "**Wilburite**" yearly meeting there in 1845. Small Wilburite secessions also occurred in New York and Baltimore. Tensions over which New England Yearly Meeting should be recognized finally led to a **Gurneyite**-Wilburite separation in Ohio Yearly Meeting in 1854. Although the leadership of Philadelphia Yearly Meeting (Orthodox) supported the Wilburite position, the Yearly Meeting avoided separation only by ceasing to communicate with any other yearly meeting.

Because **London Yearly Meeting** recognized only the Gurneyite Orthodox yearly meetings, and because Ohio (Wilburite) Yearly Meeting would not recognize any yearly meeting that had been created by secession, the Wilburites were isolated from the rest of Quakerism and partly from one another for a generation.

A small group of **Primitive Friends** with similar concerns seceded from Philadelphia Yearly Meeting (Orthodox) as Fallsington General Meeting in 1860. They corresponded with the Wilburite groups in New England, Baltimore, and New York, as well as the **Maulites** who had seceded from Ohio Yearly Meeting (Wilburite). There were additional **Kingite** and **Otisite** separations within most of the Primitive groups. Eventually, they died out, with some of their members rejoining larger Quaker bodies.

Meanwhile, the development of **revivals** and the beginnings of the **pastoral system** in Gurneyite yearly meetings caused a new round of separations, starting in Iowa in 1877, Western (in Indiana) in 1878, Kansas in 1879, and **Canada** in 1881. By 1885, these yearly meetings (now called Conservative) recognized each other's annual epistles, membership transfers, and minutes of traveling **ministers**. North Carolina's Conservative Yearly Meeting was formed in 1904. In England a small number of Conservative Friends left London Yearly Meeting to create Fritchley **General Meeting** in 1870.

For several generations, Conservative and Primitive Friends continued a way of life they believed "conserved" the Christian experience and practice of 18th-century Friends. (The Quaker use of the word "conservative" does not necessarily imply socially or politically conservative values.) Their way of life might be described as an extension of the **Quietist** Quaker culture of the 18th and 19th centuries, with emphasis on isolation from the world and on simplicity and **plain dress**, **speech**, and lifestyle (*see* PECULIARITY). Their ideal was to arrange their lives so as to provide inward space to allow the Holy Spirit or "the inward monitor" to guide all details of daily life and **ministry**. In their mostly rural or small-town settings, many meetings had their own elementary schools. Secondary boarding schools existed in Iowa, Kansas, and Ohio (*see* EDUCATION). Through the mid-20th century, a few meetings had the feel of an earlier Quakerism with surviving examples of plain dress and other aspects of Quietist culture, as well as a depth in the silent worship even in **business meetings**, on which visitors often commented. Their isolation from other Friends began to end during World War I, and by the end of **World War II**, as they sent representatives to national and international Quaker gatherings.

The 20th century has seen a decline in membership. Kansas Yearly Meeting laid itself down in 1929, as did Western in 1962; New England reunited with other groups there in 1945, and Canada did the same in 1955. Fritchley General Meeting rejoined London Yearly Meeting in 1967. Several new meetings have joined the three remaining Conservative yearly meetings—Iowa, North Carolina, and Ohio—bringing new vitality and diversity, although membership of most of the older meetings has decreased. Iowa Yearly Meeting continues to sponsor Scattergood, a secondary boarding school. Ohio Yearly Meeting turned over the management of its secondary boarding school, Olney Friends School, to alumni and friends of the school in 1999.

Conservative Friends have never had a formal organization above the **yearly meeting** level, although between 1970 and 1992, the informal Association of Conservative Friends coordinated communication between the **clerks** of the three North American Conservative yearly meetings whenever joint action was needed. Since 1965, some Conservative Friends and others have met for, usually, biennial weekend gatherings sponsored by the Wider Fellowship of Conservative Friends, a **committee** of Ohio Yearly Meeting which also sponsors a quarterly publication, *The Conservative Friend*.

In Britain, a Conservative Yearly Meeting of Friends in Christ seceded from London Yearly Meeting in the early 1990s. This group also contains members of Halcyonia Monthly Meeting in Canada whose ancestors came from Birmingham, England, and broke away from the Fritchley Meeting in 1906, seeing it as too worldly. Avon Valley General Meeting formed in 2000 in Australia has also associated with Conservative Friends. *See also* KNOLITES. [William P. Taber]

CONSOLIDATED YEARLY MEETING. A form of reunification that brings together **yearly meetings** belonging to different larger associations of Friends and in which each **monthly meeting** is allowed to choose which larger body or bodies it will relate to.

CONTINENTAL EUROPE. Apart from **Britain**, where the Quaker movement started and grew, and **Ireland**, the rest of Europe has experienced an irregular and interrupted Quaker presence—despite attempts to organize **meetings** as early as the 1650s. A continental assembly (**yearly meeting**) was formally established in Amsterdam in 1677 and lasted until 1710. Some Dutch Friends continued to meet informally for **worship** until 1851.

As a result of visitors from England and **North America**, small Quaker groups were formed in Germany in 1700. A second attempt was made a century later (*see* PEACE DALE). In southern France a mystical group, existing since 1785, became interested in the Quaker movement and made contact with the yearly meeting in London. As a result, in 1822, both English and American Friends helped to build a meetinghouse there (now a private home). In Norway, Quaker ideas and manner of worship were introduced by **Norwegian** seamen in 1818, after their return home from England where they had been held as prisoners during the Napoleonic wars. Friends also started meeting in Denmark, in 1875.

Education has always been a distinct feature of Quaker work, although little evidence remains in continental Europe. In Britain and Ireland, however, a number of Quaker schools and health-related establishments still exist.

Most existing Quaker groups in continental Europe are a by-product of Friends' service work coordinated through **Quaker International Centres**, e.g., Berlin, Geneva, Paris, and Vienna, in the aftermath of the two world wars. Mainly financed by Anglo-American Quakers, this neutral approach of offering **relief** to those in distress— particularly refugees—attracted the attention of indigenous people, and strong bonds of friendship were formed as a result.

Besides contributing to the development of voluntary service in various countries, Friends helped with campaigns for **conscientious objectors**, promoted East-West dialogue, and became further involved in international work establishing the Quaker United Nations Office (QUNO) and cooperating with UN agencies (Geneva) and the European institutions (Brussels and Strasbourg), as well as in **ecumenical** interfaith work.

Within continental Europe today, Quaker groups exist in Austria, Belgium, Denmark, Estonia, Finland, France, Germany, Hungary,

Italy, Lithuania, Luxembourg, Netherlands, Norway, Russia, Spain, Sweden, Switzerland, and Ukraine. Nine yearly meetings exist, with a total membership of about 1,000. Books, websites, and regular publications thrive in at least nine languages. [Franco Perna]

CONTINUING REVELATION. The term given to the idea that **God**'s revelation for humanity is unfolding, or that at least the human understanding of God's will may change in changed circumstances, and new **truth** may add new dimensions to received faith. In the **liberal** tradition, which emphasizes experience as the basis of religious authority, revelation is the primary means of discerning action and truth (*see* DISCERNMENT, SPIRITUAL). A tension exists between modern Friends who are clear that any valid revelation must be consistent with the **Bible** and those who seek to "be open to new **Light**." [Pink Dandelion]

CONVENTICLE ACTS. *See* BRITAIN.

CONVINCEMENT. Convincement, or "conviction" in its original 17th-century sense, was the name given to a two-stage experience common among the first Quakers. Initially, the **Light** would reveal a person's **sins** and he or she would be convicted of them. The same Light, however, would then set this person free from sin and release him or her into a new and renewed intimacy with **God** (*see* PERFECTION).

Over the centuries, the term has remained but has taken on new emphases. The chief aim of the **preaching** of Quaker evangelists is to effect a conversion in a person from being a nonbeliever to being a believer. "Conviction" and "conversion" are used to describe a spiritual process involving the relationship of the individual with God. The process of convincement specifically indicates the decision of the believer or convert that Friends' faith, practice, and fellowship are the best ways and the best place to live out this relationship.

Often (and in the past, normally) a person who experienced convincement would apply for **membership**. Many **meetings** track additions by convincement along with births and transfers. [William F. Medlin]

COOPER, WILMER A. (1920–). North American educator and theologian, Cooper grew up among **Conservative Friends** in eastern

Ohio. After serving in a **Civilian Public Service** camp in North Carolina as a **conscientious objector** during World War II and graduating from **Wilmington College**, he obtained graduate degrees from **Haverford College**, Yale Divinity School, and Vanderbilt University. Cooper married Emily Haines (1923–) in 1946. He worked for **Friends Committee on National Legislation** from 1952 to 1959 before being recruited by **Landrum Bolling** to help found **Earlham School of Religion (ESR)**. As the first dean of ESR he oversaw its formation and accreditation and served in that position from 1960 to 1978. Cooper has served as a representative to **Friends World Committee for Consultation** and represented **Friends United Meeting** at the World Council of Churches. [Margery Post Abbott]

COPPIN, FANNY JACKSON (1837–1913). One of the first two black American women to earn a college degree, Coppin was principal of the Institute for Colored Youth, a school established in Philadelphia by the **Richard Humphreys Foundation**.

CORPORATE DISCIPLESHIP. The **discipline** by which Friends hold each other accountable to **Truth**. This includes living in accord with Friends' **testimonies**, such as **simplicity** and **peace**. The **Queries and Advices** are a traditional method by which Friends have held one another accountable.

COVENANT. Early Friends were galvanized by a biblical, covenantal vision for spiritual, moral, and social renewal. They witnessed to the **Light** of **Christ** as a covenant (an eternal, mutually binding relationship) with **God**. The Light's presence within even the most **evil** person demonstrated God's covenantal faithfulness to humanity. Likewise, the quiet attentiveness required to receive and follow the Light demonstrated an individual's freely chosen covenantal commitment. Interpersonally, faithful witness to the Light of Christ within, spoken with gentle plainness to friend and persecutor alike, aimed to "reach to the witness of God" (or Light or that of God) in others, making them more aware and attentive to the inward presence. This too was a covenantal initiative, a demonstration of good faith and reconciling love. Socially, faithfulness in the Light established new foundations rooted in **truth** telling, **plain dress and speech**, **equality** of relationships, communal decision making, legal reform, **simplicity**, Christian forgiveness, **fixed-price** marketing, **peace** making, religious freedom, etc. (Indeed, "**testimonies**" is a covenantal term.)

Later periods of Quakerism have not always retained this inclusive, transforming covenantal vision. The **evangelical** renewal, with its reassertion of biblical authority, has sometimes reduced covenant to testament, in the sense of the New Testament versus the Old Testament. The **liberal** renewal has often articulated covenant mainly in its social-contract version, where human rights and personal freedoms of religious belief and expression are prized as emblems of the good society. [Douglas Gwyn]

COVERED. A "covered" **meeting for worship** has reached deeper than a **gathered** meeting. In a gathered meeting the participants feel a timeless peace in the presence of **God** and each other. In a covered meeting they also feel a special sense of the **Holy Spirit** powerfully at work among them—whether through spoken **ministry** or through the invisible energizing, transforming, and bonding work of the Holy Spirit. [William P. Taber]

CREED. "Christianity is not a notion but a way." So says the **discipline** of **Britain** Yearly Meeting, echoing the words of **George Fox**. The Quaker tradition sees any creed as an inadequate account of faith, a misleading emphasis on words instead of life, and a means of separating people from each other. **William Penn** wrote, "speculative truths are . . . to be sparingly and tenderly declared, and never to be made the measure and condition of Christian communion. . . . Men are too apt to let their heads outrun their hearts, and their **notion** exceed their obedience, and their passion support their conceits; instead of a daily **cross**, a constant watch, and an holy practice" (Penn, *Key*, v. 9).

Early Friends justified this position in three ways. First is Fox's "**opening**" that a university education did not make a person into a **minister**. He rejected intellectual speculation in favor of direct inspiration by the **Holy Spirit**. Friends also rejected teachings that were not found in the **Bible** (*see* TRINITY) seeing them as characteristic of the "papist" interpretation and thus part of the fallen nature of the **church**. Third, they understood **Truth** as a Seed which grows through faithful living, rather than as a proposition to which one assents.

Thus, Quakers sought alternative ways to express their convictions. One way has been through the discipline of the **meetings** and the power to **disown** those members who "walk disorderly and not in accordance with Truth." They also issued **queries and advices** that evolved into the books of discipline, which are distinctive of each **yearly meeting**. The **Richmond Declaration of Faith** of 1887 appears in part in many books of discipline as an authoritative statement of faith.

Some yearly meetings, London (now Britain) included, rejected the 1887 Declaration as being too similar to a creed. In the 20th century this attitude to statements of faith caused problems for yearly meetings such as Britain in seeking membership in interchurch bodies which have a basis for membership. Some **ecumenical** bodies have adapted their rules for membership to allow Quaker meetings to join without subscribing to a Basis. (Basis is a World Council of Churches term for the statement of faith adopted for membership.) Yearly meetings disagree as to whether the Basis of the World Council of Churches is a creed. Thus some Quaker bodies which do not see the Basis as a creed are members, while other bodies regard the Basis as creedal and do not apply to join. [Janet Scott]

CROSFIELD, GEORGE (1785–1847). Wilburite publicist. A series of his correspondence with **John Wilbur** was published as *Some Letters to a Friend on Some of the Primitive Doctrines of Christianity* (1832) and in its 1879 version became one of the benchmark volumes for testing orthodoxy among **Conservative Friends**.

CROSS. For all Christians the cross refers to the crucifixion and **atonement** of Jesus on the Cross. Friends have historically referred to the cross of Jesus as the way of self-denial and **simplicity** in Christian living. Early Friends often spoke of "taking up the cross daily," whereby they sought to set aside the ego and be faithful to the **Light** in their words and actions. They also defined the word "cross" as the power of **God**. [Wilmer A. Cooper]

CROSS, MARY FISHER BAYLY. *See* FISHER, MARY.

CUFFE, PAUL (ALSO CUFFEE, COFFEE) (1759–1817). Shipbuilder, merchantman, one of the few black Quakers in the early 1800s, and an important figure in American trade history. The son of a freed slave and an Indian mother, Cuffe was a member of Westport Meeting and occasionally spoke in the **ministry**. He built his own brigs and barquentines, staffed them with white and black sailors, and made commercial voyages across the Atlantic and into southern U.S. ports.

Cuffe played a major role in bringing British Quakers into the **abolition** movement and was a founder of the American Colonization Society. He worked to undercut the slave trade by forming a trading cooperative in Sierra Leone, thus linking the United States, England, and the small West African nations. Cuffe faced almost insurmountable obstacles: the War of 1812, a trade embargo, and increased power of slave traders. His life illustrates the widespread network of **African American** organizations that provided help to one another, the deep concern for education within the free black community, and the strength of the church in that community. [Emma Jones Lapsansky]

CURLE, ADAM (1916–). Mediator, **peace** activist, and author of numerous books on peace making and poetry, Curle and his wife joined the **Religious Society of Friends** while he was professor of education at the University of Ghana in 1959. Prior to that he was a staff member of the Tavistock Institute of Human Relations after having served in the British army.

Curle became sensitized to peace issues through association with a resistance movement in South Africa in 1959. In 1962, he established the Center for Studies in Education and Development at Harvard University in Massachusetts and became its director. In 1973, he founded the Bradford Peace Institute in England and was its first professor of peace studies. From his university bases, he was actively involved in long-term mediations between India and Pakistan, the Nigerian government and Biafra, and various parties in Ireland. After his retirement in 1978, he continued this work with the government of what was then Rhodesia and the Zimbabwe independence movement, and the government of Sri Lanka and the Tamil separatists. From 1992 until 1999 he worked on nongovernmental peace issues in the Balkans. Throughout this period he reflected, lectured, and wrote about the theoretical and practical implications of his work. [Margery Post Abbott]

–D–

DALTON, JOHN (1766–1844). British chemist, father of modern atomic theory (*see* SCIENCE AND TECHNOLOGY) and known for Dalton's law of partial pressures.

DARBY, ABRAHAM (d. 1717). Founder of the English iron industry in Coalbrookdale near Birmingham (*see* BUSINESS AND ECONOMICS). His lighter, inexpensive cast-iron pots and cylinders were made using his new method to smelt iron by using coke rather than charcoal as fuel. His son and grandson, both named Abraham, continued and expanded the business.

DAVIDSON, MARY JANE (ca. 1860–1918) and ROBERT JOHN (ca. 1865–1942). English missionaries to China (*see* EAST ASIA). Robert, son of a former soldier and **convinced** Friend, and Mary arrived in China in 1886, but it took until 1890 to establish the permanent Friends **mission** in Chungking. Except for leaves, Robert remained the senior British missionary in China until 1925. The Davidsons were joined in 1897 by Robert's brother Adam Warburton Davidson and, in 1901, by older brothers Dr. William Henry Davidson and Alfred Davidson. Their son, R. H. Davidson, joined the mission in 1914. [Margery Post Abbott]

DAY OF THE LORD. In 1652, **George Fox** "was moved to sound the day of the Lord" in a vision on top of **Pendle Hill** and saw "a great people to be gathered" [*Journal*, Nickalls, p. 104]. "The day of the Lord" is the biblical phrase for the time when **God** will judge all **sin**, destroy all **evil**, and free the faithful in the triumph of God's kingdom on earth as in the **prophecies** of Joel, Chapter 2 of Isaiah, and 2 Peter 3:1–13. Sounding the day of the Lord was a call to individuals to choose to respond to the **Light** of **Christ** as part of the true **church**. Those who knew Christ within grew in **perfection**, as evidenced by lives lived in accord with the **testimonies**. [Margery Post Abbott]

DEATH AND DYING. "Their burials are performed with the same **simplicity**" as they lived, noted **William Penn** when writing about the customs of early Friends in the introduction to **George Fox**'s

Journal. Penn noted that Friends had no set rites about burials other than simply burying the body near the **meetinghouse** in a plain coffin and without a marker. The mourners might pause before placing the body in the grave, take their last leave, reflect upon their own mortality, and perhaps offer some words to those gathered. They did not wear mourning, seeing it as a mark of "worldly pomp."

These early Friends had a clear sense of heavenly reward waiting for them, expecting they would continue to live on in God's abundance, sometimes anticipating death, as Sarah Camm did in 1682, as entry into the "Bride-chamber, to have the Wedding Garment . . . to enter into heavenly rest." As a person lay dying, friends and family would often gather round to hear his or her final words, vesting them with special authority as coming from one close to the next world. Beginning in the late 18th century, these sayings were periodically collected, then published in volumes entitled *Piety Promoted*, or in separate publications such as *The Death-bed of a Young Quaker* (1833), William Penn's account of the death of his son at age 21.

Today, at times, Friends still gather for **worship** and **prayer** with the dying person. Then, family and friends normally gather for a **meeting for worship** on the occasion of death. This is a time to celebrate in the **Light** of **Christ** the life of the deceased and to support those who are grieving. In Friends churches, the **pastor** may offer a message and music will be integral to the service. In meetings with **unprogrammed worship**, messages are offered out of the silence as individuals are led. Simple burials are encouraged in many meetings, or cremation. Since the 19th century, Quaker graveyards generally have had simple, low stones with the names and dates of the deceased. A **minute** of testimony to the life of the individual is usually approved at a **business meeting** and published. Some meetings encourage their members to make appropriate preparations for death, including writing wills and filing instructions for final arrangements with the meeting. [Margery Post Abbott]

DeVOL FAMILY. Missionaries, doctors, and **educators**. A long history of family service to medicine and evangelization began with the arrival of Doctor Isabella French (1869–1920) in Luho, north of Nanjing, China in 1897(*see* EAST ASIA). She was joined by George Fox DeVol in 1900. They were married immediately, remaining in China until his death in 1917. Their son Charles (1903–1989) was a recorded **minister** and held a Ph.D. in botany from Indiana University. In 1926 he and his bride, the former Leora Van Matre (1902–1995), assumed responsibility for Friends' educational and evangelistic **ministries** throughout Luho province, succeeding **Walter R. Williams**. Charles survived seven months of harsh deprivation when interned by the Japanese in 1943. Following the closure of China to Westerners, he served Evangelical Friends Church–Eastern Region as field **superintendent** of the new Taiwan Friends **Mission** from 1957 to1973 (*see* EAST ASIA).

Charles was not the only DeVol child to follow in his parents' footsteps. Catherine Isabella (1906–1986), who married **Everett Cattell** in 1927, served in India for 21 years and was the author of numerous books about the missionary experience. Brother (William) Ezra (1909–1992) and his wife Frances Hodgin (1909–1996) served Friends as medical missionaries in China, India, and Nepal. They supervised the hospital service in Bundelkhand (Madhya Pradesh), India, where Ezra was field superintendent of the mission. He spent part of each year in surgery at the Shanta Bhawen Hospital of the United Missions of Kathmandu in Nepal. *See also* EAST ASIA; SOUTH ASIA. [John Williams Sr.]

DEWSBURY, WILLIAM (1621–1688). A preacher from Yorkshire, he met **George Fox** late in 1651 or early in 1652. Influential in the organization of **meeting**s in northern England, Dewsbury was author of several pamphlets and spent many years in **prison** for his faith.

DISCERNMENT, SPIRITUAL. The gift of distinguishing **God**'s work and guidance within the human heart from other motivations. Quakers believe that all people receive a measure of this fallible, intuitive gift, trusting to receive more with faithful exercise of what has been given.

Spiritual discernment is refined in **prayer** and faithful discipleship. With experience, an individual can become increasingly sensitive to the still, small voice rising within as he or she seeks to give over personal agendas, self-centeredness, and willfulness. Quaker vocabulary underscores discernment's interior, experiential nature: e.g., coming under the weight of a **leading**, feeling at peace with an outcome.

Quakers emphasize the subtle, demanding work of discerning Love and **Truth**, prompting each heart in the midst of people, situations, and undertakings. Recognizing human fallibility in discernment, Friends rely on a few tests of authenticity. The most widespread test seen in early Quaker **journals**, and still used today, is whether the source and probable outcome manifest the fruit of the **Spirit** described in Galatians 5:22–26 ("love, joy, peace, patience, kindness, generosity, faithfulness, gentleness, and self-control"). Of equal weight is the injunction to "Choose life" (Deuteronomy 30:19–20). Characteristic queries are "Is there life in it?" "Does it come from and lead to love?" "Are Friends at peace with this?"

Early Friends also articulated another test as "taking up the **cross**." Living under the cross was consonant with authentic striving to be free of egocentricity and willfulness. These Friends also often exhorted **meetings** to be united and to love one another as Jesus commanded. Thus unity of the meeting was another sign used in discernment of Truth as was consistency with the **Bible**, when read "in the Spirit."

For many Friends today, biblical exegesis and the message and actions of Jesus also provide numerous tests along with an inward sense of peace. Consistency with the Quaker **testimonies** is another often-used test. Such comparisons cannot ignore the traditional question, "Is this guidance livingly given to this particular person, group, or meeting for this particular time?" The question focuses on dedication to life conformed to the Spirit, rather than to laws.

Spiritual discernment is part of all aspects of Quaker faith and practice. Personal prayer opens the heart to God's guidance. A person discerns whether impulses to speak in **unprogrammed meeting for worship** or to act in the world derive from the **Holy Spirit** rather than from human sources. **Business meetings** are exercises in corporate discernment of God's guidance for the meeting as a whole. The **clerk** is the servant of the meeting, articulating the meeting's discernment of God's guidance as a minute.

In the past, the progression from individual to **clearness** committee, **monthly meeting**, **quarterly meeting**, and **yearly meeting** was viewed as the Quaker hierarchy of authority. By the late 20th century, however, in some places, this model has been replaced by an image of concentric circles drawing upon an ever wider pool of experience as the process reaches even beyond yearly meetings to wider gatherings of Friends. Discernment gathers spiritual authority as wider circles of Friends unite in it. [Patricia Loring]

DISCIPLINE. The means of maintaining cohesion of the **church** community despite individualistic **theology**. Some Friends today speak of this as **corporate discipleship**. Friends early on established the practice whereby each **yearly meeting** adopted its own book of **Discipline (Faith and Practice)** and was responsible for its own internal discipline. In the 18th and early 19th centuries, **business meeting** was often called meeting for discipliine.

DISCIPLINE (FAITH AND PRACTICE). The publication of books of discipline, though developed in the late 17th century, grew widely from a renewal movement occurring between 1735 and 1790 and built upon a refinement and elaboration of Friends' practices under the inspiration of several **ministers**. Changes included the expansion of **women**'s meetings, recording of ministers, differentiation of **elders** and **overseers**, and a detailing of rules for consistent conduct.

While several **yearly meetings** had hand-written copies of a discipline in circulation in the early 18th century, the first published collection of **minutes** and advices, a *Book of Extracts*, was circulated by **London Yearly Meeting** in the early 1780s. Thus the origins of books of discipline affirm that Friends receive **Truth** corporately, expressed by **minutes** of yearly meetings. Early Disciplines were organized alphabetically by topic under which would appear actual minutes and the date they were approved. Topics addressed the right ordering of both personal conduct (e.g., gambling, moderation) and the management of the practical affairs of the **meeting** (e.g., **marriage**, oversight). *See also* OVERSEERS. Each meeting would annotate its copy with revised minutes until a new edition was produced.

When disputes over doctrines and other matters split **yearly meetings** in the United States in the mid-19th century, some Disciplines came to include statements of belief. As a public affirmation of belief became accepted as a necessary part of the discipline, these books were increasingly concerned with articulating Quaker faith as well as practice and thus entitled *Faith and Practice*. By the 20th century, this was done by most yearly meetings.

Current books of discipline or faith and practice, usually subtitled "Book of (Christian) Discipline," reflect the variety of ways Quakers have developed from their common roots. Each reflects the integrity of the yearly meeting that approved it.

For most yearly meetings, "faith" means Christian doctrine, and many Faith and Practices contain the entire 1887 **Richmond Declaration of Faith**. Others contain some derivation of the Richmond Declaration "form": a topic heading ("**God**," "**baptism**," "**peace**") with doctrinal statements justified by scriptural passages. This Richmond Declaration of Faith, together with "Essential Truths," and Extracts from **George Fox**'s "Letter to the Governor of Barbados, 1671" became the doctrinal basis of a Uniform Discipline approved by Five Years Meeting in 1900. Not all constituent yearly meetings adopted this discipline, but most followed its form. Today the disciplines of yearly meetings in both **Friends United Meeting** and **Evangelical Friends International** show the influence of the 1945 revision of this Uniform Discipline.

In 1926, **Friends General Conference** also developed a Uniform Discipline. All but one of the member yearly meetings revised their own disciplines between 1926 and 1930 incorporating most of this document. For these and other **liberal** yearly meetings, "faith"' is connected more to "spiritual experiences of Friends" and is expressed through quotations from individual Friends or yearly meetings under topic headings, often with an introductory paragraph which reflects the unity (or diversity) of opinion in that yearly meeting on the topic. The postscript from the ***Epistle of the Elders of Balby*** is often quoted near the start.

Most disciplines contain **queries**, and a lesser number contain advices; these could also be considered an expression of faith, a reminder that faith must be expressed in life. These books normally include a brief history of Quakerism in general and of that particular yearly meeting. Some in **East Africa** and **South** or **Central America** contain the statutes that allow the Church to exist in that country.

The practice section describes organization and procedures, but these are seen as a way of exercising the expressed faith by keeping the community faithful to its call and "in good order" (*see* GOSPEL ORDER). It serves as a training manual, enabling broad participation and shared **leadership** in constituent meetings. It may also contain the legal references necessary to enable Quakers to utilize the local civil laws that apply to their practices.

The disciplinary force of Faith and Practices has changed over time. In the past, persons not adhering to the stated principles or behavior could be disowned. Today there are two understandings of the authority of Faith and Practices. Some yearly meetings feel they are descriptive; they simply reflect the reality of that yearly meeting. Others continue to hold that their Faith and Practice is prescriptive, though **disownment** for nonadherence is now rare.

When a yearly meeting becomes aware of "spiritual and social inharmonies" with its Faith and Practice, a revision will be undertaken to reflect new revelations given. [Jan Hoffman]

DISOWNMENT. The formal recognition by a **monthly meeting** that a member is not in "unity" (*see* BUSINESS MEETING) with one or more essential elements of its faith and practice, or that the member's behavior reflects unfavorably on Friends' witness in the world. Prior to any formal action being taken, **overseers** or other experienced Friends meet with the individual following a process adapted from Matthew 18. Early documents, such as the ***Epistle of the Elders of Balby***, spoke of "disorderly walkers" (2 Thessalonians 3:6, Authorized Version) and set forth the process of meeting with individuals in hopes they would change their ways.

Disownment removes the offender from the **membership** lists, but the former member is still free to **worship** with the **meeting**. Most **yearly meetings** provide for an appeal process, which may involve the **quarterly** and **yearly meeting** levels. Heavily used in earlier periods of Quakerism, disownment has become increasingly uncommon over the past century. [Johan Maurer]

DISTINCTIVES. A term used to refer to the distinctive Quaker practices and interpretation of the Gospel. These include the **testimonies**, **plain dress and speech**; their manner of **worship** and inward practice of the sacraments; the conduct of **business meetings** through seeking the will of **God**; and their doctrine of **perfection**. *See* PECULIARITY.

DIXON, JEREMIAH (1733–1785). English astronomer and surveyor who was commissioned (1763–1767), along with Charles Mason

(1730–1787) by **William Penn** to settle the disputed boundary between Maryland and Pennsylvania. The Mason and Dixon line became the figurative boundary between North and South in the United States.

DOUGLAS, JOHN HENRY (1832–1911). Key figure in the **holiness** "Great **Revival**" of the 1870s. A native of Maine, in his youth he moved to New Vienna, Ohio, where he lived close to the **peace** activist, **Daniel Hill**, and adjacent to young **Walter Malone**. Douglas became the first secretary of the Peace Association of Friends in 1867. In 1876, he became the first **yearly meeting superintendent** when he was called to create that post by Iowa Yearly Meeting (**Gurneyite**). He served from 1886 to 1890 and oversaw the creation of the **pastoral system**. *See also* RICHMOND DECLARATION. [John W. Oliver]

DOUGLAS, ROBERT WALTER. (1834–1919). One of the first Friends' **ministers** to be paid for his services, he and his brother **John Henry Douglas** were founders of **Wilmington College**. Robert was the first general secretary of the Peace Association in America. *See also* PASTORAL MOVEMENT.

DOUGLASS, SARAH MAPPS (1806–1882). African American educator and one of the early members, along with her mother, Grace Douglass, **Lucretia Mott**, **Angelina** and **Sarah Grimké**, and others, of the biracial Philadelphia Female Anti-Slavery Society, founded in 1833. At these meetings, Douglass frequently presented antislavery poems, which were often later published. In 1848, Douglass helped organize the all-black **Women**'s Association of Philadelphia. Despite the strong Quaker role in **abolition**, Douglass met racial prejudice within Philadelphia **Yearly Meeting**, where, in her day, blacks were expected to sit on a back bench. She strongly protested the prejudice within Friends' meetings, but continued to worship with **Orthodox** Friends.

In 1836, she established a school for black children with the support of the Anti-Slavery Society, which then accepted responsibility for funding the school. After the school closed in 1847, she taught at the Institute for Coloured Youth. *See* RICHARD HUMPHREYS FOUNDATION. [Margery Post Abbott]

DuBOIS, RACHEL MIRIAM DAVIS (1892–1993). Born into a Quaker family in New Jersey, DuBois was active in the **Young Friends Movement** and worked for the **Women's International League for Peace and Freedom**. She was a teacher, a high school principal, a pacifist (*see* PEACE), and designer of intercultural dialogue techniques. DuBois was a pioneer in small group interactions for interracial, intercultural, international, and interreligious understanding. Because of her work with **African Americans**, she was invited by Martin Luther King Jr. to join the staff of the Southern Christian Leadership Conference. She also was invited to teach her techniques in several international venues where racial tensions flared. [Margery Post Abbott]

DUNCAN, DAVID (1839–1872). Leader of the "Duncanites," a group of free thinkers active from the 1860s, who were investigated by **London Yearly Meeting** for their views on the authority of the **Bible**. Duncan died shortly after his **disownment** in 1870. The group's position would have been more acceptable within the yearly meeting 20 years later and can be found in some of the presentations at the **Manchester Conference**. [Pink Dandelion]

DURÁN ALDANA, JOSÉ MARIA (1915–). Prominent preacher and pastor in Chiquimula, Guatemala, and founder of the Friends Ambassadors Young People's Societies. *See* CENTRAL AMERICA.

DYER, MARY BARRETT (ca. 1615–1659/60). British-born Friend who felt strongly called to visit Boston at a time when Massachusetts law prohibited Quakers in the colony. She was one of four Quakers hanged on Boston Common. *See* BOSTON MARTYRS.

–E–

EARLHAM COLLEGE. Founded in 1847 as Friends Boarding School in Richmond, Indiana by Indiana **Yearly Meeting** (**Orthodox**), it became Earlham College in 1859. As of 2002 it was affiliated with Indiana and Western yearly meetings.

EARLHAM SCHOOL OF RELIGION (ESR). From the beginning of the **pastoral system** among **North American** Friends in the late 19th century, there was discussion of the need to establish a seminary to train Quaker pastors. It proved fruitless for many years. Until 1960 **education** for Quaker pastors ranged from Bible **colleges** under Quaker auspices to the most **liberal** mainline seminaries. When **Landrum Bolling** became president of **Earlham College** in 1958, he engaged **Wilmer A. Cooper**, a **Friends Committee on National Legislation** staff member, to conduct a feasibility study. The results were favorable, and in 1960 ESR opened with 11 students and five faculty, including Cooper, **D. Elton Trueblood**, Hugh Barbour, and **Alexander Purdy**. Originally focused largely on the preparation of Quaker pastors, today ESR sees its mission as the preparation of Friends for a wide variety of **ministries**. [Thomas D. Hamm]

EAST AFRICA (KENYA, TANZANIA, UGANDA). One of the greatest concentrations of Friends in the world is in East Africa. In 2000, Kenya had 14 **yearly meetings**, Tanzania two, and Uganda one, with a combined membership totaling approximately 140,000. All are **programmed meetings** affiliated with **Friends United Meeting**.

Although **London Yearly Meeting** maintained a small **mission** in Pemba from 1896, the major story of Quakerism in East Africa began in 1902, when **Arthur B. Chilson**, **Willis R. Hotchkiss**, and Edgar Hole (1869–1943) used the new railroad from Mombasa to reach Kisumu on the shores of Lake Tanganyika. Their first station at Kaimosi, which offered both a healthy climate and a dense population not served by other churches, remained the center of Kenyan Quakerism for many decades.

The missionaries were supported by the Board of the Friends Africa Industrial **Mission** (later FAM), organized by Friends from seven **Orthodox** yearly meetings. With the development of self-supporting and self-propagating churches as its ultimate goal, the mission had a fourfold ministry that governed the development of later stations: evangelism, **education**, industrial training, and medical work. The Board of FAM was soon brought under the American Friends Mission Board of Five Years Meeting (later Friends United Meeting).

Evangelization proceeded slowly; by 1906 there were only five converts, and only 50 members by 1914. This was partly due to difficulties in communication and partly to the missionaries' attitude to the local culture, which they saw as inimical to the Christian faith. The missionaries gradually learned the languages of the Luyia peoples and translated the **Bible** into Llogooli, spoken by the Avalogoli, a subgroup of the Luyia people among whom FAM worked. Llogooli became the *lingua franca* of FAM, but not without difficulties, as it implied Avalogoli domination to nonspeakers, an issue promoting later schisms.

The missionaries simultaneously established two new missions in 1906, at Vihiga and Liranda, followed by Lugulu in 1913 and Malava in 1919, covering the geographical area allotted to Friends under the agreements of the Protestant missionaries in the region.

The first African Quaker converts demonstrated their zeal for the new faith by becoming evangelists. With little infrastructure and infrequent visits by missionaries to supply logistical support, they left the main mission stations to start outstations in remote places. Akhonya, **Maria Atiamuga,** and many others became household names identified with specific areas. For instance, **Daudi Lung'aho** and **Maria Maraga** were identified with Kaimosi, Yohana Amugune (1878–1960) and **Rabeka Amigitsi** were well known in Vihiga Station and in Chavakali, **Joseph Ngaira** and **Maria Mwaitsi** were identified with Lugulu and its adjacent areas.

The **ministry** of these Quakers included evangelism, teaching, translation, pastoral oversight of the converts, and **discipline** of the meeting. They sought to form a Christian community in line with the teachings they received from the missionaries. At the same time, however, they challenged customary injustices, such as the prohibition against females eating chicken and eggs (which were believed to cause infertility for **women**). Yohana Amugune, in particular, is remembered for allowing his wife Rabeka Amigitsi to break the taboo, after which he gave chicken to the girls who had become *Avasomi* (literally "readers," but applied to Christians in general). Despite the stir this caused in the meetings, other women broke with this taboo as they became Christians.

Mama **Rasoah Mutua,** a leading woman evangelist, interpreted this break in tradition as an opening for women to take an active role in meetings, even if they were not allowed **leadership** positions in **equality** with men. Rasoah Mutua became renowned as an evangelist, teacher, and preacher. She was among the first students to train as a **pastor** at Friends Bible College (now **Friends Theological College**) when it was started in 1943. She is remembered, too, for her ministry to women prisoners. *See* PENAL REFORM.

As well as being evangelists, the Quaker pioneers worked as Bible translators. Akhonya, Amugune, and especially **Joel Litu** contributed greatly to the translation of the Bible from English into Luragoli. The Bible provided not only the text for preaching but also the school textbook in a context where literacy and Christianity were considered inseparable. Translation of the Bible into the local language also helped to naturalize the Christian Gospel.

The African evangelists were responsible for the pastoral oversight and administration of the meetings. They presided over the converts, particularly in prayer, prepared older converts for **membership**, taught reading and writing to the young, disciplined those who failed to live up to the teaching of the **meeting**, offered preparation for **marriage**, and gave counsel to families facing difficult issues. These pioneer Quakers were the link between the missionaries and the members. Although pioneer Quakers were both men and women, it is important to note that leadership and pastoral work in the meetings was according to gender. Women did women's work and preached occasionally in the services, but the leadership roles were allocated to the men. Separate women's meetings have been established in some areas. However, the role and proximity of the Quaker pioneers to the local Christians made them the pillars of the emergent meetings.

During World War I, church membership increased as mission stations supplied people with food and treated their diseases at a time of economic crisis, famine, and epidemics. After World War I, the British colonial rule in Kenya was intensified through taxation, itinerant work, cash crop production, and the development of a monetary economy. The FAM schools and vocational training attracted local people because they offered skills that led to opportunities for work in the colonial society.

From the middle of the 1920s, Quaker converts created their own villages, known as "mission lines" (Christian villages). Drinking, smoking, dancing, polygamy, and any other practices associated by the missionaries with pre-Christian beliefs were outlawed (*see* TEMPERANCE). The mission lines both disseminated and assimilated **evangelical** Quakerism and Western culture until 1933, when the Local Native Council prohibited their creation.

After **World War II**, the struggle for independence from British rule accelerated, especially in Kenya, where settler colonialism was entrenched. The Western orientation of mission work became a focus of criticism, and Quakers were no exception. The growing nationalism throughout the country led missionaries to think about handing over responsibilities to Africans. In 1945, Five Years Meeting finally approved the establishment of East Africa **Yearly Meeting** (EAYM). **Thomas Lung'aho** was the first administrative secretary in 1958. EAYM was in charge of church extension, while the Americans continued to oversee the **education**, health, and other facets of the mission work. EAYM appointed pastors and extended its work to some parts of Uganda and Tanzania. In 1948, the first Quaker church in Kampala, Uganda, was formed.

Political independence for Kenyans coincided with religious independence for most churches. In 1962, EAYM gained full independence. In cooperation with the government, EAYM continued to provide many of the services that FAM had rendered prior to independence, especially in education and medical care (*see* JOSIAH EMBEGO). In 1968, the Manchira Monthly Meeting in Tanzania, with its eight village meetings, was registered as a church in Tanzania. In 1973, Idi Amin banned Friends from Uganda. Most of their churches were destroyed, and many members fled to neighboring countries. Many returned after the end of Idi Amin's rule in 1980 and the gradual restoration of peace since 1986.

Beginning in the 1980s, East Africa Yearly Meeting divided several times, partly as a result of its successful growth, partly because of internal ethnic tensions. [Esther Mombo]

EAST ASIA (CHINA, TAIWAN, HONG KONG, JAPAN). Friends from different branches have been active in spreading Quakerism throughout East Asia. After a faltering beginning between 1884 and 1889, China became one of the main **mission** fields (along with Madagascar, India, and Ceylon) for the Foreign Missions Association of London **Yearly Meeting**. From 13 missionaries in 1901, the number rose to 39 in 1916, including three brothers and a son of **Robert J. and Mary Davidson**, who had first gone to China in 1886. Activity was focused in Sichuan (Szechwan) Province around Chongqing (Chungking). Quakers set up schools and hospitals, including the International Friends Institute and West China University.

The North American Friend **Esther Butler** arrived in Nanjing (Nanking), China, in December 1887. Soon to join her were **Lenna M. Stanley** (1891), a teacher, and **Lucy A. Gaynor,** M.D. (1892). In 1898, Margaret A. Holme (1894) and Isabella French, M.D. (1897) opened a second area at Luho, north of Nanjing, under Butler's leadership. While the principal concern was the **Great Commission**, hospitals and schools were founded in both missions before any churches were established.

For nearly 10 years after its founding, the Ohio Friends mission in China was essentially an exclusively female enterprise. The mission was established by and for **women**. Little effort was made to evangelize among men, and male missionary candidates were denied appointment to the mission until 1899. Near the end of the century, at Butler's request, the mission was expanded to include programs for men.

Twenty-five missionaries served under the Ohio mission in China, establishing schools and hospitals as well as churches under Butler's superintendency (1887–1921), including doctors George and Isabella DeVol (*see* DEVOL FAMILY) and Myrtle and **Walter Williams**. Thirty-five missionaries served for varying periods after 1900.

By the 1930s, the Nanjing congregation reached 300 and included people from all strata of society. George and Isabella DeVol kept careful records on each patient treated at Peace Hospital, which they built in Luho, one medical, the other spiritual. Inpatients and outpatients heard the Gospel daily. Positive response by patients and families guided missionaries as they opened other preaching points in the county surrounding Luho. Under Walter R. Williams's leadership, young men were trained to assist in the hospital, teach in village schools, and preach the Gospel in villages on weekends. After 1949, the courage of Charles DeVol and other missionaries was matched by **Steven Yang** and many others who suffered severely under communism. Buildings were confiscated. The Chinese pastor of Luho church died in jail, and the Luho school principal died soon after his release from prison. Yet in 1998, the 100th anniversary of the Luho church, Pastor Liu reported 20,000 Christians in Luho Province and 31 nationalized congregations, many whose ancestral roots stem from contacts made through Peace Hospital.

British and North American Friends served in the Friends Ambulance Unit in China during **World War II** (*see* RELIEF WORK). After Mao Zedong's death in 1976, the Women's Bible Teachers Training School was transformed into the Nanjing Theological Seminary, and the Luho church building was reopened as a state-sanctioned place of worship.

Charles and Elsie Matti and Ella Ruth Hutson (1922–) pioneered work in Taiwan on behalf of Ohio Yearly Meeting. Arriving in November 1953, they settled in Chiayi City, 160 miles south of Taipei. Services in the first rented chapel began in 1954. Evangelism and church-planting were major objectives from the beginning. Twenty-six other missionaries have served in Taiwan.

Missionaries, in a role of servant-leadership, encouraged Chinese to lead in shepherding their own people from the inception of the Taiwan mission. By 2001, there were 39 self-supporting congregations, 38 of which began from Chinese vision, with a 40th being planned. These Chinese Friends supported one missionary family in the Philippines and were planning to send more missionaries abroad. Over 400 attended late 20th-century missions conferences in Chiayi and Taipei. They also assisted with needs in **South Asia**, as well as the Philippines. In 1975, Ohio Friends, David and Cindy Aufrance, began serving in Hong Kong under loan from Evangelical Friends Church–Eastern Region to the Oriental Missionary Society. A small **unprogrammed meeting** also exists in Hong Kong.

Quakerism in Japan grew out of the work of **Orthodox** Philadelphia Friends, responding to the urgings of two young Japanese men studying in America. One of them, **Inazo Nitobe**, later became one of the most important statesmen in Quaker history. Actual work began in 1884, when Philadelphia Friends sent Joseph (1851–1932) and Sarah Ann Newson Cosand (1846–1915) of Kansas to Japan. Members of several **yearly meetings** contributed to the development of the mission in Japan. The **American Friends Service Committee** gave effective help after the Tokyo earthquake of 1923 and on a larger scale after World War II. Long service was given by **Gilbert and Minnie Bowles** (1901–1941), Esther B. Rhoads, and others.

In 1940, under governmental suggestions, the yearly meeting joined other Protestant denominations to form the National Christian Church, but a small group of Friends continued to meet separately, drawing more than ever on the traditional Friends **worship** of silent waiting. Out of this group a new yearly meeting was formed in 1947, and those who had been members of the National Christian Church returned to the Japan Yearly Meeting. In 2001, six **monthly meetings** existed with about 200 members. **Sunday Schools** are held in some of the monthly meetings, and there are small groups studying the **Bible**, Quakerism, and nonviolence activities. A newsletter, *Tomo,* is published three times a year.

The Friends Girls' School, established by Philadelphia Friends in 1887, is now a self-supporting institution with several Friends on the faculty and on the school board. The student enrollment is 800. Friends Old Folks Home, *Ai-yu-en*, was founded in 1920 in Mito in Ibaraki Prefecture, where it was a pioneer project. Japan Friends Service Committee, established in 1953, is now running a nursery school, senior citizens' home and day care center at Setagaya in Tokyo. Friends Center in Tokyo is now maintained and run by Japan Yearly Meeting for various Quaker-related activities. [Jacalynn Stuckey Baker, Howard W. Moore, Michi Nakamura]

ECUMENISM. Movement for church unity. The term is derived from the Greek *oikoumene*, "the entire inhabited earth." Although both internal ("intrafaith") and external ("interfaith") relations have been an issue since the Council of Jerusalem (Acts 15), the search for greater religious unity has increased greatly over the past two centuries.

Friends' traditions provide a theological basis for ecumenism. The claim that **God** is present and working not only in oneself but in every person is fundamental to their faith. **George Fox** wrote that "**Christ** has enlightened every man that comes into the world" and "God, who made all, pours out of his Spirit upon all men and women in the world . . . whites and blacks, Moors and Turks and Indians, Christians, Jews and Gentiles, that all with the Spirit of God might know God and the things of God, and serve and worship him in his Spirit and Truth, that he has given them" (Jones, *The Power of the Lord is Over All*, Epistle 388, p. 420). **Robert Barclay**'s emphasis upon the universal availability of **salvation** was in dramatic contrast to a predestinarian

theology, which limits God's redemptive work to a select group. "The angel who declared the birth and coming of Christ to the shepherds said not that his news was for a few . . . but '. . . to all the people'" (*Apology*, Proposition 5.vi).

Grounded in theological insights of this kind, Quaker ecumenical involvement has taken many forms reflecting concerns for theology, social problems, and **peace** making. Friends were full participants in the first World Parliament of Religions in 1893. Interfaith dialogue has grown since the Quaker-initiated Zen Buddhist–Christian and the Hindu–Christian Colloquia (1967) to include some cosponsorship of the Parliament of the World's Religions (1993). Christian cooperation and dialogue have been facilitated by various organizations at state, national, and international levels; for example, **Friends General Conference** and **Friends United Meeting** are members of the National Council of Churches and the World Council of Churches (WCC), and **Evangelical Friends International** belongs to the National Association of Evangelicals. **Algie I. Newlin** of North Carolina was on the first Central Committee of the WCC, and **Everett Cattell** served as president of the World Evangelical Council. Friends regularly send delegates to these organizations and to other ecumenical efforts, such as the National Council of Churches of Kenya. Friends joined with the Mennonites and Church of the Brethren to form the New Call to Peacemaking. During the Catholic Church's Second Vatican Council (1962–1965), **Dorothy and Douglas Steere** were official observer-delegates. **Friends World Committee for Consultation** sends representatives to the Christian World Communions and has observer status at the WCC.

Not all have been enthusiastic about ecumenical associations. British Friends declined to join the WCC, because they considered the Basis for membership a **creed**. However, Quakers were instrumental in establishing the British Council for Promoting an International Christian Meeting in 1917 and are members of Churches Together in Britain and Ireland. In more recent years, the WCC's document, ***Baptism**, Eucharist, and **Ministry*** (1982), has resulted in vigorous discussion among Friends about how to respond to the idea of "one Eucharistic fellowship." As in Britain, yearly meetings in many parts of the world belong to the national ecumenical bodies. [David L. Johns]

EDDINGTON, ARTHUR (1882–1994). British astrophysicist, **conscientious objector**, and author of the first detailed account of Albert Einstein's theory of general relativity in English as well as numerous books including *Stellar Movements and the Structure of the Universe* (1914) and *The Nature of the Physical World* (1922). *See* SCIENCE AND TECHNOLOGY.

EDMUNDSON, WILLIAM (ALSO EDMONDSON) (1627–1712). Preacher, active in evangelizing in **Ireland**. Edmundson had served in Oliver Cromwell's army before becoming a Friend in 1653. On account of his faith he was in **prison** several times, and his house was set on fire while he and his family were within. They just barely escaped the flames, which destroyed the building. Edmundson was one of the first Friends to condemn slavery (*see* ABOLITION) in 1675 during a visit to **North America** with **George Fox**. His **journal** was standard reading for Friends for many years along with that of Fox. [Pink Dandelion]

EDUCATION. In 1667, **George Fox** called for educating boys and girls "in whatsoever things were civil and useful in creation." Although Friends established at least 46 schools in **Restoration** England, these were not licensed and most existed for a short time. Elias Hookes wrote a primer, along with Fox, and other Friends wrote Greek and Latin textbooks. Most early Friends could read and write at a time when many other British men and women were illiterate. Second-generation leaders like **William Penn** and **Robert Barclay** showed by example the usefulness of wide learning. The **Holy Experiment** in Pennsylvania allowed the government to erect schools, required that parents teach their children sufficient reading to be able to understand the **Bible** before age 12, and also mandated instruction in a trade. Starting in the 1690s, **London Yearly Meeting**'s epistles regularly stressed educating children. Education also referred to learning the self-control needed to observe the **plain dress and speech** and to become receptive to the Inward **Light**.

In the 18th century, Friends in **Britain** founded boarding schools, which provided a basic education and taught Latin, in spite of Quaker misgivings about the classics. The many Quaker discoveries in **science and technology** may stem from an emphasis upon studying natural history and practical subjects in school. In Rhode Island, New York,

New Jersey, and Pennsylvania, **meetings** established primary schools, although most children probably learned to read at home. Meetings emphasized the necessity for a guarded education, i.e., the need to seclude a child from **evil** and to learn only a select curriculum. A shortage of schoolmasters caused by low pay and too few students hampered Quaker education. Only a small elite progressed beyond a primary education, mainly children of merchants.

After the 1760s, Friends encouraged the establishment of schools under the control of the meeting. In order to better educate poor Friends, London Yearly Meeting in 1779 established Ackworth School, which led to several imitations in America: Westtown (Pennsylvania), Nine Partners (New York), Moses Brown (Rhode Island), New Garden (North Carolina), and Southern (Delaware). Here children could be preserved from evil in a **family**-like atmosphere and plainness could be required. As Friends **migrated** West, they established meeting schools and boarding schools. Most were later absorbed into the public school system, but a few, including Olney (Ohio) and Scattergood (Iowa), still exist.

The **Hicksite-Orthodox** separations of 1827–1828 influenced the patterns of education as each branch saw the need to found schools and **colleges**. In the late 19th century Quaker schools and colleges gradually broadened their curriculum to include novels, music, and even drama, but the emphasis remained on practical subjects plus the classics (*see* ARTS). Adding social clubs, athletic contests, student newspapers, and even fraternities and sororities made Quaker schools resemble other American schools and colleges. There was also less emphasis upon plain dress and speech, but education remained guarded with an intense religious atmosphere and strict rules.

Today many Quaker secondary schools struggle to maintain a vital core of Quaker teachers and students. The specifics differ by country, but interest in education is a concern worldwide for Friends. In Britain, for example, Friends' boarding schools are caught up in the debate over all-private, fee-paying schools. Yearly meetings in **East Africa** support over 150 primary and secondary schools, as well as several institutions of higher learning. In **North America**, boarding and private schools attract the affluent who seek a rigorous education combined with an emphasis on social responsibility, and the parents often view these institutions as a way to escape public schools. Quaker schools often seek to recruit racial minorities and the poor, but financial constraints limit their ability to offer scholarships and to pay adequate teacher salaries. Most Quaker private day schools are in the East, but many Friends elsewhere have founded schools stressing nonviolence, simple living, progressive education, and **worship**. Friends schools insist that attending the **meeting for worship** is central to a Quaker education, but they vigorously debate what else is requisite. [J. William Frost]

EICHENBERG, FRITZ (1901–1990). German-born American printmaker and illustrator of many important books for children as well as interpretations of Shakespeare, Poe, the Brontes, Tolstoy, many biblical themes, and his own fables, *Endangered Species* and *Dance of Death*. *See* ARTS.

ELDERLY. Since their earliest beginnings, Friends have been concerned for the condition of older members. Both writings and actions evidence their sensitivity to society's tendency to turn away both from the potential of the elderly for making useful contributions to the community around them and from their special needs.

As a result of a bequest, English Friends constructed homes for seniors in 1710, and the concern was mirrored in Philadelphia at about the same time with the founding of the Friends Almshouse for poor widows and elderly couples. Friends in the area of Philadelphia **Yearly Meeting** began a series of small boarding homes in the late 19th century, usually inspired by the needs of elderly Friends. Their development at the turn of the century was spurred on by generous financial support from Philadelphia **Hicksite** Friend **Anna T. Jeanes**—whose bequest continues to assist needy older Friends and Quaker senior service providers in the area.

Today Friends' senior service programs provide care and support to seniors of all faiths, and programs have emerged in other parts of the United States, although nowhere on the scale of those in the Middle Atlantic states. Their nursing homes were cited by a consumer organization in the mid-1990s as having the highest quality among all nursing home "chains" in the United States.

Friends pioneered the concept of the continuing care retirement community (CCRC) on the East Coast in the late 1960s and early 1970s with the openings of Foulkeways, Medford Leas, and Kendal in

Southeastern Pennsylvania and New Jersey. They and the others that have followed reflect Friends' belief in the dignity and potential of all people. They emphasize the role of residents in shaping the life and activities of the community, encourage active resident leadership, and stress residents' involvement in decisions that affect their lives, even when they are frail and at life's end.

In the 1990s Friends Life Care at Home in the Philadelphia area launched a unique continuing care program for seniors wishing to remain in their own homes. It is a model for similar programs elsewhere in the country.

Committed to nonviolence and **peace**, Friends created more humane conditions for patients in **mental health** hospitals and later developed models of restraint-free care of the frail elderly at Kendal and other Friends' organizations. Their special concern is for disoriented, aggressive, or physically unstable patients. Friends were among the advocates of federal standards that put severe limitations on the use of physical restraints in all nursing homes. Stapeley in Germantown (a neighborhood in Philadelphia) was one of the early Quaker boarding homes. Like several others, it grew into a more complex provider of services and today is one of the few CCRCs in the country that is based in an urban, predominantly African American community. It has emerged as a richly diverse community of residents and staff. [Warren Witte]

ELDERS. Originally, elders were responsible for both the religious and moral health of the meeting and its members. Although the office of **overseers** began to emerge in the mid-18th century, it was not until 1789 that **London Yearly Meeting** clearly specified the moral supervision role as belonging to overseers, not elders.

Today elders are the individuals responsible for nurturing the spiritual vitality of **meeting for worship**. Elders are charged with seeing to the good order of the **meeting**, with active **discernment** and encouragement of gifts of **ministry** among members, and with calling to order those who disrupt **worship**. In the 20th century, not all meetings appoint elders, absorbing this role into **committees** on worship and ministry. [Paul Lacey]

ELLWOOD, THOMAS (1639–1713). Influential English Friend. Ellwood is remembered particularly for editing and publishing the **journal** of **George Fox** in 1694. His background was among the gentry and he served for a while as John Milton's secretary. A friend of **Isaac and Mary Penington**, he first **worshipped** with Friends in their home.

EMBEGO, JOSIAH (1927–). Embego has served the Quaker church as a teacher, theological educator, and presiding **clerk** of **East Africa** Yearly Meeting South. Orphaned early, he was unable to complete Kakamega high school due to the lack of fees, but in 1946 he began teaching as an untrained teacher at Kegoye primary school, then joined the Kaimosi elementary training college, where he graduated with a teacher's certificate, which prepared him to teach at various schools in the area. In 1965, he went to Woodbrooke College, later **Woodbrooke Quaker Study Centre**, to study Quakerism, and after returning to Kenya, worked on a Harvard University anthropology research study of child development.

Embego was both the principal and a tutor at the Friends Bible Institute (now **Friends Theological College**) in Kaimosi starting in 1969 until his retirement in 1996 and has trained over half the pastors in East Africa. He succeeded in admitting **women** students to the seminary, starting in 1977, despite the opposition of board members. While principal, he took further study in Israel and at St. Paul's United Theological College in Limuru, Kenya. He has spoken at many **yearly meeting** sessions and has continued to be involved in training pastors and **preaching** at his **monthly meeting** in addition to farming. [Esther Mombo]

ENGLISH CIVIL WAR. The English Civil War of 1642 to 1648 was an unexpected explosion in the escalating conflict between Charles I and the Puritan-dominated Parliament called in 1640 (*see* BRITAIN). It ended constructive dialogue within England's propertied classes and inadvertently invited new sectors of society into the political arena. Suspension of censorship allowed new religious and political ideas to proliferate in the open. Lapsed enforcement of parish church attendance freed people to experiment publicly with new forms of **worship**, **ministry**, and **church** government (*see* BUSINESS MEETINGS). **Women** began to speak openly and publish. Finally, Oliver Cromwell radicalized the military with his innovation of a "New Model Army" in 1645 and with his millenarian rhetoric promoting the war. Regiments were tinged with a new, holy-war sensibility and a hope to establish God's kingdom in England. Millenarian expectations ran at fever pitch during the last phases of the war (*see* ESCHATOLOGY). But in 1649–1650, as the generals and moderate elements in Parliament struggled to impose a more conservative settlement of church and state, radicals were plunged into despair.

The early Quaker **Lamb's War** must be viewed partly in light of the Civil War. The violence and hollow victory of the latter helped define the pacifism (*see* PEACE) and grassroots ethic of the former. As a popular, nonviolent offensive upon the entire fabric of the new Puritan regime, the Lamb's War reasserted the "Good Old Cause" in England. From the very beginning, the Quaker movement drew disaffected dropouts from the army. Their recognition that "**Christ** is come to teach and lead his people himself" implied a new concept of sovereignty: Christ must be enthroned in the consciences of the English people. To that end, early Friends combined intense evangelical **mission** with a severe critique of state-enforced religion (*see* TITHES), new codes of social **equality**, and a revival of republican political agendas from the 1640s. [Douglas Gwyn]

ENVIRONMENT. Early Friends share with the **mystical** strand of Roman Catholicism, and other faiths, the awareness of **God**'s work in and through all creation. Further, Quakers joined in the pursuit of "natural theology," which **John Woolman** exemplified when he said: "Our merciful God hath placed a principle in the human mind which incites to exercise goodness towards every living creature" (*A Plea for the Poor*, Whittier, p. 3).

George Fox connected his knowledge of the "admirable works of the creation" with the experience of being perfected into "the state in which Adam was before he fell" (*Journal*, Nickalls, p. 27) (*see* PERFECTION). Hence, the Quaker concern for the environment is joined at the root to the spiritual experience of early Friends. Further, such spiritual experience is always interwoven with concern for all creation. As **William Penn** put it, humans will not "abuse" creation when they see "the great Creator staring them in the face, in all and every Part" of creation.

At the start of the 21st century, this concern is expressed in the Northwest **Yearly Meeting** book of **discipline**: "As a Christian steward, do you treat the earth with respect and with a sense of God's splendor in creation, guarding it against abuse by greed, misapplied technology, or your own carelessness?" For many Friends an environmental witness is integral to their lives and linked to **simplicity**. Some eschew private transport, and in particular, air travel, while many more support organic farming, and reuse and recycling programs. Quaker Green Concern in **Britain** and Friends Committee on Unity with Nature in **North America** are two more formal groups witnessing to this concern. [Lonnie Valentine]

EQUALITY. One day in 1672, while traveling in the American colonies, **George Fox** disputed with a doctor who was adamant that the **Light** and **Holy Spirit** were not accessible to all people. A man from one of the local **Native American** tribes, when asked, affirmed that there was something in him that reproved him when he told lies or behaved badly. Then, Fox says, the doctor ran off in defeat and shame. This story illustrates the early Quaker belief that the Light of **Christ** is **universal**, teaching good and evil in every human heart, without regard to race, gender, class, or even knowledge of Jesus Christ.

The work of the Spirit in his own heart, confirmed by the **Bible**, convinced Fox of the equality of all people before **God**, and of the ability of all people—like the doctor he met—to deny **Truth** and thus be subject to judgment. He also believed that those who were renewed and knew Truth were given to live out God's kingdom on earth: "In that renewal there is no longer Greek and Jew . . . slave and free" (Colossians 3:11). *See also* PERFECTION.

Friends also were ahead of their time in conceiving of **women** as "helpmeets," not as beings under the dominion of men. A popular pamphlet—authored by **Margaret Fell**—proclaimed the biblical basis for "women's speaking justified." Unlike many **Puritan** contemporaries, Quaker congregations were unperturbed by women who preached or took public **leadership** roles as **ministers**, but did not always see this equality as extending to other spheres.

Fell led in organizing the structure and communication networks of **meetings for sufferings**, **monthly meetings**, and **quarterly meetings**. Soon Quaker communities developed separate women's meetings that allowed women the opportunity to develop leadership skills, a process being repeated in parts of modern **East Africa**. From its formative period, Quaker women were empowered to travel in the **ministry**, even if such a **leading** meant leaving their young children to be cared for by the **meeting** community.

From the late 17th century, Quaker settlers in **North America** encountered Native American culture and began to grapple with equality in a new context, attempting to treat these people with respect as they created their **Holy Experiment** in a new land. Some Friends eventually advocated for people with little power to shape their own lives: slaves, prisoners, children, the mentally ill, orphans, the economically dispossessed (*see* ABOLITION; ELDERLY; MENTAL HEALTH). The efforts of **John Woolman**, **Elizabeth Gurney Fry**, and many others provided the leadership for various initiatives. By the end of the 18th century, **philanthropy** became the dominant approach. During the next century, Friends established groups to provide **relief** to civilians in war-torn areas, in economic- or natural-disaster-distressed locations, and to provide education for non-Quaker children. Always these efforts were based in the belief that each individual, regardless of background, represented an aspect of the divine. Though the actions have sometimes been clouded by paternalism and miscommunication, the intent has always been clear: to treat each person as a child of God.

By the second half of the 20th century, Friends meetings and schools had attempted to embrace and respond to people of all races, religions, and cultures (*see* AFRICAN AMERICANS). Separate women's meetings had given way to gender-integrated meetings in many parts of the world. At the start of the 21st century, awareness of the ways in which practices are inhospitable to individuals of different races or economic status is growing. Among **liberal Friends**, tolerance is increasing for atheist members, for celebration of same-sex unions, and for greater responsiveness to the voices and opinions of young people. [Emma Jones Lapsansky]

ESCHATOLOGY. Earliest Quaker eschatology (doctrine of "last things") is summarized in **George Fox**'s central message, "**Christ** is come to teach and lead his people himself," an announcement of Christ's long-awaited second coming. Fox directed hearers to look within rather than without to know Christ's return. Christ's **Light** within would reveal and enact the biblical **prophecies** of end-time events, from judgment day to the **heavenly** Jerusalem. But the power of the Light was not a matter of individual experience or personal transformation alone. It forged strong Quaker communities of seeking and following the Light in unity (*see* BUSINESS MEETINGS). It also led these communities into open conflict with civil powers deemed unjust and religions seen as false. Early Friends understood these struggles as fulfillment of the Book of Revelation (*see* LAMB'S WAR). They refused to speculate upon the millennium or the "rapture." While they did not rule out anything **God** might do in the future, their emphasis was upon God's work in the present. As such, early Quaker eschatology was not "realized" in a static, already-completed sense, but "realizing," as an unfolding present reality. It was an apocalyptic eschatology in the basic Greek sense of the word "**apocalypse**": a revelation that removes the veil from reality.

The sense of the immediacy of the Kingdom of God faded during the 17th century as religious and political powers in England reasserted themselves and it became clear the Quaker apocalypse would not overwhelm the nation. **Restoration Friends** established themselves as a "city upon a hill," a separated people whose egalitarian ethics and refined spiritual practices retained some eschatological meaning through the next century.

In the 19th century, **evangelical** renewal adopted the millennialist teachings of the wider Protestant scene. By the late 19th century, this increasingly took the form of pre-millennialism, the belief that the world will grow worse until Christ returns (in some outward manner) and begins a reign of a thousand years. However, other Friends in the same period founded utopian communities and reform movements understood in more humanistic and post-millennialist terms as God's evolving government on earth. In the 20th century, Friends divided between those with millennialist outlooks and those who gradually evolved a present-centered, noneschatological stance. [Douglas Gwyn]

ESTRELLO, FRANCISCO (1907–1959). Mexican pastor and poet. In the 1940s and 1950s he was known in the **evangelical** world as "the **peace** poet." He is author of several poetry books and anthologies. Interpreter and translator, his work includes a translation of the *Life of David Livingston* and *Gandhi*. Estrello was a member of the Hispanic American Commission for Christian Education and of the Committee for the Revision of the Translation of the *Reina Valera* version of the **Bible** in Spanish. He served as secretary of the Latin American Bible Society. [Loida Eunice Fernandez Gonzalez]

EUROPE. *See* BRITAIN; CONTINENTAL EUROPE; IRELAND.

EVANGELICAL FRIENDS INTERNATIONAL (EFI). EFI is a federation of autonomous **yearly meetings** organized in four regions, **North America**, Latin America (*see* CARIBBEAN; CENTRAL AMERICA; SOUTH AMERICA), **Asia**, and **Africa** representing about 100,000 Friends. Each region functions independently, meeting annually or triennially. They cooperate in programs of intervisitation, **missions**, leadership training, and interregional outreach.

The Association of Evangelical Friends organized conferences and publications from 1947 to 1970. This renewal movement became the catalyst for several independent yearly meetings to organize the Evangelical Friends Alliance in 1963–1965 as a vehicle for cooperative programs. The adjective "**evangelical**" affirmed a 20th-century understanding of "orthodox" Christian **theology** against a "**modernist**" formulation of Quaker thought.

The Alliance spread beyond North America and became Evangelical Friends International in 1990. A consultative Council consists of the four regional directors plus the international director. It meets triennially for minimal business, fellowship, and prayer, and publishes guidelines for leadership training and outreach. EFI has its own statement of faith, a primary tenet being the inspiration of the **Bible** as rule of faith and the **Holy Spirit** as true interpreter.

EFI/Latin America includes **Mexico**, Guatemala, Honduras, El Salvador, Bolivia (INELA), and Peru—650 congregations and 35,000 constituents, as well as various seminaries and schools. It is located in two culturally distinct and distant areas: Central America and the Andean region of South America. EFI/Asia includes 139 congregations and 9,000 constituents in Taiwan, the Philippines, India, Nepal, and Cambodia (*see* EAST ASIA; SOUTH ASIA; SOUTHEAST ASIA).

EFI/Africa covers Burundi, Rwanda, and Congo, numbering 20,000 members and attenders, in 170 congregations, mostly in **Central Africa**. Friends have created a seminary as well as numerous schools and been active in peace efforts. They have increased in numbers and vitality despite the ethnic strife in the region.

EFI/North America is the most highly organized of the regions, with permanent bodies for Evangelical Friends Mission, Christian Education, **Publications**, and Youth. It serves these yearly meetings: Alaska, Northwest, Southwest, Mid-America, Rocky Mountain, and

Evangelical Friends Church–Eastern Region, with a total membership of about 35,000 Friends. It publishes a newsletter, "The Voice," and participates in **pastors**' conferences in cooperation with **Friends United Meeting**.

Evangelical Friends Mission is a cooperative agency supporting missionary personnel in Rwanda, Nepal, India, Taiwan, Philippines, Mexico, Nicaragua, **Ireland**, at the ecumenical Bolivian Evangelical University and, in the United States, Navajo, international student, and Hispanic ministries. EFI/NA yearly meetings also support their own missions and cooperative programs in Guatemala, Honduras/El Salvador, Bolivia, Peru, Cambodia, Indonesia, Jamaica, Haiti, Palestine, China, India, and Hungary.

EFI/NA yearly meetings support institutions of higher **education** for Friends and non-Friends (*see also* COLLEGES). These include **George Fox University** (Newberg, Oregon), **Malone College** (Canton, Ohio), Houston Graduate School of Theology (Houston, Texas), **Friends University** (Wichita, Kansas), **Barclay College** (Haviland, Kansas), and the Friends Center of **Azusa Pacific University** (Azusa, California).

Across the four regions, historic Friends doctrines and practices are held with cultural variations. All are **evangelical**: they affirm the centrality of Jesus **Christ** as historically incarnate and inwardly experienced. The EFI Constitution is adapted from the **Richmond Declaration of Faith**. **Women** and men share in **ministry** roles, often as married couples. The **leadership** of the **Holy Spirit** in decision making is the norm. **Clerks** preside at **business meetings**. Representative bodies govern yearly meetings. On the issue of water **baptism** and occasional use of the elements in **communion**, some yearly meetings in Asia, Africa, and North America are divided, but traditional **testimonies** predominate, and any outward symbolism is considered secondary to immediate spiritual presence (*see* SACRAMENTS). Wesleyan modes of **holiness** expression characterize some Central and North America Friends. The **peace testimony** is taught, and Friends participate in social reconciliation. Legal status for **conscientious objectors** does not exist in many of the countries. Rwandan Friends demonstrated nonviolent behavior during the genocide of 1994 and the subsequent conflicts, and African Friends generally have been active peacemakers in strife-torn Central Africa (*see* DAVID NIYONZIMA). The **Great Lakes School of Theology** curriculum includes a major emphasis upon peacemaking, and in America, George Fox University has a strong Center for Peace Learning. [Arthur O. Roberts]

EVANGELICALISM. A movement with a rich heritage dating back to the Reformation recovery of justification by faith. From this renewal movement, evangelicalism went through a wide array of transitions and modifications as it passed through the dynamic period of **Puritanism**, assimilated the dominant influences of Pietism and culminated in the 19th century with the spiritual uprising of the Second Great Awakening (*see* HOLINESS MOVEMENT). This latter period, in particular, reshaped the **theology** and practices of **Orthodox** Friends in **North America** and, through increased **mission** work, made evangelicalism a strong influence on the majority of Friends worldwide.

While early Friends were evangelists, evangelicalism was a renewal/**revival** movement (or "Great Awakening") which began in England in the 18th century but did not significantly affect Friends until the 19th century. The Orthodox party of the **Great Separation** in 1827 was the earliest organized body of evangelical Friends. While still acknowledging most of the Quaker **distinctives**, they wanted a greater allegiance to the **Bible** than had prevailed among **Quietist** Friends. They were distressed by what they saw as heretical thought in Quaker **meetings**, many of which had been influenced by Deism and the opinions of people like **Hannah Barnard**.

Major schism was avoided in **Britain** because the majority of Friends were in general agreement. However, the leading British evangelical Friend, **Joseph John Gurney**, was seen by some, such as American **John Wilbur**, to give Scripture an authority that undermined the concept of the Inward **Light** and to be too worldly in general. Gurney's travels in North America led to a separation among Orthodox Friends into **Gurneyites** and **Wilburites** in the 1840s and 1850s. From the 1870s, Gurneyite Friends began to introduce a **pastoral system** and with this, **programmed worship**.

The remaining Gurneyites divided over allegiances to the influences of **modernism** and holiness teaching. Modernists tended to be committed to the renewal of Quakerism, seeking to make it a faith relevant to the age and open to new ideas. They were largely committed to the **social gospel** and essentially post-millennial (*see* ESCHATOLOGY). Holiness Friends, much influenced by revival movements, were less worldly and were concerned to preserve true faith in the face of a changing world. They drew their primary inspiration from their experience of **salvation** and **sanctification** leading them into a life of holiness.

The desire of some holiness Friends for water **baptism** led initially to the **Richmond Declaration of Faith**. Those evangelical yearly meetings that subscribed to it founded Five Years Meeting (later **Friends United Meeting [FUM]**). A number of holiness yearly meetings formed in turn what became **Evangelical Friends International (EFI)**. Both FUM and EFI have experienced **fundamentalist** tendencies in the 20th century as holiness spirituality and teachings have diminished.

Twentieth-first century evangelical Christianity is represented by seven controlling convictions, which include the authority of Scripture, the Lordship of Jesus Christ, the work of the **Holy Spirit**, the need for personal conversion, the priority of evangelism, participation in the life of a local church, and social responsibility toward one's local community. There are many contemporary expressions of evangelical Christian faith from fundamentalist to liberal in interpretation, but each refers to these seven convictions as the heart of its expression of orthodox Christian faith.

Today, there is a wide range of expressions of evangelical faith within both groupings and within Quakerism in general. Evangelical Friends are most often found among the yearly meetings belonging to FUM and EFI and are identified by the use of the Richmond Declaration of Faith in their books of **discipline**. Modern evangelical Friends differ in the degree to which they stress their commonalities with other evangelical Christians and hold to Quaker practices. [Gayle D. Beebe, Carole Spencer]

EVIL. Biblical tradition has held that evil began with the Fall in the Garden of Eden, but there seems to be no rational way to understand fully and account for evil. It is customary to divide evil into two categories—natural evil and moral evil. Natural evil is known in legal terms as "acts of **God**" over which humankind has little, if any, control. This includes natural disasters, such as earthquakes, floods, hurricanes, tornadoes, disease, etc., that can cause great pain, suffering, and even **death**. Moral evil, on the other hand, has been referred to as "**sin**" in the Christian and biblical tradition. It is the "not good" for which humanity is accountable before God and other human beings. Part of what it means to be human is to be able to distinguish between these two kinds of evil, to know the difference between good and evil, and intentionally to choose the good.

Early Friends regarded sin and evil as "going out of the **Truth**." In dealing with sin and evil, **George Fox** drew on the **apocalyptic** language of the Book of Revelation, which assumed a dualism between the forces of good and evil. Evil was personified in Satan and was referred to as the Dragon (Revelation 12:7). In Revelation 13 the Beast continued the image of Satan. Both Fox and **James Nayler** looked upon this as spiritual warfare, and when the **Day of the Lord** comes it will mark a victory of good over evil. They called this the **Lamb's War** in which **Christ** was the Lamb of God who would bring the victory.

In the 20th century, **Rufus Jones** drew from the Platonic tradition the belief that sin and evil represent the "absence of the good," instead of focusing on "the Fall" as an explanation for sin and evil. Failure to choose the good constituted an error in judgment. But it is a serious matter because it defies God's world of purpose and meaning. While many **liberal Friends** of the late 20th century avoided the term "sin," all varieties of Friends would agree to the importance of "living in the power of the Lord" that overcomes evil, realizing fully the measure of the **Light** God has given them. [Wilmer A. Cooper]

–F–

FAGER, CHARLES EUGENE ("CHUCK") (1942–). Fager is the author or editor of more than 20 books, including children's books, mysteries, and works on Quaker **theology** and controversial issues. A Vietnam-era **conscientious objector**, he joined Cambridge **Meeting** in Massachusetts in 1969 and is currently a member of State College Meeting in Pennsylvania. After a year on the faculty at **Friends World College** in 1966–1967, he studied theology at Harvard University from 1968 to 1971, served as a congressional staff member from 1979 to 1981, and worked for the U.S. Postal Service from 1985 until 1994. Between 1981 and 1993 he also edited and published *A Friendly Letter* (an independent newsletter). He then directed the issues program at

Pendle Hill in Pennsylvania until 1997. He has served as **clerk** of the Fellowship of Quakers in the **Arts** since 1996, and in 1998 he initiated the Lemonade Art Gallery at the **Friends General Conference** annual gathering. In 1999 he founded *Quaker Theology: A Progressive Journal and Forum for Discussion and Study*, and conducts workshops and seminars on related topics. He has worked continuously as an investigative reporter on Quaker and other topics for various national publications. In early 2002 he became director of Quaker House, a **peace** program started in Fayetteville, North Carolina, in 1969.

FAMILIED MONASTICISM. A modern term used to describe the formation of Friends in community in their first two centuries. Though they might live the uncloistered life—be employed, married, and engaged in the community—they remained separate from worldly distractions. **Robert Barclay** used the monastic analogy in his *Apology* and **William Penn** characterized Friends as living "in the world but not of it." *See* HEDGE. [Kathryn A. Damiano]

FAMILISTS. One of the precursor sects that shared elements with early Quakerism. Originating in Holland in about 1530, the Family of Love reached England in about 1550. Like early Friends, they emphasized inward religious experience and rejected oaths (*see* TRUTH), war (*see* PEACE), capital punishment, elaborate speech, and outward ceremony . *See also* CAMM, JOHN; SIMPLICITY.

FAMILY. Early Friends' beliefs on **women**'s religious **equality**, the spiritual nature of all **sacraments**, including **baptism** and **marriage**, and the lack of ordained **ministers** affected family life. Preaching the gospel seemed to take priority over family life as many men and women left their families for long periods to travel in the **ministry**. Friends defined infants as innocent and not needing baptism to cover an original **sin**. Though they talked about the need for **education** and wrote primers, persecution meant that the first Quaker schools were short-lived.

Early child rearing focused on secluding a child from **evil**. The good example of parents and teachers along with observance of **plain dress and speech** would accustom the child to self-discipline, and he or she would learn to still the will in order to experience the Inward **Light**. Quaker virtues applied to both sexes who had to learn to be "**tender**" and loving. **Certificates** would specify that a young person had her "birth and education among Friends," an indication that birthright **membership** was practiced long before being recognized in the 1737 **London Yearly Meeting Discipline**.

Eighteenth-century Friends insisted that Quakerism could not flourish in a religiously mixed family (*see* PECULIARITY). Constituting a small portion of most communities, they sought to ensure that their children associated with, and then married, other Friends. "Marriage out of unity" became the single most time-consuming task of **monthly meetings**, particularly after the tightening of discipline in the 1750s. Authority within the family rested with the father, but mutual love and forbearance rather than subordination were expected to prevail.

Demographic data on London and Philadelphia meetings show that Quakers lived longer and had fewer children than the general population, perhaps because of a child-centered family and a lifestyle stressing moderation in eating and drinking. Friends married at an older age than the general population, and many women did not marry. In the early 19th century women moved easily from responsibility within the women's meetings to organizing charitable organizations, teaching school, and participating in the **abolition** and feminist movements. Children attended **meeting**-sponsored boarding schools, or the new common schools (*see* EDUCATION).

Responding to **evangelical** impulses and declining membership, London Yearly Meeting stopped **disownment** for marriage to non-Quakers by the mid-19th century. The practice was abandoned by **Hicksite** and **Gurneyite** meetings in **North America** after the American Civil War. Under the impact of the **holiness movement**, **evangelical** Friends emphasized original sin and the necessity of a conversion experience. Hicksite and **liberal Friends** stressed an innocent child's gradual growth in grace in a Christian family. Meetings created First Day Schools whose literature reflected the contrasting views of early childhood (*see* RELIGIOUS EDUCATION).

Increasingly, Quaker views of family life have conformed to norms of the wider society. In the 20th century most meetings began to tolerate divorce, just as, more recently, liberal Friends have begun to accept homosexuality, couples cohabiting before marriage, and same-sex marriage. Some within the evangelical branches emphasize what they define as the traditional role of male authority in marriage with the wife as homemaker. [J. William Frost]

FARNWORTH, RICHARD (ca. 1630–1666). Preacher from Yorkshire, England. In correspondence with **George Fox** from 1651, Richard Farnworth was a major Quaker figure in 1651–1656 and again in 1661–1666. As a pamphleteer, his work shows the development of Quakerism from early **apocalyptic** enthusiasm to later caution and accommodation to political reality. He helped to write the important works of **discipline**, ***Epistle of the Elders of Balby*** and ***Testimony of the Brethren***.

FELL, MARGARET ASKEW (LATER FOX) (1614–1702). Born at Marsh Grange, near Dalton in Furness, Lancashire, Margaret Askew married Judge Thomas Fell (1598–1658) in 1632. She bore one son and seven daughters, six of the latter becoming Quaker **ministers** in their own right. Widowed in 1658, she married **George Fox** in 1669. Of all the Quaker **leadership** of her day, she is said to have had the clearest understanding of the early Quaker faith as proclaimed by its leading apostle, Fox. Often termed the "nursing mother" of the Quaker movement, she utilized her position and estate to establish an administrative and communication center at her home, **Swarthmoor Hall**, for the burgeoning movement. She supported ministers on an international scale with everything from pamphlets and epistles, to advice, medications, funds, and moral support.

After raising her family, Margaret devoted the years between 1660 and her death in 1702 to public **ministry**. Between 1660 and 1698, she made 10 journeys from the North of England to London to lobby the king and court, explaining Friends' principles, negotiating the release of jailed and persecuted Friends, and ministering to the spiritual needs of hard-pressed **meetings**. She was also a key figure in the establishment of **women**'s meetings through travel in ministry and extensive correspondence.

Margaret Fell suffered two imprisonments for her faith (1664–1668 and 1670–1671) (*see* PRISON). During the former, which included the sentence of *praemunire* (forfeiture of her estates for failing to swear an oath of allegiance to the king), she testified to her faith in the strongest terms, declaring "Although I am out of the King's Protection, yet I am not out of the protection of the Almighty God" (Fell, *Life of Margaret Fox*, Philadelphia, 1859, p. 36). She authored 16 books, extensive correspondence, and one poem, all defending the Quaker faith and opening it not only to Christians but also to Jews. *For Meanasseth-ben-Israel: The Call of Jews out of Babylon* (1656) was her first of five books addressed to world Jewry. The most important of her writings for the present age is her defense of women's **equality** in ministry in *Women Speaking Justified, Proved, and Allowed of by the Scriptures.* [T. H. S. Wallace]

FERGUSON, DORIS (1937–) and WILLARD (1937–). Members of Mid-America Yearly Meeting, they spent 18 years as **missionaries** in Burundi (*see* CENTRAL AFRICA). In 1987, they moved to Rwanda where Willard is field director and legal representative for the **Evangelical Friends Mission** to Rwanda. Doris serves as hostess, and does nursing and **women**'s **ministry**. The Fergusons both grew up in Kansas and graduated from the Friends Bible College (now **Barclay College**) in Haviland, Kansas. Willard went on to get a Master's of Science degree at Kansas State College, and Doris was trained in nursing. They have five children. [David Williams]

FIRST PUBLISHERS OF TRUTH. Early Quaker **preaching** activity was called "publishing **truth**." Thus, the **Valiant Sixty** and other early **ministers** have been called "First Publishers of Truth." Norman Penney used this as the title for a modern edition of reports by early **meetings** in **Britain** on how the **Quaker** message first came to their area, produced at the request of London (now Britain) **Yearly Meeting**.

FISHER, MARY (LATER BAYLY and CROSS) (1623?–1698). A servant in early life, Mary Fisher traveled widely in the **ministry**. In 1656, she and Anne Austin (d.1665) were the first Friends to sail via Barbados to Boston and were jailed there. Fisher is best known for her **mission** to Sultan Mohammed IV in Adrianople in 1657–1658. The Sultan listened to her message "from the great **God**" with courtesy. When asked her opinion of the prophet Mohammed, she said, "they might judge him false or true according to the words and prophecies he spoke," which the Sultan agreed to be true (Brinton, *Friends for 300 Years*, p. 159). She first married William Bayly, by whom she had several children. After marrying John Cross in 1678, they and her children arrived in South Carolina by 1685. She became the mainstay of the Charleston **Meeting** in South Carolina. [Margery Post Abbott]

FISHER, SAMUEL (1605–1665). Early Quaker pamphleteer. Former Baptist **minister**, he authored a number of theological works. *See* BIBLE; PUBLISHING.

FIVE YEARS MEETING. Quaker umbrella organization now known as **Friends United Meeting**.

FIXED PRICE. Setting a given, or fixed, retail price for a product, in contrast to charging a different price to each customer based on bargaining (*see* BUSINESS AND ECONOMICS). This commercial innovation is associated with some early Quaker merchants who considered it dishonest to do anything other than state what they considered a fair price to all customers (*see* TRUTH). It proved to be a highly popular and successful practice. [Thomas Head]

FOGELKLOU, EMILIA (LATER NORLIND) (1878–1972). Leading Swedish Quaker. In 1902 Emilia Fogelklou had a decisive spiritual experience of, as she used to say, "the other Reality," but did not join Friends until 1932. All through her life she taught the history of religion and engaged in **peace** work. In 1915, she represented the Swedish YWCA at the International Congress of Women in The Hague, where she discovered the connection between the **women**'s movement and peace work. While teaching at Birkagården, an adult folk high school close to Stockholm, she wrote a book on the Swedish saint Birgitta (1919). In the early 1920s she married Arnold Norlind, translator of Dante's *Divina Commedia*.

Increasingly uneasy with the Swedish Protestant church, Norlind moved closer to Quakerism. In 1929, her new book, *The Quaker **James Nayler***, caused some stir among Friends because of her somewhat critical description of **George Fox**'s treatment of Nayler. In 1932 she joined Friends, initially joining **London Yearly Meeting** until the creation of Sweden Yearly Meeting in 1937 (*see* CONTINENTAL EUROPE). In 1933–1934, she did research at **Woodbrooke Quaker Study Centre** in England for her book about **Willam Penn** (1935). **Douglas Steere** then invited her to lecture at **Pendle Hill** outside Philadelphia in 1939. Fogelklou combined feminist criticism and spiritual **mysticism** of a rare, always socially oriented, kind.

During **World War II** she worked to help both refugees and women from German concentration camps. Her interest in contemporary religious thought of every kind (Teilhard de Chardin, Martin Buber, Simone Weil) never left her as she continued to publish well into her eighties. [Karna Linden]

FORD, JEFFERSON WHITING (1879–1949). American missionary to Jamaica (*see* CARIBBEAN) and **East Africa**. While serving in Jamaica (1901–1913), he met and married Helen Farr, daughter of an Iowa missionary family who had been serving there since 1892. The Fords moved to the Africa Inland **Mission** in Kenya in 1914, where she died in 1931. The following year Jefferson Ford married **Helen Kersey**. The Fords remained in East Africa until 1943. She returned to continue her mission work in Central America after his death, then taught at Azuza Pacific College (now **Asuza Pacific University**) in California from 1951 to 1962.

FOSTER, RICHARD (1942–). Educated at the then **George Fox College** and Fuller Theological Seminary, Foster has served as a **pastor** in California and the Pacific Northwest. He taught at **Friends University** in Kansas and was the distinguished professor of spiritual formation at **Azusa Pacific University** in California. He is an **evangelical** Friend who is widely read in all branches of the **Religious Society of Friends**. His books, including *Freedom of* ***Simplicity*** (1981), *Celebration of* ***Discipline*** (1988), ***Prayer****: Finding the Heart's True Home* (1992), and *Streams of Living Water: Celebrating the Great Traditions of Christian Faith* (1998), have made him one of the most widely read modern Quaker authors. He is the founder of Renovaré, an evangelical ecumenical movement committed to the renewal of the Christian church.

FOTHERGILL, JOHN (1712–1780). Born in Yorkshire, England. Fothergill's medical career was constrained by his faith at a time when the **Test Acts** confined fellowship of the Royal College of Physicians to those from the established church. He set up a rival body, although later he became the president and a fellow of the Royal Society. He was a personal friend of Benjamin Franklin and brother to **Samuel Fothergill**. He served as **clerk** of **London Yearly Meeting** three times and republished **Robert Barclay**'s *Apology* and the works of **William Penn**. [Pink Dandelion]

FOTHERGILL, SAMUEL (1715–1772). English Friend instrumental as a traveling **minister** in the reformation of Quakerism in the mid-18th century. Fothergill encouraged Friends to withdraw from worldly compromise such as the governance of the colony in Pennsylvania (*see* HOLY EXPERIMENT). He served with **John Woolman** on a **committee**, established in 1755 by Philadelphia **Yearly Meeting**, which, among other things, urged both stricter observance of the **testimony** against military service (*see* PEACE) and immediate **disownment** of anyone marrying a non-Friend (*see* FAMILY). As part of his work for spiritual renewal among Friends, he brought a **concern** to set up the **Meeting of Ministers and Elders** in **London Yearly Meeting**. He was brother to **John Fothergill**. [Pink Dandelion]

FOX, CAROLINE (1819–1871). A British literary figure. Her diary is especially valued for her record of conversations with John Stuart Mill and others.

FOX, GEORGE (1624–1690/91). Principal founder and organizer of the **Religious Society of Friends**. Raised in Drayton-in-the-Clay, Leicestershire, England, Fox had no formal **education** and was apprenticed to a shoemaker who was also engaged in sheep and wool trading. Coming of age during the **English Civil War** of the 1640s, the youth explored the **Bible** and traveled to London at the age of 19; gradually, he began to identify with religious dissenters (*see* PURITANISM; SEPARATISTS). In 1647, after a period of personal crisis and struggle, he knew he heard a voice saying, "there is one, even **Christ** Jesus, that can speak to thy condition" (*Journal*, Nickalls, p. 11).

This inward conviction led him to proclaim his encounter with the living Christ who, in his words, "was come to teach his people himself." In a period marked by insecurity and unrest, it was a gripping message, one he preached vigorously but with little success near his home in the Midlands in 1647 and 1648. He garnered many more **convincements** (conversions) after going north in 1651. Here he attracted the disciples—the most important being **James Nayler**, and **Margaret Fell**, whom he married in 1669—destined to be leaders of the new sect. Increasingly successful in appealing to radicalized New Model Army soldiers during the rule of Oliver Cromwell, "shattered" Baptists, **women**, and other **seekers**, Fox led his followers to resist **tithes**, reject artificial distinctions between men and women, and regard all, women, children, even the uneducated, as able to take prominent roles in the simple **worship** services.

Such unorthodox stances inevitably brought Fox into conflict with the authorities; he endured **prison** at least eight times, twice for blasphemy. A prolific writer, he led his followers in taking advantage of the end of state censorship to produce hundreds of epistles and letters of admonition and advice, both to his followers and to those he hoped to convince. Less than half of these writings have survived.

By 1654, the **Children of Light** surfaced in London and spread in the south. Fox faced his first internal challenge in the popular appeal of Nayler, who rivaled him as leader but was disgraced when convicted by Parliament for blasphemy at Bristol. Fox reacted to this incident by tightening up the organization and strengthening disciplinary powers of local (or **monthly) meetings**. Over the next decade Quaker organizational structure emerged as a modified Presbyterian system of ascending authority, capped by a **yearly meeting**. This approach enabled the movement to survive two more major internal challenges, one by **John Perrot** in the early 1660s, the other by **William Rogers**, **John Story**, and John Wilkinson in the 1670s. Fox also extended the authority of women in their own meetings, especially (and most controversially) regarding **marriage** procedures.

Declining popular support for the republic provoked in Fox a major depression, while the restoration of a Stuart king, Charles II, to the throne shattered his dream of Quakers becoming England's dominant group. His 1659 work, *Great Mistery of the Great Whore Unfolded*, was a massive refutation of the movement's critics, but it did not succeed in silencing them. In 1660/1661 Fox and 11 other leaders signed a document eschewing "carnal" warfare with outward weapons, which later became a well-known statement of the **peace testimony**. Persecuted by courts and Parliament, Fox and the Friends survived large fines and imprisonment. Following one such incarceration in Worcester, Fox began dictating what became his famous ***Journal***. He made two trips to the European continent and **preached** in the New World from 1671 to 1673. By the time he died of congestive heart failure in London, the movement had spread into much of the English-speaking world and Holland.

Fox possessed a charismatic personality, one with great appeal to his contemporaries, and he collected around himself a skilled group of followers. Still, he could also be harshly severe toward any daring to disagree with him and his policies. He mostly got along well with the family of Margaret Fell, convincing all her children but one son to become active Friends. Leaders of the second generation, such as **William Penn** and **Robert Barclay**, who sided with him against dissidents, enjoyed continuing renown, while dissenters, even the brilliant **George Keith**, were relegated to the sidelines. [Larry Ingle]

FOX, MARGARET (ASKEW FELL). *See* FELL, MARGARET.

FRAME, ESTHER GORDON (1840–1920). The best-known woman Quaker **minister** to emerge from the **revival** movement among **Gurneyite** Friends in the 1870s. With her husband Nathan, she conducted numerous evangelistic campaigns, often working closely with non-Quaker ministers.

FREE QUAKERS. In 1781, Philadelphia Friends disowned from their **meetings** for various actions in support of the American revolution, including **Samuel Wetherill Jr.**, William Crispin (1742–1797), Clement Biddle (1740–1814), Benjamin Say (1755–1813), Timothy Matlack (1736–1829), Lydia Darragh (1729–1789), and legendary flag-maker **Betsy Ross**, established the Society of Free Quakers. Their book of **discipline** eliminated **disownment**. The last **meeting for worship** was in about 1836. The Society of Free Quakers continues as a Wetherill family association, and the Free Quaker Meetinghouse remains as part of Independence National Park. [Mary Ellen Chijioke]

FRIENDLY ASSOCIATION FOR REGAINING AND PRESERVING PEACE WITH THE INDIANS BY PACIFIC MEASURES. The Friendly Association was organized by Philadelphia Quakers, led by Israel **Pemberton**, in 1756 to settle the conflict between the government of Pennsylvania and the Delaware Indians. They particularly challenged the Walking Purchase of 1737, by which the proprietors of Pennsylvania had tricked the Delawares into ceding much more of their land than they had intended. Though their success was temporary and local, it was one of the first formal attempts by Quakers both to assist **Native Americans** in their dealings with the U.S. government and to remove the causes of war. *See also* HOLY EXPERIMENT; PEACE. [Mary Ellen Chijioke]

FRIENDS CHURCH. The name used by Friends in **Evangelical Friends International (EFI)** and some other evangelical Friends in preference to **Religious Society of Friends**. These Friends see themselves as part of the **church** universal under the lordship of **Christ**.

In 1892, Iowa and Kansas **Yearly Meetings** brought the suggestion to Five Years Meeting (later **Friends United Meeting**) that Friends Church be adopted as the official name of the society. This suggestion was largely ignored in the larger controversy, which ended up deciding not to allow voting in **business meetings**. The discussion continued for a number of years in various publications and as a few yearly meetings simply began to use the name, it gradually became more widely adopted. [Margery Post Abbott]

FRIENDS COMMITTEE ON NATIONAL LEGISLATION (FCNL). FCNL works with Quaker **meetings**, individual Friends, and others to bring Friends' views on a broad spectrum of **peace**, human rights, and poverty issues to the attention of U.S. policy makers. The organization focuses primarily on the U.S. Congress, which is the branch of the federal government most approachable by individual citizens (*see* CIVIL GOVERNMENT; POLITICS). FCNL is a registered lobby; a separate FCNL Education Fund carries on tax-deductible education and research.

FCNL was created in 1943 in Richmond, Indiana. Its earliest efforts were to support **conscientious objectors**, promote war **relief work** and civil rights, and prepare for the postwar world. **E. Raymond Wilson**, after years of building the Institutes of International Relations program of the **American Friends Service Committee** (1931–1942), came to Washington, D.C., with a **concern** to work on behalf of conscientious objectors in 1942. He became executive secretary of FCNL from its inception until 1962. During its history, FCNL has emphasized world disarmament, strengthening international institutions of peace and justice, reducing military expenditures, opposing military conscription, and meeting human needs at home and abroad. It has also worked to protect civil and religious liberties, advance human rights, and support the concerns of **Native Americans**.

The governing body of FCNL is its General **Committee** of approximately 240 Friends, which holds annual **business meetings**. Two-thirds are appointed by 26 **yearly meetings** and by seven other Friends' organizations in the United States; the remainder are designated at-large. FCNL has had only three executive secretaries in its long history: Wilson 1943–1962, Edward F. Snyder 1962–1990, and Joe Volk 1990–date.

The Statement of Legislative Policy reflects a consensus, although not necessarily unanimity, on a broad range of issues and does not purport to speak for all Friends. The Policy Statement concentrates in areas of traditional Quaker concerns for peace, **equality**, and justice. It is less specific on issues of economic order, the role of government, and **environmental** policy. The Statement also notes issues on which Friends are still unable to reach agreement, for example, deployment of a United Nations police force, decriminalization of drug use, abortion, and gambling on Native American lands.

One reason for FCNL's considerable acceptability among Friends, despite its stands on controversial issues, is its policy of extensive consultation with Friends and Friends' meetings as it determines its legislative priorities for each new Congress and revises its Policy Statement. [Edward F. Snyder]

FRIENDS DISASTER SERVICE. A **relief** organization that has coordinated the work of hundreds of volunteers who have given thousands of hours to cleanup and rebuilding to assist victims of natural disasters, with special attention to the elderly, handicapped, uninsured, and persons with low income. The organization, founded in 1974 after a tornado destroyed much of Xenia, Ohio, and led by Dean Johnson of Evangelical Friends Church–Eastern Region, assists with relief work in the **Americas**, **Asia**, **Africa**, and the **Caribbean**. Individuals have participated from all branches of Friends, and financial support comes from many **yearly meetings** as well as from non-Friends. [John W. Oliver]

FRIENDS FREEDMEN'S ASSOCIATION OF PHILADELPHIA. First formed in November 1863 as the Friends Association of Philadelphia and Its Vicinity for the Relief of Colored Freedmen, the Freedmen's Association worked both for **relief** and, increasingly, **education** of those freed from slavery by the American Civil War (*see* ABOLITION). The Association eventually managed 48 schools in North Carolina and Virginia. By 1900, most of the schools had been absorbed into the public educational system, and the Association concentrated on the Christiansburg Industrial Institute, Montgomery

County, Virginia. In 1934, the county took over management, although the Association retained title to the Institute until 1947. Thereafter the Association's assets were used for scholarships for **African American** students. *See also* PEACE AND SERVICE AGENCIES; PHILANTHROPY. [Mary Ellen Chijioke]

FRIENDS GENERAL CONFERENCE (FGC). A **North American** association of 14 **yearly meetings**/regional groups and five independent **monthly meetings** with roots in the **Hicksite** or **liberal** branch of Friends. Its total membership in 1998 was approximately 32,000. FGC grew out of a Hicksite tradition of conferences among yearly meetings to discuss issues of common concern: the biennial conferences of the First Day School Associations beginning in 1868, the Union for Philanthropic Labor (1881), the Friends Religious Conference (1893), and the Friends Education Conference (1894) (*see* RELIGIOUS EDUCATION). These conferences were frequently held in conjunction with each other, in what was known as a General Conference. Plans for the General Conferences, the largest of which was held at Swarthmore, Pennsylvania, in 1896, were made by a Central **Committee** whose members represented the various associations from the several yearly meetings.

In 1900, the General Conference, held in Chautauqua, New York, established the Central Committee on a permanent basis. Representatives of the First Day School, Philanthropic Labor, Friends **Education**, and **Young Friends** Associations were drawn proportionally from the seven Hicksite Yearly Meetings: Baltimore, Genesee, Illinois, Indiana (later Ohio Valley), New York, Ohio, and Philadelphia. O. Edward Janney (1856–1930) of Baltimore Yearly Meeting was named as **clerk**, and served in this capacity until 1920. In 1905, **Henry Wilbur** of New York Yearly Meeting was engaged as general secretary, working out of an office in Philadelphia. He was succeeded in 1915 by **J. Bernard Walton**, who served until 1951. With the formal establishment of Friends General Conference, the various associations became FGC standing committees.

The close connection between the standing committees and the biennial conference, both overseen by the Central Committee, gradually dissolved, but the basic structure of FGC has remained the same. Its base of support broadened in the 1950s as a result of the **reunification** of Philadelphia, New York, and the Canadian/Genesee Yearly Meetings and affiliation with the newly reunited New England Yearly Meeting.

FGC also expanded geographically as new liberal meetings grew in southern, midwestern, and western states. South Central Yearly Meeting joined in 1962; Lake Erie in 1967 and Southeastern in 1972 were quickly followed by Northern Yearly Meeting, the Piedmont Friends Fellowship, Southern Appalachian Yearly Meeting and Association, and the Central Alaska Friends Conference. FGC produces religious education materials; distributes Friends literature; supports scattered Friends and new meetings; represents Friends in **ecumenical** activities; seeks to foster the spiritual life (*see* SPIRITUALITY); and convenes the general conferences or Gatherings, held biennially until 1962 and annually thereafter. [Deborah Haines]

FRIENDS THEOLOGICAL COLLEGE. Founded in 1943 at Lugulu, **East Africa**, by **Jefferson Ford** and some local people as the Friends Bible Institute to train Kenyans to serve as pastors, it was moved to property owned by East Africa Yearly Meeting in Kaimosi in 1950. Its board is composed of members from several East African **yearly meetings** and substantial funding comes from **Friends United Meeting**.

FRIENDS UNITED MEETING (FUM) (FORMERLY FIVE YEARS MEETING). In 1887, Indiana **Yearly Meeting (Orthodox)** organized a conference of all North American **Gurneyite** yearly meetings to consider issues of unity among Friends. Key participants included **James Wood**, **William Nicholson**, **Esther Frame**, **David Updegraff**, **J. B. Braithwaite**, and **Rufus Jones**, who was then editor of *The American Friend*. The conference report included the **Richmond Declaration of Faith**, which was adopted or reported approvingly by most participating yearly meetings. Conferences of Gurneyite yearly meetings in 1892 and 1897 led to the proposal for a legislative convention to "protect them from common dangers" (especially controversies and forces of disunity) and strengthen their joint participation in Christian work. "We believe this could be accomplished by the yearly meetings conferring upon future conferences limited legislative authority within distinctly defined spheres that would not interfere with the autonomy of the yearly meetings" (Third Conference of Friends in America, Proceedings, Philadelphia: *The American Friend*, 1898, pp. 17–18).

By the 1902 conference, a draft "Uniform **Discipline**" had been prepared and had already been approved by most Orthodox yearly meetings of Friends—New England, New York, Baltimore, North Carolina, Wilmington, Indiana, Western, Iowa, Kansas, California, and Oregon. These constituted the founding members of the Five Years Meeting, known since 1965 as Friends United Meeting. Canadian Yearly Meeting was represented by fraternal delegates and joined in 1907. Nebraska Yearly Meeting was approved by the Five Years Meeting in 1907 and formally opened in 1908. **Reunification** of yearly meetings that had split in the 19th century resulted in four yearly meetings—New England, New York, Canada, and Baltimore—holding membership as annual bodies, or in the case of Baltimore, through monthly meetings, in both Friends United Meeting and **Friends General Conference**. Later, Southeastern Yearly Meeting, organized in 1963, joined both FUM and Friends General Conference. Over the years several yearly meetings have withdrawn from FUM over allegations of liberalism, and are now part of **Evangelical Friends International**.

At its inception, the Five Years Meeting incorporated the existing American Friends Board of Foreign **Missions**, whose work continues today as the World Missions office. In the **Caribbean** and **East Africa**, mission and service outreach has resulted in many members of FUM. The member yearly meetings include Bware, Cuba, East Africa, East Africa (North), East Africa (South), Elgon Religious Society of Friends, Jamaica, Nairobi, and Vokoli. Friends located in **Mexico**, Belize, Uganda, Tanzania, and Palestine also have strong connections with FUM.

Other areas of FUM's work include Christian **religious education**, consultative services in spiritual renewal and evangelism, **publishing** and distributing Christian materials (among them *Quaker Life* magazine and books published by Friends United Press), and advancement of Friends' **testimonies**. FUM is governed by a General Board representing all member groups and by general membership sessions held triennially and is served by a staff based in Richmond, Indiana. In the early 1990s, FUM was at the center of unsuccessful demands by some individuals and meetings to **realign** North American yearly meetings along doctrinal lines. Southwest Yearly Meeting eventually left FUM over this issue, and more recently, Iowa Yearly Meeting has raised this question again. FUM's purpose statement, adopted in 1993, reads: "Friends United Meeting commits itself to energize and equip Friends through the power of the **Holy Spirit** to gather people into fellowships where Jesus **Christ** is known, loved and obeyed as Teacher and Lord." [Johan Maurer]

FRIENDS UNIVERSITY. Founded in Wichita, Kansas, in 1898 by Kansas **Yearly Meeting**. The yearly meeting relinquished control in 1931.

FRIENDS WORLD COLLEGE. Experimental institution founded by New York **Yearly Meeting** in 1965, with a main campus on Long Island, New York, and additional campuses in Kenya, India, Japan, and Mexico. The academic program was largely self-directed, and students were expected to study at several of the campuses. The college became a program of Long Island University in 1991.

FRIENDS WORLD COMMITTEE FOR CONSULTATION (FWCC). During World War I, British Friends decided to invite representatives of all Quaker bodies worldwide to a conference on **peace**. In 1920 Friends gathered in London for the All Friends Conference, the first world gathering of Friends since the **Great Separation** in **North America**. The principal report of the Conference, *Friends and War*, declared that the Christian concept of love had been subverted and that true Christianity makes no allowance for war. (*See also* WOOD, JAMES; WOODWARD, WALTER).

During the next two decades, the impetus for strengthening connections among Friends continued, particularly among **Young Friends** and peace activists, even as further separations occurred in the United States. J. Passmore Elkinton (1887–1971), a member of Philadelphia **Yearly Meeting (Orthodox)**, felt a strong concern for binding Friends together. He chaired a 1924 conference in Oskaloosa, Iowa, of all North American Quakers called by the **American Friends Service Committee (AFSC)**. In Europe, **Carl Heath** (1869–1950) was a key figure in the movement toward a world body. He worked to build new connections among Friends and responded to the increasingly troubled political and economic scene in a manner "rooted in spiritual life which centers in Christ" (Herbert Hadley, *Quakers World Wide*, p. 7). In 1929, German Yearly Meeting sent an epistle encouraging Friends to see themselves as a society reaching beyond yearly meeting and national boundaries. Soon thereafter, AFSC created the Fellowship **Committee** (later the American Friends Fellowship Council, AFFC), chaired by Elkinton, with members representing all North American Friends. AFFC suggested and organized the World Conference of Friends, which was held in 1937 on the campuses of **Swarthmore** and **Haverford** colleges outside Philadelphia, with the thought of creating "An International Society of Friends." Anna Griscom Elkinton, Passmore Elkinton's wife, chaired the Conference committee beginning in 1934.

At the 1937 Conference, Friends agreed to the establishment of a world body, Friends World Committee for Consultation, designed to promote international contacts and cooperation among Friends. The word "consultation" was included in the new organization's name to make it clear that it exercised no authority over member **yearly meetings**. Carl Heath chaired the new body through its first decade with Fred Tritton (1887–1968) as secretary.

From the beginning, Friends decided that the new body would have sections in various parts of the world and over time, section committee structures and offices were established for the Americas (1938), Europe (1938, now Europe and Middle East), Africa (1971) and Asia and West Pacific (1986). The world office and a small staff are based in London.

From the start, the American section maintained close ties with AFFC, which soon became independent of AFSC. AFFC contributed significantly to the **independent meetings movement** by recognizing new **monthly meetings** as well as individual **membership** of Friends isolated from any meeting. It also created the Wider Quaker Fellowship in order to nurture informal ties with individuals who felt an affinity with Friends, but did not see their way clear to joining. In 1954 the Fellowship Council merged with FWCC/Section of the Americas. Since 1919, **London Yearly Meeting** had a Council of International Service to provide for membership of isolated Friends living abroad by developing a Register of Overseas Membership. In 1979 this responsibility was transferred to FWCC which set up the

International Membership Committee to maintain contact with and support isolated Friends and worship groups worldwide.

Most Friends supported the creation of the United Nations (UN), and in 1948, FWCC was accredited as a nongovernmental organization (NGO). A **Quaker United Nations Office (QUNO)** was established in New York, and AFSC, with its larger staff and budget, agreed to carry financial and administrative responsibilities for this program. The existing **Quaker International Centre** in Geneva, Switzerland, which had worked with the League of Nations, also became a QUNO office, with financial and administrative responsibilities carried by the then Friends Service Council in London. FWCC also established an NGO relationship with UNESCO, which was then based in Paris.

As a "Christian World Communion," FWCC has associate membership in the World Council of Churches (*see* ECUMENISM). In the latter half of the 20th century it sent representatives to Vatican conferences and delegations to the World Council of Churches assemblies. FWCC also engaged in dialogue with Hindu and Buddhist scholars.

The third World Conference of Friends was held in Oxford, England, in 1952. This Conference accepted a new purpose statement for FWCC: "To encourage and strengthen the spiritual life within the Society . . . To help Friends gain a better understanding of the worldwide character of the Society . . . To promote consultation amongst Friends of all cultures, countries, and languages . . . and To keep under review the Quaker contribution in world affairs and to facilitate both the examination and presentation of Quaker thinking and concern" (Hadley, *Quakers World Wide*, p. 43).

The fourth World Conference, in Greensboro, North Carolina, in 1967, faced the question of racial segregation. **Guilford College,** the proposed site for the event, did not admit Negro students when it issued the invitation. The event proceeded only after the college's board changed their admissions policy. The following decade saw increased contact among Friends through the Faith and Life Movement and New Call to Peacemaking (1976), which also engaged the other historic peace churches, and a series of conferences on **mission** and service. The World Conference also called on Friends to launch "an all-out attack on want" and the Section of the Americas gradually took on responsibility for a new program on Right Sharing of World Resources, which became an independent organization in 1999.

The decision to hold the fifth World Conference at three sites in 1991 recognized the fact that close to half of the world body of Friends lives in either **East Africa** or **Central** or **South America**. Friends gathered around a common theme and program at sites in the Netherlands, Kenya, and Honduras. A few individuals attended all three venues. FWCC has also held a series of Mission and Service Consultations. The Sixth Consultation, in Uganda in 1996, brought together representatives of African yearly meetings and mission and service bodies to consider Friends' work in Africa.

FWCC has also been active in supporting the activities of **Young Friends** worldwide. It encouraged the World Gatherings of Young Friends in Greensboro, North Carolina, in 1985 and cooperated with the Young Friends International Gatherings that followed each session of the World Conference in 1991. The Quaker Youth Pilgrimage, which brings together individuals from 16 to 18 years of age from all branches of Friends, started in 1957. These young people from North America and Europe travel together to several visionary Quaker meetings and historic sites, worshipping daily, and considering what it means to be a Friend. [Margery Post Abbott]

FRY, ELIZABETH (1780–1845). A pioneering **prison** reformer and **minister**, Fry was among the first to recognize the importance of rehabilitating rather than punishing criminals (*see* PENAL REFORM). Among the earliest of British women **philanthropists**, she set an example for activism among **women**.

Born Elizabeth Gurney, she was the daughter of a prosperous Norwich family of Quaker cloth manufacturers and sister of **Joseph John Gurney**. When Elizabeth was a child, her parents adopted the habits of the local gentry, abandoning **plain dress** and other Quaker **disciplines**. The Gurneys attended **meeting for worship** only on Sunday, wearing fashionable, brightly colored clothes, which shocked Norwich Friends. At the age of 17, her life was transformed by the inspirational preaching of a North American, William Savery (1754–1804). Despite family disapproval, she sought to help the poor in her village. She married Joseph Storrs Fry (1766–1855), a plain (strict) Quaker and heir to an established firm of grocery importers in the city of London.

She bore six children in eight years and was at first fully occupied as wife and mother. When her beloved father died in 1809, Fry was moved to speak in **worship**, praising **God** for his life. From then on she became more active in Quaker affairs, and her gift in the vocal **ministry** was acknowledged by her **meeting** in 1811.

The following year she began regular visits to the jail in Newgate, **praying** for the women prisoners and their small children and bringing clothes and comforts for the inmates. Two years later she initiated a school for the women of Newgate and employed a matron to supervise their activities. She arranged for devout women to visit the prisoners and teach them the scriptures. She also ameliorated the conditions of women prisoners transported to **Australia** as punishment.

In time the state took over her work, but Elizabeth Fry's devotion changed and humanized attitudes to prisoners. Her accomplishments included instituting an order of nursing sisters, organizing local **committees** to visit the poor, and providing comforts for fishermen and lifeguards. *See also* ABOLITION. [June Rose]

FUNDAMENTALISM. A movement among Protestants that came together in the early 20th century to oppose "modern thought" (higher criticism, Darwinism, and secularism; *see* MODERNISM). The term derives from booklets published between 1910 and 1915 defining the fundamentals of Christianity: the divinity of Jesus; inerrancy of the **Bible**; the second coming; creation; **sin** and redemption; **heaven and hell**; personal **salvation**; the Virgin Birth; and the reality of miracles.

To the degree that it centered on defining biblical authority, fundamentalism made a major impact on **holiness** and **evangelical** Friends. To the degree that it focused on Reformation dogma of *sola scriptura* (Scripture alone), the Quaker emphasis on direct revelation made it difficult for these Friends to be completely at home in Fundamentalism. With the rise of the New Evangelism at mid-century, Evangelical Friends commonly shifted to a more flexible orthodoxy. [John W. Oliver]

–G–

GANDHI, MOHANDAS KARAMCHAND "MAHATMA" (1869–1948). Indian political leader and proponent of nonviolence who, while not a Friend, had strong connections with and influence upon Quakers. *See* ALEXANDER, HORACE; MALLIK, GURDIAL; PEACE; SOUTH ASIA; SYKES, MARJORIE.

GARDNER, SUNDERLAND PATTISON (1802–1893). Canadian **minister**, he was a leader of the **Hicksite** Genesee **Yearly Meeting** and an active member of its Committee on Indian Affairs (*see* NATIVE AMERICANS).

GARRETT, THOMAS (1789–1871). Delaware **Hicksite** and **abolitionist**, Garrett collaborated with William Still (1821–1902) in the Wilmington to Philadelphia link of the **underground railroad**.

GATHERED. This term describes the state of a **meeting for worship** when most of those present experience a condition of deep inner quiet, waiting wordlessly before **God**, sometimes experiencing an invisible connection with the Divine and with one another. It usually takes several minutes after a **meeting** has assembled for this state to occur. Once it has occurred, the meeting continues in refreshing silence, out of which spoken **ministry** or **prayer** may, or may not, arise. *See also* COVERED. [William P. Taber]

GAYNOR, LUCY A. (1861–1912). American medical doctor and **missionary** to China (*see* EAST ASIA) who opened a hospital there in 1895.

GENERAL MEETING. Variously used to designate a gathering of Friends from a number of **monthly meetings** in a region, a regional or **quarterly meeting**, the precursor to or equivalent of a **yearly meeting**, or a public, evangelistic **meeting** of the 17th and late 19th centuries. *See also* REVIVALISM.

GEORGE FOX UNIVERSITY. Founded in 1891 as Friends Pacific Academy in Newberg, Oregon, later becoming Pacific College. The name was changed to **George Fox** College in 1949 and to George Fox University in 1995, when it merged with Western Evangelical Seminary. It is affiliated with Northwest **Yearly Meeting**, a member of **Evangelical Friends International (EFI)**.

GOD. Explicit statements about the existence and nature of God are rare in Quaker literature. For much of their history, Friends were more concerned with defending a particular view of Christianity than with engaging in dialogue with atheism. God's existence was taken as a given in this context. Friends, in common with other radical Protestants, sought to clear away the centuries of what they saw as vain intellectual inquiry by refusing to use other than scriptural terms to speak of God. In support of this, they could invoke the **Bible**, which witnesses to God as creator, judge, and savior of humanity but has little interest in metaphysics. The work of the councils of the early Christian Church, which sought to explain God's nature and attributes by refining the doctrines of the **Trinity** and the incarnation, was rejected. Instead, Friends recalled their hearers to the real and inescapable demands and promises of God. They testified to their direct experiences of God's presence among them (*see* LEADINGS; MYSTICISM). This may also, however, have left Friends with inadequate defenses against repeating the arguments and confusions of earlier Christian centuries.

One well-worn allusion to God in Quaker literature is **George Fox**'s phrase, which he himself used sparingly: "that of God" in everyone. In Fox's original 1656 letter using this phrase, those who keep in God's wisdom and power will become patterns and examples and "answer" that of God in others, rather than seek to define it. It is a call to encounter and response, a claim, not an explanation, of the immediate communication between the utterly different realms of the human and divine. The subjective experience of the human participants is the focus of interest. Some modern **liberal Friends** interpret that of God as a metaphor for the spark of human spirituality. Among some 20th-century liberal Friends "that of God" may be interpreted as a metaphor for the spark of human **spirituality**. A few reject the word "God" itself for its freight of oppressive history.

Other Friends may tend to stress the immediate relationship with **Christ**, not always distinguishing among Christ, Jesus, and God. Again, it is God in action in the human sphere, as redeemer and example, that is stressed. Though the link between the historical Jesus and the power at work in transformed lives is asserted, it is not always adequately explained. The wariness over a technical **theological** vocabulary means that it is hard for subsequent Quaker writers to distinguish between phrases that may or may not have been synonymous for Fox, such as the **Light** of Christ and the workings of the **Holy Spirit**. Words may create confusion, but may also permit necessary distinctions to be articulated. At the heart of Quaker practice is a conviction of both presence and guidance (*see* DISCERNMENT). Quaker tradition can be used to defend either the position that the word "God" simply names this awareness, or that the existence of the living God proclaimed in the Bible, the **church**, and the experience of Friends is what makes all awareness possible. [Hugh S. Pyper]

GOSPEL ORDER. The order and harmony, established by **God** at the moment of creation, transcending the chaos that seems so often prevalent, and affirmed in the **covenant** with Noah (Genesis 9:1–17). It is the right relationship of every part of creation, however small, to every other part and to the Creator. Gospel Order was the phrase most often used by early Friends to describe the nature of the **church** and society as lived by a community reconciled and in right relationship with God and each other.

The use of the term "Gospel Order" seems to have begun with **George Fox**, though it quickly spread among the **Children of Light**. The Quaker usage stems from an understanding of **Christ**'s role as the restorer of the original relationship between the Creator and creation in the New Covenant (Hebrews 8:6–12). This reconciliation enabled everyone who believes in Christ to enter into a new relationship with God. Practical aspects of living out this relationship in community were modeled on Jesus' teachings (e.g., the Sermon on the Mount and Matthew 18) and the example of the early Christian church as described in Acts.

Gospel Order and Quaker process are different things. Good Quaker process overlaps the Gospel Order but Gospel Order is much broader. Friends today use the term to remind each other that their **business meetings** are intended not just to make good decisions but to discover God's will: the Gospel Order. Though no one can know God's will in its entirety, Friends know experientially that they can, as a faith community and through rightly ordered process, know God's will for a particular time on a particular subject. [Lloyd Lee Wilson]

GRAHAM, GEORGE (1673–1751). English horologist, apprentice and executor to **Thomas Tompion**, noted for his improvements to the clock and his astronomical instruments.

GREAT COMMISSION. All **evangelical** Christians stress the importance of **Jesus**'s great commission to his disciples, "Go therefore and make disciples of all nations, baptizing them in the name of the Father and of the Son and of the **Holy Spirit**, and teaching them to obey everything that I have commanded you" (Matthew 28:19,20). Early Friends, like **George Fox** and **Mary Fisher**, went out into the world to call professing Christians into knowledge of the Inward **Christ** and to share the Good News with non-Christians. *See also* MISSIONS: MODERN MISSIONARY MOVEMENT.

GREAT LAKES SCHOOL OF THEOLOGY. Opened in April 1999 under the sponsorship of **Evangelical Friends International**–Africa Region in order to train pastors and church leaders to provide **leadership** for **evangelical** Friends in **Central Africa**. One aim is to bring leadership to the challenge of reconciliation in a region where violence has hindered the church and threatened civil order (*see* PEACE). The school opened with its African director, Ferdinand Nzohabonayo, and a board made up of representatives from the churches in Burundi, Rwanda, and Congo. [James Morris]

GREAT SEPARATION. In 1827, Philadelphia **Yearly Meeting** divided over issues of authority and **theology** into two entities, both known by the same name and claiming to be "the" Philadelphia Yearly Meeting. These two bodies were the first in what came to be known as the **Hicksite** and **Orthodox** branches of the **Religious Society of Friends**. Within a year, New York, Baltimore, Ohio, and Indiana yearly meetings had also divided into Hicksite and Orthodox bodies. **Friends General Conference** traces its roots back to the Hicksites, while the Orthodox branch has produced **Friends United Meeting** and **Evangelical Friends International**, as well as modern **Conservative** Friends. [Margery Post Abbott]

GRELLET, STEPHEN (1773–1855). French-born American **minister** and prison reformer (*see* PENAL REFORM). Grellet helped care for the victims of the Philadelphia yellow fever epidemic in 1798, visited widely in prisons, asylums (*see* MENTAL HEALTH REFORM), and hospitals, and spoke widely in Europe as well as North America on the condition of prisoners. During a trip to England he met **Elizabeth Fry** and helped spark her concern for **prison** reform.

GRIMKÉ, ANGELINA EMILY (LATER WELD) (1805–1879) and SARAH MOORE (1792–1873). The sisters were **abolitionists** and **women**'s rights activists who became **convinced** Friends in Charleston, South Carolina, before moving to Philadelphia. Both were dismayed by racial discrimination among Friends. Both women addressed the Female Anti-Slavery Convention of 1837 and spoke regularly to large crowds despite angry protests and mobs. They were criticized for speaking to "promiscuous" audiences of mixed race and gender (*see* AFRICAN AMERICANS; EQUALITY). Both women were **disowned** in 1838 when Sarah attended Angelina's wedding to the non-Quaker abolitionist Theodore Weld. *See* MARRIAGE. [Mary Ellen Chijioke]

GRUBB, EDWARD (1854–1939). British theologian and devotional writer associated with **modernism** and **liberalism**, Grubb opposed the adoption of the **Richmond Declaration of Faith** by **London Yearly Meeting** in 1887. Closely associated with **J. W. Rowntree**, he served as secretary of the **Summer Schools Movement** and later as editor of the *British Friend*.

GRUBB, SARAH LYNES (1773–1842). British Friend noted for her devotional life and writing. A **Quietist**, she opposed granting a certificate from the **Meeting of Ministers and Elders** of **London Yearly Meeting** to **Joseph John Gurney** for his travels in **North America** in 1837. *See also* WILBUR, JOHN.

GUILFORD COLLEGE. Coeducational college in Greensboro, North Carolina, founded in 1837 by North Carolina **Yearly Meeting** of Friends as the New Garden Boarding School. It became Guilford College in 1887 and is now independent of **yearly meeting** ties.

GURNEY, JOSEPH JOHN (1788–1847). Banker, biblical scholar, **minister**. Joseph John Gurney came from a long-established Quaker family in Norfolk, England. One of his sisters was **Elizabeth Fry**. Following family tradition, he was by profession a banker, but he was also an extremely erudite scholar of the **Bible** and church history who was fluent in a number of languages, including Greek and Hebrew. In addition he took a keen interest in **science**, keeping abreast of the latest developments in biology, geology, and astronomy and seeking to integrate them with his Christian faith.

From 1818 onwards, Gurney was an acknowledged Quaker minister and traveled extensively in the **ministry** in **Britain**, **North America**, and **continental Europe**. He was also heavily involved in work for **peace**, **penal reform**, and the **abolition** of slavery. He argued against slavery on economic grounds and took a winter vacation to visit the British West Indies, where slaves had been freed, to study how well that had worked. Wherever he traveled, including visits to the royal families of Holland and Denmark, he asked to visit prisons and tried to improve them. Toward the end of his life he also embraced the **temperance** cause.

Gurney's obituary in *The Friend* (London) began with words taken from 2 Samuel 3:38: "A Prince and a great man is this day fallen in Israel" (AV). So important was his influence upon the development of **evangelical** Quakerism through both his personal ministry and his many writings that it came to be known as "Gurneyism." **John Wilbur** and the **Hicksites** saw Gurney's encouragement of Bible study and **Sunday School** programs as conflicting with the **Quietist** waiting on the Spirit in silent **worship**, which was central to Friends' practice for them. Gurneyism dominated British and **Irish** Quakerism for most of the 19th century and also influenced many Quakers in North America. Many blamed British **Gurneyites** for fanning the flames of American division.

Gurney was a controversial figure during his lifetime and has remained so ever since. **Thomas Shillitoe** considered him heavily influenced by Anglican evangelicalism. In works such as his *Observations on the Distinguishing Views and Practices of the Society of Friends*, Gurney advocated a form of Christianity that was a synthesis of traditional Quaker beliefs and practices and conventional evangelical theology. He argued for belief in the immediate and perceptible guidance of the **Holy Spirit** and for the traditional Quaker form of silent worship without the outward **sacraments**. In contrast to most Friends, Gurney also stressed the supreme theological authority of the Bible as "a divinely authorized standard of revealed truth" and the necessity of **salvation** through "faith in the atoning death of **Christ**" (J. J. Gurney, *A Peculiar People*, introduction).

Friends of his day, such as Shillitoe, felt that this emphasis on the Bible and the **atonement** undermined the authority of the inward **Light** and the transforming work of Christ in the human soul. Later, **Edward Grubb** and **Rufus Jones** felt that evangelical theology had been undermined by the very biblical scholarship and scientific enquiry that Gurney advocated and emphasized the direct **mystical** apprehension of **God** rather than defense of traditional Christian orthodoxy.

Following the **Manchester Conference** of 1895, the liberal assessment of Gurney became the standard one in Britain, with the result that his works are no longer influential there. However, Gurney pioneered serious theological study among British Quakers and his works, attempting a constructive dialogue between the Quaker tradition and mainstream Protestant orthodoxy, have long been influential among North American Friends. [Martin Davie]

GURNEYITES. A name derived from **Joseph John Gurney** to refer to some **Orthodox** Friends.

GUZMAN, JUAN. Late 20th-century Cuban pastor at Holguin, Cuba, and recorded **minister**. *See* CARIBBEAN.

–H–

HADLEY, NORVAL (1928–). While superintendent of Northwest **Yearly Meeting** in the 1970s Hadley became a founder of the New Call to Peacemaking, a cooperative call for a Christian **peace** witness by the three historic peace churches—the Mennonites, Church of the Brethren, and Quakers. Robert Rumsey (1918–) who served as the staff from 1976 to 1981, Ralph Beebe (1932–), T. Canby Jones (1921–), and Duncan Woods (1910–) also contributed substantially to this work. Begun in 1975 out of the Faith and Life Movement, the New Call produced numerous written materials on peacemaking and established a dozen regional conferences to develop grassroots leadership, as well as national gatherings starting at Green Lake, Wisconsin, in 1978 with over 300 representatives from the three peace churches. Hadley was executive director of Evangelical Friends Mission through the 1990s, stepping down in 2001. [Margery Post Abbott]

HAM SOK HON (1901–1989). Teacher, farmer, theologian, scholar, prisoner, prophet, philosopher, writer, radical. Throughout his native land, he is widely known and deeply respected as the "**Gandhi** of Korea" (*see* EAST ASIA).

Ham was raised in a poor fishing village in what is now North Korea when the "Hermit Kingdom" was trying to throw off feudalism and Japanese rule. He attended Osan School, dedicated to a "thorough Christian **education**," where he began to reject blind acceptance of established religion. In Tokyo for his university education, he was impressed by the Non-Church Movement, with its simplicity of worship, strict faith, **Bible** study, and lack of form or ritual.

Returning to Korea, Ham became a teacher but was soon imprisoned for supporting the movement for independence from Japan. Released, he was not allowed to teach, and so he turned to farming, let his beard grow, and adopted traditional Korean dress. Three more times the Japanese sent him to prison, the last time for opposing the conversion of Korea into a Shinto nation. After **World War II**, when Korea was divided, he was appointed minister of **education** of his province, but his views put him at odds with the new Russian rulers, who imprisoned him twice, and he fled to the south in 1947. There, he opposed two right-wing dictators, and again he was imprisoned. He called prison his "university" because he learned so much there.

Ham conducted a series of Sunday Religious Lectures in Seoul and Pusan and was called Teacher Ham by people throughout the country. He founded a magazine, *Voice of Sial* (Seed, or People), to explore the connection between education, faith, and rural life. Seeing suffering as the keynote of Korean history, he wrote: "There is no way to meet **God** without pain." His ideas harmonized with Minjung (People's) Theology, a Korean version of liberation theology. "It is time for the world to become one."

Having learned of Quakers at Osan School, Ham was fascinated by **George Fox**. During World War II he was impressed with the large number of Quakers who were **conscientious objectors**, for he rejected violence absolutely: "Real victory can only be gained by love" (*see* PEACE). His first direct contact with Friends was in the 1950s, when he met Quakers doing **relief work** after the Korean War. He began attending **meeting for worship** in Seoul and eventually became a member. Later he spent time at **Pendle Hill**, PA, and **Woodbrooke** and attended several Friends' conferences. He wrote some 20 books, of which *Queen of Suffering, A Spiritual History of Korea* and *Kicked by God* have been translated into English. [Rose M. Lewis]

HANCOCK, CORNELIA (1840–1927). New York teacher who served as a nurse at Gettysburg, Pennsylvania (*see* RELIEF), then established the Laing School for former slaves in Mt. Pleasant. *See* ABOLITION; EDUCATION.

HARRIS, JAMES RENDELL (1852–1941). Leading British **liberal** Friend, involved in the **Manchester Conference** and subsequent **Summer Schools Movement**. A **Bible** scholar and professor at Cambridge, Johns Hopkins, and **Haverford College**, he introduced **Rufus Jones** to **J. W. Rowntree** in 1897. Harris became director of studies at **Woodbrooke** when it opened in 1902.

HARVEY, CYRUS W. (1843–1916). American **Conservative** Friends **minister**. Harvey's life is typical of a large number of Friends who traveled in the **ministry** in the late 19th century. Born to Indiana Quaker farmers, Cyrus Wilson Harvey showed early promise as a scholar. His studies at **Earlham College** were interrupted by the American Civil War. Torn, like so many other young Friends, between the **peace testimony** and the struggle for **abolition** of slavery, he served in the Union army. After the war he acknowledged his error in fighting and took up teaching and farming in Kansas. Recorded as a minister in 1875, he traveled extensively to **yearly meetings** of all branches, carrying a strong Christian message but resisting **revivalism** and the ordinances. Harvey published *The Western Friend*, a journal aimed at preserving primitive Quakerism. [Mary Ellen Chijioke]

HASLAM, FRED (1897–1979). English-born **Canadian** pacifist (*see* PEACE TESTIMONY) and **ecumenical** worker. A **conscientious objector** in World War I, he served as the first administrator of the Canadian Friends Service Committee, serving from 1941 until 1956 (*see* PEACE AND SERVICE AGENCIES).

HAT HONOR. In 17th-century England, all men were expected to doff their hats to their social peers, and especially to those of a higher class. Friends, believing it was wrong to show such deference, refused to doff their hats, even to the king. They only took off their hats in **prayer** and sought to show by their example that all were equally humble before **God**. Followers of **John Perrot** rejected even this practice as an empty form. Some Friends were disavowed by their families or lost friends for their behavior, others were treated roughly on the streets or reviled. *See* PECULIARITY; PLAIN DRESS AND SPEECH; SIMPLICITY. [Margery Post Abbott]

HAVERFORD COLLEGE. Haverford College in Haverford, Pennsylvania, was founded in 1833 as Haverford School for boys by members of Philadelphia **Yearly Meeting** (**Orthodox**) and was empowered to grant college degrees in 1856. It is now independent of yearly meeting ties. Haverford first admitted **women** in 1978, officially becoming coeducational in 1980.

HAVILAND, LAURA SMITH (1808–1898). Reformer and **abolitionist**. Born into a Quaker family in Ontario, **Canada**, Laura Smith as a child observed the abuse of **African Americans** and vowed to defend "that crushed and neglected race." She married Charles Haviland Jr. at age 17. She launched her abolitionist career in 1832 by joining with Elizabeth M. Chandler to form the first antislavery society in the state of Michigan. In 1837, she and her husband opened the Raisin River Institute, modeling it after Oberlin College by opening it to females and African Americans. Because several Friends **meetings** resisted association with non-Quakers whose antislavery methods might violate Friends' principles, Haviland began searching for another denomination that shared her abolitionistic views. In 1839, she resigned her membership in the **Religious Society of Friends**. A few months later, she joined the Wesleyan Methodist Connection, a newly formed denomination comprised chiefly of abolitionists who had seceded from the Methodist Episcopal Church.

Widowed in 1845, Haviland embarked on a full-scale abolitionist career. She plunged into activities on the **underground railroad**, escorting fugitive slaves from the home of **Levi Coffin** to freedom in Canada. Following the period of Reconstruction after the Civil War, Haviland rejoined the Quakers and traveled to Kansas in 1879 with **Elizabeth Comstock**, a fellow Quaker activist, also from Michigan. Together they labored with the Kansas Freedmen's Aid Commission to provide food, clothes, and shelter to the former slaves. In her later years she focused on other reform issues such as **women**'s suffrage and **temperance.** She also founded two orphanages at Clearwater and Adrian, Michigan. [Louisa Kaufman]

HEATH, CARL (1869–1950). British Friend who from mid-life became an ardent **peace** activist. He developed the idea of "Quaker embassies," as centers for outreach and reconciliation work after World War I (*see* QUAKER INTERNATIONAL CENTRES). After serving as secretary of the Peace Council, he became chairman of the Council for International Service, and later joint secretary of its successor body, the **Friends Service Council**. He was the first chairman of the **Friends World Committee for Consultation**. [Mary Ellen Chijioke]

HEAVEN AND HELL. Early Friends believed the "**Day of the Lord** is come." Thus, they believed that they must pronounce eternal and fiery judgment on their attackers, persecutors, and the apostate **church** around them. **God**'s judgment now was real for them. They also believed in a "Day of visitation" by God to each person, offering spiritual life if it were accepted, and spiritual **death** if rejected. God's visitation was here and now.

Many Quakers have always stressed living in the "Eternal Now," drawing on the scriptural call, "*Now* is the day of **salvation**!" (2 Corinthians 6:2). Thus, emphasis on heaven as a place of eternal joy and reward was secondary for **George Fox** to the present call to "sit down in the heavenly places in **Christ** Jesus." "Heaven" may be immediate, present and realized, when human beings live together in **gospel order** guided by the voice and presence of Christ within them.

But not when they *hear* differently what is in good gospel order. Thus, for these Quakers "hell" is all forms of **evil** expressed through envy, lust, greed, self-will, disorder, violent conflict, and war in this present world. Those who live by this evil "sword" shall perish by it.

Contemporary Friends hold widely varying views of heaven and hell. Many stress strict obedience to God's commandments in Scripture, the innate sinfulness of all human beings, and the prospect of eternal punishment if people do not seek forgiveness for their **sins**. They also affirm that God in his mercy, through the atoning death of his son, Jesus Christ (*see* ATONEMENT), offers us a life of forgiveness, salvation, **sanctification**, and the promise of eternal life in a place called heaven. By the same token, a life of disobedience and accumulated unforgiven sins will result both in alienation from God in this life and eternal punishment in the next.

Many **liberal** Quakers reject any concept of eternal punishment or bodily resurrection, often considering heaven and hell to be internal states of the human soul, either during life or continuing after death. Some find meaning in Buddhist or Hindu concepts of reincarnation; others consider questions relating to life after death as unknowable and place emphasis on right action in the here and now, without regard to later reward or punishment. [T. Canby Jones]

HEDGE. "The Hedge" and "enclosed garden" are terms often used to describe the way in which Friends, particularly during their first two centuries, shut themselves off from the influences of "the world" by their practices of **plain dress and speech** and other **distinctives**. *See also* PECULIARITY.

HERMANN, EVA (1900–1997). Pacifist Eva Hermann first met German Friends through one of her teachers with whom she stayed in contact throughout her life (*see* PEACE TESTIMONY). After her training as a teacher she married the mineralogist Carl Hermann. Both became very active members of the **Fellowship of Reconciliation**. They realized the inhumanity of the Fascist regime early on and established a support center for those who were persecuted and helped people who were not supported by Jewish organizations to emigrate. In 1943 their aid, providing refuge to a Jewish couple captured trying to cross the border, led to several years' imprisonment. That the Hermanns' actions caused suffering for their two children (whom they had adopted a few years earlier) became a persistent burden for the couple.

Hermann's report on her prison term was first published in 1947 by American Friends. After the war she deeply engaged herself in **women**'s issues and was cofounder of the Society for Christian-Jewish Co-operation. In 1970 she gave the Richard Cary Lecture at German **Yearly Meeting** with the title "In That Which Is Eternal." Throughout her life she was able to encourage others, and her house was open to foreign guests even up to her last months. Hermann accepted several public awards, including the "Medal of the Righteous" by the State of Israel, humbly pointing to others she thought were more deserving. [Konrad Temple]

HERNÁNDEZ, MAGDALENO and TITO. The first two Quaker converts in Santa Elena, Chiquimula, Guatemala (*see* CENTRAL AMERICA), in 1906. Magdaleno was the first national preacher.

HETHERINGTON, RALPH (d. 2000). British clinical psychologist, active in the Quaker **Universalist** Group, who used the tools of his profession to bring insight into the mystical experience and sought to bring awareness of the spiritual into psychological practices. *See also* MENTAL HEALTH REFORM.

HICKS, EDWARD (1780–1849). Widely known today as a major American primitive artist, Edward Hicks was also a self-taught carriage painter, sign maker, and **minister** who traveled widely among Friends. Friends at the time were suspicious of **art**, believing it to be worldly, materialistic, and counter to their **testimony** of **simplicity** and attention to **God**'s will. After his attempt at farming failed, Hicks returned to his painting and sign making. His work consistently drew on biblical topics, and his best-known works, his series of 60 or more *Peaceable Kingdom* paintings, were based on the **prophecy** of Isaiah 9 about the lion and the lamb; many also include scenes of **William Penn**'s treaty with the **Native Americans** or an assemblage of Quakers holding banners proclaiming "**Peace** on earth, good will toward men."

Hicks lived in Bucks County, Pennsylvania, and joined Friends in 1803. He was a **Quietist** who distrusted the **evangelical** strand within

Quakerism. While he strongly supported his cousin, **Elias Hicks**, and blamed the **Great Separation** on wealthy Friends seeking to impose a **creed**, he also spoke against **Unitarian** and antiscriptural tendencies among the **Hicksites**. [Margery Post Abbott]

HICKS, ELIAS (1748–1830). Surveyor, **minister**, and central figure among **Hicksite** Friends. Elias Hicks is memorable as a compelling Quaker preacher in the **Quietist** tradition, respected and beloved by many contemporaries as he traveled in the **ministry** up and down the eastern United States and **Canada** from his home on Long Island, although he became a controversial figure late in his life.

Hicks felt particularly drawn in his travels to newly settled areas where Friends were scattered and few, and hence much needing the company of experienced ministers. Among Friends, his lasting legacy is his example of deep **spirituality** and intolerance of the imposition of specific religious beliefs. Love was the first commandment for him, and behavior more important than belief. Nothing but **God**'s direct guidance, he maintained, should dictate a person's beliefs. Individuals should be open to **continuing revelation** and subdue human will and reason to God's will.

Hicks's own seeking for guidance led him consistently to support **abolition** of slavery and the use of products of slave labor, and to resist payment of taxes for war and any connection with weapons or resort to coercion (*see* PEACE). He denounced the attractions of "the world," such as seeking material wealth (*see* SIMPLICITY), security, or political power. Nor did he embrace the worldly values of **business**, commerce, or the newly burgeoning technology (*see* SCIENCE AND TECHNOLOGY). His views on some of these issues, and the blunt way he sometimes expressed them, alienated some of his listeners. He also felt great concern for the **education** of children and was a founder and trustee of the Nine Partners Boarding School in upstate New York.

His theological views, widely accepted by Friends in his earlier days, also came to be a cause of alienation. Hicks held that the **Bible** is important and helpful, but that many of its passages are to be understood allegorically: that it is not Jesus' blood that redeems us but the model of his obedience to God, if we follow it, and that we are not born sinful but may choose to be so. He saw the Sabbath and other outward observances as leftover Jewish law superseded by Jesus **Christ**'s life and gospel (*see* TIMES AND SEASONS). Hicks read widely in the Quaker **journals**, and in books of both Quaker and Christian history. In 1815, he read John L. Mosheim's book *An Ecclesiastical History, Ancient and Modern* which outlined the many different interpretations of Christian doctrine and pointed out aspects of corruption and persecution within the church over the centuries. This book seems to have confirmed Hicks's resolve that Friends should be tolerant of divergent views and his distrust of an **evangelicalism** which advocated an absolute and unquestionable authority for the Bible.

When, early in the 19th century, the Protestant churches of **Britain** and the United States took on elements of the Wesleyan **revival**, Quaker communities on both sides of the Atlantic were affected. A growing split between rural and urban Friends in Philadelphia was exacerbated by heavy-handed exercise of power and widening tensions over beliefs, until it became the **Great Separation** of 1827–1828. Hicks's popularity and strong views caused his name to became attached to this controversy, which split **North American** Quakers into two factions, **Orthodox** and **Hicksite**. He was a crucial player in this separation, since he continued to travel widely, emphasizing his views even where he knew they were unwelcome. His sermons, taken down in shorthand by listeners since he used no notes, were published and widely circulated, becoming the center of furious debate. Nevertheless, he preached openness rather than separation. He never wanted to be leader of a faction and responded with growing sadness to the splintering of his beloved community. [Cynthia Earl Kerman]

HICKSITES. One of the two branches to emerge from the "**Great Separation**" of 1827–1828 in **North America**, Hicksites were among the forerunners of those Friends now part of **Friends General Conference**.

"Hicksite" derives from **Elias Hicks**. In contrast to those Friends who emphasized the authority of Scripture and the centrality of the atoning blood of **Christ** (*see* ATONEMENT; BIBLE), Hicks directed Friends to the Inward **Light** and to an understanding of Christ as one who had achieved divinity through **perfect** obedience to that Light.

Hicks's preaching and letters drew strong criticism, especially from certain **elders** and **ministers** in Philadelphia **Yearly Meeting**, who tried to silence him. Hicks's supporters, in turn, saw such opponents, who became known as **Orthodox** Friends, as motivated by a lust for power. The Hicksite Friends determined on a "reformation" intended to return Quakerism to first principles.

These tensions reached their head at Philadelphia Yearly Meeting 1827, when Hicksite Friends in Philadelphia felt driven to separate, in the hope of returning when tensions had died down. Separations followed in New York, Baltimore, Ohio, and Indiana yearly meetings. Hicksites were a strong majority in Philadelphia, Baltimore, and New York, and of about equal in strength in Ohio, but a definite minority in Indiana. Moreover, New England, North Carolina, and Virginia yearly meetings remained entirely Orthodox. Hicksites established two new yearly meetings: Genesee in 1834 and Illinois in 1875.

After the separation, Hicksite Friends usually retained their former books of **discipline**, claiming that they advocated no new doctrines. Considerable theological diversity marked them, ranging from incipient **liberals** with **Unitarian** sympathies to Friends whose views on **theology** were not much different from those of the Orthodox, but who had been repelled by what they saw as an Orthodox lust for power.

The antislavery movement brought schism to Hicksite Friends between 1843 and 1855. **Quietist** Hicksites condemned membership in **abolition** and other reform groups as bringing dangerous ties with non-Friends. Some of the more radical Friends responded by withdrawing to form meetings of what they labeled **Congregational** or **Progressive** Friends. Others, like **Lucretia Mott**, did not withdraw. Such radicals would be important forces in the radical abolition movement epitomized by William Lloyd Garrison and in the early years of the American **women**'s rights movement. During the 1840s and 1860s, the Hicksite yearly meetings also worked jointly in furtherance of their concern for **Native Americans**.

After 1865, Hicksite Friends experienced changes that were less dramatic than Orthodox Friends, but nevertheless real. Hicksites maintained **unprogrammed worship** and a nonpastoral ministry. The **plain dress and speech** gradually faded away. Old fears of higher **education** lessened, marked by the founding of **Swarthmore**

College (*see* COLLEGES) in 1864. Hicksites also became less fearful of ties to non-Quakers, actively joining in reform movements like **temperance** after 1870. And they gave increasing attention to First Day Schools (*see* RELIGIOUS EDUCATION).

In 1881, Hicksites began a series of conferences that brought together Friends from all Hicksite yearly meetings in various areas of joint activity. In 1900, these coalesced as Friends General Conference. [Thomas D. Hamm]

HILL, DANIEL (1817–1899). Peace activist and editor. Secretary of the Peace Association of Friends from 1867 to 1898, founder and editor of the *Messenger of Peace, Christian Worker*, and *Olive Leaf*, Hill edited the peace column in the *American Friend* until his death. While most of his life as a peace activist and evangelist was in New Vienna, Ohio, he also served as an Indiana state senator, and was **superintendent** of the Children's Home in Cincinnati. He worked with **John Greenleaf Whittier** on behalf of **African Americans** in the American Civil War era. [John W. Oliver]

HOBBS, BARNABAS COFFIN (1815–1892). Midwestern American educator, he was the first Indiana superintendent of public instruction and a leader of the development of the Boarding School at Richmond into **Earlham College** (*see* EDUCATION).

HOBBS, MARY MENDENHALL (1852–1930). Gurneyite minister and teacher. Born in North Carolina, Hobbs had a major influence on **Guilford College**, along with her husband, the first president of Guilford, Lewis Lyndon Hobbs (1849–1932). She was opposed to the **holiness movement** (and the **pastoral system**) and was an ally to **Rufus Jones** and **Elbert Russell** in their campaign to "modernize" Gurneyite Quakerism. In particular she championed the idea of **continuing revelation** in opposition to the **Bible** as the primary authority. She also championed **women**'s education, and was a leader in the campaign that resulted in a Greensboro campus for women of the University of North Carolina. [Pink Dandelion]

HOBHOUSE, STEPHEN (1881–1961). British **conscientious objector** and prison reformer. *See also* PENAL REFORM.

HOBSON, WILLIAM (1820–1891). Hobson grew up in North Carolina, where he was an active **abolitionist**, then moved to Iowa where he was recorded as a **minister**, but opposed the growing use of **revivals** and the **pastoral system**. In 1878, he started a **meeting** in his home in Oregon and later helped found Friends Pacific Academy (later **George Fox University**).

HODGKIN, HENRY T. (1877–1933). British doctor, **missionary**, and **ecumenical** worker, Hodgkin served in China from 1904 until 1910 and again from 1922 until 1929. He supported the creation of the Fellowship of Reconciliation and Quaker involvement in wider Christian service. He was the first director of **Pendle Hill** Study Center, serving from 1930 until 1932.

HOLINESS MOVEMENT. Prior to the American Civil War, Methodists developed a popular form of religious revivalism, which became known as the holiness movement and spread throughout many different denominations. Beginning in the 1830s and reaching its peak in the 1870s, the holiness movement emphasized **sanctification** as a kind of second conversion experience in the life of a Christian. This experience was popularly referred to as the "second blessing."

The theological roots of the movement are found in John Wesley's doctrine of Christian **Perfection**, as the culmination of the spiritual journey from **sin** and separation from **God** to perfect love of God and neighbor, drawn in part from early Quaker teaching. The beginning of the American holiness movement is usually traced to the ministry of a Methodist laywoman, Phoebe Palmer (1807–1874), and it gathered momentum through camp meetings, traveling evangelists, and religious publications. The movement spread to the British Isles primarily through the influence of a Philadelphia Quaker couple, Robert Pearsall Smith and **Hannah Whitall Smith**.

Although the holiness movement began as a unifying and **ecumenical** force for renewal within a broad spectrum of churches, by the 1870s it had become more controversial and divisive. More radical holiness advocates, promoting "instantaneous sanctification" and a more separatist mentality, began leaving their churches and forming new denominations.

Starting in the 1860s, holiness teachings, methods, and expressions transformed many traditional silent Quaker **meetings for worship** into **revivals**. By the 1880s the holiness movement had made huge inroads into Quakerism, particularly in Ohio, Indiana, Iowa, Oregon, and California. Many midwestern Quaker **meetings** began to adopt Methodist practices and doctrines, including the introduction of **pastors** to provide church **leadership** and **preaching**, congregational singing, and among some, even water **baptism** and occasionally, speaking in tongues (*see* PENTECOSTALISM).

Holiness moderates and holiness radicals debated various interpretations of the sanctification experience and argued over the abandonment of distinctive Quaker traditions and the adaptation of new forms and practices. The most visible and controversial Quaker holiness evangelist during this period was **David B. Updegraff**, from Ohio **Yearly Meeting**, who questioned the doctrine of the Inward **Light** and identified it as a **Hicksite** belief incompatible with **evangelicalism**. Renewal leaders from the moderate wing increasingly found the radicals an embarrassment to the cause of holiness among Friends. Updegraff was **disowned** for performing water baptism and offering the bread and wine of **communion**. Some Quaker holiness leaders joined with other "come-outers" as they were called, to form new denominations. Quaker evangelist Seth Cook Rees, for example, joined with Methodist evangelist Martin Wells Knapp to form the Pilgrim Holiness Church in 1897.

Other holiness leaders, such as **Walter and Emma Malone** of Ohio Yearly Meeting, remained loyal to a Quaker tradition in which they believed holiness had always been central. The Malones adapted traditional Quaker **spirituality** with its emphasis on holy living, egalitarianism, and social concern to Wesleyan theology, polity, and worship to create a new evangelical form of Quakerism. The branch of Quakers known as **Evangelical Friends International (EFI)** is one legacy of the holiness movement among 19th-century Friends. [Carole Spencer]

HOLMES, THOMAS (1627?–1666). English Quaker **minister** from Westmoreland who joined with **George Fox** in 1652. His field of activity was Wales, where he lived with his wife, **Elizabeth Leavens**.

HOLY EXPERIMENT. William Penn saw his colony, Pennsylvania, which he once referred to as "the Holy Experiment," as a refuge for

Friends and other religious dissenters. Penn visualized Philadelphia as a new Jerusalem on the Delaware River, a place of brotherly love committed to peaceful relations with **Native Americans**. The early laws guaranteed religious liberty, that is, no established **church**, no **tithe**, no persecution, although non-Friends were expected to conform to Quaker customs. At a time when many colonies had strict laws about religious practice, the Charter of Privileges of 1701 stated that "all persons living in this province, who confess and acknowledge the one almighty and eternal **God** . . . and that hold themselves obliged in conscience to live peaceably and justly in civil society, shall, in no ways, be molested or prejudiced for their religious persuasion or practice." The Quaker Party held a majority in the legislature until 1756 when many Friends resigned rather than vote to support the French and Indian War (1754–1760). *See* CIVIL GOVERNMENT; POLITICS. [Margery Post Abbott]

HOLY SPIRIT. Quakers have long held that there is a direct correspondence between the Holy Spirit and the early Quaker view of the **Light** of **Christ** within. The Holy Spirit was in many respects synonymous with other early Quaker terms—the Inward Light, the Seed, the Measure, and **George Fox**'s claim there is "that of **God** in everyone." The first Friends believed that the living Christ continues to be present to guide and to direct their lives. This is why individuals and the worshipping community can have firsthand experience of the living God. It is also the spiritual basis for religious authority and the means of **discerning** the will of God.

Another reason for emphasizing the Holy Spirit was Friends' identification with the Christian biblical tradition (*see* BIBLE). Acts 2 is the account of the early church's experience of the presence and power of the Holy Spirit. The Spirit of God is not only a personal experience, it can also be a corporate experience for the community of faith—the Quaker **meeting for worship**. Friends have relied on the Scripture's promise that upon Jesus' death he would send another Counselor, Comforter, and Advocate in his place, namely, the Holy Spirit (John 14:25–26).

For many Christians the Holy Spirit constitutes the third person of the **Trinity**. But for Friends the Holy Spirit is a living experience of the Godhead. It is also a **prophetic** voice which can empower the **ministry**.

Some **liberal Friends** have substituted the Spirit and Inner **Light** for the Holy Spirit without reference to its biblical and Christian origins. Historically, Friends used "Spirit" in ways such as "God is Spirit" and the "Spirit of Truth." Since the 19th century, inheritors of **Orthodox Quakerism** have continued to use "Holy Spirit" coupled with christological and biblical references, but have tended to neglect "Inward Light" and "Light Within" language. [Wilmer A. Cooper]

HOOTEN, ELIZABETH (ALSO HOOTON) (ca. 1600–1671/72). Hooten had a **convincement** experience in 1646. An early ally of **George Fox**, she lived in the east Midlands of England where Fox made his home at the end of 1640s. Her home at Skegby, Nottinghamshire, became a main center of early Quaker activity. After the events of 1652 when the movement first took shape, Elizabeth Hooten remained an influential and formidable Friend, moving to New England with her daughter. There she was whipped and imprisoned. She died in Barbados. [Pink Dandelion]

HOOVER, HERBERT CLARK (1874–1964). Mining engineer, international **relief** administrator, author, and president of the United States. Orphaned at age eight, Iowa-born Herbert Hoover was raised by a Quaker uncle, John Minthorne, a **missionary** and head of Friends Pacific Academy, later **George Fox University**, in Newberg, Oregon, which Hoover attended for three years. Hoover studied mining engineering in the first class at Stanford, and joined a London mining firm. He married Lou Henry, an Iowa-born geologist, in 1899 on his way to China as chief engineer in the imperial Department of Mines. The next year, he organized aid for Americans and Europeans in China trapped by the Boxer Rebellion. Based in England during World War I, he arranged for the return of 120,000 American tourists who were in Europe at the outbreak of the war and managed the transport of food through the Allied blockade to nearly 10,000,000 people in Belgium and France. After the war Hoover administered the U.S. relief effort to feed Germans and others, overseeing the distribution of food to people in 30 countries. He worked with the Red Cross and the **American Friends Service Committee**, organizations already involved in European relief efforts, to respond to the Russian famine of 1922–1923, then directed relief work after the Mississippi River flood of 1927.

After 1921, Hoover served in Washington, D.C., where he attended Florida Avenue **Meeting** that was built with a gift from the Hoovers. He was secretary of commerce under Presidents Warren G. Harding and Calvin Coolidge and was elected president in 1928 as a Republican. He proved sensitive to **women**'s issues, hostile to racial segregation (*see* EQUALITY), and a vigorous supporter of **temperance**. During his administration, he also participated in disarmament conferences and other efforts to extend world **peace** and initiated the "Good Neighbor" policy toward Latin America. Although Hoover was elected as a symbol of prosperity and the New Era, his policies relying on privately organized poor relief were unsuccessful in coping with the Great Depression that hit the United States in 1929. Makeshift communities of impoverished families became known as "Hoovervilles." In 1931, he pushed the creation of the Reconstruction Finance Administration and other actions to counter the effects of the Depression. He was defeated for reelection in 1932 by Franklin Delano Roosevelt (1882–1945).

Hoover retired to his home in Palo Alto, California, authored 30 books, including *The Problems of Lasting Peace* (1942), advocated alternatives to the policies of the Cold War, and chaired the Hoover Commissions of 1947 and 1953 to recommend ways of simplifying and economizing federal administrative structures. He donated his substantial library and funds to Stanford University, out of which was founded the Hoover Institution on War, Revolution and Peace. [Margery Post Abbott]

HOPPER, ISAAC TATEM (1771–1852). Isaac T. Hopper early spoke against all laws protecting slave owners and became a legal expert on manumission (*see* ABOLITION). However, he opposed illegal actions adopted by other Friends active in the **underground railroad**. Among the many former slaves he aided was Richard Allen (1760–1831), a freed man who had been captured by slave hunters. Allen later founded the African Methodist Episcopal Church.

HOTCHKISS, WILLIS RAY (1874–1948). Graduate of the Malone's Friends Bible College, Cleveland, Ohio (later **Malone College**), Willis R. Hotchkiss was the principal founder of the Friends Africa Industrial **Mission** to **East Africa** with **Arthur B. Chilson** and Edgar

Hole. Hotchkiss was also a leading speaker on college campuses for the Student Volunteer Movement and an author of books on Africa.

HOVDENAK, EGIL (1927–) and TURID (1933–). As active members of Norway **Yearly Meeting**, the Hovdenaks initiated a European Quaker Service Program in Algeria following Algerian independence (*see* PEACE AND/OR SERVICE AGENCIES). The couple worked as volunteers for this **relief** effort from 1963 to 1969. From 1971 to 1992, Egil worked at the information division of the Norwegian Agency for International Development (NORAD). Egil is a board member of Quaker Service Norway. Since 1992, he has been the contact person for the Change Agent Training Programme in Uganda, which was initiated by and is led by Stan Burkey.

Following the **Friends World Committee for Consultation (FWCC)** Mission and Service Conference on Quaker work in Africa, held in Kampala, Uganda, Egil and some African participants took up the idea of a Change Agent **Peace** Programme for the Great Lakes Region in Central and East Africa. This program started in 1998 and is active in six countries: Rwanda, Burundi, Democratic Republic of Congo, Uganda, Kenya, and Tanzania. The program is run by the Quaker Service Norway, in cooperation with FWCC Africa Section and the local yearly meetings. Stephen Collett is the international coordinator. The program is supported financially by the Norwegian Ministry of Foreign Affairs.

The Hovdenaks have been engaged in helping asylum seekers since 1996 and have hosted refugees in their home periodically. Turid is a retired primary school teacher. Egil was **clerk** of the FWCC-Europe & Middle East Section from 1996 to 1998 and is currently the chair person of the council of the Norwegian Peace Center. [Margery Post Abbott]

HOWGILL, FRANCIS (1618–1669). Quaker preacher from Westmoreland in northern England. The former leader of a separated congregation (*see* SEPARATISTS), he joined with **George Fox** in 1652, and became leader of Quaker London **mission** in 1654–1656 with **Edward Burrough**. A pamphleteer, he was condemned to life imprisonment for refusing to take an **oath** of allegiance 1664 and died in Appleby jail (*see* PRISON).

HOWLAND, EMILY (1827–1929). New York teacher and **abolitionist**, she was a nurse at Gettysburg during the Civil War and taught in a freedmen's camp in Virginia after the war (*see* AFRICAN AMERICANS).

HUBBERTHORNE, RICHARD (1628–1662). Quaker preacher from Westmoreland, who joined with **George Fox** in 1652. His field of activity was at first mainly in eastern England, but he took over the London **mission** in 1657. A political pamphleteer, he was arrested in 1661 and died in London **prison** in 1662.

HULL, HANNAH CLOTHIER (1872–1958) and WILLIAM ISAAC (1868–1939). American **peace** activists. After advanced study in Berlin, Leyden, and Paris, William Hull taught international relations at **Swarthmore College** from 1892 to 1938. In 1929 he become the Howard M. Jenkins Professor of Quaker History. His works on the history of 17th-century Quakerism in Holland and on **William Penn** remain classics. He was also a major figure in the international peace movement, a commitment shared with his wife, Hannah, an 1891 graduate of Swarthmore and daughter of prominent Philadelphia retailers. He was a noted proponent of arbitration and disarmament, she a founder and later national president and honorary president of the **Women's International League for Peace and Freedom**. She also served as vice chairman of the board of the **American Friends Service Committee**, 1928–1947. [Mary Ellen Chijioke]

HUMPHREYS, RICHARD (1749–1832). North American silversmith and benefactor. *See also* RICHARD HUMPRHEYS FOUNDATION.

–I–

INDEPENDENT MEETINGS MOVEMENT. During the 20th century, many new Quaker **meetings** formed in the United States as Friends moved to college towns and other communities that had no **meeting for worship**. These meetings tended to attract Friends from several different **yearly meetings**, and, in many cases, several different branches of Friends. Instead of seeking oversight and permission from one or all of the attenders' home meetings, some of these new groups formed without any structural affiliation with an existing **monthly**, **quarterly**, or **yearly meeting**. The first such independent meeting is considered to be the College Park Association of San Jose, California, formed in 1889 by **Hannah and Joel Bean** and their followers after Iowa Yearly Meeting (**Gurneyite**) refused it recognition. Other early independent meetings were Friends Meeting of Washington (D.C.) (*see* HOOVER, HERBERT) and Friends Meeting at Cambridge (Massachusetts).

Independent meetings share some characteristics with "united meetings"—monthly meetings that belong to more than one yearly meeting, usually across branches. Their independence enabled the new meetings to experiment with and to some extent reinvent Quaker faith and practice, free of the strictures of a particular book of **discipline** or established **oversight** structures. Each meeting to some extent worked out its own **membership** practices, **committee** structure (if any), and **worship** emphasis. Some meetings sought to introduce the practice of joint membership in more than one monthly meeting in order to encourage prominent Friends to join these new meetings. Such meetings have tended to be **liberal** in **theology** and active in social and political affairs, with a highly educated membership of professionals and college professors.

Initially, independent meetings were supported and nurtured by the College Park Association (later Pacific Coast Association), and by a joint committee of the **Hicksite** Yearly Meetings. Many members of these meetings did not, however, wish to be affiliated with any one of the branches that divided Friends. The American Friends Fellowship Council provided guidance and encouragement during the 1930s and 1940s (*see* FRIENDS WORLD COMMITTEE FOR CONSULTATION). As yearly meetings along the Eastern seaboard reunited (*see* REUNIFICATION), the independent meetings in those regions joined the merged bodies. Independent meetings in other sections of the country have formed new yearly meetings, or have affiliated with **Friends General Conference** as monthly meetings. Five Years Meeting (*see* FRIENDS UNITED MEETING) also supported a few independent meetings, as in Elmira, New York.

New independent, **unprogrammed,** liberal meetings continue to form in the United States and a number of other countries. Some of these groups are under the care of the **Friends World Committee for Consultation**'s International Membership Committee, which recognizes monthly meetings as they become large and strong enough. [Elizabeth Cazden]

INDIRE, FILEMONE F. (19?–). Born and raised in Kenya, Indire was a university professor in Nairobi. From 1971 until 1991, he served as the first clerk of **Friends World Committee for Consultation**–Africa Section, which is based at the Friends International Centre on N'Gong Road in Nairobi.

IRELAND. Quakers first arrived in Ireland in 1654. Historically, Irish Friends have followed a similar pattern to those in **Britain** without embracing **liberal** theology to the same degree in the 20th century. Christian witness and evangelism remain important elements for Irish Friends. **Worship** remains **unprogrammed**. The membership of Ireland **Yearly Meeting** of about 1,600 is divided between Northern Ireland, which is still part of the United Kingdom, and Eire, where most Friends are centered in Dublin. [Pink Dandelion]

–J–

JANNEY, SAMUEL McPHERSON (1801–1880). Member of Baltimore **Yearly Meeting** (**Hicksite**) who maintained close connections with the **Orthodox**. A merchant and a strong **abolitionist**, he founded a school for freed slaves in Virginia. Author of a four-volume *History of the Society of Friends*, Janney later became superintendent for the Northern District under President Ulysses S. Grant's "Peace Policy" for **Native Americans**.

JAY, ALLEN (1831–1910). An Indiana Friend, Jay combined a moderate permissive **revivalism** with successful evangelism in a career as minister and **pastor**, mainly in North Carolina. After an 1866 visit to Baltimore **Yearly Meeting** (Orthodox), he was asked by businessman Francis T. King (1817–1891) to work on rebuilding schools and

meetings throughout North Carolina in the aftermath of the American Civil War. He helped transform New Garden Boarding School into **Guilford College** and was involved in the establishment of Friends Board of **Missions** and Five Years Meeting (*see* FRIENDS UNITED MEETING). Highly popular and much loved by all **evangelical** Friends, his association with **modernists** such as **Elbert Russell** moderated the reaction against them. [Pink Dandelion]

JEANES, ANNA THOMAS (1833–1907). Philadelphia **Hicksite philanthropist**. Heiress to much of the Pennsylvania coal industry, Anna T. Jeanes used her wealth to support a number of local charities, such as the Jeanes Hospital in Abington. She was particularly interested in African and **African American education**, funding the Negro Rural School fund in the American South and a similar fund for industrial education in **East** and **Southern Africa**. *See also* LITU, JOEL. [Mary Ellen Chijioke]

JESUS. *See* CHRIST.

JOHNSON, RONALD G. (1941–). Johnson has been president of **Malone College** since 1994, after serving as provost and vice president for 13 years. His home **meeting** was Tecumseh **Friends Church** in Michigan, and he is married to the former Marjorie Van Valkenberg. Johnson served as presiding **clerk** of Evangelical Friends Church–Eastern Region (EFC-ER) (now a member of **Evangelical Friends International**, formerly Ohio **Yearly Meeting**, a **Gurneyite** meeting) from 1983 until 1993. He was clerk at Canton (Ohio) First Friends Church from 1977 until 1983, and clerk of Jackson Friends Church (North Canton, Ohio) from 1990 until 1999. Johnson is on the Executive Board of EFC-ER, the Board of Directors of the Christian College Consortium, and the Presidents Council for Christian Colleges and Universities. He earned his bachelor's degree from Eastern Michigan University and his M.A. and Ph.D. in radiation biophysics from the University of Kansas. [Jacalynn Stuckey Baker]

JONES, ELI (1807–1899) and SYBIL (1808–1873). Friends from Maine who traveled widely in the **ministry** and were concerned for **education** and abstinence from alcohol (*see* TEMPERANCE). Sybil, the daughter of Quakers Ephraim and Susannah Jones, had a strong call to **ministry**, traveling initially in eastern **Canada** starting in 1840. In later years, Eli (from a different Jones clan, whom she married in 1833) accompanied her as they traveled among Quaker **meetings** in the United States and to Liberia to visit recolonized black freedmen and **preach** to non-Christian ethnic groups. They also were called to preach in the West Indies, and to speak against alcohol use and visit meetings in Europe. In 1867–1869, their travels in the **Middle East** led to the founding of schools in Brummana, Lebanon, and Ramallah, Palestine, which are still in operation. Eli also was elected as a state legislator in Maine and was president of Oak Grove Academy. [Margery Post Abbott]

JONES, RUFUS MATTHEW (1863–1948). North American scholar of **mysticism**, **peace** activist, and reformer. Born into a devout Friends family in South China, Maine, Jones was educated at **Haverford College**, and later taught philosophy there from 1893 to 1934. He studied ethics, social psychology, and New Testament in obtaining his master's degree from Harvard University in 1901. Influenced by Ralph Waldo Emerson (1803–1882), Josiah Royce (1855–1916), and William James (1842–1910), Jones focused on the centrality of religious experience, and the direct intuitive contact with the Divine, which he called mysticism.

Jones worked closely with **William Charles Braithwaite** and **J. W. Rowntree**, whom he met in 1897, on a comprehensive, multivolume history of Quakerism, designed to show its mystical roots and spirit. As editor of *The American Friend* and drafter of the 1902 *Uniform Discipline of Five Years* (later Friends United) *Meeting*, he encouraged the **modernist** wing of the **Gurneyite** branch and actively built bridges with both **Hicksite** and **Orthodox** Philadelphia **Yearly Meetings**. He was instrumental in forming **Friends World Committee for Consultation (FWCC)**, presiding over its 1937 World Conference, and the Wider Quaker Fellowship.

Jones was a popular speaker at college chapels throughout the United States. Many of his talks were reprinted in his 56 books and innumerable magazine articles. He also lectured widely in England and continental Europe, gave lectures in China for the YMCA, and spent six months in Asia conducting research for the Laymen's Foreign

Mission Inquiry. His extensive speaking and writing led many to regard him as the informal head of the **Religious Society of Friends** in America.

Jones's confidence in "that Love which works . . . triumphantly at the Heart of Things" led him into practical service. In 1917, following the lead of British Friends, he started training volunteers at Haverford for **relief work** in France, the beginnings of the **American Friends Service Committee (AFSC)**. Jones served as AFSC chairman or honorary chairman until 1944, providing a "buoyant spirit of radiant expectation" that motivated others to do more than they thought possible. In 1938, he and two other Philadelphia Friends met with leaders of the German Gestapo to get permission for Friends to help Jews emigrate. One of Jones's final achievements was the 1945 **reunification** of New England **Yearly Meeting**, bringing together his own Yearly Meeting of Friends for New England (Gurneyite), its **Wilburite** counterpart, and five **independent meetings**. [Elizabeth Cazden]

JONES, THOMAS ELSA (1888–1973). Jones served as the first staff person for the National **Young Friends**. He married Esther Balderston in 1917 after they met at Hartford Seminary, then followed her to Japan, where he worked for the **American Friends Service Committee (AFSC)**. In 1926, he became president of Fisk University in Tennessee, a position he held until 1946. In 1940–1941, Jones organized the **Civilian Public Service (CPS)** camps on behalf of AFSC. From 1946 to 1958, he served as president of **Earlham College**, attracting many veterans of the CPS camps. [Margery Post Abbott]

JOURNALS. Journals are narrative accounts of the lives and travels of Friends, usually published after their **death**, that provide a spiritual interpretation of these events (*see* SPIRITUALITY); they represent a distinctive Quaker **theological** genre. Quaker journals evolved out of autobiographical elements in religious tracts. Quaker journals eventually came to be written mainly for Quaker readers. The first *Journal* published was that of William Caton (1636–1665), in 1689. Probably about a thousand Quaker journals are in existence.

Most journals in the 18th and early 19th centuries were written by traveling **ministers**. For their own times, journals set the example of what was expected of a serious Friend. They provide modern students an invaluable source for the outlook and spiritual life of Friends in different times and places. The *Journals* of **George Fox** and **John Woolman** are widely recognized as classics of Christian literature. [T. Vail Palmer Jr.]

JUSTIFICATION. *See* SALVATION.

–K–

KEITH, GEORGE (1638–1716). Intellectual as well as mentor and friend of **Robert Barclay**, George Keith came from eastern Scotland and joined Aberdeen Friends in 1662. For a time a leading Friend, he took a major part in theological controversies and traveled to Germany with **George Fox**, **Robert Barclay**, and **William Penn**. He increasingly advocated greater exactitude in doctrine, trying to express the Quaker faith as a list of precise tenets. He proposed that Quakers should adopt a public confession of faith, but **London Yearly Meeting** did not agree (*see* CREED). He influenced Barclay in the development of formal Quaker **theology**.

In 1685, Keith took up appointment in America as a teacher and surveyor. He became concerned about the condition of North American Quakerism, considering that emphasis on the Inward **Light** was leading to a "**spiritualism**" and neglect of **fundamental** Christian doctrine. Expelled by Philadelphia Friends in 1692 for printing tracts critical of Friends and causing a schism, he then returned to England and put his case to British Friends, but was **disowned** by London Yearly Meeting in 1695. After this he then set up his own meeting of "Christian Quakers," exposing what he called "Quaker errors," until he joined the Church of England in 1700, becoming a priest in 1702.

Keith was associated with the foundation of the Society for the Promotion of Christian Knowledge in 1699, and also with the Society for the Propagation of the Gospel in Foreign Parts (SPG), founded in 1701, both bodies being set up, among other things, to counteract Quakerism. In 1702 he was sent to America by the SPG, and toured the colonies, converting many of his followers to the Anglican church. After his return to England he continued to write and preach against

Quakerism for some years. His lasting influence in **Britain** is within the Church of England, through his part in the foundation of two important Anglican societies. Many of his American followers later became Baptists or Anglicans. [Rosemary Anne Moore]

KEKOYI, MARITA (1889–1984). East African leader, wife of **Joel Litu**, and one of the founders of the **yearly meeting** for **women**.

KELLY, THOMAS RAYMOND (1893–1941). North American college professor and devotional writer. Born in Ohio in 1893, son of **evangelical** Friends, Carlton and Madora Kersey Kelly, Thomas R. Kelly graduated in chemistry from **Wilmington** and **Haverford Colleges**. He received his B.D. and Ph.D. degrees from Hartford Theological Seminary, where his research focused on ethics and epistemology. In further study at Harvard University he concentrated on the philosophy of science. In 1917 and 1918, he served Quakers in **Britain** working with German prisoners of war, then in 1924–1925, he headed the **American Friends Service Committee** food **relief** program in Germany. Kelly married Lael Macy (1893–1959) in 1919 and taught **Bible** at Wilmington College from 1919 to 1921. His teaching at **Earlham College** and the University of Hawaii led to an interest in Asian religions. He then taught philosophy at Haverford until his death of a heart attack in 1941.

Kelly's failure to gain a second doctorate from Harvard devastated him and contributed to the strong religious experience which followed. This experience changed the direction of his writings and **ministry** in the last three years of his life (*see* MYSTICISM). His devotional writings, collected posthumously as *A Testament of Devotion* (1941), remain Christian classics, using vivid language to evoke the personal experience of **God**'s universal presence.

The life of devotion and of promise, according to Kelly's description, finds God searching for us, not just us searching for God. Such a life requires living on two levels at the same time—the secular level of work and external affairs and the spiritual level of **prayer** and adoration—not living on one or the other or alternating between the two from time to time. It also draws us deeper into the arena of social concern where we readily share in the sufferings of others, not away from that arena or into avoidance of suffering. [Ron Rembert]

KERSEY, HELEN (d. 1973). Missionary from California to Guatemala (*see* CENTRAL AMERICA) and later **East Africa** (1933–1948), where she became the second wife of **Jefferson Whiting Ford** and was in charge of the Girls Boarding School at Kaimosi from 1935 to 1943.

KERSHNER, HOWARD ELDRED (1891–1990). A graduate of **Friends University**, Kershner served with **American Friends Service Committee** during the Spanish Civil War of 1936–1939 and organized Quaker **relief work** for European children. He was a member of the Committee on Food for Small Democracies, vice president for Save the Children, and a founding member of CARE. He was also a founder of the Christian Freedom Foundation and editor of *Christian Economics*. Kershner's books include *The Menace of Roosevelt and His Policies (1936), Quaker Service in Modern War (1950),* and *God, Gold and Government* (1956). He was awarded the Order of Leopold by the Belgian government, the Order of Merit by the International Union for the Protection of Children, and the French Legion of Honor. [John W. Oliver]

KING, FRANCIS T. (1817–1891). Orthodox Baltimore businessman and supporter of the revival of North Carolina Quakerism after the American Civil War. *See also* JAY, ALLEN.

KINGITES. One of the factions that divided the small **Wilburite** New York **Yearly Meeting** in 1859 into "**Otisites**" and "Kingites." The split occurred over interpretation of a single passage in a vision of Joseph Hoag, for which John King, their **clerk** was serving as principal editor. A similar separation took place in the Wilburite New England Yearly Meeting in 1863.

KNOLITES. One of the factions of Primitive Friends in Ohio General Meeting that broke with the **Maulites**. *See also* CONSERVATIVE FRIENDS.

KUHN, ANNE WICKER (b. 1907) and HAROLD BARNES (1911–1994). Harold Kuhn was known as a **minister**, **educator**, and humanitarian, and his wife, Anne, as a college professor and humanitarian. A member of the Ohio **Yearly Meeting**, he served as a Friends' minister in Rescue, Virginia (1934–1936), Beacon, Iowa, Methodist Church (1938–1939), Allen's Neck Friends Meeting, Dartmouth, Massachusetts (1939–1941), and Waldon Congregational Church, Brockton, Massachusetts (1941–1944). He served on the faculty of Asbury Theological Seminary from 1944 to 1978. Kuhn was the founder of the *Asbury Seminarian*, which he edited from 1946 to 1978 and was a contributing editor to *Christianity Today*. His published articles appeared in the *Harvard Theological Journal, Asbury Seminarian, The Pentecostal Herald, Evangelical Friend*, and *World Vision*. After **World War II**, Harold and Anne Kuhn, who taught German at Asbury College from 1964 to 1978, did extensive **relief work** in East Germany and Poland. [Bill Kostlevy]

–L–

LAMB'S WAR. In the 1650s, early Friends understood the **Light of Christ** in apocalyptic terms (*see* APOCALYPSE; ESCHATOLOGY). They interpreted their experience, identity, and **mission** using imagery from the Book of Revelation. Convinced, transformed, and empowered by the Light of Christ within them, Friends saw themselves as the followers of the Lamb (Revelation 14:1ff), gathered to engage in nonviolent conflict against the forces of the Dragon: **evil** within and in the world. They viewed coercive, state-sponsored religion as the embodiment of Babylon, drunk on the blood of Christian martyrs (Revelation 17:1ff), riding on the Beast (Revelation 13:1ff). The beast was the newly established **Puritan** regime that had already begun persecuting religious dissent. The third person of this unholy trinity was the False Prophet (Revelation 13:11), embodied by the state-supported clergy, the linchpin of the Dragon's anti-Christian rule on earth. Friends felt that the "priests" kept people dependent upon their teaching, collecting unjust **tithes**, and justifying the arrogance and power of England's economic and political elites.

The martial images of the Lamb's War appear in the writings of **George Fox** and other early Friends throughout the 1650s. The most programmatic statement is **James Nayler**'s *The Lambs Warre* (1657, expanded in 1658), written in **prison**. He described this conflict as "not against Creatures, not with flesh and blood but spiritual wickedness . . . against the whole Work and Device of the god of this World, Laws, Customs, Fashions, Inventions, this is all Enmity against the Lamb and his followers." The Lamb has come "to take the Government to himself that God alone may wholly rule in the heart of Man" (D. Gwyn, *The Covenant Crucified*, p. 185). [Douglas Gwyn]

LAY, BENJAMIN (1677–1759). North American **abolitionist**. A hermit prone to dramatic action-statements against slavery, he was **disowned** for publishing criticisms of Friends who owned slaves or dealt in the slave trade, but Lay remained an important voice in the reforms of the mid-18th century.

LEADERSHIP. For Quakers, leadership is a gift of **God**, a charisma, which is discerned and affirmed by the worshipping community. True leadership grows from a **leading**. In the Quaker movement's earliest days, the leadership functions required by Friends in addition to vocal **ministry** and evangelism fell under two headings: visiting the widows and orphans in their affliction, and keeping from the "spots of the world." The practical needs of caring for the sufferings of members for their religious convictions, supporting **families**, educating children, documenting **marriages**, inheritances and wills, relieving the poor, **publishing** the **Truth**, maintaining and protecting property owned by the Society, and setting up simple arrangements for calling people together for **worship** formed the first focus of Friends' corporate efforts. The second set of issues, "keeping from the spots of the world," concerned keeping the spiritual **discipline** of the fellowship and arose from the need of local groups of Friends to correct "ranters" and "disorderly walkers": individuals whose immoral behavior brought scandal to the fellowship. Thc ***Epistle of the Elders of Balby*** is an early written expression of this process.

Gradually, the process of formal recognition of the gifts of leadership appropriate to roles as **ministers**, **elders**, and eventually **overseers** evolved. Over the next two centuries, this led to a system whereby individuals were essentially appointed to key positions for life, resulting in an entrenched leadership. In the mid-19th century, tensions over the powers of elders, in particular, contributed to the **Great Separation**, and the traditional system started to break down.

Present-day Quaker **church** government involves giving individuals authority and responsibility as **clerks**, elders, ministers, overseers, **pastors**, and **superintendents**. The nomination process for clerks, elders, and other **committee** members requires reflecting on the **meeting**'s needs, the known gifts of members, and potential gifts that might be brought to full expression by appointing the individual to the right committee. Faithfulness to the individual's degree or "measure" of spiritual and practical wisdom is essential in discerning leadership qualities. Wise mediators might serve as clerks of the **monthly meeting**, responsible for the right ordering of the **business meeting**. Good writers might serve as recording clerks, responsible for accurate minutes of the meeting's decisions. Good listeners may be called to serve as elders, those especially charged with the spiritual health of the **meeting for worship**, or as overseers working with the personal needs of members. People are often appointed to leadership in such tasks for limited, fixed terms, so their skills may be encouraged and strengthened, and so that responsibilities for leadership may be as widely diffused and shared among members as possible.

Ministers are identified by a process whereby the monthly meeting, and often the **yearly meeting**, formally recognizes, or records, a gift in the **ministry**. Pastors are called by individual monthly meetings or churches. They may or may not be recorded ministers. A number of yearly meetings hire superintendents or general secretaries, and other professional staff, in a **discernment** process involving the consideration of appointed committees and the business meeting of the yearly meeting at annual session or its executive committee. [Paul Lacey]

LEADING. An individual may "feel a leading" from **God** to speak or to make some act of witness, or to commit to a new way of living. Early Friends came to apply at least four major tests to **discernment** of leadings: moral purity, patience, the self-consistency of the Spirit, and bringing people into unity. These tests were applied together as a means for a community to discern the dynamic of a particular individual or group leading. Moral purity would be demonstrated by "not fleeing the **cross**," but by obeying calls from God which were difficult and sent simply as tests of obedience. Patience is a sound test of a leading because "self-will is impatient of tests." Self-consistency tests a leading against scriptural and historical analogues and examines how consistently one keeps faith with one's leadings. The test of unity is also called the test of the fruits of the Spirit, and starts from the premise that a sound leading to action will enrich the spiritual life of the whole worshipping community. Such a leading increases concord and has the possibility of increasing "love, joy, peace, patience, kindness, goodness, faithfulness, gentleness, self-control" (Galatians 5:22–23).

If the spiritual fellowship recognizes the leading as genuine and in good order, the individual may be given both responsibility and authority to take **leadership**, whether in **committee** work, as a **recorded minister**, in a professional capacity, or in following an individual concern. **Meetings** today vary in their process of testing a leading. They may use the normal meeting structures, or in some cases, they may appoint an ad hoc **clearness** committee to aid in the discernment process. The meeting may also **release** one of its members to travel in the **ministry**, to found a school, or undertake a new ministry. Such leadership is not a status conferred but a spiritual readiness recognized. [Paul Lacey]

LEAVENERS. Modern British musical group active in performing new works about Quakers such as *The Fire and The Hammer*, an oratorio based on the **journal** of **George Fox**. Started by Alec Davidson in 1978 as the Quaker Youth Theatre, the project has expanded to offer wider opportunities for Quaker men and women to use music and drama to express their faith. The Quaker Festival Orchestra and Chorus began in 1986. The Leaveners Experimental Arts Project (LEAP), begun in 1987, became independent in 1999 as LEAP Confronting Conflict, working with youth on conflict resolution and mediation skills. Since 1995, the "Words, Sounds, & Vibes" project has provided opportunities in the community for both thc hearing and deaf. *See also* ARTS. [Pink Dandelion]

LEAVENS, ELIZABETH (d. 1665). Preacher from Westmoreland in northern England, who joined with **George Fox** in 1652. She was attacked and badly beaten in Oxford 1654. Leavens later married Thomas Holmes, a Quaker **minister** who also joined with Fox in 1652. They lived and preached in Wales.

LEDDRA, WILLIAM (1596–1661). Last of the **Boston martyrs**.

LE SHANA, DAVID C. (1932–). Le Shana was born in India where his parents were serving as missionaries and first came to the United States in 1949 to attend Taylor University in Indiana. He received his master's degree at Ball State University in Ohio and his Ph.D. at the University of Southern California. He was introduced to Friends by his wife, Becky, and served as a **pastor** in Ohio **Yearly Meeting** as a young man. In the 1970s, he was a leading figure in the St. Louis and Houston Faith and Life conferences that encouraged dialogue among different groups of Friends. Le Shana is the author of *Quakers in California*. He served as president at **George Fox University** from 1969 until 1982, then at Seattle Pacific University in Washington State until 1992, when he became president of Western Evangelical Seminary in Portland, Oregon. The seminary merged with George Fox University under his leadership in 1996, when he became president emeritus of both institutions. [Margery Post Abbott].

LEVERING, MIRIAM LINDSEY (1913–1991) and SAMUEL R. (1908–). Members of North Carolina **Yearly Meeting**, active in **Friends United Meeting** and **Friends Committee on National Legislation**. Starting in 1972, they worked extensively on behalf of the 1982 Law of the Sea Treaty.

LEWIS, LUCY BIDDLE (1861–1941). North American suffragist, prohibitionist, and **peace** activist. Born to an important Pennsylvania **Hicksite** family, Lucy Biddle married John Reece Lewis in 1884. Following his death in 1898, Lucy Biddle Lewis returned with her son to her parents' home, where she spent the rest of her life working for **women**'s suffrage, **temperance**, and peace. She accompanied **Jane Addams** to The Hague in 1915 for a women's conference protesting the fighting in Europe. At the end of the war, she helped organize the **American Friends Service Committee**'s **relief work** in Belgium and Germany. Lewis was a founder, with Addams, **Emily Greene Balch**, **Hannah Clothier Hull**, and others, of the **Women's International League for Peace and Freedom**, of which she was later president of the American organization. Her success in persuading Addams not to destroy her papers laid the foundation for the **Swarthmore College** Peace Collection. [Mary Ellen Chijioke]

LIBERAL FRIENDS. A phenomenon of the late 19th century, liberal Friends currently form about 20 percent of the global Quaker population. Influenced by Darwinian theories of evolution, scientific inquiry, and the biblical scholarship of the 19th century, some Friends questioned a faith that placed central emphasis on scriptural authority (*see* BIBLE). In **North American** radical egalitarian political movements, transcendentalism and **Unitarianism** were among the influences, and it is possible to identify a proto-liberalism among some **congregational** meetings as early as the 1840s. The mix of liberal Friends in the United States today include all the former **Hicksite** meetings, some **Orthodox** meetings influenced by **modernism**, and most bodies arising out of the **independent meetings movement**. In **Britain**, the **Manchester Conference** of 1895 marked the emergence of liberalism.

For liberal Friends it was easy to marry an enthusiasm for a renewal of Quaker faith, including some of this new thinking, with certain original Quaker **distinctives**. As **George Fox** had placed the **Light** of **Christ** before Scripture, so liberal Friends sought to return to a faith rooted in experience, an experience found and confirmed in corporate **unprogrammed worship**. These Friends wanted to have a faith relevant to the age, ever open to new Light, and one which, in structure, liturgy, and testimonies, was distinctively Quaker. Liberals at the turn of the 20th century saw Quakerism as a key player in world affairs, proud of its distinctive witness. After World War I, Friends reaffirmed these distinctives as a reminder of the potentially tragic consequences of worldliness.

Continuing revelation and the emphasis on experience formed a Quaker **theology** that was keenly interested in the history of its past, yet in a way had no place it needed to go back to. Scripture was given less emphasis. Although early liberals were Christian, there has been an increased diversity of beliefs among this group since the 1950s, and liberalism has entered a second stage of "permissive liberalism" or "liberal liberalism." Within this new liberalism, the emphasis on silence and hesitations around the authority and appropriateness of words has hidden this diversity and encouraged an attitude of "perhapsness" to theological statements. Ever seeking new Light, theological statements are often provisional. The belief that **God** is "beyond words" allows a present-day sense that **theology** is also personal or only partially true: a human attempt to make sense of an experience that cannot be described.

Meetings for worship among liberal Friends are unprogrammed, and **monthly meetings** are generally permissive in terms of beliefs, tending to be liberal in their **politics** (*see* CIVIL GOVERNMENT). The lack of an authority rooted in text or tradition has allowed such **yearly meetings** to take on radical politics, for example in terms of feminism, and lesbian and gay issues relatively easily (*see* MARRIAGE; SEXUALITY; WOMEN). These shared values and the adherence to the way of being a religious group offer these Friends a cohesion and coherence in spite of the diversity of belief. They differ from other Friends in their increased ambivalence toward Christianity, their provisional attitude toward theology, a discomfort with **leadership**, overt emotion, and evangelization. They define Quaker faith more in terms of practice than belief. Liberal yearly meetings are numerically stable, with a large portion of **convinced** Friends attracted by the form of worship, the **testimonies** to **equality** and **peace**, and the lack of proselytization or confession of faith. [Pink Dandelion]

LIGHT: INWARD LIGHT, LIGHT OF CHRIST, INNER LIGHT. Variously referred to as the Light of **Christ,** the Inward Light, or the Inner Light, the Light is one of many ways Friends speak of Christ's work in the human heart, although its meaning has changed over time. A central understanding is that the Light will show **sin** and **evil** just as it will show the way to **salvation**. The Light is within though from without, and if a person stands in the Light, responds to Christ, and is obedient, the power will be given to the individual to end all his or her wrongdoing and forsake all that is contrary to the Light. In the Light, a person will know to deal justly with all people, and not to be proud or covetous. Swearing, lying, envy, hatred, cheating, fraud, and committing adultery will all become clearly wrong when seen in the Light. Having cleansed or "convicted," the Light becomes a source of power and joy.

The Light acts both in the individual heart and among the **gathered**, worshipping community. Central to the Friends **business meet-**

ing is a belief that the Light will lead all people who wait in its Power into unity and to walk in the **Truth**.

For **George Fox**, the Light is of Christ and the Light is Christ. The Light is an active, **universal** principle which functions in the human heart (John 1:9 and John 8:12). Fox used the terms "Light," "Spirit," "Christ," "Seed," and "Truth" interchangeably and often spoke of the "voice" of the Light, just as he spoke of the **Holy Spirit** as "it." The Light, thus, while it was personal in its actions, did not have personality, and early Friends did not speak in terms of a personal relationship with Jesus. Fox also believed that the Light would open the scriptures so that they might be read in the Spirit in which they were written and would not teach anything that would contradict the **Bible**, correctly understood.

Fox regularly encouraged others to wait in the Light, which comes from Christ, whereby a person will come to know delight in **God** and the Power that comes of God. To find true peace is to wait in the Light and receive that Power. The Light also offers God's comfort to the soul, which no person can give. The Light will lead the individual out of the darkness into salvation and teach all to **worship** in Spirit and in Truth (John 4:24).

Like other Friends of her day, **Elizabeth Bathurst** affirmed the Light as the Universal Witness in every conscience. If the Light is denied often enough, the person will no longer be aware of it. If the person responds, the Light will teach repentance and lead to rejoicing. **Isaac Penington** further emphasized that salvation does not occur without human participation. Each person must respond to the call of God by turning to the Light and letting it work within. The individual must then be willing to become one with the Light, to suffer with it and take up the **cross**, daily if need be. This is an ongoing process. The Light, or Seed, will grow within and strengthen as the person continues to respond, giving victory over sin. The process of increasing unity with Christ is central to early Friends' doctrine of **perfection**.

In the 19th century, the Light became a controversial concept and influenced the **Great Separation** of 1827–1828. **Hicksites** held to the doctrine of the Inward Light and tended to spiritualize Christ. **Orthodox** Friends emphasized the resurrection and the atoning nature of Jesus' death, often distrusting those who spoke of the Light. In the 20th century continued unease exists among some Friends when the term is used without a clear indication that the Light is of Christ as identified with the historic Jesus.

Liberal Friends have taken to heart the early Quaker assertion that the Light is available to all people even if they know nothing of Jesus. However, unlike early Friends, they do not see Christ's atoning death as essential, or necessarily even relevant, to the action of this Principle in the human soul. **Howard Brinton** was one of the most influential Friends in the 1950s and 1960s to actively explore the concept of the Light as it appears in different religions.

Modern liberal interpretations of the Light vary greatly. It may be synonymous with "that of God within," the divine aspect of every human being or a metaphor for the transforming Spirit within. The Light speaks of truth, love, rightness, and beauty. Those who are biblically oriented refer to the opening verses of the Gospel of John or occasionally to Acts 9, when Paul was struck blind on the road to Damascus. The Light, often spoken of as the Inner Light, has become a unifying phrase among liberal Friends because of the multiple ways it can be interpreted, ranging from views similar to those of George Fox to the more frequent sense of the Light as a universal force of Love and **discernment** which is present in the human heart. The modern phrase "to hold someone in the Light" is often used to mean "pray for them." [Margery Post Abbott]

LITU, JOEL (also JOELI) (1890–1977). East African educator and **Bible** interpreter. He was born in western Kenya, Mbale village, the second son to Majani, a village elder, and his wife, Jaluha. Litu attended the school at Mbale started by Quaker missionaries in 1911. A promising student, he was recommended by Yohana Amugene, his teacher, to work with **Emory Rees** on the translation of the Bible into Luragoli. Litu completed the **Bible** translation with **Jefferson Ford** following Rees's departure for the United States.

Litu married **Marita Kekoyi**, from Vihiga where they settled to raise a family and work at the **mission** station. Twelve children were born, nine boys and three girls. When a boarding school was started at Vihiga, Litu taught Bible studies, **preached**, and led hymn singing. After Emory and Deborah Rees returned to the United States in 1926, Litu was left in charge of the mission station at Vihiga. During the 1930s, Quakers offered him the opportunity to attend the **Jeanes**

Teacher Training Centre at Kabete (near Nairobi) to study practical hygiene and farming. On his return he was named as the first African inspector of the schools under the management of Friends Africa Mission and also became locally known for his produce and animals.

In the early 1940s, Litu taught Bible at the Kaimosi Boys School, where he was joined by his eldest son, Joseph Adede, a new graduate of Makerere College in Uganda. Litu also taught at the Kaimosi Girls Boarding School. Over the years he was responsible for raising funds for building **meetinghouses**, and at times would even supervise their construction.

When East Africa **Yearly Meeting** was established in 1946, his son Joseph translated directly from English to Luragoli during the opening ceremony attended by thousands of Kenyan Quakers. Litu served as the presiding **clerk** for the first three years. In 1948, Litu was appointed as a magistrate to the Court Tribunal to execute justice at the village level on behalf of the government. For 17 years, Litu served in the courts at Mbale among the Maragoli people, at Mumias among the Wanga people, at Lurambi among the Kabras and Butsostso people, and finally at Ikolomani among Idakho and Isukha people. He was widely known for his honesty and refusal to take bribes (*see* TRUTH).

Throughout his life, Litu remained involved in East Africa Yearly Meeting and a member of the General Board, and was chairman of the Board of Trustees at his death. [Rose Adede]

LLOYD, DAVID (1656–1731). Welsh-born lawyer and **politician**, Lloyd was a leader of the popular (antiproprietary) party in the Pennsylvania Assembly.

LOE, THOMAS (d. 1668). Early British Quaker **missionary** whose only convert was **William Penn**.

LOGAN, JAMES (1674–1751). Irish-born agent for **William Penn**, Logan protected proprietary interests in Pennsylvania from 1699 to 1747 in a variety of **political** and legal roles.

LONDON YEARLY MEETING. The name given to the **yearly meeting** for England, Scotland, Wales, the Isle of Man, and the Channel

Islands prior to 1994, when it changed its name to **Britain** Yearly Meeting.

LONGWOOD. The Pennsylvania Yearly Meeting of **Progressive Friends** was founded in 1853 at the Friends meetinghouse at Old Kennett, Chester County. After a dispute over the use of the meetinghouse, they built their own hall at Longwood Farm, Chester County. Known as the Progressive Friends of Longwood they continued to meet to promote religious, economic, political, and social reform activities until 1940. [Andrea Constantine Hawkes]

LORING, PATRICIA (1936–). Loring is a released Friend who travels in the **ministry**, leads retreats, and writes about Quaker **spirituality** under the care of Bethesda **Monthly Meeting** in Maryland. Her most recent work is a series of books on Quaker **theology** and practice entitled *Listening Spirituality*. After receiving her undergraduate education from St. John's College in Annapolis and studying at the Hartford Theological Seminary in Connecticut, she attended five terms at **Pendle Hill**, the Quaker Study Center, and trained in spiritual guidance and group leadership at the Shalem Institute for Spiritual Formation in Washington, D.C.

LUFFE, JOHN (ALSO LOVE) (d. 1658/1659). Early Quaker **missionary**, companion to **John Perrot**. He was hanged after his attempts to convert Pope Alexander VII.

LUND, SIGRID HELLIESEN (1892–1987). Norwegian worker for **peace**, she was active in the Norwegian underground protecting Norwegian Jews and refugees during **World War II**. In 1947, she became the first member of the fledgling Oslo Worship Group to become a member of the **Religious Society of Friends**.

LUNG'AHO, DAUDI (ca. 1872–1967). Pioneer **East African** church leader. When **Arthur Chilson**, Edgar Hole, and **Willis Hotchkiss** arrived in East Africa, one of the first Africans to join in their work in Kaimosi was Daudi Lung'aho. The local people were at first suspicious of these white men and called them "amanani" (man-eaters); since they wore long, black coats, the local people also joked about their "tails."

Daudi and others took on the difficult task of making these missionaries accepted. Daudi learned carpentry as well as reading and writing at the **mission** station. As other Americans arrived, he learned to cook European food and keep house, as well as to erect houses sent from England. Dr. Elisha Blackburn (1873–1958), who served in Kenya from 1903 to 1906, took him on as a medical assistant as well.

Daudi Lung'aho married **Maria Maraga** in the first Christian **marriage** at Kaimosi. Later this couple, believing that men and **women** are **equal** before **God**, broke the taboo against women eating chicken. Daudi became active in spreading the Good News around the mission station and further afield, often meeting with local chiefs, becoming known as a preacher. Over the years he also taught at many schools in the region.

In 1935, Daudi Lung'aho and several other men were detained when the Tiriki elders accused them of encouraging young people to refuse to accept tribal customs (*see* PRISONS). Daudi refused to agree to stop **preaching** but was eventually freed by the government officials in Kakamega. [Margery Post Abbott]

LUNG'AHO, THOMAS GANIRA (1919–1999). Educator, and first administrative secretary of **East Africa Yearly Meeting**. Thomas Lung'aho, son of **Maria Maraga** and **Daudi Lung'aho**, grew up among **missionaries** in western Kenya. After teaching and serving as a school administrator, he became district chair of the Christian Churches Association, then served on a commission established by the Ministry of Education shortly after Kenya's independence in 1961 to survey the national **education** system. He and his wife, Leah, had seven children and created a model small farm at their home. Lung'aho took on major administrative responsibilities in the yearly meeting in 1958, in preparation for Kenya's independence. As administrator for "institutions and projects," he oversaw the teachers' education college, four secondary schools, a hospital, a health center, a rural service program, and Friends Bible Institute (later **Friends Theological College**, at Kaimosi). In 1962, he became chair of the National Christian Council of Kenya. [Margery Post Abbott]

LUPTON, LEVI RAKESTRAW (1860–1929). Born near Beloit, Ohio, to Emmor and Rebecca (Rakestraw) Lupton, he established a

Quaker community in Lupton, Michigan. After a Wesleyan **holiness** conversion experience in 1885, he was recorded a **minister** by East Goshen **Monthly Meeting**. In 1900, he began evangelistic services in Alliance, Ohio, where he founded a **Friends Church**. In 1901, he started an annual camp meeting in Alliance which Gary McGee calls the first **Pentecostal** camp meeting in the eastern United States. He then founded the World Evangelization Company (1904) in an unsuccessful attempt to convert Africa, sending William M. Smith (1872–1964) along with Helen (Farr) and **Jefferson Ford** to Nigeria. Having resigned from Friends, a year later he opened a **missionary** training school in Alliance that competed with **Walter and Emma Malone**'s school in Cleveland. Lupton's reputation suffered when an affair with his secretary was reported by *The Alliance Daily Review* in 1910, but after a period of repentance he continued to serve in the new Pentecostal movement. [John W. Oliver]

–M–

MADLALA-ROUTLEDGE, NOZIZWE (1953–). Pacifist and legislator, Nozizwe Madlala was born in KwaZulu-Natal, South Africa. During the antiapartheid struggle, she served a year in solitary confinement for her political activism. She and her husband, Jeremy Routledge, director of the Friends **Peace** Center in Cape Town, are members of Central and South Africa **Yearly Meeting**. In 1994, she was elected to Parliament in South Africa's first democratic elections following the end of apartheid (*see* CIVIL GOVERNMENT; POLITICS). She was named deputy defense minister for South Africa by President Thabo Mbeki in 1999 as part of his program for transforming military culture, a foreign policy that enhances peacemaking and building peace and development in Africa through the New Plan for Africa's Development (NEPAD).

MALLIK, GURDIAL (1895/96–1970). Gurdial Mallik was the Hindu Quaker in whom "the two religions were said to flow together in one clear, sparkling stream." For more than 20 years Mallik gave himself generously, but not exclusively, to the Quaker fellowship; but he was never willingly absent from any who were in trouble or in need.

Mallik spent 22 years as a teacher at Santiniketan, Rabindranath Tagore's Ashram in Bengal. This all began with a longing to meet Tagore, going there, and after a few moments of silence, having Tagore stretch out his arms and say, "I have long known you. Come and stay with me." He did, and during those years became a bridge between **Mahatma Gandhi** and Tagore. [Martha Dart]

MALONE, EMMA ISABEL BROWN (1860–1924) and JOHN WALTER (1857–1935). Bible teachers, "soul winners," **publishers**, Quaker **mystics**. Walter (as he was called) received his **evangelical** Quaker faith in New Vienna, Ohio, from his mother, Mary Ann (Pennington) Malone, evangelist **John Henry Douglas**, and **peace** activist **Daniel Hill**. Both Douglas and Hill lived beside young Walter Malone. As a young woman, Emma inherited a theologically liberal faith from her father Charles and grandfather Ira, brother of Nicholas Brown who was a friend of **Elias Hicks**. Emma was converted to holiness evangelicalism in 1879 by Dwight L. Moody and to evangelical Quakerism in 1882 by **Esther Frame**. With Walter, she experienced holiness, or "instant **sanctification**," in 1884, which they learned from **Dougan Clark Jr.** and became part of the **holiness movement** among Friends.

Married in 1886, Walter and Emma cofounded the Christian Workers Training School for Bible Study and Practical Methods of Work in Cleveland, Ohio (now **Malone College**), in 1892. While the school was located one block from Euclid Avenue, then known locally as "the most beautiful street in the world," they focused their "practical work" among Cleveland's poor, focusing on evangelism while providing various sorts of poor **relief** and job training. Thirteen **women** and 11 men from the first year were recorded by Friends or ordained by other denominations as **ministers**, while at least 68 women from the school were recognized as ministers by 1907. Also by 1907, missionaries from the school were serving overseas in Brazil, China, Cuba, India, Jamaica, Japan, Kenya, Mexico, South Africa, and Venezuela. In no small part, the fact that most Friends today live outside Europe and **North America** is due to Walter and Emma Malone (*see* MISSIONS).

The Malones published *The Christian Worker,* the largest Quaker periodical in the United States in the later 1880s and early 1890s. In

1894 the *Worker* merged with the smaller *The Friends Review* to become *The American Friend*, edited by **Rufus Jones**. They also published *The Young People* and *The Bible Student*, which merged with *The Christian Arbitrator* and *Messenger of Peace* in 1897 and was renamed *The Soul-Winner* in 1902. It became *The Evangelical Friend* in 1905.

Mary Ann, Walter, and Emma Malone also can be studied in the tradition of Quaker **mysticism** and **testimonies**. They opposed all killing, whether by war, capital punishment, or abortion. Most of all, Walter was remembered for his glowing countenance and kindly ways. Almost 20 years after his retirement, his death was the lead story in the *Cleveland Plain Dealer*, which called him "one of the best loved conservative clergymen in the history of Greater Cleveland." [John W. Oliver]

MALONE COLLEGE. Founded in 1892 as the Friends Bible Institute and Training School by **Walter and Emma (Brown) Malone** in Cleveland, Ohio. The name was changed to Cleveland Bible College in 1937. In 1957 the school moved to Canton, Ohio, and the name was changed to Malone. It is affiliated with **Evangelical Friends International**–Eastern Region.

MANCHESTER CONFERENCE (1895). The major turning point in the history of modern British Quakerism, away from the **evangelical** faith espoused by **Joseph John Gurney** and his followers, and toward the **liberal** perspective associated with Friends such as **John Wilhelm Rowntree**, **Rufus Jones**, and **Edward Grubb**.

By the end of the 19th century all mainstream churches in **Britain** were responding to a number of challenges to traditional forms of Christian belief. Developments in the natural sciences (especially geology and biology) called into question the biblical account of how the world came into being. An increasing number of people saw aspects of orthodox Christian teaching—such as the beliefs that **God** ordered the extermination of the inhabitants of Canaan, that on the **cross Christ** took the punishment for the **sins** of the world (*see* ATONEMENT), and that after death the wicked would suffer forever in **hell**—as morally incredible. Literary and historical criticism appeared to undermine the authority of the **Bible** by seeming to show that large parts were not the work of their traditional authors and were both historically inaccurate and internally contradictory.

Response to these challenges among British Quakers, as among Christians in general, was mixed. Some rejected them in their entirety and held on to their traditional beliefs. Some shifted toward **fundamentalism**. Some abandoned Christian belief altogether. **Modernists** saw these challenges as presenting an opportunity to develop a new form of Christian and Quaker **theology** that to their eyes was more intellectually and spiritually credible.

Until 1895 those liberal Quakers who held to the latter view were a small and uninfluential minority among British Friends. The modernist viewpoint was not accepted by the Conference itself or by **London Yearly Meeting** when it considered the report of the Conference the following year. Nevertheless, the Conference was a turning point because liberals were able to express their opinions at a representative Quaker gathering without being censured or condemned. [Martin Davie]

MARAGA, MARIA (1873–1956). Early Friends **leader** and evangelist in **East Africa**, she arrived at the Kaimosi **mission** station in 1902. Maraga married **Daudi Lung'aho** in 1903 and in 1905 became the first woman convert in East Africa. She was the first **woman** to break the taboo against eating chicken. In pre-Christian Luyia society chicken was believed to cause women to become barren, and the taboo against eating chicken became a symbol of the lack of **equality** between men and **women**.

MARRIAGE. Marriage is seen by Friends as a **covenant** relationship before **God**. **Equality** in marriage has had a special place in Quakerism since its earliest days, as a man and woman of faith were each seen to be a "helpmeet" to the other in the image of God, restored by **Christ** to thc condition before the Fall. Historically, wives as well as husbands who felt called to travel in the **ministry** left household and childrearing responsibilities to the stay-at-home spouse. Others in the **meeting** were also supportive although the domestic patterns within families did not generally change. Until the late 19th century, Quakers were expected to marry other Friends or else face **disownment** for "marrying-out" of the meeting.

Initially, Quaker marriages were not recognized under English law, as they took place in an **unprogrammed meeting for worship** with no **minister** to preside or to declare the couple married. **George Fox** noted that marriage "is the work of the Lord only, and not the priest's or magistrates'; for it is God's ordinance and not man's. . . . For we marry none; it is the Lord's work, and we are but witnesses" (Fox, *A Collection of Epistles*, 1698, epistle 264, 1669). From 1661 onwards, several civil law judgments upheld Quaker marriage. Although much diversity existed in early Friends' relationships, the marriage of George Fox and **Margaret Fell** in 1668 set an example both in the form of the ceremony and in establishing the equality of the man and woman in marriage. Their marriage certificate cited the marriages of Jacob, and of Ruth and Boaz, as precedents. Fox, who was from a more humble background, took great care that the rights of Fell's children to her substantial estate should not suffer. After they were married, she continued to make decisions regarding her estate.

Today, in North America once a couple has expressed their intention to marry, either the **pastor** or a meeting-appointed **clearness** committee meets with the couple to ascertain their readiness for marriage and freedom from other entanglements. Assuming no impediment, the marriage ceremony itself takes place in a specially called meeting for worship appointed by the monthly meeting. The pastor or a **committee** of **overseers** helps the couple follow legal procedures established by the local jurisdiction. If the ceremony is held in an unprogrammed meeting for worship, according to custom, the couple will rise after a period of silent worship to make their solemn declarations of commitment to one another. The **clerk**, or another person, will then read aloud from the certificate of marriage prepared in advance, repeating the declaration just made, and the newly married couple will sign the **certificate**. The meeting for worship continues with spoken **ministry** from the gathered Friends, and at the close of the meeting all those present sign the certificate as witnesses. The legal systems in different countries and states accommodate Quaker marriages in widely varying ways. When the marriage is held in meetings where **programmed worship** is practiced, the ceremony may take a more traditional Protestant form with the pastor presiding and signing the appropriate legal documents.

Friends are divided on the question of whether marriage can be recognized for any other than one man and one **woman**. Few, if any,

Friends churches permit same-sex marriages, considering marriage to be the divinely ordained union of a man and a woman. **Liberal Friends** are most open to same-sex unions, which they may call either a marriage or a ceremony of commitment. Friends who support same-sex marriage feel that the **Holy Spirit** can be as much present in a home established by two partnered men or two partnered women as in one established by a man and a woman. Similarly, biological or adopted children can be equally cherished where love and peace reign.

In **East Africa**, Friends allow the continued practice of "bridewealth" but seek to regulate its use so that families set a fair value, which is acknowledged as "a token rather than a price," and encourage feasts that are inexpensive rather than ones that might bankrupt the family. Polygamy is banned for those who profess to be Christians. However, those who became Christians while in polygamous marriages were and are allowed to keep their wives but not take **leadership** roles in the church or marry more wives. Generally, only the first wife is allowed full **membership** in the meeting, often inadvertently causing hardships.

Divorce was rarely known among Friends until the 20th century. Acceptance of the modern reality of divorce has varied among the different branches of Friends. More liberal meetings may offer clearness committees to either or both members of a couple considering divorce in hopes of either reconciliation or a less destructive separation. Occasionally, individuals may seek a called meeting for worship at the time of the divorce. More evangelical churches are stricter in stating that marriage is for life and not to be broken by divorce except on scriptural grounds, but accept individuals who have been divorced, but are living consistent Christian lives, to join the church and work for it. *See also* SEXUALITY. [Margery Post Abbott, Elise Boulding, Esther Mombo]

MAULITES. A group (named for Joshua Maule, their leader) which separated from the **Wilburite** Ohio **Yearly Meeting** in 1863 because the yearly meeting would not recognize other, small Wilburite yearly meetings. In 1867 these **Primitive Friends** (officially called Ohio General Meeting) divided into Maulites and **Knolites**. In 1870, Joshua Maule and his family withdrew from the Maulite Ohio **General Meeting** one year before it ceased to exist. [William P. Taber]

McCLINTOCK FAMILY. North American radical **Hicksites, abolitionists**, and feminists. Thomas (1793–1876) and Mary Ann Wilson McClintock (1799–1884) were married in Philadelphia in 1820. A druggist and biblical scholar, Thomas was in 1827 the first secretary of the Free Produce Society, organized to boycott slave-made goods. In 1833, Mary Ann was a founding member of the Philadelphia Female Anti-Slavery Society. They moved to Waterloo, New York, in 1837. Both served in **leadership** positions of Genesee **Yearly Meeting** until 1848, when they joined the faction that split to form the Yearly Meeting of **Congregational Friends**, of which Thomas was first co-**clerk** (with Rhoda De Garmo). That same year, Mary Ann was one of the five **women** (of whom four were Quaker) who called the **Seneca Falls Woman's Rights Convention** in July 1848. Thomas presided for the final session. Their two older daughters, Elizabeth (1821–1896) and Mary Ann (1822–1884), helped edit the proceedings, and Elizabeth joined **Elizabeth Cady Stanton** in calling the Rochester Convention in August. Elizabeth married abolitionist lawyer Burrough Phillips in March 1852. Following his accidental death in 1854, she returned to Philadelphia to earn her living as a storekeeper. Her marriage and later departure from Philadelphia left a void in Stanton's life that was eventually filled by friendship with **Susan B. Anthony**. Following Thomas's death in 1876, Mary Ann also returned to Philadelphia, until her own death in 1884. Elizabeth retired to **Vineland**, New Jersey, in 1885, where she died in 1896. [Mary Ellen Chijioke]

MEADE, WILLIAM (1628–1713). London Quaker merchant and co-defendant with **William Penn** in the Bushels case in 1670, which established the right of a jury to return a verdict contrary to the judge's opinion. In 1681, Meade married **Margaret Fell**'s daughter Sarah.

MEETING. The term is found in the 17th-century records of Quaker faith and practice (*see* DISCIPLINE) and used in a variety of distinctive and important ways, although by the 20th century it has been replaced by "**church**" in many congregations springing from the **Gurneyite** tradition.

First, "meeting" is the shorthand name for **meeting for worship**. This refers to the appointed period of silent **unprogrammed** worship (in the 20th century, about an hour) in which anyone may be moved by the **Holy Spirit** to offer vocal **ministry** (any vocal contribution arising out of the worship). Instead of asking if somebody's going to church, or to the Mass, these Friends ask, "Are you going to meeting?"

Secondly, "**business meeting**," "meeting for worship for church affairs," or "meeting for worship for business" are common alternative uses of the term. However, as Friends' churches do not have ordained **ministers**, all members are responsible for the running of the organization, even where there is a **pastor** or other **released** staff (*see* PASTORAL SYSTEM). This, coupled with the early Quaker insight that **God** can be encountered through expectant silence, and that God's will can be discerned most effectively and reliably by a **gathered** group, led to creation of "meetings for church affairs" or business meeting in which the whole congregation participates in decision making. In this **gospel order** the worshipping group is thus also the executive body responsible for its church affairs.

"Meeting" is also a suffix or prefix for a range of different kinds of worship events, other than the basic meeting for worship. **Clearness** meetings, for example, are gatherings held in worship to help somebody or a couple or a group forward in their **discernment**. "Meetings for Learning" or "Meetings for Healing," for example, denote other kinds of corporate worshipful events.

Finally, "meeting" is used to refer to the corporate body of members at various levels, named by their frequency of occurrence: **monthly**, **quarterly**, or **yearly**. Any decision which can be taken locally is thus the responsibility of that local group. Yearly meetings differ in their authority over constituent groups, i.e., whether they operate on **congregational** or hierarchical models. Most yearly meetings adopt their own book of **discipline** or faith and practice today, although historically, many looked to the London and Philadelphia bodies. In more congregational yearly meetings, these volumes simply describe usual belief and practice; in hierarchical organizations, the yearly meeting may take steps to discipline monthly meetings that do not adhere to prescribed faith and/or practice

The basic unit of organization, which records **membership** and makes basic local decisions, is the monthly meeting. Traditionally, and in **Britain** and a few other areas today, the monthly meeting is made up of several congregations, or **preparative meetings**, which come together monthly to transact business. (In this case, the preparative meeting meets monthly to prepare business *for* monthly meeting.) In **North America**, the congregational movement eventually prevailed, so that today each local congregation is its own monthly meeting. (Here, a preparative meeting is a local group too small to stand on its own, preparing to *become* a monthly meeting.)

These descriptions are, thus, used to describe both an event and a constituency. A member might belong to a monthly meeting and also attend worship at a location given the same name.

Larger groupings, which incorporate monthly meetings in increasingly wider geographic areas, include the **general** or quarterly meetings, half-yearly meetings, and the yearly meetings. The business in these is conducted, as the names suggest, usually quarterly, every half-year, or every year. The annual session of the yearly meeting is the largest gathering and will include Friends from all meetings belonging within this larger body. [Pink Dandelion]

MEETING FOR SUFFERINGS. The name given to the executive **committee** of **Britain Yearly Meeting** that dates back to 1668, when it was set up in order to petition the government to alleviate the sufferings of Friends who were imprisoned or had their goods confiscated. It became the representative body that conducts business on behalf of the yearly meeting. Other than in Britain Yearly Meeting, the name has over time been changed to Representative Meeting, Interim Committee, or Steering Committee.

MEETING FOR WORSHIP. A gathering for **worship** in the manner of Friends, either **programmed** or **unprogrammed**. Regularly scheduled **meetings** on Sunday, or during the week, are now usually about an hour long, although originally the **elders** who closed the meetings by shaking hands would wait until they sensed that the **Holy Spirit** was ready for the meeting to end.

MEETING OF MINISTERS AND ELDERS. Historically the standing body at each level of Friends' **meeting,** responsible for ensuring the spiritual health of the worshipping group, that included all recorded **ministers** in the **meeting** and selected **elders** who were not ministers. The first nationwide meeting of ministers in **Britain** was held in 1661. The meeting of ministers was annual from 1668 and coincided with the **yearly meeting** for business after 1678. Soon some quarterly and half-yearly meetings included elders in this group. In 1721 **London Yearly Meeting** mandated that ministers and elders meet regularly at all levels.

Until the 20th century, ministers were generally recorded for life; elders could be removed by the meeting that appointed them. Resistance to perceived abuse of power by the meeting of ministers and elders was a key factor in the **Progressive Friends** movement of the 19th century. In the 20th century, lifetime recognition of ministers was often abandoned. In **North America**, many yearly meetings replaced the meeting of ministers and elders with a limited-term meeting/**committee** on ministry and worship (*see* LEADERSHIP). In smaller meetings, the spiritual and pastoral nurture roles may be combined in a committee on ministry and oversight. In Britain Yearly Meeting, this takes the form of the elders and overseers. [Mary Ellen Chijioke]

MEETINGHOUSE. Term used by Friends for the building where they meet to **worship**, seeing the **church** as the body of believers rather than a building. They do not consecrate this building, and the old-style meetinghouses do not have steeples or other adornment. In the 21st century, many Friends holding **programmed worship** prefer to use the term "church," and in **Britain**, it is two words: "meeting house."

MEJÍA GONZÁLEZ, RAÚL (1891–1919). Well-known, early Quaker poet and teacher at the Friends School, Chiquimula, Guatemala. *See* CENTRAL AMERICA.

MEMBERSHIP. Membership is a corporate recognition of a person's unity with Friends' faith and practice and is recorded in the **minutes** (and thereby included in membership lists) of a **monthly meeting**. Membership developed in the 17th century to enable Friends to know who could speak on their behalf, and thus be defended if attacked, and who was entitled to physical or material aid when in need. Procedures for membership were solidified in the 18th century by the requirement that Friends marry only other Friends (*see* HEDGE).

In the first generation of Friends, all who joined with them in **worship** and **corporate discipleship** were considered Friends (without formal distinctions as to members or attenders). Their status might become recorded in documents for any of several reasons: as public **ministers**, as recipients of assistance, as prisoners or martyrs, and eventually as born or married in the fellowship. On the other hand, a person might be named in the minutes as not being in unity with Friends for reasons of belief or behavior. This was particularly important at a time when Friends were regularly under threat of imprisonment and needed clarity about acceptable behavior. As early as 1667, **George Fox** referred to **disownment** of disreputable persons "if they go under the name of **Quakers**." By 1675, **meetings** were also concerned to identify which body was responsible for financial aid as well as moral oversight.

This "going under the name of Quakers" became more important to record as they become a settled fellowship, including births, **deaths**, and instances of new people joining by **convincement** instead of just noting special circumstances. Books of **discipline** instructed monthly meetings to maintain lists of births, deaths, **marriages**, and removals (transfers) as well as to record applications for membership and disciplinary actions, including disownments, in the meeting's records. Friends did not regularly list the names of members until the 19th century. Unity with faith and practice was assumed for adult members, but until the 20th century, children born and educated among Friends had the express right (birthright) of membership. **Birthright membership** has been modified in many **yearly meetings** to require a decision or expression of unity at some point for membership to be continued. "Unity" has also changed in meaning in some yearly meetings, gaining a doctrinal emphasis in some places, an emphasis on correct practice in others, and personal comfort in still others.

Most meetings have a procedure, usually a visit by a small **clearness** committee from the monthly meeting, or participation in a "membership class," to verify that a membership applicant truly has been convinced of the validity of Friends' faith and practice, based on accurate understanding and personal commitment. Membership is then decided by the **business meeting**. [Johan Maurer]

MENDENHALL, NEREUS (1819–1893). A North American educator, he served as head of New Garden Boarding School through the

American Civil War, then oversaw the rebuilding of the school as **Guilford College**.

MEN'S MOVEMENTS. Men's movements emerged in the United States in the mid-20th century, complementing **women**'s organizations, such as the **United Society of Friends Women**. The earlier organization of women's societies reflects economic and social factors. In the agricultural/industrial society men were more job-bound than women. And in America's westward moving culture, activities such as service to the needy devolved upon women. In rural areas, quilting and praying together strengthened bonds of Christian fellowship for Quaker women and fostered a concern for organized activity, ranging from assistance to freedmen in the 1860s (*see* ABOLITION) to support for **missions** later in the century.

By the mid-20th century, Quaker men sought comparable opportunities for spiritual fellowship and service. The most inclusive organization, Quaker Men International (QMI), is a part of **Friends United Meeting (FUM)**. It was organized in 1950 under a concern to strengthen Quaker fellowship and service. L. Glenn Switzer, a California businessman, gave initial leadership to the organization.

The purpose statement for local groups of QMI includes witnessing **Christ**'s way of life in **business** dealings, through social actions, and by **evangelistic** outreach. Major service projects include raising funds for the FUM office building, purchasing land for a new Phoenix, Arizona, **meetinghouse**, constructing youth camp facilities in various **yearly meetings**, building a facility for the Mesquakie Indian Reservation (*see* NATIVE AMERICANS), and expediting disaster **relief work** projects.

Triennial conferences are held, in conjunction with the United Society of Friends Women. Persons from groups within non-FUM **yearly meetings** often participate in these gatherings. During the 1990s, some North American Quaker men participated in an **ecumenical** movement, "The Promise Keepers," finding spiritually fulfilling the male and interracial bonding that occurs at rallies and responding to its summons to faithful Christian discipleship. [Arthur O. Roberts]

MENTAL HEALTH REFORM. Friends have always had a great empathy for the mentally ill. Even in the 17th century, Quakers did not consider the insane as animals or comic, filthy and/or dangerous, as many others did. Although it was not acted on for nearly a century, **George Fox** issued an early call for Friends to create institutions for the humane care of the mentally ill. Overcoming hindrances to the work of the **Light** of **Christ** in the human heart was an ongoing motivation for work with the mentally ill, as well as in **prison** reform, **abolition** and **temperance**.

Until the 19th century, "madhouses" were the accepted institutions for the mentally ill. Chains were normal modes of restraint. The growth of medical professions in the 18th century led to treatments based on the medical standards of the day—bloodletting, purging, etc.—but no reduction in restraints. **William Tuke** led a revolutionary movement, based on the belief that even the mentally ill retained a divinely granted capacity to respond to a loving but controlled environment. In 1796, Tuke established The Retreat at York, England, after the suspicious death of a Quaker widow at the York Asylum. "Moral Treatment" emphasized talking, occupational therapy, diet, fresh air, and exercise in addition to medical treatment. Spacious, attractive grounds furnished space for patients to walk and for their occupation in the gardens and fields as part of their treatment. Patients would also attend **meeting for worship**. Soothing and gentle treatment was used whenever possible with the attempt to instill self-discipline rather than use external restraints, although they were used when necessary. Underlying the approach was a view of the individual as an indivisible whole of mind, soul, and body, which in turn invited treatment in each of these aspects.

Samuel Tuke (1784–1857), grandson of the founder, wrote *Description of the Retreat in 1813* and gave talks throughout Europe on the methods developed in York. His work contributed to the creation of many similar institutions, particularly in **Britain** and **North America**.

While Pennsylvania Hospital had a special unit for the mentally ill, which emphasized humane treatment, moral treatment became central only in the 19th century. In 1811, Thomas Scattergood (1748–1814) urged Philadelphia Yearly Meeting to create an institution similar to The Retreat at York. Friends Asylum opened in 1817 "for such of our members as may be deprived of the use of their reason," although it soon was open to non-Quakers. Thomas Kirkbride

(1809–1883), resident physician in 1832–1833, became the first **superintendent** of Pennsylvania Hospital's separate institution for the insane, where he continued use of "moral suasion" in his treatment of patients. He was later instrumental in establishing the Association of Medical Superintendents of American Institutions for the Insane, the parent organization of the American Psychiatric Association.

Friends Asylum was the first facility in the U.S. designed for humane treatment of the mentally ill and remains a leading psychiatric institution. Later the **Lindley Murray** family of New York gave their estate of Bellevue to become the (second) site of New York Friends' reform school, hospital, and mental hospital, which served mainly non-Friends.

In the 20th century, many young men elected to take their service while **conscientious objectors** at Friends Hospital and in other institutions caring for the mentally ill, often in menial positions. Individuals, such as **Ralph Hetherington**, who was the first secretary general of the British Psychological Society, challenged the trend in psychiatric thought that equated movements of the **Holy Spirit** with "hearing voices" and thus associated with psychopathology. Friends pointed rather to the importance of **mysticism** as part of understanding the human mind and mental health.

In the United States, **Howard Brinton**, Elined Prys Kotschnig, and others initiated the publication *Inward Light* in 1938 to explore aspects of bodily and mental health alongside worship, contemplation, and the ways in which the "beloved community" might best express itself. **William Camp**, a Quaker psychiatrist, was founder of Physicians for Social Responsibility. The Friends Conference on Religion and Psychology was founded in 1943 (as the Conference on the Nature and Laws of Our Spiritual Life) and continued with annual meetings and publication of the *Inward Light* through most of the rest of the century. [Margery Post Abbott]

MEXICO. Gulielma M. H. (b. 1850) and Samuel A. B. Purdie (1843–1897) arrived in Mexico in 1871, sponsored by the Foreign Missionary Association of Indiana Yearly Meeting, and remained until 1895. At the invitation of the Tamaulipas state government, they moved to the capital city, Ciudad Victoria, where the first **monthly meeting** was established in 1888. Their printing press, the first one in the state capital, was used to spread the Gospel in tracts, small booklets, and a newsletter, *El Ramo de Olivo* (The Olive Branch). Purdie also published textbooks used in both private and public schools. He died of tetanus from a cut finger. While the Purdies were not **recorded ministers**, nor primarily preachers, they helped establish many churches and schools in the northeastern states of Mexico, the first one in Matamoros, Tamaulipas.

In 1947**, Heberto M. Sein** helped found the Mexico City Meeting and *Casa de los Amigos* (Friends House). In the early 1950s his concern for dialogue among different groups of Friends in Mexico was the catalyst to the formation of the *Reunion General de los Amigos en Mexico* (General Meeting of Friends in Mexico) in 1958, which consists of meetings in Cuidad Victoria, Monterrey, Mexico City, and Nuevo Leon. The *Comite de Servicio de los Amigos* (Mexican Friends Service Committee) is engaged in support of Guatemalan refugees and construction of community housing and other work in Mexico City.

Roscoe S. and Tina Patterson Knight came to Mexico in 1967 under sponsorship of Evangelical Friends Alliance (*see* EVANGELICAL FRIENDS INTERNATIONAL) with the purpose of opening a new mission field. In 1993 they saw the opening of the *Iglesia de los Amigos Evangelicos* (Evangelical Friends Church) in the metropolitan area of Mexico City, which today has several congregations. [Loida Eunice Fernandez Gonzalez]

MIDDLE EAST. Following **George Fox**'s missionary impulse, individual **ministers** from **Britain** ventured to the Mediterranean area, visiting places such as Rome, Jerusalem, and Constantinople (*see* MISSIONS). However, it was only in 1868, in Brummana, near Beirut, Lebanon, that **North American** Quakers succeeded in establishing a **worship** group; this was followed later by one in Ramallah, near Jerusalem (*see* JONES, ELI and SYBIL). In both those areas, Friends schools were opened, an important and valued service, which still continues (*see* EDUCATION). **Meetings** or informal worshipping groups continue in Lebanon, Egypt, and Palestine at the beginning of the 21st century. *See also* ZARU, JEAN. [Franco Perna]

MIGRATIONS. In **Britain** rural Friends moved into towns starting in the mid-17th century. Even before a Quaker enterprise in West New

Jersey (half of the present state) attracted the first large groups of Friends to **North America** in 1676, there were local migrations, for example, from New England to Long Island (New York) and thence to East New Jersey. When Charles II granted **William Penn** the charter for the colony of Pennsylvania in 1681, the way opened for large numbers of Friends from England, **Ireland**, and Wales to engage in the "**Holy Experiment**." Smaller numbers of Friends came into Maryland, Virginia, northeastern North Carolina, and Charleston, South Carolina. These migrations from Britain weakened **meetings** and contributed to the end of numerical growth there after 1680.

By 1760, 50,000 to 60,000 Quakers lived in the coastal colonies in North America. As land became scarce, they began to move west and south. Quakers on Nantucket Island and in other parts of New England and southern New York moved to an area on the Hudson River above Poughkeepsie, New York. Others joined large numbers of Pennsylvanians and Virginians who moved into central North Carolina. This migration extended into northern South Carolina and Georgia. Within two generations of the first settlement of these regions, many Quakers began to emigrate to eastern Tennessee, Ohio, and Indiana. During this period of time Friends also moved from the Delaware Valley to western Pennsylvania and from the Hudson River settlements across the Mohawk Valley to the Finger Lakes region of New York. *See also* NORWEGIAN EMIGRATION.

By 1800, three streams of migration were evident in North America. Friends moved both from the east and south, westward to Ohio while others moved northward to Ontario. Many of the emigrants to **Canada** were Friends who preferred, or were forced, to live under British rule after the American Revolution.

When the Northwest Ordinance of 1787 opened land north and west of the Ohio River, including land in Indiana, as territory free from slavery (*see* ABOLITION), a flood of Quakers moved in from both the east and the south. Southern meetings were drained by migration, especially those in South Carolina and Georgia. In 1835, land in Iowa opened up and attracted Friends from New England, Indiana, and Ohio, and from there some moved into Kansas. As early as 1847, a few Friends settled in the Willamette Valley of Oregon; in 1875, another group, mainly from Iowa, settled near Newberg, Oregon. Other smaller settlements grew in Washington and Idaho. By the 1880s, a land boom and cheap railroad fares made it possible for many midwestern families to move into Southern California.

Many sound reasons to migrate were shared with other migrant groups. For Quakers the decision to move was also frequently grounded in religious inspiration and purpose. The movement in England from rural to urban areas avoided persecution for not paying **tithes** to the church and enabled Friends to live close together for mutual support and community. Immigrants to America sought social and political stability and religious freedom. Those who came to William Penn's colony were drawn at least in part by the desire to participate in a new vision of Christian society and **civil government**. The scarcity of land for growing families and younger sons influenced many decisions to migrate to America and to participate in the great westward migration from the east. For southern Quakers the desire to live where slavery was illegal was a powerful incentive as well. [Carole B. Treadway]

MINISTERS. In the Quaker faith, every believer is a minister, witnessing to the central message that "**God** was in **Christ** reconciling the world to himself." Some Friends have felt a special calling to minister in a particular manner, or place. **Ministry** is what one does to fulfill God's calling. Public ministry is the calling to repeated **preaching**, **prophecy**, or other vocal spiritual **leadership**. This calling is to be verified by the **gathered** meeting. Historically, if this ministry required the person to be away from home, the **meeting** would help care for the family, **releasing** the individual to fulfill his or her ministry. The call to travel in the ministry, speaking to a particular concern, is usually minuted by the local **monthly meeting** which releases the individual to fulfill God's calling. Examples are **Mary Fisher** traveling to Turkey and **John Woolman** traveling to speak to Friends about slavery (*see* ABOLITION).

The call to public ministry leads to a process of recording, or recognizing, that gift. Friends believe that God ordains ministers; humans simply record what God has done. Most **yearly meetings** have developed a procedure to record the gift of ministry. A person who has completed that process is recognized as a recorded minister. The recording process can stress different skills and gifts, depending on the yearly meeting. A recorded minister is usually given all the privileges of an ordained person in other fellowships. While the practice of recording has died out in some areas, the majority of Friends in the world still practice the recording of ministers.

For Friends whose manner of **worship** has grown to depend upon a minister, or **pastor**, recording tends to focus on recognizing the training and skills as well as the gift. One of the earliest cases of a Friend being paid to preach, to pastor, and to conduct weddings, was in Wilmington, Ohio, in 1868, when Robert Douglas received a license from the local court to conduct weddings.

While **George Fox** recognized that it was not training or education at Oxford or Cambridge that qualified one to be a minister, it is important to have adequate preparation to minister, including caring for the spiritual needs of the meeting. Graduate study in **theology** and religion has become more common. Friends have developed their own seminaries, such as **Earlham School of Religion**, which trains **leadership** for both **programmed** and **unprogrammed** meetings. [Larry Barker]

MINISTRY. Ministry may be defined as **God**'s call to speak to the spiritual and personal needs of others. There is also a ministry of silent "waiting upon the Lord." There is a ministry of enabling others in their spiritual journey. And there is a ministry of the written word to edify others in their religious faith.

Ministry is the vocation of all who respond to God's call in their lives. It is not just the chosen few, whether ordained clergy or Friends recognized and recorded as **ministers**, who are called to this service. Historically, any Friend who exercised a special gift in ministry, particularly the spoken ministry, was recorded. Instead, some emphasize that anyone may be moved by the Spirit of God to share a message in **meeting for worship**, or carry out loving service to others. Friends have always recognized the **equality** of **women** and men in ministry, though their practice in this regard has not always been consistent.

It has been the general belief and practice of Friends that spoken ministry is a gift from the **Holy Spirit**. In this sense, it is a **prophetic** ministry inspired by the **leading** of the Holy Spirit. In the Christian context the authority for ministry is from **Christ** through the Holy Spirit. It usually takes place in the Friends' meeting, which is the gathered community of faith for mutual sharing, **prayer**, and **worship**. Thus, authority for Quaker ministry is not by apostolic succession, as many churches believe, but is by endeavoring to be in the same Spirit as the apostles were. Ministry is not an office or profession, it is above all a response to the divine initiative. Historically, Friends believed in the "free Gospel ministry" without monetary remuneration. This is still true for some Friends, particularly those who still hold to **unprogrammed worship**. However, since the late 19th century, Friends' **pastoral** ministers generally have been paid. All too often, the practice has been the "poorly paid ministry," and the quality of the pastoral leadership at times has suffered. [Wilmer A. Cooper]

MINUTE. A statement of the sense of the **meeting** on an item of business by those in attendance at a given **business meeting**. The sense of the meeting may be unity on a given course of action, a stop about moving forward, or an indication of the need for further seasoning. In the past, and sometimes today, individuals traveling in the **ministry** carried formal minutes approved by their meeting to indicate their acceptability. [Jan Hoffman]

MISSIONS. The Friends' missionary movement emerged in **Britain** and **North America** in about 1650. **George Fox**'s spiritual awakening created a missionary movement, first within Britain and later to **Continental Europe** and the American colonies. He had a vision that Friends should go to the farthest parts of the globe. Many were unclear about geography and culture, but they traveled, armed with a concept of the **Lamb's War** from the Book of Revelation. They believed Christians were to suffer with **Christ**, follow his model of sacrificial self-giving, and transform both individuals and societies. Fox saw a great sea of **Light** overcoming the darkness. Christ was the commander who promised his followers they would walk cheerfully over the earth if they responded to the work of his Light within their hearts. Friends of the Lamb, as some early Quakers referred to themselves, spoke as **prophets** to the world, urging personal faith and obedience and working to prepare Christ's kingdom on earth.

Restoration Quakerism saw a waning of this zeal to reform the whole world and an end to the confidence that everyone would soon share their experience of Christ present. Eighteenth-century Friends were active in **evangelizing** and social reform within the Anglo-Saxon world. They sought to establish new **meetings** throughout

Continental Europe. Public Friends traveled widely in the **ministry**, evangelizing in "appointed meetings" aimed at non-Quakers, and nurturing existing, often isolated, Friends' communities in North America as well as in Britain and **Ireland**.

Friends also actively worked with **Native Americans**. Often their work was more focused on providing **education** and training, which would allow the tribes to adapt to English social norms than on conversion. By the 1780s, Friends were forming **meetings** for **African Americans**, although they were reluctant to allow blacks into membership in established **monthly meetings** (*see* ABOLITION; EQUALITY). **James Backhouse**, who helped establish meetings in **Southern Africa** and **Australia**, was one of a number of British Friends who felt led to travel more widely overseas in the early part of the 19th century.

The mid-19th century marked the start of the **modern missionary movement**. Friends in the American **Orthodox** and **Evangelical** branches were energized by the **revivals** to save souls for Christ. Both they and British Friends were influenced by the broader Protestant missionary movement to initiate a new, institutionally supported, and at times **ecumenical**, form of missionary work. Modern **liberal Friends** have eschewed the missionary movement and focus primarily on social justice work, but pattern their ministry after 18th-century Friends like **John Woolman**. Programs of intervisitation and outreach are established both by individual **yearly meetings** and through **Friends General Conference**, most recently in their Traveling Ministry Program. [E. Anna Nixon, Ron Stansell]

MISSIONS: MODERN MISSIONARY MOVEMENT. In the 19th century, Friends' conception of the **Great Commission** took on new forms as **yearly meetings** began to establish mission boards to support and encourage this work. Between 1850 and 1900, **Gurneyite** yearly meetings in **North America**, transformed by the **revivals**, sent missionaries through much of the world, evangelizing and setting up hospitals and schools in South and **East Asia**, the **Middle East**, **East Africa**, the **Caribbean**, and Alaska. The American Friends Board of Foreign Missions, officially formed in 1894, led the way for the creation in 1902 of the Five Years Meeting (**Friends United Meeting [FUM]** from 1965). For the next century, most evangelical Friends missionaries, like **Everett and Catherine Cattell** (India), **Charles and Leora DeVol** (China and Taiwan), Roscoe and Tina Knight (**Mexico**), and **Arthur and Edna Chilson** (East Africa), stressed conversion, **evangelism**, and church planting along with **education**, human **equality**, **women** in ministry, and the guidance of the **Holy Spirit** in **worship** and service.

Philadelphia Yearly Meeting (**Orthodox**), which was independent of FUM, began missionary work in Japan in 1885. With the **reunification** of the two Philadelphia Yearly Meetings, the Japan **Committee** became the core of the merged Outreach Committee.

British missionaries were instrumental in early work in **Southeast** and **East Asia**, Pemba, and Madagascar. The Friends' Foreign Mission Association was created in 1868, and a similar effort was made to evangelize at home. Through Friends' work in the Adult School movement, it was estimated that by 1875, as many people belonged to Adult School "mission meetings" in **Britain** as to Friends' meetings. The Home Mission Committee was formally established in 1881 and had over 43 missioners at work a decade later. After 1927, British Friends mostly ceased a sense of active conversion evangelism, but continued peace and service efforts and loose ties with mission-founded groups of Quakers in Africa, India, and elsewhere. Social Witness and **Outreach** and **Advancement** committees are the visible heirs to the earlier British Quaker missionary concerns. *See* PEACE AND SERVICE AGENCIES.

A second wave of missions occurred from the turn of the century into the 1930s when Friends meetings were planted first in East Africa, then in **Central** and **South America**, and in **Central Africa**. The overwhelmingly largest of these church plants is in Kenya, under the direction of FUM, where the original Friends African Industrial Mission was begun in 1903. In the beginning, it was a blend of technical training, medical ministry, founding of schools, and evangelistic church planting. **Willis R. Hotchkiss**, the prime mover of the Kenya mission, eventually left the Friends mission and paved the way for the large and prosperous work of World Gospel Mission, a process repeated by other Quaker pioneers in Bolivia, Honduras, and elsewhere. Central Yearly Meeting, of Westfield, Indiana, began its mission in Bolivia in 1919. This resulted in several yearly meetings separate from the Bolivian meetings formed by the work of Northwest Yearly Meeting. In 1934, Mid-America Yearly Meeting started Friends Africa Gospel Mission in Burundi (*see* CENTRAL AFRICA) which is now related to **Evangelical Friends International (EFI)**.

The **Friends World Committee for Consultation (FWCC)** came into being in 1937 to promote better understanding among Friends the world over. One leader commented, "Under the leadership of **Christ** differences of opinion can be distinguished from matters of conscience." With awareness of the differences that separate and the commitment to transcend them, FWCC can be an effective force in the care of and communication among Friends worldwide including those who have become and are becoming Friends through missionary efforts.

The third modern wave of mission work began in 1978 when Evangelical Friends Mission (EFM) was created by EFI to bring together the work of a number of yearly meetings and create new, joint efforts. New conversion evangelism and church planting occurred in Mexico City, the Philippines, North India, Nepal, Rwanda, eastern Russia, Indonesia, and Cambodia.

Evangelical Friends Church–Eastern Region had missions in India (Chatarpur) (1896–), China (1887–1950), and Taiwan (1953–), and supported staff in Hong Kong, Kenya, Haiti, and Jamaica. Northwest Yearly Meeting supported missions in Bolivia (1931–), and Peru (1961–), and some staff in Ramallah in Palestine (*see* MIDDLE EAST). Mid-America Yearly Meeting worked in Urundi (Burundi) (1934–1985) and Rocky Mountain, in Rough Rock, Arizona, among the Navajos (1954–1991). In 1994, Friends Church Southwest Yearly Meeting (FCSW) brought its entire missions program under the umbrella of EFI, including missions and newly established yearly meetings in Alaska (1897), Guatemala (1906), Honduras (1914), El Salvador, and Nicaragua. In 1987, work in Indonesia was undertaken, and in 1995, in Cambodia. The fruits of evangelical Friends missions are loosely organized worldwide by the Evangelical Friends International Council with regional directors in Africa, Asia, Latin America, and North America.

Today, FUM field staff work in East Africa (Kenya, Uganda, and Tanzania), Palestine (Ramallah Friends School and Monthly Meeting), inner-city Chicago (*see* URBAN MINISTRIES), and Belize, and maintain ties with Friends in Cuba, Jamaica, Mexico (Ciudad Victoria), and among **Native Americans** in the United States. They also minister as "project partners" in Turkana Friends Mission, Samburu Friends Mission in Kenya, and Swift-Purcell Boys Home and Lyndale Girls Home in Highgate, Jamaica (*see* CARIBBEAN). New works in the 1990s include contacts in Moscow, Russia, and in Tecuci, Romania.

At the beginning of the 21st century, the largest bodies of mission-related Friends were in Kenya, Central America, and South America, with significant new growth in Asia. The vast majority of non-Caucasian Friends everywhere in the world were of an **evangelical** Christian persuasion. The two American Friends missions agencies (FUM and EFM) are phasing out of older fields and phasing into new ones. Strong national leadership has arisen in East and Central Africa, Central and South America, and Taiwan. Non-Western Quakers have now joined the missionary movement with the commissioning of workers to Nepal, Nicaragua, Peru, the Philippines, Siberia, and Congo. [E. Anna Nixon, Ron Stansell]

MITCHELL, MARIA (1818–1889). Astronomer and professor at Vassar College from 1865 to 1888, Mitchell observed and plotted the course of a new comet in 1847. She was the first woman elected to the American Academy of Arts and Sciences in 1848 and became its president in 1850. In 1868, she was the first woman member of the American Philosophical Society. Born into a Nantucket, Massachusetts, Quaker family, she was **disowned** for refusing to give up her piano; she afterwards considered herself a Friend in belief while attending the Unitarian church. [Margery Post Abbott]

MODERNISM. A movement among religious groups in the late 19th century that can be found within Quakerism from the 1870s onward. Modernism held that faith must be relevant to its age and context, that **God** works in and through the world, particularly via the experience and creativity of humanity, and that religion needs to be open to new ideas as history and humanity progress toward the reign of God. It was inspired and supported by new scientific discovery, the fresh interest in ideas of evolution and progress, and the Higher Criticism, which had started to question claims about the authorship and authority of the **Bible.** It was essentially optimistic, moderate, and committed to the **social gospel**. For **Hicksites**, **independent meetings**, and other **liberal Friends**, it allowed a reaffirmation of the Inward **Light** critiqued by **evangelical** Friends.

Modernism also had a major influence on part of the evangelical movement, dividing it into a modernist renewal wing and a **holiness** revival wing. **Rufus Jones** was an **Orthodox** Friend who became a modernist in the 1890s and then campaigned to frame American Quakerism, of whichever strand, within a modernist perspective. **Friends United Meeting** became essentially modernist, allowing **reunification** and consolidation of some member **yearly meetings** with liberal yearly meetings belonging to **Friends General Conference** in the 20th century. [Pink Dandelion]

MONTHLY MEETING. A traditional term referring to the monthly gathering for the conduct of **church** business, the **business meeting**. Traditionally, a monthly **meeting** consisted of three to four local congregations called **preparative meetings**. In 20th-century **North America**, **congregationalism** has prevailed, and each established worshipping group generally forms its own monthly meeting.

MOORE, HOWARD (1925–). Moore served as **superintendent** of Taiwan **Missions** on behalf of Evangelical Friends Church–Eastern Region from 1973 to 1989 (*see* EAST ASIA). He holds a Doctor of Missiology from Trinity International University Evangelical Divinity School in Deerfield, Illinois. Presently he is **minister** of missions at First Friends Church in Canton, Ohio.

MOORE, JOSEPH (1832–1905). North American **minister** and biologist, he served as president of **Earlham** and **Guilford** Colleges, and was an early proponent of evolution.

MORNING MEETING. Beginning 1673, **ministers** (later joined by **elders**) in the London area met weekly on Second Day (Monday) mornings. This group, sometimes called Second Day meeting, supervised all visiting ministers. Until 1860, it also reviewed all manuscripts by Friends intended for **publication** and made full use of this power of censorship.

MORRISON, NORMAN (1933–1965). Executive Secretary of Baltimore **Yearly Meeting** who self-immolated on the steps of the Pentagon as a protest against the Vietnam War (*see* PEACE TESTIMONY). Morrison's death helped change defense secretary Robert McNamara's stance on the war.

MOTION OR INWARD MOTION. A term once common and still sometimes used to describe the subtle but clear prompting of the **Holy Spirit** to speak in **meeting** or to take a specific action.

MOTT, LUCRETIA COFFIN (1793–1880). North American traveling **minister**, **abolitionist**, and pioneer of **women**'s rights. Educated on Nantucket, in Boston, and at Nine Partners School in New York, Lucretia Coffin became a gifted teacher. At the age of 18 she married James Mott (1788–1868) of Long Island, a fellow teacher and abolitionist. Together the couple had six children, of whom five survived to adulthood. After the death of her second child, Tommy, Lucretia Mott turned more deeply to the **Bible** and Quaker writings, became at age 28 a recognized minister, and thereafter traveled in the **ministry** all her life.

In 1833, Mott helped to organize the Philadelphia Female Anti-Slavery Society, an interracial, interdenominational organization that played an important role in the antislavery struggle. She also became a member of the Pennsylvania Anti-Slavery Society and the American Anti-Slavery Society. In 1840, she was sent as a delegate to the World Anti-Slavery Convention in London, but was not seated because of her gender. This led her and **Elizabeth Cady Stanton**, the wife of another delegate, to plan with three other Quaker women the **Seneca Falls Convention** of 1848, at which the world's first declaration of women's rights was proclaimed (*See* McCLINTOCK FAMILY).

While she continued to work against slavery and racial discrimination and for the rights of women all her life, Mott was also an advocate of nonresistance, of peaceful settlement of conflicts (*see* PEACE), and an end to capital punishment. She espoused the rights of the **Native Americans**, especially of women, and of working-class women, and was concerned with **temperance** and prison reform (*see also* PENAL REFORM). Her courage was matched with a sweet spirit, which made her a beloved figure both within and without the **Religious Society of Friends**. [Margaret Hope Bacon]

MUGESIA, ENISI (1912–). Born at Chandumba in **East Africa**, the daughter of Elazia Vunuli and Ziporah Mbai, Mugesia began schooling at Chandumba in 1924 and was accepted as an associate member of the **Friends church**. In 1926, she went to school at Chavakali and was made a full member of the Quaker **Meeting** by **Jefferson Ford**. In 1927, she attended the Girls Boarding School (GBS) at Kaimosi, then under the leadership of **Laura Haviland**. A month later, she returned home to care for her widowed mother and also began teaching the girls and **women** of her village to read and **preaching** to them about the **Word** of God.

In 1929, she married Ezekiel Mudegu, **clerk** of Kegondi Friends **Meeting,** and began preaching at Kegondi Meeting. She had five children, three of whom died as infants. In 1940 her husband died, leaving her with two small children. A year later, after a consultation among her family, the meeting, and her husband's clan, she returned home, as there was no one to take care of her as was the custom. In 1943, she married a widower, Jeremiah Mkutu, in a ceremony conducted by Jefferson Ford. Mugesia joined Mkutu in Kisii and helped found the meeting there. She served there as clerk and preacher to the Women's Meeting

Mugesia worked to form the Women's **Yearly Meeting** in the then East Africa Yearly Meeting of Friends. She heard about prison ministry when she was attending the women's annual conference at Budaywa in 1962 (*see* PENAL REFORM). Moved by a speech about prisoners and prison ministry, she felt that God was calling her to take up this ministry. The women's **committee** appointed her to the Kisii prison where she met with women prisoners each Sunday between 1962 and 1982. As well as leading the services, she talked with the prisoners, listening to them and giving counsel on spiritual matters. She was delighted to see lives of prisoners change when they left prison after their sentences ended. Mugesia is retired and lives at Birongo, where she advises the young **leaders** of the church. [Esther Mombo]

MURRAY, LINDLEY (1745–1826). Member of a prominent New York Quaker family, Lindley Murray's grammar texts were used for the education of generations of North American and British school children. He was exiled to England after the American Revolution. His family, after whom a section of Manhattan in New York City is named, donated their estate for the present Bellevue Hospital. *See* MENTAL HEALTH REFORM.

MUSTE, ABRAHAM JOHN (1885–1967). Pacifist, union organizer, and labor education pioneer, A. J. Muste trained **Bayard Rustin**, James Farmer (1920–1999), and other civil rights leaders in the theory and practice of nonviolence. First joining Friends in New York, he was secretary of Fellowship of Reconciliation and a leader in defense of civil liberties, support for **conscientious objectors**, and **peace** making.

MUTUA, RASOAH (1895–1996). The first woman to train as a **pastor** at the Friends Bible School in **East Africa** and one of the first **women** to serve on the board of East Africa **Yearly Meeting**. Starting in the 1960s, Mutua also regularly visited women's prisons (*see* PENAL REFORM) as a volunteer on behalf of the Women's Yearly Meeting. She married Kefa Sakari (d. 1939) in 1923.

MWAITSI, MARIA (ca. 1888–1946). Early Friends leader in **East Africa** who helped **Edna Chilson** organize **women**'s work such as planting vegetable gardens.

MYLANDER, CHARLES (1941–). As **superintendent** of Evangelical Friends Church Southwest (California, Arizona, Nevada, and Utah) from 1984 until 2001, Mylander oversaw the creation of the Friends Center at **Azusa Pacific University**, the start of several new Friends churches, and the opening of new **mission** fields in Indonesia and Cambodia. In 2001, he became director of Evangelical Friends Missions, the North American missionary-sending body for **Evangelical Friends International (EFI)**. He was a key figure in the efforts to **realign** Friends in the mid-1980s. The formal proposal for realignment was to ask the affiliate member meetings of **Friends United Meeting (FUM)** to explore new alignments with like-minded Friends via new structures by joining either EFI or the more **liberal** body, **Friends General Conference**. Under his leadership, the then Southwest **Yearly Meeting** left

FUM and joined EFI in 1992. Mylander is also the author of several books and many articles.

MYSTICISM. Mysticism, in general, refers to a sense of Divine Presence, and encompasses the experiential aspect of all religions. Its meaning and usage among Quakers, as in Christianity in general, has changed throughout its history. Mysticism can also refer to an entire way of life, including the spiritual practices, such as prayer and contemplation, that are part of the desire for encounter and ongoing relation with the divine. **Rufus Jones** defined it as "a type of religion which puts emphasis on immediate awareness of relation with **God**, on direct and intimate consciousness of the Divine Presence."

Quaker history also provides instances of the popular notion of mysticism as altered states of consciousness such as ecstasies, visions, raptures. **George Fox** records several visionary experiences in his *Journal*, such as the classic description of his being "caught up in the spirit through the Flaming Sword, into the Paradise of God" (*Journal*, Nickalls p. 27). But for most mystics, Quakers included, such vivid visionary encounters are not the essence of mysticism. The mystical life is growth toward Christian **perfection**, the perfect love of God, the **discernment** and doing of God's will, which culminates in thorough **sanctification** in body, soul, and spirit. The early Quaker **theology** of perfection emerged from their direct experience of the divine, resulting in total transformation of the self and becoming manifest in the fruit of perfect obedience.

The most mystical aspect of Fox's teachings, and the keynote of his preaching is his claim that he knew **Christ**, and Christ alone, by direct revelation, without the help of any book or writing. The appeal to direct, personal experience and deemphasis of traditional forms of religious authority is common to most mystical movements. Fox's mysticism was not, however, a solitary pilgrimage, nor a form of illuminism, in which the individual hears God directly and becomes his or her own authority. Direct **leadings** and revelations were to be confirmed and verified within the community of Friends. The **Bible** remained the lens through which experience was interpreted and articulated. Because early Quakers believed that Christ had returned in Spirit to the world, all outward practices such as **creeds**, liturgies, rites, and **sacraments** were no longer necessary, only a waiting in silence for the present Christ to speak. **Thomas R. Kelly** speaks of this phenomenon as "group mysticism."

The mysticism of George Fox can be categorized as highly kataphatic (images and visions being a prominent element), active (evangelistic, this-worldly), and **prophetic** (ethical and reform-oriented). Mysticism as it developed in 18th-century Quakerism emphasized an increasing detachment from the world's ways. **Worship**, as communal contemplation in silence, became the distinguishing feature. The active, prophetic approach to mysticism remained visible in the lives of many Friends like the social reformer **John Woolman**, who was one of America's most important prophetic mystics. In the 19th century, mysticism was eclipsed by a turn toward **Unitarianism** and rationalism on one side, and **revivalism** and **evangelicalism** on the other. Both movements tended to disparage mysticism as a peculiar relic of the past.

In the early 20th century, Jones reinterpreted Quaker mysticism in a positive light. He considered himself an affirmative mystic and described Quaker mysticism as prophetic, active, and ethical. But he overlooked the apophatic dimension (the imageless, *via negativa* of St. John of the Cross) inherent in Quaker mysticism. Quakers, particularly in the **liberal** tradition, retain a strong apophatic dimension in their spirituality, through their emphasis on silence and the inward **Light**, and their disuse of nonuse, symbols, and sacraments.

Louis Bouyer in his *History of Christian Spirituality* claims that Quakers, in contrast to other Protestant groups, "have been most ready to give a warm and instinctive welcome to the highest teachings of the Catholic mystics." At the same time, liberal Quakers are among the most open to the apophatic way of Eastern spiritual traditions, and to a blending of mystical elements from other nontheistic religions. Mysticism in contemporary Quakerism ranges widely from a charismatic, evangelical devotion to Christ, to a mystical experience of the human spirit apart from any appeal to God. [Carole Spencer]

–N–

NATIVE AMERICANS. Seventeenth- and 18th-century Friends held a distinctly Quaker understanding that Native Americans, though without knowledge of the **Bible** or of historical Christianity, were both religious and moral beings, whose **spirituality** confirmed the Quaker understanding of the **universality** of God's grace. For brief periods Friends were influential in the colonial governments of Rhode Island, East and West Jersey, North Carolina, and for a much longer period in Pennsylvania (*see* CIVIL GOVERNMENT). Though not always consistent in practice, Quaker government policy toward the Native American tribes was based on a belief that the Native Americans held valid title to their lands and should be justly compensated for land sales, that **peace** and brotherhood be maintained between the English and Native Americans, and that disagreements between the two groups be mutually resolved. Eventually, this policy came into direct conflict with European land hunger and the imperial wars of the colonial powers.

In the 1750s, Quakers left the Pennsylvania government, but worked to influence governmental policy through the **Friendly Association for Regaining and Preserving Peace with the Indians by Pacific Measures** (1756) and the New Jersey Association for Helping the Native Americans (1757). In the 1790s, Philadelphia, New York, and Baltimore **Yearly Meetings** took the lead in providing education in agricultural and the domestic arts to Indian tribes. In addition, Quaker delegations attended treaty negotiations as independent observers and acted as cultural mediators and sources of advice and assistance to Native Americans. In the 1830s and 1840s, a Joint **Committee** representing four **Hicksite** yearly meetings successfully worked to revise the 1838 Treaty of Buffalo Creek, which, if implemented, would have forced the bulk of the Iroquois to leave New York State.

In 1869, under the "Peace Policy" initiated by President Ulysses S. Grant (1822–1885), Quakers were given direct responsibility for overseeing government agencies in the western plains. **Orthodox** Friends, who organized the Associated Executive Committee (AEC) on Indian Affairs (1869) had responsibility for several tribes in the Central Superintendency, covering parts of Kansas and Oklahoma. Hicksite Friends formed their own Joint Executive Committee on Indian Affairs to supervise the Northern Superintendency in Nebraska. The direct involvement of Friends in supervision of Indian agencies ended in the 1880s, though individual Friends served on the United States

Board of Indian Commissioners. Individual Friends were also active in organizing the periodic Lake Mohonk Conference on Indian Rights from 1883 to 1916 and again in 1929, and with other organizations.

In the mid-19th century, the efforts of the Orthodox yearly meetings and the AEC began to focus more on traditional **missionary** work. By the 1880s, Friends meetings were established among Native Americans in Oklahoma and Kansas, and missionary efforts were beginning among Native people in Alaska and **Mexico**.

In the 20th century, Friends' concerns shifted from the 19th-century focus on economic development to a renewed concern for the treaty and other rights of indigenous peoples. In this effort in **North America**, the several yearly meetings and the AEC were joined by Quaker-based organizations including the **American Friends Service Committee (AFSC)**, the Canadian Friends Service Committee, and the **Friends Committee on National Legislation**. Several **Friends churches** continue work among the Shawnees, Delawares, Osages, and other tribes. Alaska Yearly Meeting, a primarily Inuit church formed in 1970, grew out of the work of Friends Church Southwest Yearly Meeting and now has a Bible Training School. In **South America**, Friends churches consist of significant numbers of Native Americans, particularly the Aymara people of Bolivia and Peru. [Christopher Densmore]

NAYLER, JAMES (ALSO NAYLOR) (1618?–1660). Nayler, a Yorkshire farmer, served in the Parliamentary army during the **English Civil Wars** of the 1640s (*see* PURITANS). He probably met **George Fox** during the autumn of 1651 and became known as the Quakers' finest speaker and most capable theological author. Many saw him as a leader equal to Fox.

In June 1655, Nayler came to London in order to support the mission of **Edward Burrough** and **Francis Howgill**, and developed a high reputation as a **preacher**. During the summer of 1656, questions of **leadership** and the right to judge the actions of other Friends came to a head. Burrough and Howgill found fault with the **ministry** of several, including one **Martha Simmons**. Simmons asked Nayler for support, which he at first refused, but then changed his mind. George Fox was then in **prison**, and leading London Friends decided that Nayler must be taken to see him. The meeting between Fox and

Nayler led to a complete rupture between them. Meanwhile, Simmons and her friends were publicly speaking and writing of Nayler in strongly messianic terms. (Various Friends also used similarly terminology regarding George Fox and **Margaret Fell**, but privately.) In October, Nayler, accompanied by a small group of followers, entered Bristol in a reenactment of Christ's entry into Jerusalem. He was arrested and charged with blasphemy, and after a famous trial before Parliament, was sentenced to be flogged, branded, and imprisoned.

The consequences of this affair reverberated among Quakers for many years. Nayler's conviction had a serious effect on the public reputation of Friends, and from this time, Quakers made an obvious effort to improve their public image. Efforts underway to establish a more formal organization were intensified. Nayler was released in 1659, but Fox would not meet him. Fox was not reconciled with Nayler until 1660, and still begrudged it. Nayler died in 1660, following a mugging. His supposed dying words, affirming a "spirit that delights to do no evil," remain an inspiration for modern Friends. [Rosemary Anne Moore]

NEW FOUNDATION FELLOWSHIP. In 1976, **Lewis Benson** gave a series of talks on "A New Foundation to Build On," which became the impetus for small groups in **North America** and **Britain** who called themselves the New Foundation Fellowship (or "Group" in Britain). The masthead of the newsletter bears the inscription "We Seek the Good of All," taken from the words of Stephen Crisp in 1688. The Fellowship has reinforced the concept that 17th-century Friends are the measure of true Quakerism. They rely on **Christ** and call for a prophetic Gospel message as preached by the apostles and by the **Valiant Sixty**, which they believe has not been fully retained in any living Quaker tradition. [Margery Post Abbott]

"NEW LIGHTS." A label applied to schismatic Quaker groups in the 1790s in **Ireland** and in the 1820s in New England, although no direct connection existed between the two.

The Irish New Lights found their most eloquent leaders in Abraham Shackleton and John Hancock. Both men found it impossible to reconcile Old Testament accounts of warfare and a **God** of vengeance with **Christ** and the New Testament God of love. The leaders of

Dublin **Yearly Meeting**, pushed by the American **minister** William Savery (1777–1848), saw such questioning as deistic and condemned it, disowning Shackleton, Hancock, and their sympathizers.

Thirty years later, in Lynn, Massachusetts, certain members, especially the minister Mary Newhall (1785–1829), troubled some of their peers by spiritualizing certain passages of the **Bible**, and by making claims of **perfection**. Attempts to silence the New Lights at Lynn brought charges of oppression and intolerance. **Disownments** brought the Lynn troubles to an end by 1822. Soon, Mary Newhall preached in nearby New Bedford meeting, where some **elders** attempted to silence her. Two other elders, Mary Rotch and her sister, Elizabeth (Rotch) Rodman (1757–1856), defended Newhall. Attempts to remove the sisters as elders by accusations of deistic sympathies made this an issue of liberty of conscience. It ended with the disownment of Rotch, Rodman, and their supporters, nearly all of whom became **Unitarians**.

Historians have seen parallels between the New Lights and **Hicksite** Friends. Indeed, it seems likely that the expulsion of the New Lights removed the influence from New England Yearly Meeting that would have been most likely to sympathize with **Elias Hicks** in 1827. [Thomas D. Hamm]

NEWLIN, ALGIE INNMANN (1895–1985). Professor of history and political science at **Guilford College** in North Carolina from 1924 to 1966 and member of the first Central Committee of the World Council of Churches. *See* ECUMENISM.

NEW ZEALAND. British Friend Samuel Strong established the first **meeting for worship** in New Zealand in 1842. A general meeting was formed (under London) in 1914. In 1964 New Zealand became an independent yearly meeting, and nine monthly meetings existed at the end of the century.

The school at Wanganui opened in 1920 and lasted 50 years. It was then sold, and the proceeds support a Friends Settlement House for conferences and outreach. New Zealand Friends have maintained the **peace testimony** over many years, opposing both conscription and nuclear weapons, and work through the New Zealand Friends Service Committee (now called Quaker Peace and Service New Zealand).

Aotearoa/New Zealand Yearly Meeting is a member of the National Council of Churches. [David Purnell]

NGAIRA, BENJAMIN S. (1915–1968). Son of Joseph Ngaira (d. 1960), an early Friends leader in **East Africa**, and his wife Maria Mwaitsi (d. 1948), Benjamin Ngaira served as vice-chair of **Friends World Committee for Consultation** for nine years, starting in 1955.

NICHOLSON, SAMUEL EDGAR (1862–1934). Recorded **minister**, journalist, legislator, and **temperance** crusader. Member of the Indiana legislature and later presiding **clerk** of Indiana **Yearly Meeting** (1919–1926), Nicholson was a founder and national secretary of the Anti-Saloon League (1898–1931).

NICHOLSON, WILLIAM (1826–1899). Nicholson, who was born in North Carolina and died in California, was involved in Friends Associated Executive Committee under President Ulysses S. Grant's "peace policy" for **Native Americans**. He was also a member of the Kansas legislature, was active in the Prohibition movement, and participated in the Richmond Conference of 1887. *See* RICHMOND DECLARATION.

NITOBE, INAZO OTA (1862–1933). Inazo Nitobe served as the president of the First National College, Tokyo (1906–1913) and of Tokyo Women's Christian College (1918–ca. 1925), and as professor at Sapporo Agricultural College (1891–1898) and the Imperial Universities of Kyoto and Tokyo. He was a central figure in Japan **Yearly Meeting** for many years (*see* EAST ASIA). Nitobe became a Friend in 1886 while studying at Johns Hopkins University in Maryland. There he also met his wife, Philadelphian Mary Patterson Elkinton (1857–1938). Along with many books, his work included efforts to improve living standards in Taiwan and attempts to decide the ownership of the Ålands Islands in Bothnia Bay between Finland and Sweden when he was Under-Secretary of the League of Nations, as well as improving relations between Japan, China, and Taiwan. [Mary Ellen Chijioke]

NIXON, E. ANNA (1916–). Nixon represented Evangelical **Friends Church**–Eastern Region (EFC-ER) for 44 years as a **missionary** to

India (*see* SOUTH ASIA) starting in 1940, and now lives in Newberg, Oregon. She has written six books on missionary life and history. Her influence in **ecumenism**, theological **education**, and Christian education reaches well beyond Friends. During **World War II**, she was captured by the Japanese on her way to India and held for 39 months in Santo Tomas Internment Camp (STIC) in the Philippines, beginning in January 1942. There, she served as secretary of the STIC Religious Committee, which planned services for the 4,000 prisoners, and taught Sunday school class for the teenage girls. After recuperation, she arrived in India in 1946 where she managed the Friends mission school in Nowgong, Madhya Pradesh. She later did adult literacy, health lessons, and evangelism in rural villages.

From 1955 until 1973, EFC-ER loaned her to work with other missions and churches associated with the Evangelical Fellowship of India. She established a Christian Education department to organize conventions and to produce literature and Christian education materials in 20 languages for all of India for many denominations. From 1973 until 1980 she taught in the Union Biblical Seminary in Yavatmal, Maharashtra (now located in Pune). The seminary opened in 1953 as the first project of the Evangelical Fellowship of India with the sponsorship of 11 denominations. The seminary is supported now by 24 cooperating groups, of which EFC-ER is one. Nixon left India in 1980, but worked until 1984 as a missionary of EFC-ER writing the history of the American Friends Mission in Bundelkhand, India.

NIXON, RICHARD MILHOUS (1913–1994). Thirty-seventh president of the United States. Nixon was born of Quaker parents in Yorba Linda, California, remaining a member of East Whittier **Friends Church** all his life. Educated at **Whittier College** and Duke Law School, Nixon served in the navy during **World War II** and, following his discharge, was elected to the House of Representatives in 1946 and the Senate in 1950. He served as vice president from 1953 to 1961, only to lose an extremely close race for president in 1960. Eight years later he succeeded, this time promising to end the war in Vietnam, a conflict most Quakers opposed; his win was capped by reelection with a substantial victory in 1972. Often displaying evidence of personal insecurity, on more than one occasion he cited his Quaker heritage to answer charges of war making or racism, even as he distanced himself from this background. In 1971, for example, while Cambodia was bombed on his orders, he told the nation that he was a "deeply committed pacifist, perhaps because of my Quaker heritage from my mother." *See* PEACE TESTIMONY.

Refusing to attend regular church services, Nixon initiated and presided over private Sunday gatherings in the White House. His presidency saw the war intensified and extended as he began a process of Vietnamization and gradually removed American forces from Vietnam. Eastern **unprogrammed** Quakers pressed East Whittier Friends Church to discipline Nixon as a member leading the country into war, a move its **leadership** rejected. When facing impeachment for matters associated with the "Watergate affair," he abruptly resigned the presidency in August 1974. For the next 20 years he traveled, wrote numerous books, and delivered speeches in an attempt to vindicate his career. He also assisted succeeding presidents in diplomatic initiatives in China and Russia. As the best-known Friend in the 20th century, Nixon exercised more power than any modern Quaker. [Larry Ingle]

NIYONZIMA, DAVID (1959–). The child of Quaker parents who lived at the Kwibuka **mission** station in Burundi (*see* CENTRAL AFRICA), Niyonzima became deeply involved in **peace** work following the tragedies in Burundi when his brother, many of his friends, and fellow church members were killed. In October 1993, four days after the assassination of Burundi's president, several of his students at the Kwibuka Pastoral Training Center (now succeeded by the **Great Lakes School of Theology**) were killed with no warning. After burying 25 bodies near his home, Niyonzima found himself called to find a way to forgive those who were involved in the killing, rather than seek revenge. He visited others in the area, encouraging reconciliation and ministering to the physical needs of both Hutus and Tutsis, forming a peace committee in 1994. In 1996, the family had to seek refuge in Kenya, where Niyonzima continued to work for peace. In 1998 David, a Hutu, his wife Felicity, a Tutsi, and their family returned to Burundi. He received his bachelor's degree at Kenya Highlands Bible College and a graduate degree in trauma counseling **George Fox University**. Niyonzima is currently **superintendent** of

Burundi **Yearly Meeting** of Friends and coauthor of the 2001 book, *Unlocking Horns: Forgiveness and Reconciliation in Burundi*. [Margery Post Abbott]

NOEL-BAKER, PHILIP JOHN (1889–1982). British pacifist, scholar, and parliamentarian. Philip Noel-Baker was instrumental in suggesting and forming the Friends Ambulance Unit (FAU) in 1914 and was its first commandant (*see* PEACE TESTIMONY). He took part in the creation of the League of Nations and joined its secretariat, working on the problems of refugees. In 1932, he served as principle assistant to the president of the Disarmament Conference in Geneva, Switzerland. He also served as minister of state in the British government starting in 1945 and actively supported the creation of the United Nations; he then became Britain's first representative on the UN Security Council. He served as Britain's secretary of state for air in 1947. During the Berlin Crisis of 1948–1949, he suggested the airlift as a solution to the international stand-off. Noel-Baker received the Nobel Peace Prize in 1959.

Born into a Quaker family near London where his father, Allen Baker, was a manufacturer and politician as well as being active in the Adult School Movement, Noel-Baker's career started as an academic with specialties in economics and international law. He became vice principle of Ruskin College, Oxford, in 1914. Philip Baker married Irene Noel, a driver in the FAU, in 1915. They later adopted the name Noel-Baker. He was first elected to Parliament in 1929. His books include *Disarmament* (1926), *The Juridical Status of the British Dominions in International Law* (1929), and *The Private Manufacture of Armaments* (1937). While not active in Friends organizations most of his adult life, ties remained close, and his 90th birthday party was held at Friends House in London. [Margery Post Abbott]

NORTH AMERICA: UNITED STATES. The first Quakers arrived in North America in 1655 or 1656. By 1660, Friends had won converts in New England, especially in Rhode Island, on Long Island, and in the Chesapeake region. As in **Britain,** Friends faced persecution in some colonies, climaxing in the execution of four Friends in Boston between 1659 and 1661 (*see* BOSTON MARTYRS). In the

1670s and 1680s thousands of Friends settled in West New Jersey and Pennsylvania, colonies that Quakers established (*see* HOLY EXPERIMENT). By 1700, Friends were the third largest denomination in the British colonies.

After 1700, while the number of Quakers remained relatively static in Britain, they grew in North America, largely through natural expansion, though their percentage of the population declined. Individual Friends like **John Woolman** exercised considerable influence as reformers. They were early leaders of antislavery movements and defenders of the rights of **Native Americans** and free blacks (*see* ABOLITION; EQUALITY). When the first **women**'s rights convention was held in **Seneca Falls**, New York, in 1848, Friends dominated it, and Quaker women, such as **Lucretia Coffin Mott** and later, **Susan B. Anthony**, provided much of the movement's leadership. Friends also followed the general movement of the American population westward, with one significant exception—they avoided lands in which slavery existed (*see* MIGRATIONS).

After 1820, American Quakerism splintered. In 1827–1828, **Hicksite** Friends, who were associated with **Elias Hicks** of Long Island, separated from **Orthodox** Friends. While Elias Hicks emphasized the primacy of the Inward **Light**, issues of church governance tended to be more central to the Hicksites than **theology**. The Orthodox, who tended to be wealthier, urban Friends, at least in Philadelphia, emphasized the divinity of **Christ** and the authority of the **Bible**. Although a majority in New York, Philadelphia, and Baltimore **yearly meetings**, Hicksites were a minority among all American Friends. Hicksites experienced a secession of radical reformers in the 1840s and 1850s, who called themselves **Congregational** or **Progressive** Friends. In the 1840s and 1850s the Orthodox divided into **Wilburites**, unbending **Quietist** traditionalists, and **Gurneyites**, more open to non-Quaker influences.

Gurneyite Friends experienced the greatest growth after 1850, establishing seven new yearly meetings. They also changed most rapidly. After 1870, they experienced a wave of **revivalism** in which the traditional **plain dress and speech** was swept away. Most Gurneyite Friends embraced **pastors**, music, higher **education** (*see also* COLLEGES), and **programmed worship**. Some went so far as to embrace the ordinances, **baptism**, and **communion**, (*see also* HOLINESS

MOVEMENT; PASTORAL MOVEMENT). This in turn led to a new round of separations, forming **Conservative** yearly meetings in North Carolina and Iowa that joined with Wilburites.

The last century has seen growing theological and ideological diversity among North American Friends. Friends of Hicksite heritage are now embraced in **Friends General Conference**. Their faith and practice has now merged with that of **independent meetings**. They still practice **unprogrammed worship** and tend to political and religious **liberalism**. Conservative Friends also worship without pastors but retain a more Christo-centric theology. The most diverse Quaker entity is **Friends United Meeting (FUM)**, formed as the Five Years Meeting by Gurneyite Friends in 1902. The **reunification** of Hicksite and Orthodox yearly meetings in New York, and **Canada** and Baltimore's **consolidation**, have brought more diversity into FUM. Influenced by **fundamentalism**, and responding to what they saw as excessive liberalism, other Gurneyites formed the Association of Evangelical Friends (now **Evangelical Friends International**) in 1947. Since 1900, Quakers have been most visible to the larger world as social activists, especially through the **American Friends Service Committee**, founded in 1917. At the beginning of the 21st century, the 93,000 North American Quakers range from New Age **universalists** to fundamentalists. *See also* CANADA; CARIBBEAN; MEXICO. [Thomas D. Hamm]

NORWEGIAN EMIGRATION. Between 1825 and 1900, 30 to 50 percent of Norwegian Quakers emigrated to **North America**, settling initially in New York, later mainly in Iowa, Wisconsin, Illinois, and **Canada**. Their motives were variously religious, political, and economic. Some Friends including Asbjørn Kloster (1823–1876), noted Quaker and **temperance** leader, viewed the departures with ambivalence. For a time, the newcomers set up Norwegian-speaking Friends' **meetings**, but gradually most became integrated within local American **yearly meetings**. [Pink Dandelion]

NOTION. Used by 17th-century Friends as a derogatory term for abstract theological reasoning and concepts considered to be out of the **Truth**.

–O–

OPENING. Early Friends often spoke of the spirit of **God** opening their understandings and their hearts or opening the principles of **truth** to them. This sense of immediate, **continuing revelation** of divine purpose was central to their faith of **Christ** present and **leading** them directly. When describing **worship**, they might speak of the power of the Lord over all creating openings in which one of them was led to speak to the **gathered meeting**. [Margery Post Abbott]

OPPORTUNITY. A time of **unprogrammed worship** held at any time or place, sometimes occurring without human prearrangement. This ancient Quaker practice, drawn from Matthew 18:20, has been revived in recent years as Friends rediscover its value for spiritual friendship or mentoring and for visits in the homes of members.

ORTHODOX QUAKERISM. Orthodox Friends are those who emerged from the **Great Separation** of the 1820s with views on certain doctrinal questions similar to those of **evangelicals** of other denominations. Orthodox Quakerism has proved the most prolific of Quaker parent stems, with **Beanite Friends**, **Conservative Friends**, **Friends United Meeting**, and **Evangelical Friends International**, as well as some unaffiliated **yearly meetings**, tracing their ancestry to it.

Quakers and historians of Quakerism still debate the sources of Orthodox Quakerism. In the 1820s, **Hicksite** Friends argued that Orthodox **theology** represented a fundamental break with traditional Quakerism. Certain facts that lend themselves to such an interpretation are beyond dispute. Many Friends in **North America** had by the 1820s formed strong ties with non-Quaker **evangelicals** in **philanthropic**, reform, **business**, civic, and political groups (*see* CIVIL GOVERNMENT; POLITICS). Many Friends in **Britain** had formed similar ties. For many Hicksites, such ties had drawn Orthodox Friends away from primitive Quaker beliefs. In turn, the Orthodox perceived Hicksites as tainted by association with **Unitarianism** and with skeptics like Robert Dale Owen (1801–1877) and Frances Wright (1775–1852). Orthodox Friends claimed simply that they were holding to early Quaker beliefs.

Orthodox Friends in the 1820s saw themselves as defending certain fundamental beliefs. These included the authority of Scripture, the divinity of **Christ**, and the nature of the **atonement**. Orthodox Friends argued that the **Bible**, rather than appeals to other revelation or the Inner **Light**, should be the final arbiter of doctrinal questions. They bitterly attacked **Elias Hicks**'s argument that Jesus Christ achieved divinity through perfect obedience, rather than being born as **God** incarnate. And they emphasized the redeeming power of the blood of Christ as shed on the **cross**, which Hicksites tended to spiritualize. Most Quaker **distinctive** beliefs and practices were not an issue—both sides embraced the Inward Light, a nonpastoral **ministry**, pacifism (*see* PEACE), and **plain dress and speech**.

Historians of the separation have seen other common characteristics of the Orthodox. In the urban parts of Philadelphia Yearly Meeting the Orthodox tended to be those Friends who were successfully adjusting to the new market economy. Orthodox leaders there tended to emphasize authority, especially that of **elders**. It is unclear whether these characteristics were true of Orthodox Friends elsewhere.

Orthodox Friends embraced virtually all of the yearly meetings in New England, Virginia, and North Carolina, and about 80 percent of Indiana Yearly Meeting. Ohio Yearly Meeting probably divided about evenly. In New York and Philadelphia yearly meetings, Orthodox Friends made up only about a third of the membership; in Baltimore only about 20 percent.

After the separation, Orthodox Friends gave increasing attention to doctrinal statements in their books of **discipline**. They also tended to deal swiftly with doctrinal deviation. That brought conflict in the 1840s and 1850s, as Orthodox Friends divided into **Gurneyite** and **Wilburite** parties. Today, the Orthodox emphasis on doctrines shared with other evangelical Christians continues to be central to many Friends. [Thomas D. Hamm]

OTISITES. One of the two factions (named for James Otis, their **clerk**) that divided the small **Wilburite** New York Yearly Meeting in 1859. A similar separation of Otisites and **Kingites** took place among New England Wilburites in 1863.

OUTREACH. A term used particularly among **liberal Friends** since the mid-20th century to describe efforts to publicize Quakerism and to introduce inquirers to it. It is distinctive from **mission** in its low-key approach. Those involved in outreach seek to inform rather than convert.

OVERSEERS. Individuals charged with the pastoral care of the **meeting**, overseers visit families, keep in touch with distant members and give confidential attention to family crises, special needs, conflicts between individuals needing mediation, and labor with members whose actions cause scandal or violate Friends' principles (*see* LEADERSHIP). In the past, overseers also had responsibility for physical property. [Paul Lacey]

–P–

PAINTER, LEVINUS KING (1889–1983). North American pastor, **mission** supporter, and social activist, Painter worked with coal miners in western Pennsylvania (1936–1939) and helped establish clothing and food **relief** for Palestinians in 1949 and 1950. He was instrumental in the establishment of **East Africa Yearly Meeting** and made five visits to Kenya over a period of 25 years.

PARNELL, JAMES (1637?–1656). Noted writer and preacher. One of the **Valiant Sixty**, Parnell was a teenage convert to Quakerism in 1653 who became its first martyr when he died in **prison** in Essex aged 19.

PASTOR. The majority of **Friends churches** today have full or part-time paid pastors. The **pastoral movement** of the late 19th century changed both the manner of **worship** and the way pastoral care is provided in many **meetings**. Pastors generally offer a message and arrange the program for **worship**, although the latter is often done in conjunction with the **elders** or a **committee** on worship and **ministry**. In some churches responsibility for offering the message may rotate among members of the congregation as well as the pastor or members of the pastoral team. Because **preaching** is expected to be led by **God**, many instances can be cited where pastors have left an unscheduled period of **unprogrammed worship** when they found no inspiration for a message.

Normally, the local congregation extends the call for pastoral leadership. The **superintendent** of the **yearly meeting** may suggest possible names or provide other assistance in the process as requested. The pastor is a recorded **minister** when possible, but too few Quakers are available for this service, and churches may find themselves hiring pastors from other denominations. The pastor and the elders or **overseers** share responsibility for the spiritual and pastoral care of the congregation. [Margery Post Abbott]

PASTORAL MOVEMENT. After 200 years of encouraging each individual to find his or her meaningful **ministry** as an expression of the leading of the **Light** of **Christ** within, the pastoral movement developed among Friends in **North America** between 1850 and 1890. The reasons for this development are as varied as they are complex. The external forces driving this innovation included urbanization, industrialization, the westward **migration** (enhanced by the telegraph and the railroad), the ongoing Methodist **revivals**, and the **holiness movement**. The revivals brought an influx of converts from non-Quaker backgrounds, rising demands for full-time ministry, and a shift from spirit-centered waiting to pulpit-centered **worship**.

While there were few pastors before 1870, by 1880, many **Gurneyite** Friends had moved away from the early forms of Quaker life and worship (*see* PECULIARITY). They had come to place a premium on the authority of the **Bible** and the primacy of **preaching** while diminishing the **distinctives** of Quaker life and thought. This trend resulted in the elevation of the pastoral office and the development of a full-time, professional clergy by the 1890s to oversee the life and ministry of the **church**. These **meetings** began to look similar to churches in other denominations, especially those influenced by the great revivals sweeping the American frontier. The results of this change included the decline of the itinerant and largely impromptu preaching **ministry**, acceptance of regularly scheduled and prepared sermons by pastors, and eventual significant decline in the recording of **women** ministers.

By 1900, the pastoral movement was so deeply entrenched and so widely embraced that it had incorporated every Gurneyite **yearly meeting** except Baltimore into its fold. This development signified the shift in power from **elder-**led meetings to pastor-led churches and worship became **programmed**. The professionalization of the pastorate led to a decline of **women** in the ministry in Gurneyite churches for much of the 20th century, a trend that has recently reversed to some degree.

Throughout the 20th century, the pastoral movement continued to garner widespread interest and support and was the form of worship spread by most modern **missionaries**. As a result, a practice begun in North America has proliferated as Friends' ministry spreads throughout the world. [Gayle D. Beebe]

PAUL, ALICE (1885–1977). American feminist, alumna of **Swarthmore College** and leader first in the **women**'s suffrage movement and then for an Equal Rights Amendment to the U.S. Constitution.

PEACE. One of the best-known statements of **George Fox** and other early Friends, the declaration to King Charles II in 1660/61: "We utterly deny all outward wars and strife and fightings with outward weapons, for any end or under any pretence whatsoever. And this is our testimony to the whole world." Friends came to understand in the early years of the movement that the spirit of **Christ** would never move a person to kill either for human kingdoms or for the kingdom of **God**. They believed in accord with the New Testament doctrine of James 4, that "lusts," such as greed, hatred, and pride, were at the root of all war and that they lived under the new **covenant** whereby all people would come to live in peace. This belief was at the root of what has come to be known as the Friends' **peace testimony**.

Friends' understanding of peace has always involved pacifism, or the refusal to fight, and **conscientious objection** to war. It also includes active peacemaking efforts, reconciliation, **relief work** for victims of war, and actions to remove the causes of war. In the 20th century, Friends were central to the formation of a wide variety of peace groups such as the **Women's International League for Peace and Freedom** (*see* BALCH, EMILY GREENE) and the Fellowship of Reconciliation (*see* MUSTE, A. J.) and many programs promoting personal nonviolence, such as the Alternatives to Violence Program (*see* ANGELL, STEPHEN). [Margery Post Abbott]

PEACE AND/OR SERVICE AGENCIES. Quaker bodies recognized by a **yearly meeting**(s) to promote **relief** and development programs, and/or address issues of **peace**, human rights, human flourishing, justice, and/or a sustainable **environment** in the world.

In the 17th and 18th centuries, Friends took collections to help other persecuted groups in **prison** and for the relief of war victims and refugees. They played a prominent part in the national human rights campaigns against slavery (*see* ABOLITION). The humility of **John Woolman** in expressing his intention to love and learn from America's **Native American** peoples in the 1760s became a model for future generations of Quaker service work.

The 19th century saw Friends in **Britain** continuing to join relief operations of other agencies on the European mainland before establishing the first Friends Relief **Committee** in 1823 to help "distressed Greeks." Friends were also deeply involved in Irish famine relief. The first Standing Committee or Association, as such, the Friends Foreign **Mission** Association, was founded in 1868 to share the Gospel but soon turned to building schools, hospitals, and orphanages. In the United States the **Friends Freedmen's Association** was created during the American Civil War. The first official Friends War Victims Relief Committee adopted the black and red Quaker Service star emblem in 1870–1871 during the Franco-Prussian War. These institutions were sometimes quasi-autonomous and not official **yearly meeting** bodies.

The 20th century's wars, armaments, refugees, and recognition of world poverty and pollution enhanced public recognition of Friends' **peace testimony**. Friends developed better organized war relief work emphasizing reconciliation; **Quaker International Centres** in world capitals (*see* HEATH, CARL), including the United Nations (*see* QUAKER UNITED NATIONS OFFICE); off-the-record conferences for diplomats; discrete peace missions to political leaders in violent conflicts; techniques of sustainable development, and campaigns to increase official overseas aid; and support to national anti-war and disarmament campaigns. Other global issues at the new millennium include the environment, child soldiers, race relations, training in nonviolence, the regulation of world trade, peace education, and HIV/AIDS.

By the early 21st century, approximately 15 main international peace and/or service agencies or committees have evolved in wealthier industrial countries. They are distributed in North America (6), **Asia** and Pacific (2), and Europe (7). They vary in size from the **American Friends Service Committee** and British Quaker Peace and Social Witness, the successor to Friends Service Council (1928–1978), and Peace and Social Service (1978–2001) to small individual yearly meetings with peace or service committees (or institutions) but no paid staff. **Friends World Committee for Consultation** keeps a database of overseas service projects, which are mainly in the **Middle East**, **Africa**, Indochina, **Central** and **South America**, and Eastern Europe. Practically every yearly meeting has its own indigenous programs, institutions, and advocacy. [Andrew Clark]

PEACE DALE. "Friedenstal" (Peace Dale), the first and only Quaker settlement in **continental Europe,** was founded in 1792 near Pyrmont in the heart of Germany. This utopian settlement consisted of several modern communal houses, workshops, and the first German Quaker school, directed by Theodor Marschhausen. The main significance of the settlement lay in its **educational** endeavors, such as a new pedagogy, new books, and the founding of a girls boarding school by Judith Bawier (1759–1807), attracting visitors such as Johann Wolfgang von Goethe. Daily life in Peace Dale was in sharp contrast to "the world": social behavior was strict, and religious life was pietistic.

The Napoleonic Wars ended the settlement's initial prosperity. Bankruptcy, internal conflicts, and Prussian rule accelerated the decline, despite extended stays by **Thomas Shillitoe** and **Elizabeth Fry** in 1840–1841. The majority of the 70 inhabitants emigrated to the United States, the last **meeting** was held in 1870, and the houses sold. Some of the old Quaker houses still stand on the outskirts of Bad Pyrmont, and the restored meetinghouse has been used as the center of German **Yearly Meeting** since 1932. [Claus Bernet]

PEACE TESTIMONY. Early Friends adopted a consistent policy of opposition to participation in war only after their first decade. **George Fox** refused to join Oliver Cromwell's army, but many soldiers became Friends (*see* PURITANISM). After the revolt of the Fifth Monarchy Men shortly after the restoration of a Stuart king, Charles II, in 1660/61, Friends declared their opposition to war "for any end, or under any pretense whatsoever" (*see* PEACE). However, in **Britain** for the next century the peace testimony meant not rebelling and not serving in the army. Colonists in early **North America** faced different conditions. In Pennsylvania, **William Penn**, as proprietor, was responsible for military defense, but Friends in the Assembly refused to create a militia (*see* CIVIL GOVERNMENT). When the British Crown demanded money for war, the Assembly on several occasions voted funds, but always stipulated that such monies be used for grain or feeding **Native Americans**.

After Major General Edward Braddock's defeat in 1755 at the beginning of the French and Indian War, the Pennsylvania Assembly voted a war tax and to create a militia. As a consequence, Philadelphia **Yearly Meeting** brought sufficient pressure on Quaker Assembly members to cause a number to resign, leaving Friends without a majority in wartime. Some Friends refused to pay the war tax, though the yearly meeting could reach no consensus on whether to endorse or oppose this practice. Members who served in the militia were **disowned**.

The American Revolution brought an end to Quaker political power in Pennsylvania and New Jersey. American yearly meetings advised against participation in **politics** when it became apparent that constitutional protest would lead to a war for independence and political office would require collaboration with the military effort. Friends officially became neutral in early 1776 and declined to take loyalty oaths (*see* TRUTH) or affirmations of loyalty to either side, refused to pay a fee for not serving in the military, and opposed paying taxes to governments of uncertain legitimacy. Friends in all the colonies compiled a list of goods seized by the new states and disowned approximately one-fifth of the eligible adult males for having served in the military. *See also* FREE QUAKERS.

British Quakers played an influential role in the emergence of early 19th-century peace societies. Under the leadership of **Joseph Sturge**, the British Peace Society broadened its focus from a biblically based opposition to war to advocate arbitration, peace congresses, expanded suffrage, and free trade. Sturge and **John Bright** created a newspaper to advocate peace in opposition to the Crimean War (1853–1856). Although a few North American Quakers became prominent in antebellum nonresistance societies, most yearly meetings advised members to avoid participation in outside organizations.

Even while seeking to end slavery, Friends feared a war. During the American Civil War, Friends often felt compelled to choose between **abolition** of slavery and peace. Many Indiana Quakers joined the Union armies, and no disciplinary action was taken. Other Friends, particularly in Philadelphia, paid for substitutes. Yearly meetings provided aid for the freedmen and supported teachers and schools during Reconstruction (*see* AFRICAN AMERICANS).

In World War I, some 30 percent of eligible British Friends joined up. Some served in Friends ambulance units, a few went to jail as **conscientious objectors (COs)**, and more joined in reconstruction work in France. British Friends, who sought to provide service as an alternative to fighting, pioneered most of the aid techniques in France that would be used after 1917 by the **American Friends Service Committee (AFSC)**. As a way of promoting reconciliation at the end of the war, British and American Friends took charge of a program to feed German children and instituted aid projects in Russia, Poland, Austria, and Serbia. Providing **relief** to the victims of war would remain a central focus of the peace testimony during the 20th century.

During the 1920s, Friends insisted that the causes of war were deeply embedded in society and worked to counter racism, colonialism, economic exploitation, and extreme nationalism. They sought disarmament and approval of the League of Nations. During the 1930s, Friends were inspired by the nonviolent techniques of **Gandhi** as a means of resolving international grievances. British and American Friends helped Jews escape from Nazi Germany, but also opposed rearmament and, in 1939, sought a negotiated settlement.

During World War II, while only 15 percent of eligible British Quakers enlisted, most North American young Friends served in the military, but all yearly meetings upheld the official policy of pacifism. AFSC helped administer the **Civilian Public Service Camps** for COs and visited "absolutists" who were in **prison**. Friends opposed the confinement of the Nisei (Americans of Japanese ancestry) to internment camps, spoke out against saturation bombing of Germany and Japan, and worked for the creation of a United Nations.

During the Cold War, some Friends attempted to promote dialogue between the Soviet Union and the West, and many opposed the arms race, deplored the reliance on nuclear weapons, and worked with Arabs and Israelis in seeking peace in the Middle East, while some supported the campaign against Communism. During the Vietnam War, a few Quakers sent medical supplies to both sides, and more joined demonstrations against the war. They also attempted to serve as intermediaries in civil wars in Nigeria, Northern and Southern Rhodesia, and South Africa. Friends were also active in many peace groups such as the New Call to Peacemaking (*see* HADLEY, NORVAL).

By the 1990s Friends expanded the definition of the peace testimony from negative peace (i.e., the absence of war among nations) to positive or structural peace, which included a focus on the causes of poverty, domestic violence, **environmental** degradation, racism, and sexism (*see* EQUALITY). Following the terrorist attacks in the United States in September 2001, many Friends actively called for a response based on international law enforcement and social justice, rather than military action, to remove the cause of world terrorism. Recognizing the correlation between foreign policy and how a nation handled internal disputes, Friends sought to apply the techniques of nonviolent conflict resolution to families, schools, and the nation. In more than three hundred years of opposition to war, Friends have often redefined and expanded their peace testimony. [J. William Frost]

PEASE, EDWARD (1767–1858). Scion of a banking family (*see* BUSINESS), Pease financed the Stockton and Darlington Railway, Britain's first steam-powered railway. He was the father of Britain's first Quaker Member of Parliament, Joseph Pease.

PECULIARITY. Friends from the beginning refused to engage in "normal" everyday practices such as greeting their peers or betters by doffing their hats (*see* HAT HONOR), or using the polite plural form of "thou," "you." From quite early on, Friends were advised to be wary of the "worldes fashions," believing them to be counter to true Christianity. **Testimonies** against the swearing of oaths, the payment of church **tithes**, excess profit, and the bearing of arms, which they initially saw as **Truth**, applicable to all people, gave these Quakers an innate peculiarity. **Robert Barclay** in his *Apology* affirmed this increasing sense of Friends as "His people," set apart from a corrupt world.

With the advent of **Restoration** Quakerism, these practices began to be institutionalized and regulated on both sides of the Atlantic.

Friends moved away from being active fighters with **Christ** in the **Lamb's War** who would overcome "the world" and its **evils**. They became more concerned with protecting themselves from the corrupt physical world in which they lived, while seeking a greater intimacy with **God**, drawing increasingly on Paul's characterization of Christians as "peculiar people" (Titus 2:14 AV). Reinforced by the **Quietist** mistrust of human desire, these Friends enlisted outward conventions of **plain dress and speech** to support the inward state of purity they sought to achieve. For a group wary of outward religious forms, these outward codes of peculiarity acted as a continual reminder of all they sought amidst the "wearisome pilgrimage" of life.

In the late 17th and 18th centuries, spiritual delinquency included the **arts**, attending the theater, playing music (even owning a piano was a offense that could lead to **disownment**), and reading novels, all of which Barclay described as vain customs and pursuits. The testimonies to plain dress and speech were continued. Even men's wigs were policed. Marrying a non-Quaker was outlawed (*see* MARRIAGE). Quakers built a **hedge** between themselves and the world to protect their own purity and to model true Christianity to others. Given the state of human nature and of the world, it was only to be expected that many would fall from the path and "walk disorderly." As the number of offenses rose during the 18th century, so did the volume of delinquency. The appointment of **elders** to visit Quaker households increased adherence to the **discipline**, but the number of Friends who were disowned caused many meetings to shrink.

By the 1850s and 1860s those Friends who questioned the theological basis and pragmatic value of the hedge began to win reforms. Between 1845 and 1850, for example, **yearly meetings** first permitted gravestones if they were all of equal height and bore no more than names and dates. In 1860 **London Yearly Meeting** allowed marriage to non-Quakers. In 1861, the advice on plain dress and plain speech was dropped, as Friends argued they would maintain a testimony on **simplicity** inwardly. The rate of such changes varied greatly among **North American** yearly meetings, but all moved in the same direction. [Pink Dandelion]

PEMBERTON FAMILY. Eighteenth-century **North American** merchants, reformers, and **abolitionists**. Israel Pemberton (1684/85–1754) bequeathed to his sons— Israel (1715–1779), James (1723–1809), and John (1727–1795)—not just a successful merchant house and prominence in Pennsylvania **politics** but a commitment to the affairs of the **Religious Society of Friends**. In the late 1740s, the three brothers became leaders of the reform movement. John, a recorded **minister**, accompanied **John Churchman** on his religious travels in England from 1751 to 1753. Either Israel Jr.—head of the family firm and sometimes called "the king of the Quakers"—or James was **clerk** of Philadelphia **Yearly Meeting** for all but three years between 1750 and 1781. Both served significant periods in the Pennsylvania legislature. By 1756, Israel had retired from politics, but James resigned with other Friends rather than vote for measures in support of the French and Indian War (*see* PEACE TESTIMONY). All three were among the 19 Quakers exiled to Winchester, Virginia, from September 1777 to April 1778 for refusing to take an **oath** of loyalty to the revolutionary government, after which Friends never again exercised the same commercial power in Philadelphia (*see* BUSINESS AND ECONOMICS). All three brothers supported the antislavery movement within Philadelphia Yearly Meeting. James was a founder and later president of the Pennsylvania Society for Promoting the Abolition of Slavery. [Mary Ellen Chijioke]

PENAL REFORM. The foundation of Friends' modern concern with penal reform started with the Quaker experience of imprisonment in the 17th century. **Margaret Fell** and **John Bellers**, in particular, encouraged **prison** visiting. They consistently, and eventually absolutely, opposed capital punishment. Friends helped establish the first penitentiary in America where their endorsement of solitary confinement as a means of reform was later seen as misguided and was much-regretted. **William Penn**'s "**holy experiment**" liberalized criminal justice in the American colonies. Individual Friends were involved in an **ecumenical** effort to create the Walnut Street Jail in Philadelphia in 1790, which replaced whipping and the death penalty (for burglary as well as murder) with a view of criminals as redeemable human beings. It introduced the ideas of trained staff, single cells for men and women, and the use of silence and solitude for hardened criminals. Members of the organization that founded the jail later became the Pennsylvania Prison Society, and many of their ideas became the foundation of the modern prison system.

These, and above all the work of **Elizabeth Fry**, are part of Friends' heritage.

In the 19th century, in both **Britain** and **North America**, individual Quakers supported every effort to reform prisons (only sometimes at the formal behest of their **meetings**). Quakers formed Britain's first penal reform body, and were key figures in the second: William Tallack (1831–1908), hitherto a leading campaigner against capital punishment, was the Howard Association's first chairman.

After World War I, a wave of Quaker and socialist-inspired penal reform occurred, based on the testimony of imprisoned **conscientious objectors (COs)**. One CO, Stephen Hobhouse (1881–1961), coauthored an immensely influential report on prisons. British Friends revived ideas about victim compensation and put objection to capital punishment on a statistically stronger footing. After **World War II**, the support system that wartime British Friends had established for imprisoned COs evolved into the present system of Quaker prison **ministers**. The Penal Affairs **Committee** campaigned against capital punishment until its abolition in 1969 and promoted alternatives to prison.

In the 1960s, various Quaker probation officers developed new ways of working with homeless offenders and helped evolve "intermediate treatment" for young offenders. They established Glebe House in Britain, building on the lifework of David Wills, a pioneer of therapeutic communities for young people. In 1962, the Women's **Yearly Meeting** in **East Africa** undertook a program of prison ministry at the urging of **Rasoah Mutua**. These women gave spiritual support to women prisoners, communicating the Christian faith as they knew it.

Historically, a similar pattern of support for rehabilitation of criminals had occurred in North America, until, suddenly, in 1971, the **American Friends Service Committee (AFSC)** condemned the hypocrisy of a system that claimed to rehabilitate prisoners but which actually abused civil liberties and involved essentially punitive practices. In *Struggle for Justice*, AFSC argued that a fair form of retributive punishment was the best way forward. It was hugely influential in international debate on prison reform, but may have accidentally contributed to the later expansion of incarceration in America. Later in the 20th century, many meetings and individual

Friends championed the idea of restorative justice, which seeks to *restore* as far as practical all parties—victim, offender, the community at large—to wholeness.

The Alternatives to Violence Project was created in 1975 by Friends in New York Yearly Meeting as an extension of the nonviolence training techniques developed for the civil rights and antiwar movements (*see* ANGELL, STEPHEN). The program, which attempts to get at some of the root causes of violence by working with inmates to change their behavior, has since been adapted for use in schools as well as prisons, and its use in prisons has spread around the world to such places as **Central Africa**.

In 1982, several English Friends formed Quakers in Criminal Justice as a support group for Friends working in the system as professionals or volunteers. Jan Arriens (1943–) established Lifelines, offering support, via letters, to prisoners on death row in America. The Alternatives to Violence Project was introduced from America and supported by Britain Yearly Meeting until it became independent in 1997. Prison psychiatrist Bob Johnson (1937–) campaigned against the orthodoxy of "untreatability" in his profession. Entering the 21st century, Friends sought to broaden the field from "penal affairs" to "community justice," encompassing crime prevention as well as prison and probation issues. [Mike Nellis]

PENDLE HILL, ENGLAND. In Lancashire, in the north of England. Pendle Hill was the site of **George Fox**'s 1652 revelation that there was a "great people to be gathered." This was the start of his highly successful **missionary** activity that summer when the **Valiant Sixty** gathered around Fox and a time popularly acknowledged as the beginning of what became the **Religious Society of Friends**.

PENDLE HILL (WALLINGFORD, PENNSYLVANIA). Founded in 1930, Pendle Hill is a Quaker center for study and contemplation offering programs open to people of all faiths. **Anna and Howard Brinton** established many of its programs, aiming to balance the inner and the outer life, relying on daily **meeting for worship** and for business, and focusing on the Quaker way of life. Pendle Hill also **publishes** a regular series of pamphlets and books on Quakerism. [Margery Post Abbott]

PENINGTON, ISAAC (1616–1679) and MARY PROUDE SPRINGETT (1625?–1682). Isaac Penington was the eldest son of the wealthy **Puritan** politician and lord mayor of London, Isaac Penington (1587?–1660) and his wife, Abigail Allen Penington. The younger Isaac went to Cambridge University, but did not pursue a profession. He was deeply searching spiritually and in a state of spiritual darkness, when he met and married Mary Proude Springett in 1654. She was the only child of the wealthy John and Anne Proude (both died in 1628), and widow of William Springett, a devoted Puritan and Cromwellian officer who died in camp of a fever in 1644.

The Peningtons were **convinced** and joined Friends about 1658 after many struggles to give up their lives totally to the guidance and direction of the Inward **Christ**. Their struggle to center their lives on living out **God**'s will led to a total transformation of their lifestyle. **Thomas Ellwood** took them as foster parents after he became a Friend. As wealthy Friends, they suffered greatly for adopting the **plain dress and speech** of the Quakers and for their refusal to take **oaths**, forfeiting much of their property (*see* TRUTH).

Penington was imprisoned six times for his Quakerism. This destroyed his health but deepened his faith, which he shared freely with others. He was recognized as a gifted and inspired **minister** of the Gospel. Both were involved in establishing Jordans **Meeting,** and in spiritually encouraging others. He wrote many letters of encouragement and spiritual counsel as well as tracts explaining the Quaker faith, and she, a moving spiritual autobiography. They had five children (John, Isaac, William, Edward, and Mary). Gulielma Maria Posthuma Springett (1643/44–1693), the daughter of Mary Proude and William Springett, became the first wife of **William Penn**. [Virginia Schurman]

PENN, WILLIAM (1644–1718). Minister, theologian, advocate of religious liberty, and the founder of Pennsylvania. Son of Admiral Sir William Penn (1621–1670), one of England's great naval commanders, William Penn attended a grammar school. He was expelled from Oxford in 1661 because of his **Puritan** sympathies. Sent to France, Penn returned a gentleman, studied law briefly at the Inns of Court, managed his father's estates in **Ireland**, and considered becoming a soldier.

As a young boy, Penn had heard the Quaker **Thomas Loe** preach. In Ireland he heard Loe again and was **convinced**. In spite of strong parental opposition, Penn identified publicly with Quakers and began writing in defense of his new faith. His tract, *Sandy Foundation Shaken* (1668), brought imprisonment in the Tower of London on a charge of heresy. There Penn wrote the first edition of *No **Cross**, No Crown*, a plea for a life of surrender to **God**. Released from prison after publishing a tract clarifying his beliefs, Penn became a leading **minister**, active defender of his faith in public debates, advocate with the Crown to release imprisoned Friends, and supporter of religious toleration. Arrested with **William Meade** in 1670 for violating the Conventicle Act, his trial—termed Bushels Case—established the precedent that the verdict of an English jury cannot be coerced.

In 1680, in payment for a debt owed to his father, Penn obtained a grant for a colony in **North America**, that Charles II named Pennsylvania in honor of the admiral. Before this, Penn had spend six years in helping to establish West New Jersey as a Quaker enclave. Penn envisioned Pennsylvania, which he once called the "**Holy Experiment**," as a refuge for Friends and other religious dissenters where they could practice their religions freely and be guaranteed their property and political rights. The early laws guaranteed religious liberty, i.e., no established **church**, no **tithe**, no persecution. Penn visited Pennsylvania in 1682, laid out Philadelphia, and ratified the laws.

A dispute with Lord Baltimore over the Maryland–Pennsylvania border required Penn's return to England where James II had become king. Penn saw in James's friendship an opportunity to achieve religious toleration. After the Glorious Revolution of 1688, Penn's association with James brought suspicion, and he went into hiding. Here he produced some of his most creative writings, including the "Preface" to **George Fox**'s *Journal* (reissued as *Rise and Progress of People called Quakers*) and *Fruits of Solitude in Reflections and Maxims*.

Pennsylvania proved difficult to control. From the beginning Penn and the Quaker settlers disagreed over the role of the Assembly and the necessity to pay taxes (*see* PEACE). Penn was careless about finances, spent beyond his income, and received little money from his colony. He lived for nine months in debtors' prison in 1707 until a group of Quakers paid his debts. He was negotiating a possible sale of his right of government to the Crown when he had a stroke in 1711.

In 1672 Penn married Gulielma Maria Posthuma Springett (1643/44–1693). He remarried in 1695, to Hannah Callowhill (1670–1727), daughter of a Bristol merchant. She managed his affairs after his stroke and later acted as proprietor of Pennsylvania. None of his children who survived to adulthood remained Friends. [J. William Frost]

PENNEY, NORMAN (1859–1933). Librarian to **London Yearly Meeting** from 1900 after years of **mission** work. Penney was a major historian, bringing to light original Quaker documents, including the *Spence Manuscript* (a 1674 version of **George Fox**'s *Journal*, prior to the major editing in 1694 by **Thomas Ellwood**). The document had been lost for much of its existence.

PENNINGTON, LEVI TALBOTT (1875–1975). North American **minister** and educator, Pennington served as president of Pacific (later **George Fox) College** in Newberg, Oregon, from 1911 until 1941.

PENTECOSTALISM. At the day of Pentecost in Jerusalem following the death and resurrection of Jesus, his followers gathered in an upper room. "All of them were filled with the **Holy Spirit** and began to speak in other languages, as the Spirit gave them the ability" (Acts 2:4). By the 20th century, speaking in tongues had become an issue for Friends as other churches that recognize ecstatic gifts have rapidly spread worldwide.

While some Friends experience speaking in tongues as a personal spiritual practice, modern Friends have generally not accepted ecstatic gifts as a part of the church service, recognizing instead gifts given for the common good in accordance with Paul's teachings in 1 Corinthians 12–14. In **East Africa**, a separation occurred in 1927 as Kifa Ayuba became the founder of the new *Avakambuli* (African Holy Spirit) or *Dini ya Roho* (Church of the Holy Spirit) with its headquarters at Lugala, Kakamega in Kenya. In **North America**, the Vineyard Movement was formed in the 1970s by John Wimber, after he resigned as **pastor** of Yorba Linda Friends Church in California. *See also* LUPTON, LEVI. [Margery Post Abbott]

PERFECTION. Many pilgrimages of faith have begun from hunger for moral perfection, dedication, and personal purity. Early Friends took seriously Jesus' admonition to his disciples to "Be perfect, therefore, as your heavenly father is perfect" in loving everyone impartially (Matthew 5:48) and to the rich young man: "If you wish to be perfect, go, sell your possessions. . . . Then come, follow me" (Matthew 19:21). Quakers, like many Christians—and also Hindus, Buddhists, Jews, and Muslims—rejected moral compromise.

In his boyhood, **George Fox** struggled with the issues of human frailty, moral compromise, and perfection, until he found that the "oceans of light and darkness" were also within himself. He also experienced a sense of purity like Adam's before the Fall. He seldom later claimed perfection, but like most Friends in 1652–1672, preached that perfection and sinlessness were possible for everyone, though only after months or years of agonizing self-searching and inner surrender to the **Light** that illuminated **evil**.

Friends rejected self-originated good deeds as sternly as did the **Puritans**. Puritans called Friends self-righteous and blasphemous. When Puritan pastors urged parishioners to be aware of their lifelong weaknesses to accept divine forgiveness, Friends accused them of "pleading for **sin**." When **Richard Baxter** said, "Christ's kingdom is an hospital; he has no subjects in it but diseased ones," **James Nayler** replied that **Christ** cures them. Responses to Puritans and Nayler's disgrace at Bristol forced Friends to explain carefully that they claimed perfection not for themselves as humans but for the **Holy Spirit** as it led them.

Early Friends sought perfect response to **God**'s will and guidance, rather than perfect humility (like Saint Francis), perfect love (like John Wesley), or perfect following of biblical commands (like Mennonites). In the late 19th century this would underlie the clash of traditional Friends and Wesleyans over the nature of Holiness: slow-won or instant (*see* HOLINESS MOVEMENT).

Isaac Penington, **Robert Barclay**, and **William Penn**, the best schooled of the second generation of Friends, admitted that the perfect obedience of children would differ from that of mature adults, according to "the measure" of Light each had been given. The resulting relativity allowed such Friends to plead for tolerance and honesty from people not yet Friends, and to avoid mere condemnation of conscientious people who had not yet rejected war or **sacraments**. They still assumed that **Truth** would lead everyone to unity as they became Friends when more Light was given them. The contrast between divine guidance in personal decisions and "**openings**" of truth regarding **testimonies** underlay Friends' belief that the outward **discipline** of customs and behavior was required (*see* PECULIARITY).

The belief that there is one Truth broke down in the 19th century. Conflicting doctrines held as Truth by earnest Friends led to the **Hicksite/Orthodox** separation of 1827. In the American Civil War, Quaker men were torn over the dictates of the **peace testimony** and their desire to volunteer and thus fight to end slavery (*see* ABOLITION). In the years after the American Civil War, the holiness movement appealed strongly to Friends, with its central doctrine of perfect love and reaffirmation of a doctrine of perfection. By the 20th century, Quaker perfectionism turned into more individual and inward channels. [Hugh Barbour]

PERROT, JOHN (d. 1665). Irish Friend, **convinced** in 1655 by **Edward Burrough**. In 1657, Perrot left **Ireland** and, with five other Friends including **Mary Fisher** and **John Luffe**, set out for Turkey to meet with the sultan in Constantinople. It proved difficult to get into Turkey and the group divided. Feeling led to speak with the pope, Luffe and Perrot ended up in Rome. By the end of the year 1658/59, Luffe was dead, and Perrot, imprisoned as mad, was tortured. He remained in jail until 1661.

Perrot's accounts of his confinement elevated his status among British Friends. However, he created controversy and schism when he wrote that **God** had instructed him that it was wrong to follow the Quaker practice of removing hats in prayer (*see* HAT HONOR). Perrot later also stated that setting fixed times for **meeting for worship** was counter to divinc guidance. Perrot won the support of **Isaac Penington** and others for a time, but as **George Fox** asserted his opposition with clarity and firmness, Perrot's support fell away.

The controversy continued when Perrot moved to Barbados in 1662, and Perrot, hurt by his treatment, came to distance himself from Friends. In 1665, a few months before his death, he claimed Quakerism had failed its mission. The hat controversy was calmed although "the spirit of the hat" would emerge in schismatic tendencies within **British** Quakerism in the following decades. [Pink Dandelion]

PHILANTHROPY. Quaker charity began at home. As they first came together as a movement, Friends assumed responsibility for caring for their own widows, orphans, and those suffering for **Truth**'s sake. Their attention was directed outward in the 1740s by reformers, like **John Woolman** and **Anthony Benezet**. Responding to growing prosperity and assimilation, the reformers matched their call for a tighter enforcement of the **discipline** on **simplicity** and Quaker **peculiarities** with concern for the indigent and powerless in the world around them. In the 18th century, American Friends gave particular assistance to **Native Americans** and free **African Americans**.

Until the later 19th century, most Quaker philanthropy was done through associations, some of which were limited to Friends, others dominated by them. Examples of the latter in North America include the Pennsylvania Society for Promoting the Abolition of Slavery, the Relief of Negroes Unlawfully Held in Bondage, and for Improving the Condition of the African; and the Female Association of Philadelphia for the Relief of the Sick and Infirm Poor with Clothing. By 1800, philanthropic societies became an important form of Quaker **women**'s organization, especially for single women, on both sides of the Atlantic. After the American Civil War, women supplied many of the teachers for the **Friends Freedmen's Association** that organized Quaker efforts to aid liberated African Americans in the South. Other areas of Quaker philanthropic activity in the 19th century included hospitals, schools (*see* EDUCATION), **penal reform**, assistance to poor women and children (including prostitutes), and **mental health reform**. They embraced the settlement house movement led by **Jane Addams**. Meanwhile, Friends established funds to assist necessitous members, including the **elderly**.

As individual fortunes grew, a number of Friends became known for their personal philanthropy. Among the early examples are two Philadelphians, **Richard Humphreys** and **Roberts Vaux**. Major philanthropists of the 19th and early 20th century include **William Allen**, **Anna Jeanes**, and Joseph Wharton (1826–1909). These individuals supported local charities and endowed institutions that continue today. By the late 20th century, not only were there fewer large

Quaker fortunes but many Friends became suspicious of traditional philanthropy and its paternalistic style. Current Quaker philanthropy tends to be in the form of personal service and donations to Quaker institutions, missions, and service agencies. [Mary Ellen Chijioke]

PICKETT, CLARENCE EVAN (1884–1965). Pastor and **American Friends Service Committee (AFSC)** leader, Clarence E. Pickett was raised in a large, Midwestern **Gurneyite** farm family. He attended **William Penn College** in Oskaloosa, Iowa, and in 1913, graduated from Hartford Theological Seminary with a B.D. degree. Immediately following his marriage to Lilly Dale Peckham (1882–1973) of Iowa, he served as pastor of the Toronto, **Canada**, Friends **Meeting**. In 1917 he became pastor of the College Avenue **Friends Church** in Oskaloosa, Iowa.

In 1919 Pickett began work as secretary of the Board of **Young Friends** Activities of the Five Years Meeting of Friends (*see* FRIENDS UNITED MEETING) based in Richmond, Indiana. In 1923 he was appointed professor of Biblical Literature and Church History and also served as pastor at **Earlham College** in Richmond. His association with several programs of AFSC since its founding in April 1917 led to his appointment as its executive secretary in 1929.

In his 35 years of service with AFSC—as executive secretary until 1950, then as honorary secretary and executive secretary emeritus until his **death**—Pickett was prominently involved in **peace** education, the furtherance of **equality** between whites and blacks, refugee and **relief work** during and following **World War II**, and personal diplomacy between U.S. and Soviet officials during the Cold War. He had a close working relationship with Eleanor Roosevelt (1884–1962) that gave Quakers access to the president, and was much in demand as a public speaker. [Lawrence McK. Miller]

PINKHAM, WILLIAM PENN (1841–1919). Gurneyite minister. Pinkham spent most of his life teaching in Quaker institutions, including **Earlham College**, the Cleveland Bible Institute (later **Malone College**), and the Huntington Park Institute (later **Azusa Pacific University**). Author of *The Lamb of God*, which defended the doctrine of the **atonement**, and a founding editor of the *Evangelical*

Friend (1905), he was one of the most influential critics of **modernist** theology among Friends. [John W. Oliver]

PITMAN, DOROTHY (1902?–). North American **pastor** and **missionary** to the **Native Americans** in Oklahoma and North Dakota. She served in **East Africa** from 1943 to 1962.

PLAIN DRESS AND SPEECH. For over two centuries, Quakers were easily identified by the **distinctives** of their plain dress, which became stylized by the 19th century as gray or dark brown dress with simple bonnets for the women and broad-brimmed hats for the men. Individuals were also meticulous in use of "thee" or "thou" when speaking to one person rather than using the more common, but plural, "you." These practices started in the earliest days of Friends as testimonies against the vain and empty customs of the world and became a mark of their "**peculiarity**." Friends were encouraged to lay aside vanity and to live as in the presence of Jesus.

The use of "you" when addressing an individual not only violated the **testimony** of integrity (see TRUTH), it also was seen as a means of flattery and contrary to the fact that all people are created equal before **God**. In 17th-century England, superiors were addressed as "you" and all servants were addressed as "thee." Friends also refused to use formal titles and would even address the king as Charles Stuart. Titles, such as "Grace" or "Lord," were also reserved for **Christ**, and their use to single out individuals based on heredity or position seemed blasphemous (*see also* TIMES AND SEASONS).

Simplicity in dress was initially linked to moderation in the use of possessions and restraint from vain display. Friends were urged to make proper use of creation and not encourage greed, lust, or arrogance by their dress. Plain dress was also a witness against the way in which dress supports social position and customs. It later became controversial as **elders** sought to regulate the details of dress to a ridiculous degree. By the late 19th century, changes in the English language and the growth of the ready-made clothing industry made the use of plain language and dress seem empty forms to most Friends, and their use generally ended. [Margery Post Abbott]

PLUMMER, JONATHAN WRIGHT (1835–1918). Pharmacist and **minister**. Raised in Richmond, Indiana, Jonathan Plummer became partner in a small pharmacy in 1854. The following year he married Hannah Ballard. As minister, he helped form both the Friends First-Day School Conference and the Friends' Union for Philanthropic Labor, precursors to **Friends General Conference**. After moving to Chicago in 1874, he opposed the use of tobacco and introduced profit sharing into his business. He was clerk of Illinois **Yearly Meeting** (**Hicksite**) from 1875 to 1883. [Mary Ellen Chijioke]

POLITICS. Quaker participation in public policy discussions and interactions with government officials reflects the contrasting approaches embodied by two early Quaker leaders, **George Fox** and **William Penn**. George Fox was confrontational in his dealings with government officials. Like an Old Testament **prophet**, Fox admonished Oliver Cromwell to govern with righteousness and justice, not worrying about gaining favor. Fox recorded in his ***Journal*** that he had exhorted Cromwell to "keep in the fear of **God**, that he might receive wisdom from Him, that by it he might be ordered, and with it might order all things under his hand unto God's glory."

During the English Commonwealth under Cromwell, early Friends echoed the political ideas of radicals in the New Model Army, calling for an end to **tithes**, for religious toleration, for laws written in plain English, for strict enforcement of the moral laws, and an end to oppression by the wealthy. Friends, who supported the Commonwealth, resisted the movement to make Cromwell king and denounced the increasing conservatism of the government. Friends did not negotiate with the authorities over policies. Rather, they issued prophetic calls for justice and threatened God's judgment on those who ignored reforms. After the death of Cromwell, Friends refused to get involved in the rcsulting power struggles and withdrew from politics.

From the restoration of the monarchy in 1660 until the mid-19th century, the English government did not allow Friends a direct role in governance. Eighteenth-century British Friends enjoyed limited religious toleration and made few efforts to influence the policies of the government, except on issues that directly affected them like oath taking (*see* TRUTH) and their colony of Pennsylvania.

Quakers have been more comfortable as prophets than as kings. Friends have worked tirelessly to persuade public officials to act with justice and righteousness at least since the 1660 petition of **Margaret Fell** to the king and parliament. In this and other documents, they reacted to charges of subversion by declaring their **peace testimony**, which renounced the use of outward weapons for any reason, and by clearly stating that Friends were loyal subjects of civil authority except when there was a direct conflict with **leadings** of the Spirit. Early Quaker leaders regularly met with public officials to seek fair treatment for Quakers and for all persons of conscience. Unlike the Anabaptist "two kingdoms" view that concentrated on developing godliness among believers, Quakers became a small, but strong voice in public life on both sides of the Atlantic.

William Penn became a prominent advocate for religious toleration. Penn's political success was always limited, however, and his later connection with James II ensured conflict with William and Mary when they ascended the British throne. William Penn's "**Holy Experiment**" in Pennsylvania gave Friends the opportunity to participate in and directly shape **civil government**. Penn believed that "government was a part of religion itself, a thing sacred in its institution and end."

For several decades after the end of Quaker governance of Pennsylvania, Friends in **North America** followed the counsel of **Thomas Shillitoe**, who urged them not to get involved in politics. As Quakers became a strong force for the **abolition** of both the slave trade and slavery itself, they also found themselves in internal conflict over their place in the world of politics. In **Britain**, Friends remained legally restrained from national public office until the English Reform Bill of 1832, which repealed the Test Act, permitting them to join the Parliament by expressing their loyalty with an affirmation instead of an oath.

Before the American Civil War, Friends in the United States overwhelmingly supported the Republican Party, seeing it as antislavery. Until the early 20th century, most Quakers continued to support the Republican Party, although the corruption of big-city politics brought them to support reform candidates. Many North American Friends supported the reforms identified with the Progressive movement: **women**'s suffrage, **temperance**, **penal reform**, ending child labor, regulation of big **business**, and arbitration of international disputes. Active lobbying by Friends established the right to **conscientious objection** status and alternatives to military service. While minuscule in numbers, and rarely holding any political power, Friends continued to make their mark. From 1933 to 1945, the tiny German Yearly Meeting distinguished itself by its refusal to collaborate with Nazism. Since 1960, Cuban Friends have maintained a clear witness to their faith despite varying levels of government harassment.

The desire to establish an ongoing, organizational means of influencing public policy in the U.S. led to the creation of the **Friends Committee on National Legislation** (FCNL) in 1942. While they have no exact counterpart to the FCNL, many European Friends became committed to such causes as nuclear disarmament and preserving the **environment**. Others sought penal reform by serving as magistrates, parole officers, and social workers.

Political views of modern Quakers reflect their theological divisions, but most still feel comfortable with William Penn's call to political activism: "True godliness does not turn men out of the world, but enables them to live better in it, and excites their endeavors to mend it" (William Penn, *No Cross, No Crown*, p. 12). [Lon Fendall, J. William Frost]

POWELL, AARON MACY (1832–1899). Lecturer for **abolition** and **woman** suffrage, Powell later gave leadership to the American Purity Alliance. Powell edited the National **Temperance** Society's monthly, *National Temperance Advocate*, from 1873 to1894 and helped make scientific temperance instruction part of the school curriculum in the United States. Belonging to New York **Yearly Meeting**, he and his wife, Anna Rice Powell (ca. 1834–1915), were active in and through the Union for Philanthropic Labor of the **Friends General Conference**. [Sabron Newton]

PRADO, SALAMÓN (d. 1955). Early teacher at the Friends School in Guatemala. *See* CENTRAL AMERICA.

PRAYER. In his *Apology*, **Robert Barclay** wrote, "Inward prayer is the secret turning of the mind toward **God**, where it looks up to him and constantly breathes some of its secret hopes and aspirations toward him" (Barclay, *Apology*, Freiday, p. 286). The essence of prayer is thus waiting to feel and respond to God's Spirit.

For Friends, outward, vocal prayer traditionally was seen as dependent on the **motion** of the Spirit; thus they did not use formal written prayers. Barclay noted that "The breathing of the Spirit of God arises in the soul so powerfully that audible sighs, groans or words are brought forth. This can arise in either public assemblies, or in private, or at mealtimes" (Barclay, *Apology*, Freiday, p. 290). Historically, when someone knelt to pray in **worship**, all others present would stand and remove their hats (*see* HAT HONOR). Today, Friends who worship in **unprogrammed** meetings generally prefer silent prayer. However, among Friends who attend **programmed worship**, vocal prayer, including intercessory prayer, is a regular part of the worship service and other gatherings. This is most often spontaneous, but may sometimes be written in advance. [Margery Post Abbott]

PREACHING. Quakers are commonly known for holding "silent" **meetings for worship**, but silence among early Friends and most contemporary Quakers is not seen as an end in itself, but as a means of quieting the inward person to hear the voice of **Christ**. Particularly among early Friends, words spoken in **meetings** by both men and **women**—and there were few gatherings that were entirely silent—were regarded as words from **God**, because the speakers believed they acted as God's oracles or **prophets**. Quaker preaching, until the late 19th century, had been entirely impromptu, ostensibly motivated by the Inward **Light** of Christ speaking to individuals in the silence, prompting the spoken word to be delivered to the gathering.

The sources on early Quaker preaching are surprisingly rich, considering the impromptu nature of the discourse. A number of early Quaker sermons were taken down by auditors and published. Additionally, Samuel Bownas's *A Description of the Qualifications Necessary to a Gospel Minister* (1750), a practical book on **ministry**, reflected the practice of Quaker preachers. Early sermons were not written out prior to meeting and reflected the Quaker rejection of any style employed strictly to display the speakers' knowledge or facility with words. A simple style and spontaneous nature continue to describe vocal ministry at **unprogrammed** Quaker meetings. In addition, early sermons were characterized by the expression of **theo-**

logical beliefs largely in terms of metaphors rather than **creedal** statements. Eighteenth-century **ministers** developed a sing-song style of preaching that survived among **Conservative Friends** into the 20th century.

Some of the most commonly used metaphors in surviving early Quaker sermons include the light/dark family, the Voice (part of a metaphor cluster that includes several terms for sound and silence), hunger and thirst metaphors, growth metaphors (including early Quaker use of the term "seed" to denote the new life and potential for growth through the Light of Christ), and the metaphor of the journey.

During the later 19th century many **Gurneyite** Friends in the United States were influenced by a **revivalistic** preaching style (*see* REVIVALS) and moved to a paid **pastoral system**, which in turn encouraged the practice of preparing sermons ahead of time. In the 20th century, the majority of meetings and churches worldwide came to prefer **programmed worship** with times designated for a prepared message, **Bible** readings, and hymns. Many also encourage or allow spontaneous vocal ministry during a comparatively brief period of silent waiting before the Lord, a part of the worship service which some call "Friends Communion" (*see* SACRAMENTS). The predominant mode of preaching among these Friends, however, remains the delivery of sermons by the **pastor** or other Friends with a recognized gift in the ministry. [Michael P. Graves]

PREPARATIVE MEETING. In traditional Quaker organization, the local congregation that prepared to take business to the **monthly meetings**. In 20th-century **North America**, a preparative meeting is a congregation under the care of a monthly meeting until it is strong enough to stand on its own as a monthly meeting. In the 18th and 19th centuries, the Preparative **Meeting of Ministers and Elders** also met prior to monthly meeting to discuss matters affecting the spiritual health of the meeting. [Mary Ellen Chijioke]

PRIMITIVE FRIENDS. Members of the smaller **Wilburite** bodies in **North America** who were willing to secede from established **yearly meetings** in order to preserve original "primitive" Quakerism. This did not include Ohio **Yearly Meeting** (Wilburite), which did not for many years recognize any group created by secession.

PRISON. In the 17th century over 11,000 Friends in **Britain** were imprisoned, often more than once, including **George Fox**, **Margaret Fell**, **Edward Burrough**, **Dorothy White**, and **William Dewsbury**. In Britain, 243 died in prison and the four **Boston martyrs** were hanged in the colonies. Friends were regularly persecuted under a number of laws for actions such as blasphemy, the refusal to take oaths (*see* TRUTH), and nonpayment of **tithes**. The Quaker Act of 1662 made it illegal for Quakers to worship together. Friends **meetings** organized support of those who were imprisoned, fined, or otherwise penalized for their faith and cared for the children whose parents were in jail. Lists of sufferings incurred by Friends on account of their faith were regularly compiled by meeting for sufferings. Friends continued to be imprisoned after the 17th century, chiefly for adherence to the **Peace Testimony**. *See also* PENAL REFORM. [Margery Post Abbott]

PROGRAMMED WORSHIP. A **meeting for worship** that has at least some preplanned program. In its simplest form, it may include a few planned activities like **Bible** reading, hymn singing, and **prayer** to begin and end a longer period of **unprogrammed** or "open" **worship**; at the other extreme it may take the form of a Protestant-type church service with little or no silence. *See* MEETINGS.

PROGRESSIVE FRIENDS. In the 1840s and 1850s disaffected **Hicksite** Quakers in Michigan, New York, Ohio, Indiana, Iowa, and Pennsylvania left their established **meetings** to form independent religious associations of **Congregational** or Progressive Friends. They left because they felt larger meetings exercised "despotic authority" over smaller meetings; they objected to the undue influence of the **Meeting of Ministers and Elders**; and they wanted to participate more fully in "worldly" reform societies, especially those concerned with the **abolition** of slavery.

Individual liberty of conscience and social reform were the main objectives of Progressive Friends. They attended to concerns and **discipline** in their own independent congregations; they regulated the **ministry** among themselves; and they came out with a broad platform of reform that actively supported antislavery, **women**'s rights, pacifism, **temperance**, prison reform, **Native American** rights, and the abolition of capital punishment (*see also* PEACE; PENAL REFORM). The "Basis of Religious Association," a document written in 1848 by the Congregational Friends of **Waterloo**, New York, and later adopted by most of the other associations, best articulates their grievances, founding principles, and aims.

Chief among the aims of Progressive Friends was the "perfect" recognition of the **equality** of women, and they quickly did away with separate meetings for men and women. While all the associations promoted the coalescing women's rights movement, the Waterloo Congregational Friends in New York, in particular, were instrumental in initiating the first women's rights convention at **Seneca Falls** in 1848.

Progressive Friends did not restrict their membership to Quakers, and most associations later changed their name to The Friends of Human Progress, or Friends of Progress, to reflect both their decision to be nonsectarian and their humanist vision. They consciously created an environment of tolerance and skepticism in their various meetinghouses and halls, opening them to a variety of speakers expounding the most radical reforms of the day. **Spiritualism**, which evoked early Quaker **mysticism**, was adopted by many Progressive Friends.

Most associations of Progressive Friends ceased to exist by the end of the 19th century, although some meetings such as **Longwood**, Pennsylvania, North Collins and Milton, New York, and **Vineland**, New Jersey (established in the 1860s), continued well into the 20th century. Progressive Friends adopted a radical stance for individualism in the Quaker balance between individual and community and opened avenues for social justice in **North America**. Their commitment to reform and their reforms of Quakerism have become accepted practice among **liberal Friends**. [Andrea Constantine Hawkes]

PROPHECY. The first-generation Friends clearly saw themselves in the prophetic tradition and considered their vocal **ministry** in **worship** as an extension of prophecy.

The books of the Old Testament show that prophets, by their words and by their lives, signaled **God**'s presence, power, and purpose in the world. Contrary to popular misunderstandings, the prophets were not primarily engaged either in predicting the future or in correcting social ills. Their service grew directly from their personal encounter with God as an overwhelmingly present reality. They knew God directly, intimately, and they faithfully went on missions, carrying the messages with which they were charged. Like early prophets, early Quakers sometimes spoke words of warning or judgment; at other times they offered words of hope and restoration.

Quakers have often identified closely with the prophetic tradition, with its emphasis on direct encounter of all with God (Acts 2:14–18) and on Spirit-empowered insights, tasks, and messages (*see* HOLY SPIRIT). They have emphasized the prophetic "office" of **Christ** as teacher and guide. **George Fox** invited people to "come to the life of the prophets." The New Testament not only speaks of a "gift" of prophecy that some receive (Romans 12:6, 1 Corinthians 12:28, Ephesians 4:11), but also suggests a more universal gift of prophecy to be enjoyed by all upon whom the Spirit has come: young and old, **women** and men (Acts 2:14–18). Friends took this literally, with women like **Margaret Fell** being prominent in the ministry from the start.

George Fox and **John Woolman** are the Friends most widely regarded as "prophets," but the possibility and reality of prophetic ministry among Friends has been widespread. Interest in and awareness of prophecy grew among Friends in the late 20th century. **Lewis Benson**, in particular, has argued that prophecy is a major characteristic of early Friends who understood that "the people of God in the new **covenant** would be gathered to Christ through the prophetic experience of hearing and obeying." [Howard R. Macy]

PUBLISHING. Beginning in the 1650s Friends issued thousands of sermons, **prophecies**, **journals**, defenses of their faith, attacks upon outsiders, and accounts of sufferings. At first, they mainly published short tracts or broadsides, but even during the periods of persecution after 1660 they began issuing substantial volumes like **Robert Barclay**'s *Apology* and the collected writings of influential martyred early Friends, including **Edward Burroughs**, **Isaac Penington**, and **Francis Howgill**. In the 1690s, **George Fox**'s *Journal*, Epistles, and theological writings appeared in large folio volumes. While the quantity declined in 18th-century **Britain**, Friends continued to publish substantial new works and the collected writings of influential Friends like **William Penn** and **Thomas Chalkley**.

Friends soon realized that they needed some controlling mechanism to make sure that what was published represented Friends accurately. So a **committee** of the Second Day Morning **Meeting of Ministers and Elders** in London (*see also* MORNING MEETING), and similar committees in other **yearly meetings**, read all manuscripts with the right to make changes and to recommend publication, circulation in manuscript, or suppression. Early Quaker publications can be taken as authoritative for the group.

After 1700, Quakers primarily published journals and *Piety Promoted*, a collection of the sayings of devout Friends close to **death**. Both promoted an ideal Quaker lifestyle that changed little until the 1850s, and survive to this day as spiritual autobiographies and memorial **minutes**. In Georgian England, Friends produced a diversity of writings: **theology**, poetry, essays, schoolbooks, scientific treatises. American Friends published much less, partially because there were few Quaker printers but also because they seemed to prefer handwritten materials. Minutes, epistles, **marriage** certificates, and **disciplines** remained handwritten. This changed when first London in 1783, and then most American yearly meetings, published their books of discipline.

The 19th century witnessed technological breakthroughs that made printing much cheaper. The new technology, coupled with the schisms (*see* GREAT SEPARATION), led Friends to reissue collections of the writings of early Friends, e.g., the *Works of George Fox*, the *Friends Library*, and *Friends Miscellany*. In addition the **Orthodox**, who blamed the schism on insufficient **religious education** in the beliefs of Christianity, sought through Quaker **Bible** and Tract Societies to make sure that every Friend learned what they defined as basic truths. **Hicksites** and the Orthodox published defenses of their conduct, while blaming the other branch, and began issuing periodicals. Each of the theological controversies and separations in Britain and **North America** resulted in extensive publications. After Friends began creating First Day Schools, they published materials for the use of teachers and pupils.

Friends' periodicals aimed at Quaker readers grew during the 19th century. Today, several Quaker bodies either subsidize or control a press: **Quaker Life** in Britain; **Friends United Meeting** Press in

Richmond, Indiana; Barclay Press in Newberg, Oregon; and **Pendle Hill** and **Friends General Conference** in eastern Pennsylvania. [J. William Frost]

PURDY, ALEXANDER CONVERSE (1890–1976). North American biblical scholar and **minister**, Purdy was professor at **Earlham College** (1916–1923), then professor of New Testament at Hartford Theological Seminary in Connecticut from 1923 until 1960, where he shaped two generations of Quaker **pastors** and teachers.

PURITANISM. The uneven Reformation of the national Church of England under Henry VIII (1491–1547) and Queen Elizabeth I (1533–1603) drove a nucleus of the most dedicated clergy together to form a "puritan" party. Those who escaped to Geneva, Switzerland, from Mary Tudor's (1516–1568) persecution of Protestants brought back the Calvinist theology and presbyterian church patterns by which, for three generations thereafter, they hoped to remake the Church of England. Puritan clergy meanwhile remade the lives of congregations with sermons and lectures every Sunday, family prayers and Bible study, self-examination and journal keeping by laymen and women. Some stressed the Spirit's power (*see* HOLY SPIRIT). The Puritans' lifestyle grew from a belief that salvation was through election by God for no merit of one's own and that there was a consequent need to demonstrate election through a life of visible piety and to make England a model Christian nation. Puritans became a majority among merchants and leaders in Parliament.

Charles I's efforts to rule by divine right and his policies of heavy taxation helped drive the country into the **English Civil War** in 1642. Both working-class **separatists** and Puritans returnees from New England enrolled in Oliver Cromwell's (1599–1658) "New Model" Army, which defeated the Royalists. They executed the king in 1649, setting up the Commonwealth. The "Puritan Revolution" abolished bishops, monarchy, and the House of Lords and set up other reforms. But the working-class Baptist and separatist congregations turned against the middle-class Puritans and prevented enforced uniformity. In this crisis, the Quaker movement seemed to Puritan pastors a mortal threat, notably when Friends entered Puritan-led parish churches to proclaim against them. In Massachusetts, Puritans imposed the death penalty on banished Quakers who returned to the colony after deportation (*see* BOSTON MARTYRS). In **Britain**, Friends were arrested for disturbing the peace, as vagabonds, or for refusal to pay **tithes** to support parish churches, but clashes with Puritan clergy mainly led to verbal debates and to tracts, over 750 by each side.

Quakers rejected all parish churches and clergy and made the Bible secondary to the Spirit's inner power and **leadings**. Though Puritans believed that only the Spirit could bring the gospel message to the heart of each converted person, they denied the possibility of ethical **perfection** and infallible inner guidance. Debated too was **George Fox**'s belief that Jesus **Christ** was simply a "prepared body" for God as Spirit, and that Jesus' historical actions, healings, miracles, and even the **cross** primarily reflected timeless "types" to be reenacted in each Christian life, as **James Nayler** tried to do. Puritans separated Father, Son, and Spirit, which **William Penn** called making God "three He's." Such debates continued into the 18th century.

The **Restoration** Parliament of Charles II (1630–1686) enacted an Act of Uniformity in 1662, enforcing use of Episcopal liturgies and bishops. Over 2,000 Puritan clergy conscientiously refused and were evicted from their parish churches. Some were jailed. Many others "conformed," reluctantly. The Toleration Act of 1689 reduced all surviving Puritan congregations in Britain to the status of "Nonconformist Conventicles." [Hugh Barbour]

–Q–

QUAKER. The term was allegedly first used to describe Friends in 1650 by Justice Gervase Bennet of Derby, England, at a trial of **George Fox**, who had been imprisoned under the Blasphemy Act. Fox recorded that "This was Justice Bennet of Derby that first called us Quakers because we bid them tremble at the word of **God**." By this he meant that they trembled at the power of God. Friends like **Robert Barclay** equated quaking to the trembling experienced in **worship**. The term Quaker was soon widely used by Friends as well as by their detractors.

Friends originally called themselves **"Children of the Light"** (cf. John 12:36, Ephesians 5:8, 1 Thessalonians 5:5). "Publishers of

Truth," "Friends of Truth," and "Friends in the Truth" were other early names used starting with the second generation of Friends. As the formal name **Religious Society of Friends** became standard, many friends rejected the term Quaker as an unwanted nickname. By the late 20th century, most liberal **Friends** accepted the popular name along with the more formal one, while **evangelicals** more consistently spoke of the **Friends Church**. *See also* CELESTIAL FLESH. [Margery Post Abbott]

QUAKER HILL CONFERENCE CENTER. An independent conference and retreat center located in Richmond, Indiana, whose mission is to be "a special place apart from the routines of daily life for groups and individuals to nurture spiritual life." It is most closely related to Indiana, Western, and Wilmington **Yearly Meetings**. The Center is owned and operated by Quaker Hill Foundation, a not-for-profit foundation created in 1940 to operate this historic property. It shares a campus with the office of **Friends United Meeting**, Friends United Press, and the Quaker Hill Bookstore. [David Edinger]

QUAKER INTERNATIONAL CENTRES. As a response to World War I, Friends in **Britain** and **Ireland** sought to create Quaker embassies in strategic centers of the world that could help establish a lasting **peace** (*see* HEATH, CARL). In 1919, London and Dublin **Yearly Meetings** created the Friends Council for International Service. The continued need for **relief work** delayed the development of the centers, but the first was soon established in Paris. By 1939, the Friends Service Council had centers in China, France, Germany, India, Madagascar, Pemba, Spain, Switzerland, and Syria. While their specific activities varied according to time and local circumstances, all tried to combine service with spiritual outreach to the local communities. Many concentrated on services to students; others worked with local farm or industrial groups. Many found themselves organized relief efforts in the crises leading to **World War II**. Quaker centers today are generally under the care of particular yearly or local **meetings**. *See also* PEACE AND/OR SERVICE AGENCIES. [Mary Ellen Chijioke]

QUAKER LIFE. Central department of **Britain Yearly Meeting**, formerly known as Quaker Home Service, responsible for helping nurture the spiritual life of the constituent **meetings**. Sections include **Outreach,** Children (*see* FAMILY), and **Publishing**.

QUAKER THEOLOGICAL SEMINARY. Founded on June 1, 1985, in Chiquimula, Guatemala, by Amigos de Santidad (Holiness **Yearly Meeting**). *See also* CENTRAL AMERICA.

QUAKER UNITED NATIONS OFFICE (QUNO). A few individual Quakers were instrumental in the founding of the United Nations (UN) in 1945–1946. The UN granted **Friends World Committee for Consultation** (FWCC) consultative status in 1948, and Friends have had official representatives at the UN, and offices in New York and Geneva, since that time. Both QUNO offices seek to help the international community solve its problems through words rather than weapons (*see* PEACE TESTIMONY). The role of Friends primarily has been as behind-the-scenes facilitators and informal mediators, although on occasion they have taken strong advocacy positions on issues such as disarmament, economic justice, and **abolition** of slavery. [Margery Post Abbott]

QUARE, DANIEL (1648–1724). English Quaker horologist. Quare developed the repeating watch.

QUARTERLY MEETINGS. Regional gatherings of Friends from a number of **monthly meetings** for the conduct of **business meetings**, **worship**, and mutual support were first recommended by **George Fox** in 1666. Meeting two to four times a year, they are sometimes called area, regional, **general**, or half-yearly **meetings**. **Yearly meetings** typically are comprised of several quarterly meetings.

QUERIES AND ADVICES. Having rejected the idea of a **creed**, early Friends developed their own mechanisms for maintaining **church** unity, including a process of self-examination and a cluster of exhortations to strengthen faith and practice.

The earliest queries were sent to **monthly meetings** in the 17th century: "What ministering friends have died in the past year?" and "How does **Truth** prosper among you?" New queries have been added, both to collect further information and to sharpen reflection on particular topics. Originally, written responses were prepared by the **business meetings**, and forwarded to the **quarterly** and **yearly meetings**. Currently, queries are seen by both individual Friends and meetings or churches as a means of engaging their hearts, minds, and spirits in an examination of their spiritual condition. Only rarely today are written responses to the yearly meeting expected.

Friends differ on the origin of the advices. Some say they derive from the Advices and Regulations drafted by **George Fox** in 1668, while others hold that advices first appeared in the form of epistles sent among Friends to encourage and strengthen each other in their faith. Whatever their origin, their articulation of the gathered wisdom and experience of Friends over time still has the power to inspire and encourage many. In many yearly meetings, however, this power has diminished, and in the majority of books of **discipline**, no advices appear. Outside **Europe** and **North America**, queries or advices rarely appear. [Jan Hoffman]

QUIETISM. The 18th century is often described as the Quietist period among Friends. Quietism called for an emptying of all actions motivated by human will to be open to the guidance of **God** in **worship**, in the conduct of **business meetings**, and in attending to **leadings**. External authority such as the clergy, or even the **Bible**, was seen as a distraction or, at most, secondary to inner guidance. **George Fox**'s 1658 message to "be still and cool in thy own mind and spirit from thy own thoughts, and then thou wilt feel the principle of God" (Fox, *Journal*, Nickalls, p. 346) was reinforced by the Continental Quietist movement against the influences of the "Age of Reason," a common term to designating the dominant 18th-century thought. The mystical writings of Jeanne de la Motte Guyon, François Fenelon, and Migual de Molinos were influential among Friends. A sampling of the work of these Continental Quietists was compiled and published as *A Guide to True Peace*. This small volume was often carried by 18th-century Friends and is still read today.

For the second generation of Friends, the tensions between the world and their vision of living faithfully in community as the manifestation of God's New Order on earth (*see* GOSPEL ORDER) led to increasing withdrawal from interactions with non-Quakers. Quietism helped reinforce the movement toward **peculiarity**. These Friends solidified the spiritual practices that served to create a culture of listening to **Christ**'s guidance as a **hedge** to the values of "the world."

The hedge did not prevent action on **peace** and justice issues. This commitment allowed Friends to encourage those **tender** in the **Holy Spirit** and to admonish others in love. Further fruits of faithfulness were the **prophetic** witness to governments that advocated violence or to practices such as slavery that were a hindrance to hearing the guidance of God. At its best, Quietism is above all a return to nourish the inward life, not a withdrawal from the world. Today some Friends still find inspiration from the Quietist vision. [Kathryn A. Damiano]

–R–

RAMÍREZ, BERNARDINO (1880–1949). Prominent preacher who, like many early Guatemalan Friends, worked for the United Fruit Company. *See* CENTRAL AMERICA.

RAWSON, A. PERRY (1906–1996) and L. MARJORIE MOORE (1902–1991). Friends missionaries to Burundi (*see* CENTRAL AFRICA) under Kansas **Yearly Meeting** for 25 years beginning in 1947. Perry Rawson established hospitals at Kibimba and Kwisumu and served as medical director for a leprosarium at Nyankanda. Marjorie Rawson ran a hostel for missionary children and ministered house-to-house to women in the hills of Burundi. Their son **David Rawson** served as ambassador to several African countries. *See* MISSIONS. [John W. Oliver]

RAWSON, DAVID (1941–). Born in Michigan, Rawson moved to Burundi (*see* CENTRAL AFRICA) in 1947 with his parents, **Marjorie and Perry Rawson** who served as Quaker medical missionaries. Rawson attended Rift Valley Academy in Kenya, graduated from **Malone College** in 1962, then earned his M.A. and Ph.D. from American University in Washington, D.C. He taught political science at Malone College from 1965 until 1971. From 1971 to 1999, he worked for the United States Foreign Service (*see* CIVIL GOVERNMENT) in various posts, including head of the Africa desk at the State Department.

He served as ambassador to Rwanda from 1993 until 1996 and ambassador to Mali from 1996 until 1999. He currently teaches at Spring Arbor University in Michigan, where he is a member of Rollin Friends Church. [Jacalynn Stuckey Baker]

REALIGNMENT. A movement among some evangelical Friends in the 1980s and 1990s to reorganize the major national organizations of American Friends **yearly meetings** along consistent theological lines essentially by dividing members of **Friends United Meeting** between **Evangelical Friends International** and **Friends General Conference**. *See* MYLANDER, CHARLES.

REES, DEBORAH A. and EMORY J. (1870–1947). American **missionaries** to **East Africa** from 1904 to 1926. He supervised the translation of the **Bible** into Luragoli, and she worked with the **women**, earning a Luyia name *Avugutsa* (seeds) for her stress on the creation of vegetable gardens. *See also* LITU, JOEL.

RELEASED FRIEND. A person whose **monthly meeting**, having recognized his or her calling to the **ministry**, provides the spiritual and practical support for the individual to respond to the call.

RELIEF WORK. Friends have always been involved in the relief of suffering, basing such work on their belief that the Inward **Light** of **Christ** is available to all people and that there is "that of **God**" in each human being. They persistently work to relieve human suffering, whatever its cause, its source, or the political complexities surrounding it.

Quakers have been particularly active in relief campaigns following wars, providing food, clothing, medical assistance, education, training, relocation for refugees, and rehabilitation, as well as community development and nonviolence training meant to deal with the root causes of suffering.

Friends' relief began in the crucible of their own persecution and suffering among the original followers of **George Fox**, **Margaret Fell**, and other seekers, as they helped each other and began **ministries** and **committees** for sufferings. But very soon the **concern** reached out beyond the original circle. Friends in **Britain** provided relief to Quakers in the former colonies during and after the American Revolution, and individual Friends assisted Russian seekers during the time of Catherine the Great.

Quakers provided relief in **Ireland** during the great Potato Famine of the 1840s, sent food and medical supplies accompanied by relief workers during the Crimean War (1853–1858) and to freed slaves during and after the American Civil War (*see* AFRICAN AMERICANS). They became heavily involved in relief on both sides of the Franco-Prussian War (1870–1871) and sent workers and relief to the Great Russian Famine (1891–1892). In the midst of this work, a debate emerged between individuals who believed in providing disinterested humanitarian relief to all, regardless of political or religious considerations, and those more interested in spreading Christianity among people who received relief. This debate reflected the theological and organizational ferment among Friends, particularly in Britain and **North America**.

The 20th century saw a tremendous variety of international relief efforts emerge. Refugee and postwar reconstruction efforts in Belgium, France, Germany, the Netherlands, Poland, Russia, and Serbia followed World War I, and then famine relief and reconstruction work occurred in Russia from 1920 to 1927. **World War II** relief included the Friends Ambulance Unit work in China and refugee relief throughout Europe, for which the **American Friends Service Committee (AFSC)** and the Friends Service Council received the Nobel Peace Prize on behalf of Friends in 1947.

Postwar relief has included such diverse initiatives as the pioneering **educational** work with Palestinian refugee children in Ramallah on the West Bank, then part of Jordan, humanitarian relief and education in Japan, and numerous community development efforts throughout the world. The tradition of war relief to both sides of conflicts continued during the Vietnam War (1965–1973), as AFSC and a Quaker Action Group both provided medical assistance to North Vietnam, in addition to operating AFSC Rehabilitation Center in Quang Ngai, South Vietnam.

Today Friends worldwide continue to be active in relief efforts, and the debate about their meaning and importance continues. *See also* PEACE AND SERVICE AGENCIES; PEACE TESTIMONY. [David W. McFadden]

RELIGIOUS EDUCATION. In the enthusiasm of direct spiritual experience that accompanied the birth of the **Religious Society of Friends**, there was no organized structure for the religious education of children or adults. Assuming the Inward **Light** of **Christ** present in everyone, children were seen as "**tender** plants" in whom the **Holy Spirit** was gently nurtured. From infancy, children participated in **meeting for worship**, usually twice a week, and often held daily in the home. At its best this **Quietist**, **family**-centered Quaker culture was a gentle all-encompassing lifestyle based on listening for God's guidance (*see* FAMILIED MONASTICISM). At its dry extreme it resulted in neglect of outward teaching of biblical or spiritual material on the assumption that the Inward Teacher was sufficient.

What 18th-century religious education that existed took place in schools that used the **Bible** as a textbook. In the early 19th century, the **Sunday School movement** encouraged churches to sponsor Sunday Schools for basic literacy and religious instruction. But it was not until later that this form of Bible education was seen as important for the children of middle-class church members. Quakers followed their Protestant neighbors in sponsoring First Day (Sunday) Schools first for the poor, and then later for their own children and youth (*see* TIMES AND SEASONS).

After the separations in **North America**, the **Orthodox** concentrated increasingly on biblical literacy. "First Day Schools for Scriptural Instruction" grew rapidly in the 1830s. By 1850, most Orthodox Friends were moving closer to the dominant culture in the United States and **Britain**, and they adopted First Day School methods that resembled those of non-Friends. By 1860, the First Day School had become established in most **Gurneyite** Friends **meetings**. **Wilburites** resisted. Lessons were published in several Quaker magazines and used by both Orthodox and **Hicksite** meetings in North America. Both branches used the *International Sunday School Lessons*, a systematic, nondenominational Bible study begun in 1873.

About that time, Hicksite Friends also began to organize First Day Schools in the 1850s. By 1869 Hicksites were **publishing** *Scattered Seeds*, a periodical containing lesson plans. The curriculum included readings from the Bible, books of **discipline**, and other inspirational literature. The Lord's Prayer, a **temperance** pledge, and memorized Bible verses were recited. Hicksite **yearly meetings** sent representatives to a Conference on Religious Education held in 1867 and biannually thereafter until 1900, when it helped form the **Friends General Conference (FGC)**.

The 20th century has seen a growing sensitivity to the developmental needs and abilities of children of different ages. Friends have generally done what Protestant churches have been doing. This was explicit in the 1980s when **Friends United Meeting (FUM)** and FGC participated in the **ecumenical** Joint Educational Development of biblically based curricula. In the 1970s FUM and FGC cooperated in the development of the *Living Light* series of graded materials. In the 1990s FUM and **Evangelical Friends International (EFI)** collaborated on *The Adult Friend* curriculum, based on current *International Sunday School Lessons*.

Today, in FGC and Britain Yearly Meeting some materials are prepared for sale to local meetings for both adults and children, but local meetings are responsible for developing their own programs. Often children participate in part of the **unprogrammed worship** and have First Day School classes the remaining time. There are many small meetings with few children of widely spread ages.

In both FUM and EFI the congregations tend to be somewhat larger than in FGC meetings, with religious education more formally organized. EFI has several very large churches with a wide spectrum of classes and activities. Many monthly meetings in all branches also pursue active religious education for adults. [Martha Grundy]

RELIGIOUS SOCIETY OF FRIENDS. At the start of the 18th century Friends began to speak of "our religious society" when corresponding with non-**Quakers**, such as in formal petitions to civil government. With the increased availability and use of printing, the name became formalized as the Religious Society of Friends so that by the 19th century this was the normal title used by Quakers. While this is still the name used by many Friends, by the start of the 20th century, **evangelical** Friends began to use **Friends Church** instead. [Margery Post Abbott]

RESTORATION. Following the death of Oliver Cromwell in 1658, the **Puritan** revolution imploded. A new Parliament acted to restore the monarchy by recalling Charles Stuart from France to rule as

Charles II. With this final collapse of their hopes for **Christ**'s rule on earth, Friends began more rapidly to develop formal structures, modify their earlier grand claims, and change their views on the **Lamb's War** and the Second Coming of Christ. This pragmatic restoration Quakerism is often called the second period of Quaker history.

RETIREMENT. A term in use among Friends from the 17th to the 19th century to describe times of withdrawal from activity for personal meditation and waiting upon **God**. The value placed on retirement is summarized by **Thomas Clarkson**:

> Retirement is considered by the Quakers a Christian duty. The members, therefore, of this Society are expected to wait in silence, not only in their places of **worship**, but occasionally in their **families**, or in their private chambers, in the intervals of their daily occupations, that in stillness of heart and in freedom from the active contrivance of their own will, they may acquire both directions and strength for the performance of the duties of life. (*A Portraiture of Quakerism*, 1808, Vol. I, p. 34)

George Fox's cultivation of solitude during four years of wandering preceding active **ministry** might be considered the first example of Quaker use of retirement. **William Penn** emphasizes and expands on the concept in *No **Cross**, No Crown*, encouraging times of retreat.

An increased awareness of, need for, and cultivation of retirement exists today. A renewed appreciation exists for daily times of personal devotion as well as use of both group silent retreats and solitary retreats. A few Friends are also exploring the monastic tradition for the light it can throw on Friends' practice. *See also* FAMILIED MONASTICISM. [Frances Irenc Taber]

REUNIFICATION. In 1945, after more than a century of discord, the New England **Yearly Meeting** of the Religious Society of Friends rejoined its fractured parts into one united community. In 1955, Canada, Philadelphia, and New York Yearly Meetings followed suit. In 1968 Baltimore Yearly Meeting **consolidated**, allowing each **monthly meeting** to chose affiliation with **Friends United Meeting**, **Friends General Conference**, or both. These formal reunifications, actually the result of a long series of informal contacts between the **Gurneyites** and **Wilburites** in the first instance, and **Hicksites** and

Orthodox in the others, were spurred by an increasing understanding that a community that was at odds with its own members could hardly be a credible advocate for "world **peace**."

A half-century after the **Great Separation** of 1827–1828, decreases in membership, magnified by tensions over doctrine and practice, helped fuel voices for change. Led by **Rufus Jones** and others, the journal *American Friend* began to advocate a common doctrine (*see* CREED) and a greater tolerance for differing methods of **worship**. By the early 20th century, combined Hicksite/Orthodox **committees** to address social problems were soon followed by gatherings of businessmen and combined women's service committees. In response to World War I, the **American Friends Service Committee (AFSC)** was organized by individuals from Orthodox, Gurneyite, Hicksite, and **Conservative** meetings, in pursuit of the common goal of world peace. A forward-looking group of "**Young Friends**" also sought ways to build a united Quakerism to replace the discordant world of their parents.

By the 1930s, this mood of cooperation led to individual **monthly meetings** electing to become "united" meetings, to the dissolution of the last few separate meetings for **women**, along with a general opening of Quaker communities to embrace people of many different backgrounds. Friends' meetings appointed women as **clerks**; Friends schools admitted **African American** children; and Orthodox meetings relaxed their restrictions against "marrying-out." These reunifications reinvigorated many Friends communities. One long-range effect, however, was to decrease among **liberal** yearly meetings the long-held focus of Quakerism as a Christian-centered religion. At the same time, moves to strengthen the Christian center of Friends occurred as some Gurneyite yearly meetings eventually formed **Evangelical Friends International**. In the 1980s and 1990s a few sought **realignment** of Friends based on their acceptance of **evangelicalism**. [Emma Jones Lapsansky]

REVIVALISM. A form of evangelism that emerged in 19th-century **North America**, primarily after the Civil War. Its aim, like that of earlier nominal "awakenings," was to "revive" sinners and bring people to Jesus **Christ**. Revivalism was distinguished from previous awakenings by its use of "new methods," pioneered by Charles

Grandison Finney (1792–1875) and Phoebe Palmer (1807–1874) in the **holiness movement**. These methods included emotional preaching, music, public testimonies, public prayers, the "mourners bench," and the "altar of prayer." Many revivalists embraced Wesleyan holiness theology, which posited a second experience of "instant" and "complete" **sanctification**, following conversion, in which one become victorious over **sin**.

The earliest Quaker revival meeting appears to have been held at Indiana **Yearly Meeting** (**Orthodox**) in 1860. In 1867, revival meetings were held at Walnut Ridge, Indiana, and Bear Creek, Iowa, leading to the spread of the movement primarily in the American Midwest (Ohio, Indiana, Kansas, and Iowa) and South (North Carolina) among **Gurneyite** Orthodox Friends. The publication, *The Christian Worker*, served as the principal organ of the movement. Prominent among Quaker revivalists of the late 1870s were **Dougan Clark Jr**., **John Henry Douglas**, and **Esther G. Frame** in Indiana, **David B. Updegraff** in Ohio, John Y. Hoover (1834–1909) in Iowa; Luke Woodard (1832–1925) in New York, and **Allen Jay** and Rufus P. King (ca. 1843–1923) in North Carolina. Later Quaker revivalists carried the movement into the West (California and Oregon) and into Quaker foreign **missions**.

Revival meetings gave an outlet to mostly younger Friends who had no other vehicle for expressing religious emotion. Outwardly quite different from the typical Friends **meeting for worship** based upon silent waiting, there were points of similarity. The traveling revivalist was, in some ways, like the traveling **minister**. "Gifts of the Spirit" remained more important than formal education or church sanction. Acceptance of the inspiration of the **Holy Spirit** was similar, at least in theory, to Quaker worship. **Women** as well as men preached. Some Friends believed that revivals were a return to the spirited **preaching** of early Quakers and used the early term for evangelistic gatherings, **general meetings**, to refer to their revivals.

Profound changes resulted from revivalism. Quakers who had been converted in revival meetings found much in common with those from Methodist and holiness churches. New or "revived" Friends meetings sought the regular paid services of ministers, many of whom came from these other churches (*see* PASTORAL MOVE-

MENT). The insularity of pre–Civil War Orthodox/**Gurneyite** Quakerism was shattered in the United States, along with the **plain dress and speech**. The silent worship gave way to musical instruments, hymn singing, and preaching. By the late 19th century yearly meetings in Iowa, Indiana, Kansas, and North Carolina separated into Gurneyite and **Conservative** bodies as a result of the revivals.

Quaker numbers increased dramatically, most impressively in the South where revivalism reversed a prewar trend toward extinction. Controversy over the use and advocacy of the ordinances by revivalist David B. Updegraff and others led to the Richmond Conference of 1887 and the **Richmond Declaration**, which, in turn, led to the formation of the first nationwide American Quaker denomination, the Five Years Meeting (now **Friends United Meeting**). Revivalists **J. Walter** and **Emma Malone** revived Quakerism in urban Cleveland, Ohio, establishing a Bible school there (now **Malone College** in Canton, Ohio) that encouraged women as leaders and welcomed students of all races, well before the Friends' schools of the East were racially integrated. Walter Malone also founded the publication, *The Evangelical Friend*, which became an important factor in the **fundamentalist-modernist** controversy among Friends in the early 20th century. **Joel Bean** wrote the most famous criticism of revival methods. [Damon D. Hickey]

RICHARD HUMPHREYS FOUNDATION. At his death in 1832, silversmith Richard Humphreys (b. 1749) bequeathed $10,000 to 13 members of Philadelphia **Yearly Meeting** (**Orthodox**) to establish a school for "descendants of the African race" for training in useful trades and as teachers, The Institute for Colored Youth (ICY) opened in 1837. The ICY, chartered in 1852 and administered by a Quaker board, was the only such private school in the Philadelphia area. **Fanny Jackson Coppin** and Mary Jane Patterson, the first two black American **women** to obtain college degrees, served as principal and assistant principal. **Sarah Mapps Douglass**, a Quaker **abolitionist**, served as principal of the Preparatory Department. After the American Civil War the school became known as the leading **educational** institution for blacks in America.

In 1889, when a night school was added with a vocational education program, over 600 men and women applied during its first year.

The ICY moved to Cheyney, Pennsylvania, in 1902. The name was changed in 1916 to Cheney Training School for Teachers. Taken over by the state of Pennsylvania in 1920, the ICY eventually became **Cheyney University**. After the state takeover, the remaining assets of the Foundation were used to provide scholarships for **African American** students. [Mary Ellen Chijioke]

RICHMOND DECLARATION OF FAITH. In the mid-1880s, the **Gurneyite yearly meetings** found themselves badly split by a controversy over the practice of the holy ordinances, especially **baptism** (*see also* SACRAMENTS). Leading revivalists like **David B. Updegraff** and **John Henry Douglas** argued that Friends should at least tolerate water baptism. For others, including many active in the **revival** movement, this was too great a departure. By 1886, all of the Gurneyite yearly meetings save Ohio had ruled that they would retain no one in the station of **minister** or **elder** who had undergone water baptism. Ohio, Updegraff's stronghold, refused to endorse that position, leading some to call for "sound" Friends there to separate and join Indiana Yearly Meeting.

To meet this divergency, Indiana Yearly Meeting called for a conference of the Gurneyite yearly meetings in Richmond, Indiana, in the fall of 1887. All sent delegations, as did **Ireland** and **London yearly meetings**. Four members of Philadelphia Yearly Meeting (**Orthodox**) were also present. Ironically, the conference quickly decided that the actions of the preponderance of yearly meetings had resolved the question on baptism. Instead, participants sharply debated such questions as the mission of Friends, the nature of **worship**, Quaker missionary work (*see* MISSIONS), and the proper role of the **ministry**.

One of the first actions of the conference had been to resolve that it was desirable that "some method should be taken to form a common declaration of fundamental doctrine, which might prevent the tendency toward the disintegration of the Society." Although preparation was entrusted to a **committee**, the final Richmond Declaration of Faith document was largely the work of the British minister **Joseph Bevan Braithwaite**, drawing on statements found in the **disciplines** of the various yearly meetings.

The Richmond Declaration is a monument to the impact of **evangelicalism** on Gurneyite Friends in the 19th century. Almost half of the document is devoted to statements on **God**, **Christ**, the Fall of Man, the Resurrection, and the Sabbath, indistinguishable from those of contemporary evangelicals. The statements on justification and **sanctification** are more ambiguous, reflecting deep divisions among advocates of instantaneous and gradual **holiness**. The sections on baptism and communion, **peace**, and **oaths** are more traditionally Quaker.

In the aftermath of the conference, most Gurneyite yearly meetings endorsed the Declaration. **Wilburite** Friends blasted it as further Gurneyite apostasy. Other yearly meetings thought it too **creedal**. Radical holiness revivalists like Updegraff repudiated it as an infringement on liberty of conscience.

With the rise of a **modernist** wing among Gurneyite Friends after 1890, the Richmond Declaration became more controversial. When the Five Years Meeting (*see* FRIENDS UNITED MEETING) was formed under a Uniform Discipline in 1902, it was left to yearly meetings whether to include the Declaration. Some Friends subsequently pressed to have the Declaration incorporated into the Uniform Discipline, leading to a series of debates that culminated in the withdrawal of two yearly meetings in 1925 and 1937. An effort to reaffirm the Declaration at the 1987 sessions of Friends United Meeting failed. [Thomas D. Hamm]

ROGERS, WILLIAM (d. 1707). A Friend from Bristol, England, Rogers joined with **John Wilkinson** and **John Story** in challenging **George Fox** in the 1670s. Rogers continued his own opposition to the centralization and formalization of church government within Quakerism in **Britain** into the 1680s.

ROSS, ELIZABETH GRISCOM ("BETSY") (1752–1836). Free Quaker and supporter of the American Revolution, Ross is supposed to have designed and stitched the first Stars and Stripes American flag.

ROWNTREE, JOHN STEPHENSON (1834–1907). Author of the highly influential *Quakerism, Past and Present,* winner of a Prize Essay Competition in 1859 on the causes of decline within British Quakerism. Rowntree, an **evangelical**, labeled **Quietism** as "the degeneracy of the second generation of Friends" and encouraged the ending of **peculiarity**. [Pink Dandelion]

ROWNTREE, JOHN WILHELM (1868–1905). Probably the leading Friend associated with the **modernist** reinvention of Quakerism in **Britain** at the end of the 19th century and the beginning of the 20th. Vocal as a **young Friend** at **yearly meeting** in 1892, he toured extensively in America in 1895 and spoke at the **Manchester Conference** the same year. He was instrumental in the foundation of the **Summer Schools Movement**, gatherings of hundreds of Friends to hear and learn about the new thinking on biblical scholarship and Darwinism. It was his vision to instigate the writing of a comprehensive multivolume history of Quakerism. He began work on this, but died prematurely at the age of 37. The task was taken over by **Rufus Jones** and **William Charles Braithwaite**. Their collection of books are known as the Rowntree Series.

Rowntree's impact on Rufus Jones should not be underestimated. Upon meeting in Switzerland in 1897, the two struck up a deep and close friendship. Their letters to each other testify to their love for one another but also for their shared vision for the future of Quakerism. Jones, in a sense, was converted to Rowntree's **liberalism**, and their meeting marks the beginning of Jones's modernism.

Jones and Rowntree were frequent visitors in each other's family homes, and it is on the way to America that Rowntree contracted his final fatal pneumonia. He died in Rufus Jones's arms. His death shook British Friends, but his work was far enough advanced to find a secure base to continue. [Pink Dandelion]

ROWNTREE, JOSEPH (1836–1925). Manufacturer, civic leader, **philanthropist**. Leaving his father's grocery business 1869 to enter a cocoa and chocolate partnership with his brother, Joseph Rowntree was active in the firm until 1923 (*see* BUSINESS AND ECONOMICS). He sat briefly on York City Council in northern England and chaired the York Liberal Association. He took a philanthropic interest in the city's library, Quaker schools, and the Retreat at York (*see* EDUCATION; MENTAL HEALTH REFORM) and supported adult **religious education** work of Friends. In 1904, he established a model village for his workers and the Rowntree Charitable Trust. He collaborated in 1897 on the ***Temperance** Problem and Social Reform*, and published four other volumes on regulation of the liquor trade. His son, Seebohm, made a scholarly study of *Poverty*, published in 1901. [Sabron Newton]

RUIZ, GENARO G. Quaker teacher and **pastor** in Ciudad Victoria, Tamaulipas, **Mexico**. In the early 1950s the *Reunion General de los Amigos en Mexico* was formed under his leadership.

RUSHMORE, JANE PALEN (1864–1958). For over 30 years general secretary of the Central Bureau of Philadelphia **Yearly Meeting** of the **Religious Society of Friends** (**Hicksite**) (1911–1945), Jane Rushmore also served as **clerk** of the Yearly Meeting and of its Representative **Committee**. Prior to that she had served as the first staff person for the **Friends General Conference (FGC)** Religious Education Committee, work she continued after 1911. As a result, the FGC and Philadelphia **religious education** programs were virtually merged for nearly a half-century. Rushmore was a frequent speaker and writer of essays and pamphlets interpreting **liberal Friends** in the first half of the 20th century. [Margery Post Abbott]

RUSSELL, ELBERT (1871–1951). Teacher, Quaker historian, and writer. Russell's was a leading voice, along with that of **Rufus Jones**, to bring **modernist** insights on the primacy of revelation and the importance of scholarship in the renewal of faith into **Gurneyite** Quakerism. Russell accepted the **pastoral system** but was opposed to the **revivals** of the **holiness movement**. Professor of **Bible** at **Earlham College** starting in 1895, he also served as chaplain. He resigned his position in 1915 after his proposal to strengthen the Quaker nature of the **college**, by building a large **meetinghouse** on campus for both students and the **yearly meeting**, was rejected. He later taught at Johns Hopkins University, in Maryland, then became dean of the Duke Divinity School, Duke University in North Carolina. [Pink Dandelion]

RUSTIN, BAYARD TAYLOR (1912–1987). Civil Rights leader and **peace** activist. Bayard Taylor Rustin was born in West Chester, Pennsylvania, and raised by his grandparents. Although Janifer, Rustin's grandfather, was a member of the African Methodist Episcopal Church, his grandmother, Julia, was a Quaker. The children attended the African Methodist Episcopal church, but Julia infused in all of her "children" Quaker ideals of tolerance, love of justice, nonviolence, and the conviction that there is "that of God" in everyone. *See* EQUALITY; LIGHT; PEACE.

Rustin attended Wilberforce University and later **Cheyney** State Teachers College. In 1937, he moved to New York City and soon joined New York **Monthly Meeting**. He became involved in issues of racial and social justice, as a member of the Young Communist League prior to **World War II**. He spent time as a **conscientious objector** in prison during and after the conflict, and serving on the staff of the Fellowship of Reconciliation. In 1956, Rustin was arrested for "indecent behavior" with two other men, at a time when homosexual conduct was a felony in all American states. The disgrace that this arrest brought upon him caused him temporarily to withdraw from his political endeavors, but by the early 1960s he was a comrade of Martin Luther King Jr. (1929–1968). In 1963, he was superintendent of the March on Washington, D.C., that propelled King to international renown. Shortly thereafter, Rustin became director of the A. Philip Randolph Institute, and by the early 1980s he also was active in Freedom House, which observed elections in various developing countries to make sure they were held honestly. Rustin died after an inspection of the elections in Haiti. He stated throughout his life that it was his Quaker love of justice and **peace** that animated many of his activities. [Buzz Haughton]

–S–

SABBATH. *See* TIMES AND SEASONS.

SACRAMENTS. Within the Christian church the governing question of the sacraments is "How is the divine reality communicated?" In orthodox Protestant Christianity, **baptism** and **communion** (also known as the Holy Ordinances), have readily identifiable signs of **God**'s invisible Presence—water or bread and wine. For example, the wine and bread "communicate" **Christ**'s risen, real Presence. The Presence is what makes the sacrament effective. This Presence is divinely communicated, not a human endeavor.

The classical Quaker understanding of sacrament develops from this context. It is rooted in the firm conviction that God "communicates" the divine Presence directly and immediately to human beings. Early Friends spoke of baptisms of fire and of the **Holy Spirit**, which surpassed water baptism, and the communion experienced in the **gathered meeting for worship**. **George Fox** looked to the inward, true sacramental experience, knowing God does not need designated visible signs to communicate the grace of the divine self (cf. Luke 3:16). Fox believed that practice of the ordinances was spiritually barren and an invitation for people to mistake the substance for the form.

In his *Apology,* **Robert Barclay** takes Fox's position, then moderates it. Barclay says, "for we are certain that the day has dawned in which God has risen and dismissed all those ceremonies and rites. He is to be worshipped only in Spirit. He appears to those who wait upon him." Barclay goes on to state that the sacraments, as traditionally practiced, were not wrong. On the contrary, he says, "If there are any in this day who practice this ceremony (communion) with a true tenderness of spirit, and with real conscience toward God, and in the manner of the primitive church . . . I do not doubt but they may be indulged in it" (*Apology*, Freiday p. 361), but he was skeptical of how often this occurred in practice and rejected outward sacraments for Friends.

Prior to the 20th century, Friends were often **disowned** for being baptized with water or taking communion. A crisis triggered by **David Updegraff**'s insistence on the right to be baptized led to the Conference in Richmond, Indiana, in 1887, which affirmed that no one who had undergone baptism should be retained as a **minister** or **elder** in the **church**. However, Friends in Ohio, such as Updegraff, ignored this aspect of the **Richmond Declaration of Faith** adopted at that Conference.

Modern Friends believe that God initiates a sacramental encounter each time men and women gather to worship God in Spirit, as Barclay said. Then and there, God graciously and freely communicates "the real presence." This presence is variously understood as the risen Lord, the living Christ, the **Light** of Christ, or the Holy Spirit.

Today, Quakers do not condemn the traditional practice of sacraments among non-Quakers. Friends argue, rather, that the use of bread and wine or water is not necessary for communication of the divine reality. In fact, most Quakers reject the practice of the outward sacraments within their **meetings**.

Clearly, Quakers "believe in the sacraments," although Friends usually do not use the outward practices. They also consider the Catholic sacraments such as **marriage**, ordination, penance, and extreme unction to be a direct matter or **covenant** between the individual and God (*see* DEATH AND DYING). Other individuals may only stand witness to this inward reality. Friends affirm that the divine reality is communicated not through particular visible signs, but, rather, immediately and directly into human hearts. [Alan Kolp]

SALVATION. Quaker views on salvation have varied widely, but the traditional stance, as articulated by **George Fox**, **Robert Barclay**, and others maintains the scriptural position that salvation is received by faith in what **God** has done through **Christ** Jesus. Fox's letter of 1671 to the governor of Barbados is his statement closest to an orthodox Christian view and is often included in modern books of **discipline**, but this and other statements about salvation also stress the essential nature of the inward work of **Christ** in the human heart. They point to the conviction that the saving work of God involves a dynamic reality rather than a mechanistic transaction.

Robert Barclay developed several aspects of this reality including tensions between: opportunities for salvation being limited and God's grace being sufficient; an emphasis on universal access to the **Light** of Christ and the necessity of **preaching** to the world; the importance of inward faith and an emphasis on faith without works being dead. **Joseph John Gurney** continued along these trajectories, emphasizing both the universal nature of the Light and the particularity of that Light being none other than the presence of the Spirit of the risen Christ working within the hearts of humanity.

Friends, however, have not simply viewed salvation as an object of interest regarding one's eternal destiny. Rather, Friends have emphasized three aspects of salvation: the transformative character of Christ's saving power, its universal accessibility, and its societal impact. All of these are central aspects of salvation through Christ. Friends, thus, have long held that the saving power of Jesus Christ not only leads to the triumph over **sin** at the last judgment, but that Christ destroys the grip of sin and **evil** in persons' lives, reversing—at least in part—the curse of human fallenness (*see* PERFECTION). The power of Christ and the **Holy Spirit**, early Friends held, was more than enough to deliver persons from any habit or pattern of sin, and **sanctification** through Christ was held to be central to the saving Christian Gospel. These views have influenced various **holiness movements** over the past three centuries.

Second, while accepting the scriptural teaching that all who come to the Father do so by Christ Jesus (John 14:6), Friends have also held high the scriptural injunction that the **Light** of Christ enlightens all who come into the world (John 1:9). This has balanced the particularity of means with the universality of access (*see* UNIVERSALISM) and has underlain Friends' evangelistic efforts from the **Valiant Sixty** to the **modern missionary movement**.

Third, Friends have understood the realm of Christ's saving work to involve societal, moral, and economic realities and have thus sought to become agents of actualizing the Divine Will on earth as it is in heaven. The world is the object of God's saving love and the sphere in which the good news of salvation is to be played out. Quaker **peace** work and social **concerns** likewise illustrate the belief that the Christian Gospel indeed has radical social implications.

For more than a century, salvation has not been viewed with unanimity across the various Quaker traditions. Even biblically, some Friends have emphasized Paul's teaching on the atoning effect of Christ's sacrifice as the central issue, while others have looked more to John's emphasis of the revealing work of Christ as compelling (*see* ATONEMENT). In the modern era some Friends have either diminished the traditional emphasis Friends have placed on salvation, or they have adopted an all-inclusive universalism, which makes the issue irrelevant. These moves, however, risk departure from the historic Friends' understanding, whereby salvation is received solely by means of a believing response to God's saving initiative as opposed to trusting in anything which is of human origin. While God's saving love is revealed through Christ, this revelation is not confined to Christian presentations of it. In that sense, Friends have embraced the essence of the Christian Gospel: getting at its core, rather than focusing on its manifestations. [Paul N. Anderson]

SANCTIFICATION. Derived from the Latin term for holiness, "sanctification" means to make holy; to be set apart for a special work of **God**: to be full of love and free of **evil**. Early Friends spoke of this as "**perfection**," a doctrine that at times resulted in imprisonment for blasphemy. (*See* PRISON)

The earliest Friends believed in the possibility of total eradication of **sin**, emphasizing the active work of God in this life. **George Fox** believed that complete sanctification was both possible and the intended design for Christian living. **Robert Barclay** modified Fox's position, seeing perfection in this life as attainable, but rare. Neither man emphasized sanctification and conversion as separate works of the **Holy Spirit**. Both saw the **Light** of **Christ** working to seal human **salvation** and ensure conformity to the life of Jesus Christ. **William Penn** articulated clearly Friends' view that every individual must experience the **cross** and daily die to sin. In this way the cross—the power of God—would obliterate sin and sanctify those who submitted to its discipline.

For the next two centuries Friends often spoke of "baptisms" in the plural (*see* SACRAMENTS). These inward baptisms of fire and of the Holy Spirit were sometimes described as a daily experience and often ones of tribulation. These "deep baptisms" not only washed away sin, but also the desire to sin. The individual could not control this process of coming under the will of Christ, but could cooperate with it by silent waiting on the Lord (*see* QUIETISM).

Until the 1870s, Friends explicitly rejected the formulation of instantaneous and complete sanctification of the Wesleyans. **Joseph John Gurney**'s insistence that simple faith in the **atonement** was enough to ensure salvation opened the way among **Gurneyite** Friends for the Wesleyan holiness doctrine of sanctification as an instantaneous experience often called the "second blessing," or second work of grace, producing a perfect love for God. The Methodist leader John Wesley, like Fox and Barclay, believed that an individual could be made perfect in love in this life. Wesley, like John Calvin and early Friends, believed that sanctification begins at conversion. Unlike Calvin, Wesley held that one can live in the fullness of God's love as the highest expression of entire sanctification. Unlike Wesley, Phoebe Palmer (1807–1874), a key figure in the **holiness movement**, and **David Updegraff** believed that sanctification was both "instantaneous" and "complete." In late 19th century, many Gurneyite Friends could report the day and even the time of their sanctification. In contrast, the **Wilburites** thought that Gurney was seeking an easy way to **heaven** and bypassing the discipline of taking up the cross, which they believed was an essential part of Friends' understanding of perfection.

In the 20th century, **Everett Cattell** has constructed a contemporary alternative to both the absolute position of Fox and the holiness position. Cattell noted that although it is possible for the perfection of love and holiness to happen instantaneously, it is rare. More often, an instantaneous experience in which one awakens to a deeper life with God is followed by a process of growth in this love in which one gains an understanding of the absolute holiness of God.

Cattell's unique contribution in this creative synthesis is to say that sanctification does not eradicate the sin nature, but rather cleanses human nature in order to free it of its self-centeredness and the inherent temptation to sin. For those Friends who still take sanctification seriously this has become their normative position, although some Friends, particularly in Evangelical Friends Church–Eastern Region, clearly qualify this with a statement that while the Holy Spirit empowers believers to have victory over sin, it does not make them incapable of choosing to sin. [Gayle D. Beebe]

SANCTUARY MOVEMENT. A number of **North American** Friends were active in the movement by several churches to offer sanctuary for refugees from violence in Central America in the 1980s. One of the founders of the movement, **Jim Corbett**, a member of Pima Monthly Meeting in Tucson, was eventually acquitted, along with several non-friends, in a highly publicized trial in Arizona in which the U.S. government attempted to end the practice of churches offering sanctuary. [Margery Post Abbott]

SARGEANT, JOHN (1813–1883). Leader of the Fritchley Schism of 1868 in **Britain**. This was a **Conservative** group concerned with the revision of **discipline** (e.g., the acceptance of **marriages** to non-Quakers and dropping the use of **plain dress and speech**). The group set itself up as Fritchley **General Meeting** and remained outside **London Yearly Meeting** until 1968.

SCHOFIELD, MARTHA (1839–1916). American Quaker **abolitionist** and **educator**. A native of Chester County, Pennsylvania, Schofield was one of the few northern women to continue working with freedmen in the South after Reconstruction. The Schofield School is now part of the Aiken, South Carolina, public school district.

SCIENCE AND TECHNOLOGY. George Fox's decisive 1652 meeting with the Westmoreland **Seekers** came 10 years after the death of Galileo (1564–1642) and the birth of Isaac Newton (1642/43–1727). Despite their different goals, the new religion and the new "natural philosophy" shared a practical orientation and rejected the validation of **truth** through appeal to tradition, authority, or majority opinion. Their bent to the practical sphere was reinforced by their suspicion of the **arts**.

The remarkable contribution of Quakers to science is most clearly seen in **Britain** where Friends for many years were excluded from the classic professions. It has been estimated that 46 times more Friends were elected to the Royal Society, Britain's premier scientific body between 1850 and 1900, than would be justified by their actual numbers. The first woman to be elected was the crystallographer Kathleen Lonsdale (1903–1971), later the first woman president of the British Association for the Advancement of Science. The foundations of both atomic and cosmological science were laid by Quakers. **John Dalton** proposed the atomic theory of matter in his *New System of Chemical Philosophy* in 1808. Sir **Arthur Eddington** almost single-handedly founded the science of astrophysics and was among the first to espouse Edwin Powell Hubble's theory of an expanding universe in 1929. In 1967, the radio-astronomer **Jocelyn (Susan) Bell Burnell** codiscovered the X-ray pulsar, a major step toward unifying quantum physics and cosmic evolution.

In **North America**, Friends played a major role in the American Philosophical Society in its early years, the botanist **John Bartram**'s name being the second in the original membership roll after that of the non-Quaker Benjamin Franklin. Bartram was only the most prominent in a long line of Quaker naturalists and horticulturists (*see* COLLINSON, PETER and MITCHELL, MARIA).

The physicist and engineer Silvanus Thompson (1851–1916), whose classic textbook on calculus is still used in American colleges, was an influential member of the reform group at the 1895 **Manchester Conference**, which set a **liberal** course for British Quakerism. So taken for granted was the scientific bent of Quakers that **William Charles Braithwaite** pleaded at the Manchester Conference for a broader "witness to the Glory of God," noting that "while Friends have been among the pioneers of modern science, they have until recent years repressed all taste for the fine arts."

No social group played a greater role than Quakers in developing technology for **business** and industry. The take-off point of the Industrial Revolution is generally acknowledged to be the iron-smelting and forging processes introduced by the **Darby** family at Coalbrookdale in the mid-18th century. Quakers were prominent in canal building, engineering, pump manufacture, and instrument making. Closely associated with lead mining and china clay extraction, the modest amount of silver they produced was of such purity that it became, in effect, a Mint standard, and from 1705 to 1737 so-called "Quaker shillings" were issued, specially marked as a warrant of their quality. North American Friends were also engaged in early industrial technology, including Josiah White (1781–1850), the prominent ironmaster, Curtis Hussey in copper and crucible steel production, and Joseph Hussey in the early oil industry.

The most eminent of English horologists, **Thomas Tompion**, is recorded as a Quaker, as were his close peers, **Daniel Quare** and **George Graham**. Surveyor **Jeremiah Dixon** gave his name to the politically important Mason-Dixon boundary line between Pennsylvania and Maryland.

In the railway era Quaker banking, manufacturing, and engineering expertise came together in an extraordinary synergy. James Tangye, a deeply spiritual man as well as the successful founder of large industrial company, was typical of Friends in seeing technology as an integral part of the divine creative action. **Edward Pease**, who financed George Stephenson's first railway in 1825, was only the first of many Quakers involved in railroad development.

In the 20th century, several North American Friends were in the forefront of the social sciences and public health. **Kenneth Boulding**'s work has offered new approaches to economics, using biological images and models to describe economic and social processes. The geographer Gilbert White (1911–) has been a leader in the improvement of public water supplies and flood protection worldwide. He has set new standards for understanding water management issues within environmental systems. **Mary Steichen Calderone** (1904–1998), a medical doctor and New York Friend, has been a pioneer in the study of human sexuality and acceptance of family planning as part of public health practice.

In the late 20th century, **Conservative** Friends and others became increasingly concerned about the dangers of excessive dependence on technology, both as a practical matter and as a threat to the **testimony** of **simplicity**. In contrast, some liberal Friends have been excited by the discovery of quantum physics as being parallel to the both/and views of God. [Frank Parkinson]

SCOTT, JOB (1751–1793). American teacher, theologian, and traveling **minister** whose version of **Quietism** served as a prelude to **Elias Hicks**.

SEEGER, DANIEL A. (1935–). While an attender at Morningside **Meeting** in New York, Seeger sought **conscientious objector (CO)** status in 1962. Because at that time he claimed to be an agnostic, the U.S. Justice Department denied his application. In May 1964, after being sentenced to a year in prison, Seeger, supported by the **American Friends Service Committee (AFSC)**, appealed the decision as a violation of the constitutional provision that "Congress shall make no law respecting an establishment of religion." In 1965, the U.S. Supreme Court ruled in Seeger's favor, expanding the Selective Service and Training Act to cover cases like Seeger's. Seeger and his wife, Betty Jean, soon joined Friends, and Seeger served for many years as head of the AFSC New York office, then became executive director of **Pendle Hill** Center for Study and Contemplation in Pennsylvania from 1991 to 2000. He has also been active in the Quaker **Universalist** Fellowship and **Friends World Committee for Consultation (FWCC)**, and served as **clerk** of the FWCC Interim Committee and as presiding clerk of the World Conference of Friends in 1991 in Kenya. Many of his writings on spiritual and social concerns themes have been published.

SEEKERS. During the **English Civil War** (1642–1648), stalemated religious and political conflicts led some idealistic young **Puritans** to give up on all churches. They were dubbed "Seekers," or "Waiters," as they waited for the Kingdom of **God** to be revealed. Some stayed home, while others met in groups for religious discussion, **prayer**, Scripture reading, and "waiting upon the Lord" in silence. Without official leaders or outward **sacraments**, these Seekers already practiced some key aspects of Quaker **worship**. Some looked for new apostles who would work signs and wonders and reestablish the purity of primitive Christianity. Others did not expect to return to New Testament practices but anticipated that God would move them forward into a new age of "spiritual Christianity." By 1650, however, both types were disillusioned. It was among these informal seeking groups that **George Fox** and other Quaker apostles found the most fertile ground for their new movement. [Douglas Gwyn]

SEIN, HEBERTO M. (1898–1977). Born in Matehuala, San Luis Potosi, **Mexico**, Sein was a founding member of Mexico City **Meeting** and Friends House. In the early 1950s, his **concern** for dialogue among different groups of Friends in Mexico, was the catalyst to the formation of the *Reunion General de los Amigos en Mexico*. He also advocated the development of international workcamps sponsored by the **American Friends Service Committee (AFSC)** (*see also* CÉRÉSOLE, PIERRE). As international interpreter, he participated in the sessions of the formation of the League of Nations and later with the International Labour Organisation in Geneva, Switzerland. Living out the **peace testimony**, he was a well-recognized promoter of nonviolence in Mexico and beyond. [Loida Eunice Fernandez Gonzalez]

SENECA FALLS WOMAN'S RIGHTS CONVENTION. In 1848, **Lucretia Mott** gathered for tea with three other Quakers, Mary Ann McClintock (*see* McCLINTOCK FAMILY), Jane Master Hunt, and Martha Wright (1806–1875), and also **Elizabeth Cady Stanton**. These **women** composed a call to a women's rights convention to be held on July 19 and 20 in nearby Seneca Falls, New York. James and Lucretia Mott and Thomas McClintock chaired the large, public sessions, which reviewed the status of women around the world. The convention ended with numerous resolutions on behalf of women's rights including a Declaration of Sentiments modeled on the United

States Declaration of Independence and a call for women's suffrage. [Margery Post Abbott]

SEPARATISTS. A term most often used to describe self-governing or separated churches not part of the English national parish church system. From 1540 to 1640, congregations of committed adults who had rejected state-church ties emerged in many lands, but risked death penalties except in Holland (*see* ANABAPTISTS). During the **English Civil War** (1642–1648), radical **Puritan** and Baptist "believers" groups who rejected the parish system flourished in England. They mushroomed under self-chosen leaders, such as John Bunyan, and produced most of the recruits to early Quakerism. The groups, which worshipped in silence and found **sacraments** empty, were nicknamed **Seekers**.

After the restoration of the English bishops and kings in 1660, Independents, Congregationalists, and Friends did not give up hope for converting England, but were jailed under the Conventicle Acts of 1664 and 1670. Though freedom of worship was granted in 1689, Friends and other Dissenters or Nonconformists were excluded from the English universities, Parliament, and the army until the 19th century, except in the **North American** colonies. [Hugh Barbour]

SESSIONS, FREDERICK (1836–1920). English-born missionary to **South Asia**.

SEXUALITY. Until the late 20th century, Friends accepted sexuality only within monogamous marital relationships. The first sign of a major change came with the1963 publication in **Britain** of the pamphlet *Toward a Quaker View of Sex*.

Many Friends today still believe that sexuality should only be expressed within the traditional **marriage** relationship and they frown on divorce, polygamy, and premarital sex, as well as homosexuality, as sinful behavior outside biblical norms. Other Friends accept a variety of loving, committed relationships. They believe that those whose sexual orientation is toward another of their own gender rather than the opposite sex are responding to what is physiologically normal for them, but may find this socially painful because it can be treated by others as deviant, even immoral. They believe that to reject people on the grounds of their sexual orientation may be considered a denial of God's creation.

In 1965, Quaker **women** in **East Africa** first addressed the issue of initiation rites with respect to female circumcision and requested the government ministry of health to study this question and make recommendations. No strong stance has been taken in part because many Friends came from areas where female circumcision was not practiced, and it only slowly became an issue as the church expanded. [Elise Boulding, Esther Mombo]

SHAKING QUAKERS (SHAKERS). The nickname given to followers of the Wardle family who broke with Bolton **Meeting** in England in 1747 and established a more charismatic liturgical form, involving dancing. Later led by "Mother" Ann Lee (1736–1784) to America in 1774, the group developed as communitarian and celibate. It became officially known as The United Society of Believers in Christ's Second Appearing but is commonly referred to as the Shakers. Highly successful in the 19th century, the group continues today albeit with a membership of only six people living in one community. [Pink Dandelion]

SHARPLESS, EVI (1844–1913). First North American **missionary** to Jamaica, sent by Iowa Yearly Meeting in 1881. *See* CARIBBEAN.

SHARPLESS, ISAAC (1848–1920). North American mathematician and astronomer, he served as professor from 1875 until 1884, then dean for three years, and eventually as president of **Haverford College** until 1917.

SHILLITOE, THOMAS (1754–1836). A **Quietist minister** from **Britain** whose response to divine commands led him to choose work as a shoemaker, then, at age 51, to leave this vocation and use the small capital he had accumulated for full-time traveling **ministry** in England, **Ireland**, **continental Europe**, and **North America**. Raised an Anglican in London, he attended chapel services in later youth and then became a Friend against the wishes of family and acquaintances. His **theology** retained many **evangelical**, Anglican influences mixed with a Quaker quietism. His **mission** to both the ordinary and the powerful called for repentance, living a devout Christian life, and enforcement of Sabbath observance. He also advocated **temperance**, rejection of luxuries, reliance on **God**'s power rather than arms, release of slaves, and care of the poor and of prisoners. He thus formed an example in several ways: dedication to mission; demonstrating use of intuitive feeling as a test of **leading;** and giving up a **business** in favor of God's work.

Shillitoe's theology (*see* ORTHODOX QUAKERISM) involved **salvation** by both faith and works; personal acceptance of **Christ'**s full divinity and the **atonement**; the dominating authority of the **Bible**; repentance for **sin**; living a righteous life following God's commands; and avoiding Satan's wiles. His sense of the necessity of these beliefs for all Friends, his powerful evangelical **preaching**, and his dogged insistence on separation where beliefs differed made him the key opponent of **Elias Hicks** and a major precipitating factor in the **Great Separation** of 1827–1828. [Cynthia Earl Kerman]

SHITEMI, SIMEON (1931–). Born and raised in the Kakemega District in Kenya (*see* EAST AFRICA) Shitemi and his wife, Beatrice, are members of East Africa (North) **Yearly Meeting** based at Kitale. Educated in London, he taught at Kaimosi Teachers College and was lecturer in the Kenya Institute of Administration in civil service and diplomacy, later receiving an honorary doctorate from **Earlham College**. Shitemi has served the Kenya government as under-secretary in the office of the president, permanent secretary in the ministries of health, tourism, wildlife and fisheries, and director of the department of foreign trade. He represented Kenya on the United Nations Disarmament Commission in Geneva from 1979 to 1981. Shitemi served as **clerk** of **Friends World Committee for Consultation** (FWCC) from 1986 until 1991 and has been chairman of the board of **Friends Theological College**. He currently is on the Board of Trustees of **Friends World College**, clerks the FWCC-Africa Section until 2004, and is head of a nongovernmental organization based in Nairobi. [Margery Post Abbott]

SIMMONS, MARTHA (ALSO SIMMONDS) (1624–1665) and THOMAS (fl. 1650s). Martha Simmons was a well-known London Friend, a sister of Giles Calvert (1612–1663), and a leading supporter of **James Nayler**. Later reconciled to the main body of Quakers, she died on a journey to Maryland. Thomas was a printer of Quaker books, his establishment being on the same premises as the London Quaker office and meeting room, at the old Bull and Mouth tavern.

SIMPLICITY. In order to live in the **Truth**, 17th-century Friends stripped away whatever appeared to be superfluous. This process of stripping led to what is now called simplicity, the by-product of a single-minded intention toward **God**. Its root lies in the understanding that for the inward life to grow, the outward life must respond and that the growth of the inward life depends in part on *doing* what one knows to be right. This approach means that stripping away whatever hinders relationship with God becomes of primary importance.

Before the end of the 17th century this determination to strip away superfluities became a demand for the **plain dress and speech** that became characteristic of **Quietist** Friends for the next century. Expectations for a life consistent with faith had been formalized. These expectations never became so rigid as with Amish and some Mennonite groups, but retained an underlying assumption that each individual's plainness grew out of personal spiritual **leading**.

By the latter part of the 19th century, expectations for plain dress and speech were relaxing in many regions, though they persisted to a degree well into the 20th century among **Conservative** Friends. During this period the term "simplicity" came into favor, denoting a less formalistic, more flexible approach. The concept also came to have relevance to simplification of activity and schedule which, a century later, **Thomas R. Kelly** saw could grow out of attention to the Quaker understanding of **concern**.

John Woolman is often quoted for his attention to the relationship between the **spirituality** and its outward manifestations, with simplification of the outward. In *Plea for the Poor*, he explored the societal and economic implications of personal choices for the roots of war, poverty, and slavery as well as effects on the individual soul. Later Friends used Woolman's work to show simplicity as a root of concern for the **environment**.

As the Quaker **distinctives** disappeared in the 20th century, the avoidance of excessive consumption, ambition, and activity as advocated by Woolman and Kelly became seen as primary expressions of simplicity in **Europe** and **North America**. [Frances Irene Taber]

SIN. George Fox said that sin came from transgression and disobedience, obeying the Serpent (in the Garden of Eden) rather than **God**. Fox also was clear that in **Christ** all could come into "the state of Adam which he was in before he fell": a state of **perfection**, without sin, whereby one could live subject to the spirit of God. **Robert Barclay** describes the implications of the Fall in his *Apology*. As descendants of Adam and Eve, all humans are like them in the natural propensity to disobey and inability to overcome this propensity alone. Adam and Eve, however, sinned as a consequence of their actions, not by simply existing, and the same is true of their descendants. While weak and subject to temptation, no one is sinful until he or she actually sins. In Barclay's words, "This seed [of disobedience, sown by the Serpent] is not imputed to infants, until by transgression they actually join themselves therewith" (*Apology*, Freiday, p. 66).

Early Friends spoke **prophetically** to institutionalized sin when they called for justice in economic and political relationships (*see* POLITICS), but most of their theological writings focused on sin as a concern affecting the individual's relationship to God. In more recent years, more attention has been given to sin as a social as well as individual phenomenon.

A first consequence of this "functional" way of thinking about sin was a natural integration into understanding the power of Christ, leading to the doctrine of **perfection**. If sin is a matter of disobedience rather than our essential nature, then freedom from sin requires the power to know God's will and be obedient to it. Friends saw that power as coming from the **Light** of Christ Jesus. According to Fox, "With the light you come to know the Messiah, your Saviour, to save you from your sin . . . this light shews you your **evil** deeds, and evil ways, when God is not in all your thoughts, when your heart revolteth" (Fox, *Works*, 4:73). The assertion that Christ's power enables his followers to overcome sin was a terrible scandal to other Christians of the time. Fox and Barclay accused other Christian leaders of seeking to keep their followers in their sinful states, in the Devil's custody, denying the full power of the Savior.

The emphasis on actual behavior rather than a theoretical state of depravity or innocence helps explain why there has been very little systematic thinking about sin in Friends' **theology** since the first generation, or in the development of Friends' books of Christian **discipline**. Today, many Friends consider sin to be disobedience to the will of God. Some Friends accept the essential depravity of humanity and others believe that human nature is essentially good. Yet among most Friends past and present, progress toward freedom from sin is (assuming genuine faith and a desire for **holiness** or **sanctification**) a matter of practicing obedience in **worship**, study, personal relationships, and service. [Johan Maurer]

SMITH, HANNAH WHITALL (1832–1911). Holiness **minister**, writer, born into a Philadelphia **Orthodox** Quaker family. Smith's two books—*The Christian's Secret of a Happy Life* (1870) and *The Unselfishness of God* (1903)—established her reputation in the **holiness movement** and are still read today.

An ardent seeker after **salvation**, Smith discovered the Plymouth Brethren in 1865 and became immersed in the holiness movement and camp meeting **revivals**. After a long struggle with her own self-will, she became an adherent of holiness, preaching **sanctification** as the "the second blessing."

Unable to find a similar enthusiasm among Philadelphia Friends, she and her husband, Robert Pearsall Smith (1827–1898), both resigned their membership in 1872. As a husband and wife evangelistic team, the Smiths visited England from 1873 to 1875, leading large gatherings dedicated to the promotion of holiness. Their teachings laid the groundwork in 1876 for the Keswick Convention, one of many institutionalized forms of the holiness movement. Later she repudiated some of the teachings of the more extreme revivalists and became a militant suffragette and socialist. She eventually rejoined Quakers through Baltimore **Yearly Meeting**. [Margery Post Abbott]

SMITH, RUTH ESTHER (1870–1947). Early missionary to Guatemala. Smith was the main forger of Friends' missionary work in **Central America**. At the age of 36, in San Francisco, California, she was called to **mission** work, after hearing the voice of **God** saying: "Chiquimula, Guatemala." She arrived in Guatemala on November 22, 1906 Under her leadership, the churches expanded widely in Guatemala and Honduras. [Édgar Amílcar Madrid]

SMUCK, HAROLD V. (1920–1995). Educated at Marion College (now Indiana Wesleyan University), Christian Theological Seminary (Indianapolis), and **Earlham College**, Harold Smuck served Friends as a missionary, **pastor**, missions executive, and leader within **Friends United Meeting (FUM)**. His first missionary service was at the Friends Center in Kingston, Jamaica (*see* CARIBBEAN), under joint appointment by FUM and the **American Friends Service Committee (AFSC)**. Later he served in Ramallah, Palestine, and in **East Africa**. He was head of the FUM **missions** program from 1966 until 1981, and was the presiding **clerk** of FUM from 1993 to his death in 1995. He was also active in Indiana **Yearly Meeting**, AFSC, the Associated Committee of Friends on Indian Affairs (*see* NATIVE AMERICANS), and **Friends World Committee for Consultation**, Section of the Americas. His writings include the books *Friends in East Africa* and *I Do Not Climb This Mountain Alone*. In 1944, he married Evelyn Sutton, whom he met while she was preparing for service as a missionary nurse; he died four days short of their 51st anniversary. [Johan Maurer]

SOCIAL GOSPEL. Although Quaker literature contains little specific mention of a social gospel, many joined the Religious Society of Friends because they saw it as a historical expression of this movement which, after World War I, emphasized **Christ**'s teachings as the basis for social reform.

The first Quakers believed that "Christ has come to teach His people Himself," and waged a "**Lamb's War**" against **sin** and **evil**, holding all systems—political, religious, economic, and social—to the standards of a "restored" Christianity. Following the restoration of the Stuart monarchy by Charles II in 1660, social concern gradually evolved from an expectation of **apocalyptic** triumph to the approach of changing the world by small degrees.

Until the late 18th century, much of the notable social action taken by Friends was individual rather than institutional: **William Penn**'s policies of religious freedom and **peace** in Pennsylvania; **John Bellers**'s proposals for addressing poverty, illiteracy, health, and international peace; **John Woolman**'s and **Anthony Benezet**'s influence on the antislavery movement and promotion of **Native American** rights; **William Tuke**'s creation of a pioneering **mental health** hospital.

During the 19th century, individual efforts continued to bring significant results: **Elizabeth Fry (penal reform)**; **Lucretia Mott (abo-**

lition and **women**'s suffrage); **Levi and Catherine Coffin** (the **underground railroad**); **John Bright** (political and social reform). Increasingly, however, Friends shared in the wider **evangelical** Christian "voluntary" movement, and abolition of slavery, suffrage, peace, **temperance**, women's rights, and other reform causes were taken up by Quaker institutions.

Growing wealth from Quaker **business** and industry was applied in the 19th and 20th centuries to workers' housing, education, and social improvement. Especially noteworthy in this regard were the British confectioners and bakers Carr, Cadbury, Rowntree, and Palmer.

Rufus Jones, **Emily Balch**, and many others felt the influence of the social gospel through slum pastors like the Baptist Walter Rauschenbusch (1861–1918). British, Canadian, and American **peace and service agencies** provided major **relief** efforts during and after the wars of the 20th century and addressed the systemic ills that "sow the seeds of war." In the United States in the latter 1900s, some Friends formed the **Friends Disaster Service** to tie relief efforts more directly to Christian witness.

Individual Friends of all traditions in the 20th century continued to distinguish themselves in areas of social concern. Examples include Swiss **Pierre Cérésole** (peace); Korean **Ham Sok Han** (reconciliation); Norwegian-born **Elise Boulding** (**family** and social issues); **African American Bayard Rustin** (civil rights); Kenyan **Simeon Shiteme** (**education** reform); and England's **Adam Curle** (peace). Many others attempt to integrate the social **testimonies**—**integrity**, **simplicity**, peace, and **equality**—in their private and professional lives, and institutional Quakerism continues to channel religious and social concern through peace and service agencies. [Max L. Carter]

SOUTH AMERICA: BOLIVIA AND PERU. Friends in Bolivia and Peru are primarily Aymara, a pre-Columbian Andean people. From beginnings around Lake Titicaca in the early part of the 20th century, Friends' congregations have also spread to the high valleys and southern coastal area of Peru and to the valleys and semitropical regions of Bolivia.

In 1919, the first missionaries came to Bolivia from what would later become Central **Yearly Meeting** in the United States. At about the same time (1921), a **Native American** from California, William (Guillermo) Abel, came to Bolivia, only to die shortly after his arrival. One of Abel's converts, a Bolivian named **Juan Ayllón**, began a work that was turned over to Oregon Yearly Meeting (later to become Northwest Yearly Meeting) in 1930 and eventually grew into *Iglesia Nacional Evangélica "Los Amigos" Boliviana* (National Evangelical Friends Church of Bolivia). The work in Peru can be dated to 1961 when missionaries from Oregon Yearly Meeting began working with the Aymara peoples located around the Peruvian side of Lake Titicaca.

Today Andean Quakers belong to several separate yearly meetings, reflecting different historical North American **mission** origins. The main groupings in Bolivia include *Amigos Central* (Central Friends—with origins from Indiana Yearly Meeting), *Amigos Santidad* (**Holiness** Friends—a group that separated off from Central Friends), and *Iglesia Nacional Evangélica "Los Amigos"* (the National **Evangelical** Friends Church—related to the Northwest Yearly Meeting). Other smaller groups represent various separations from these primary organizations. Peruvian Friends are concentrated in one yearly meeting, *Iglesia Nacional Evangélica "Los Amigos" del Peru* (the National Evangelical Friends Church—related to the Northwest Yearly Meeting). These yearly meetings, while remaining separate, cooperate in various **educational** programs. One of these is Friends Center, a theological study program linked to the Bolivian Evangelical University in Santa Cruz.

The 2001 estimates for people affiliated with Friends in Bolivia list some 20,000 people with Holiness Friends (the largest single group) and under 10,000 for all other yearly meetings combined. These statistics may be high and should be held tentatively. People affiliated with Peruvian Friends numbered around 5,000 in 2001.

The several yearly meetings in both countries have various characteristics in common. Andean Friends are **evangelical**, holding to a belief in a triune **God** and in Jesus **Christ** as the Son of God. They focus on **preaching** the message of **salvation** in Christ and actively strive to see people converted and brought into the church. Andean Friends hold to the **Bible** as the written word of God and attempt to follow and teach its precepts. Andean Friends have adopted the **pastoral system**. Andean Friends are indigenous in the administration of their churches. Although all yearly meetings have origins in North American missions, each group is now independent, some maintaining partnerships with Friends missions. Andean Friends emphasize appropriate social response to the problems their people face. This has resulted in primary and secondary schools, medical and agricultural work, and other projects.

The face of Quakers in Bolivia and Peru is changing as people from rural areas increasingly move to the cities and as young people go through the educational system and become professionals. A small **unprogrammed** worship group also exists in Bolivia. [Nancy Thomas]

SOUTH ASIA: INDIA AND NEPAL. Friends' **meetings** in India grew out of the work of **British** and **North American** Friends from several branches. Later, Indian Friends started work in Nepal.

Rachel Metcalf (d. 1889) from England was the pioneer Quaker **missionary** to India in 1866. She was supported by a special committee of British Friends, which evolved into the Friends Foreign Missionary Association. In 1869, Metcalf was joined by two Americans, Elkanah and Irena Beard. Soon the Mid-India Yearly Meeting was established. Since 1890, the Ohio **Yearly Meeting** (now Evangelical Friends Church–Eastern Region) has been responsible for a mission in the Bundelkhand district. Independently, Indians in Calcutta were led to start a **meeting for worship** after reading Quaker literature.

After Metcalf's death in 1889, a Quaker businessman, Frederick Sessions (1836–1920), helped set up an industrial training unit at Rasulia near Hoshangabad, which has continued as the Friends Rural Centre. Delia Fistler (1867–1916) and **Esther Baird** arrived in December 1892. They relieved famine victims, cared for orphans, opened dispensaries, and later a hospital, where Ruth Hall Bennett (1887–1998) and Ezra and Frances **DeVol** served. They also opened the first Hindi school for girls in Bundelkhand.

Beginning in the 1920s, many Friends came to India to study Hinduism and related religions. Among those who studied with or were otherwise influenced by Rabindranath Tagore (1861–1941) were **Harry and Rebecca Janney Timbres** and **Marjorie Sykes**. Sykes and **Horace Alexander** were both closely associated with **Mahatma Gandhi**.

As other Quakers came to the large cities of India for a variety of individual pursuits, meetings were established.

As the political situation grew more tense with the "quit India" movement in the 1940s, **Ranjit and Doris Chetsingh** felt led to establish a "**peace** garrison" amid the stresses of Delhi, founding the Delhi Quaker Centre in 1943 as a meeting place to which all open-minded people of goodwill might come.

Friends also have been active in India-wide cooperative work. **Everett L. Cattell** helped form and lead Evangelical Fellowship of India (EFI); **Anna Nixon** organized its Christian Education Department; Robert Hess was principal of Union Biblical Seminary; Milton Coleman served the EFI's Committee on Relief; and Clifton Robinson led International Christian Leadership. Forty-six missionaries have served in India during the past century.

In 1959, the General Conference of Friends in India was established, to bring together scattered Friends in India in annual gatherings which continue to date. Presently, **evangelical** Friends are also active in a home for children of temple prostitutes, a ministry of health care to small villages in Central India, evangelizing the Garhwali people in North India, and assisting P. K. Sam, a **Malone College** graduate, who plants churches in Kerala, South India.

John and Sangi Vanlalhriata, nationals of India who previously directed and taught in the girls English school in Chhatarpur, started Friends Nepal work in 1994. Bob and Debbie Adhikary joined the team in 1995. There now are 15 congregations with over 400 believers. Nepali Friends care for the poor, teach skills that empower people to supplement their living, and help with medical needs wherever possible. [Martha Dart, Howard W. Moore]

SOUTHEAST ASIA. Friends Churches in Southeast Asia are primarily connected with **Evangelical Friends International**. Jaime and Lydia Tabingo have led **evangelical** Friends' work in the Philippines from its beginning in 1978. **Bible** study evangelism in homes introduces Filipinos to **Christ** and provides opportunities for **ministries** to neighbors who are poor and neglected, as well as meeting spiritual needs. The work has grown to 16 congregations. Pastor Tabingo equips the students he teaches at Manila Bible College, who then put learning into practice by planting new churches. (*See also* EAST ASIA.)

Southwest **Yearly Meeting** began their Indonesia **mission** in 1987. By 2001, they reported an estimated 51 congregations with 2,500 adherents. Ray Canfield and Alan Amavisca, missionaries who have served in Guatemala, visit Indonesia periodically to assist in the work.

Yiv Poa, nephew of a member of the Cambodian Friends Church in Long Beach, California, became a Christian while a refugee in Thailand. Upon his return to Cambodia in 1995, he began preaching Christ in his home. There, he discipled four young men, able to teach others. Groups now meet in Battambang and Phnom Penh. Christine and Gary Colfax were appointed as missionaries in 1997. Ray and Virginia Canfield also spend nearly half their time there. [Howard W. Moore]

SOUTHERN AFRICA. For more than 60 years, Friends' **meetings** in South Africa and later those in Botswana, Lesotho, Malawi, Mozambique, Namibia, Swaziland, Zambia, and Zimbabwe have gathered in Central and Southern Africa **Yearly Meeting** (CSAYM). Some of these are expatriate, temporary gatherings. Other meetings have taken root and become indigenous. Yearly Meeting sessions, held each December, include a **Summer School**. **Monthly meetings** take turns editing and publishing the quarterly *South Africa Quaker Newsletter*.

Throughout the region **unprogrammed worship** is customary. In response to individual and communal needs additional activities include **Bible** studies, fellowships, retreats, music, singing, discussion groups, and social witness.

In Zimbabwe, Hlekweni Quaker **Peace and Service** has promoted an agricultural training college near Bulawayo. Regular **meetings for worship** also occur in Maseru (Lesotho), Lilongwe (Malawi), and Windhoek (Namibia) and worship groups exist in Botswana. Occasional meetings are held by resident Friends in Mbabane (Swaziland), Zambia, and elsewhere.

A number of meetings exist in South Africa and the Quaker **Peace** Centre in Cape Town engages in a variety of development and peace education projects. Transvaal Monthly Meeting has corporately adopted the Alternatives to Violence Project in Johannesburg.

During the devastating years of apartheid, individual Friends from Kenya, **Britain**, the United States, and CSAYM sustained and encouraged those in South Africa. The U.S./South Africa Leader Exchange Program initiated by the **American Friends Service Committee (AFSC)** in 1959 has been a powerful agent of change in South Africa.

Throughout Central and Southern Africa, work continues to remove racism, discrimination, and oppression, and the roots of violence. Worship and activities continue to be "color-blind." In their daily work, individual Friends have been in the forefront of developmental work, **education**, and social and political change. Notably, two Zambian Friends are engaged in a uniquely successful rural development through the Gwembe Agricultural Mission and Imwe Muyama. A Cape Town Friend, **H. W. Van de Merwe**, facilitated the early negotiations between the former white government in South Africa and the "government in exile." In 1999, **Nozizwe Madlala-Routledge**, a Friend and committed pacifist, accepted appointment as deputy minister for defense in South Africa. [Jennifer Kinghorn]

SOUTHLAND COLLEGE. Quaker-run boarding school and college for **African Americans** in Helena, Arkansas. Founded in 1864 by Indiana **Yearly Meeting** as an orphanage for African American victims of the Civil War, Southland developed after 1869 into a teacher training institute. In the 20th century, its mission changed to "practical and industrial" **education**, and the name was changed to Southland Institute. Following a series of natural and financial disasters, it closed in 1925. Southland **Monthly Meeting**, based at the College, was recognized as a monthly meeting by Indiana Yearly Meeting in 1873, the only such meeting with a predominantly African American membership. [Mary Ellen Chijioke]

SPIRITUALISM. The practice of communicating with the spirits of the dead through a medium. Some radical **Hicksites** of the mid-19th century experimented with spiritualism as part of their exploration of the boundaries of **mysticism**. For example, Elizabeth McClintock (*see* McCLINTOCK FAMILY) was known as a medium.

SPIRITUALITY. Quaker spirituality centers around **George Fox**'s hearing, "There is one, even **Christ** Jesus, who can speak to thy condition." Fox experienced Jesus as alive, present, and active in each soul as Seed or **Light**, two of his many terms that describe the inward work of Christ. As this Light drew people toward **God**, it would at some early stage in the spiritual journey starkly reveal how each person was an alienated, selfish entity separate from God. Then as the Light continued to "speak to the condition" of each unique person, it would lovingly show how to let go of self-centered, willful individualism and to accept the healing mystery of Grace, which early Friends understood to result from the atoning sacrifice of Jesus, or his "outward work" (*see* ATONEMENT). However, this *outward work* was of little effect unless one accepted the continuing *inward work* of Christ, which transformed a person from the inside and led to a palpable sense of communion with Divine Reality, especially during long periods of silent **worship** (*see* SACRAMENTS). The nourishing and transforming power of this group **mystical** experience continues to be an essential part of the life-long spiritual journey of many Friends.

Early generations believed that the continuing inward work of Christ went on throughout a lifetime (*see* PERFECTION). Their ideal was always to be alert to the Inward Presence and responsive to its guidance in order to move toward a state of **sanctification** as the human will becomes increasingly aligned to the Divine will and in which even automatic responses are in tune with the spirit that Jesus demonstrated on earth. Fox sometimes described this as "living in the **Cross**," an attitude in which one is so alert to the Presence as to be able to recognize and let go of negative emotions, selfish cravings, and personal willfulness in order to make appropriate choices in every situation.

Such attentiveness to all that the Light reveals still typically reorients priorities and values so that many aspects of lifestyle and outreach may be altered. A quiet passion for rearranging one's life and affairs according to a new sense of harmony and balance often emerges. Thus, the spiritual path has always had an outward as well as an inward side. The spirit of Jesus becomes manifest in all relationships as well as in faithfully living out **testimonies** and **concerns** in the world.

The 18th century saw a flowering of the **Quietist** emphasis on a deeply contemplative spirituality and total dependence on the Inward Guide. At the same time, official Quaker spirituality came to emphasize conformity to the outward aspects of a culture that was separate from all the world. Differences in **theology** and practice in the following centuries have caused Quakerism to divide into several streams, each of which has tended to emphasize some of the aspects of the early body.

A majority of the world's Quakers now hold **programmed**, or pastoral, **meetings**. Most of these, like early Friends, place acceptance of **salvation** though Jesus Christ as a primary and essential step in the spiritual journey. They also stress the availability of God's presence and guidance through the resurrected Jesus Christ, the **Bible**, and the **Holy Spirit**. Like George Fox and the early Friends, some of them are strong evangelists, believing that all Christians are called to fulfill the **Great Commission** of Matthew 28:19. In many parts of the world, personal devotions and worship services often demonstrate their faith in a very exuberant way.

The spirituality of a substantial minority of world Quakers still centers on the **unprogrammed meeting for worship**, although they now share a wide variety of understandings about the theology underlying the spiritual journey. [William P. Taber]

STANLEY, LENNA M. (1856–1920). North American missionary sent by Ohio **Yearly Meeting** to **East Asia** who worked in China from 1891 to 1920.

STANTON, ELIZABETH CADY (1815–1902). The non-Quaker housewife from upstate New York who collaborated with **Lucretia Mott** and **Mary Ann McClintock** and three other Quaker **women** to organize the **Seneca Falls Woman's Rights Conference** of 1848. After 1855, she and **Susan B. Anthony** became the acknowledged leaders of the American women's rights movement.

STEERE, DOROTHY LOU MacEACHRON (1907–) and DOUGLAS VAN (1901–1995). Ecumenists, writers, educators. Rhodes Scholar at Oxford in 1925–1926, Douglas Steere later received his doctorate at Harvard University. He succeeded **Rufus Jones** in the Philosophy Department at **Haverford College**, where he taught until his retirement in 1964. A founder of **Pendle Hill** Study Center, his numerous scholarly works and writings about Friends, **prayer**, **worship**, and **mysticism** are widely known. Steere was one of several

Quaker mystics of the mid-20th century who were sympathetic to mystics of other faiths and who studied Buddhism in Japan.

Dorothy Lou MacEachron met Steere at age 17 while a freshman in college, planning on a career as a Congregationalist **missionary**. Married in 1929, both Steeres were soon drawn to the work of the **American Friends Service Committee (AFSC)**. In 1930 they joined with several others to revitalize Radnor Meeting as a united **meeting** (*see also* REUNIFICATION). They joined the **Religious Society of Friends** in 1932. Dorothy also contributed several well-loved writings on Quaker **spirituality**.

Both Steeres traveled throughout the world on behalf of AFSC. Douglas Steere served as a delegate-observer at three sessions of Vatican Council II (1963–1965). In 1967, while he served as **clerk** of that body, the Steeres drew together, on behalf of **Friends World Committee for Consultation**, a colloquium of Zen masters and Christian spiritual leaders in Japan and a similar group of Hindus and Christians in India. *See also* ECUMENISM. [Margery Post Abbott]

STEPHEN, CAROLINE (1835–1909). British author of the devotional *Quaker Strongholds* (1890) and *Light Arising* (1908) at the beginning of the **liberal** movement in **Britain**. Both books remain popular. Stephen was aunt to and an influence on the novelist, Virginia Woolf.

STORY, JOHN (d. 1681). One of the **Valiant Sixty**, in the 1670s, he challenged **George Fox** and was one of the leaders of the Wilkinson–Story separation (*see* WILKINSON, JOHN).

STURGE, JOSEPH (1793–1859). Activist for **peace**, **abolition**, and **temperance**. A grain dealer from Bristol area, Sturge gave up a profitable barley and malt **business** in 1844 for reasons of conscience. One of the first English Friends to join the new total-abstinence temperance movement of the 1830s, he was also a leader in agitation against the opium trade in the 1850s. Having advocated abolition, he visited the West Indies in about 1836 and bought property where freed slaves could settle. In 1854, he was part of a delegation of Friends who met with the czar in St. Petersburg in an effort to end the

Crimean War, and later was a major organizer of **relief** aid to Finnish cities, then under Russian rule, which the British had shelled. [Sabron Reynolds Newton]

STURGE, MARY DARBY (1862–1925). Mary Sturge was a physician affiliated with the Birmingham and Midland Hospital for **Women** in England and directed **relief work** for children in the northern Tyrol after World War I. She coauthored with a well-known British physiologist, Victor Horsley, *Alcohol and the Human Body,* which went through six editions between 1907 and 1920 and was revised again after her death. [Sabron Reynolds Newton]

SUMMER SCHOOLS MOVEMENT. A program of adult religious education started in Scarborough, England, in 1897, growing out of the enthusiasm of the **Manchester Conference** of 1895. One purpose was to show that **modern** biblical criticism could enhance rather than hinder faith. *See* GRUBB, EDWARD; ROWNTREE, JOHN WILHELM.

SUNDAY SCHOOL MOVEMENT. The Sunday School movement began among Protestants in **Britain** in 1780 to provide basic literacy and **religious education** to the working poor, often using the **Bible** as the primary textbook. In 1803, the London Sunday-School Union was formed to encourage the establishment of nonsectarian Sunday Schools, provide materials, and improve teaching. By the early 19th century it had taken root in the United States. Individual Friends were involved early on; **meetings** sponsored Sunday Schools for the disadvantaged in the second half of the 19th century. In the 20th century the term Sunday School (or First Day School) came to mean programs for **religious education** within the **meeting** community, particularly for children. [Martha Paxson Grundy]

SUPERINTENDENTS. In the mid-20th century, the term "superintendent" became increasingly common for the chief paid executive of the **yearly meeting**, especially among **Gurneyite** Friends. It reflected the desire for coordination and general supervision over the ministries of the yearly meetings. **Unprogrammed** yearly meetings use variations of the term "general secretary" for such positions, emphasizing the authority of the **meeting** over all staff.

SWARTHMOOR HALL. Built between 1600 and 1620, Swarthmoor Hall was the estate of Judge Thomas and **Margaret Fell** in Lancashire, one mile south of the market town of Ulverston in northwest England. After the **convincement** of Margaret Fell and her daughters in 1652, the Hall became the national and international administrative center for Quaker **ministry** for many years, with the tacit approval of Judge Fell. The main structure and immediate grounds are largely intact today, though the interior of the former has been extensively renovated and a new building added to accommodate a small conference center. [T. H. S. Wallace]

SWARTHMORE COLLEGE. Located in Swarthmore, Pennsylvania, Swarthmore was chartered in 1864 and opened in 1869 as a coeducational college by members of New York, Philadelphia, and Baltimore **Yearly Meetings (Hicksite)**. It is independent of yearly meeting ties.

SYKES, MARJORIE (1905–1995). Alice Barnes (1907–1968) and Marjorie Sykes were first drawn to Friends while in India and subsequently joined through **London Yearly Meeting**. Along with Mary Barr, they became the nucleus of Quaker work in South India. Sykes joined the Ashram Santiniketan of Rabindranath Tagore from 1939 to 1947 and was with **Gandhi** at Sevagram in 1947–1948. Barr and Barnes were coeditors of the *Friendly Way*, a quarterly newsletter about Friends and their associates in Pakistan and India, which was continued by Sykes after their deaths. *See also* SOUTH ASIA. [Martha Dart]

–T–

TABER, FRANCES IRENE (1930–) and WILLIAM P. (1927–). Members of Ohio **Yearly Meeting** (**Conservative**) where Bill is a recorded **minister**. Fran grew up among Conservative Friends in Iowa and Ohio. They both attended Olney Friends School in Barnesville, Ohio. Bill then received a bachelor's degree from **William Penn College** and a M.A. from **Earlham School of Religion**, and Fran received her bachelor's degree from Boston University. As a

conscientious objector, Bill was a nonregistrant, serving a nine-month **prison** term just after **World War II.** He later registered and did alternative service. In 1965– 1966, he was a T. Wistar Brown Fellow at **Haverford College**. For six years he served Ohio Yearly Meeting as a "**released** Friend," which allowed him to reach out to other Quakers and work on **ecumenical** projects within the yearly meeting.

After 20 years at Olney Friends School, the Tabers were at **Pendle Hill** study center in Philadelphia from 1981 until 1994. Fran initially joined the cooking team and Bill taught various aspects of Quakerism and **prayer**. Following study at Pendle Hill and at the Shalem Institute for Spiritual Formation, Fran established a spiritual retreat program and was a core teacher in the Spiritual Nurturer program of the School of the Spirit, which came under the care of Philadelphia Yearly Meeting. Both have written substantially about their faith; they lead retreats and are respected interpreters of Quakerism out of their background in the Conservative stream with its **Quietist** emphasis (*see* SPIRITUALITY). They currently live near Barnesville, where they are coordinators of a small Ohio Yearly Meeting conference and retreat center, and have two adult daughters, Anne Marie and Debora, and three grandsons.

TEMPERANCE. George Fox and his associates condemned drunkenness. One of the first temperance tracts was Fox's 1682 letter to vintners and innkeepers, handed out widely and posted where Friends sold alcoholic beverages to the public. **William Penn** held up temperance as a virtue, and his 1682 criminal code for Pennsylvania made drunkenness punishable by fine or imprisonment. Quaker colonists in America refused to sell liquor to **Native Americans**.

North American Friends helped shape regulations on licensing of taverns and sale of liquor at fairs and public auctions. After 1700, the populace had access to cheap distilled beverages. Resultant social disorder was apparent in English and Irish cities by 1725, leading, in England, to the Gin Acts of 1736 and 1751. Old Quaker records alluded to a worsening situation as early as 1721 in Maryland, and 1737 in Pennsylvania. Friends were warned against excess.

French-born **Anthony Benezet** published a pamphlet in Philadelphia in 1774 making a strong case against hard liquor. Focusing on "spirituous liquors," Friends began asking members to avoid distilling, importing, retailing, or transporting, "handing out," or consuming them, except medicinally. Use of beer and wine continued, but if excessive, led to **disownment**. Friends became clear that they should refuse to pay harvest help in rum, and publicized the close tie between the slave and rum trades.

Friends began to join local temperance societies in the early 1800s and also worked in the regional and national bodies that developed later. The first societies took a pro-moderation, anti-strong-drink stance, but from the 1830s they increasingly promoted total abstinence from all alcoholic beverages. Friends in all parts of the world contributed to the membership and leadership of the Woman's Christian Temperance Union (WCTU), founded in 1874, and its national affiliates. Friends also worked through their own channels. **Samuel Bowly**'s prodding resulted in the formation of the Friends Temperance Union in **Britain** in 1852. Most American **yearly meetings** had temperance **committees** by 1890.

Quaker reform enthusiasts also established temperance towns for workers; developed popular nonintoxicating beverages, including cocoa and root beer; donated drinking fountains for public places; opened temperance lunchrooms, coffee houses, hotels, and resorts; and devised insurance for abstainers. Homes were expected to be alcohol free. Late 19th-century temperance leaders included Asbjørn Kloster (1823–1876), **Aaron Powell**, **Joseph Rowntree**, and **Joseph Sturge**. Notable in the 20th century were **Hannah J. Bailey**, Muriel Heath, **S. Edgar Nicholson**, and **Mary Darby Sturge.**

National prohibition was a hot political issue in the United States as the 20th century began. Some Friends voted for or worked within a third, Prohibition, Party, which also had Quaker opponents. The Anti-Saloon League generated similar controversy. Many Friends rejoiced when Prohibition became the law in 1920, but then became complacent. As the 12-year national experiment came to an end, temperance and prohibition **committees** began to be merged into bodies working on **peace** and other issues.

Cultural pressures to use alcohol, and, from the 1960s, new and illegal drugs as well, increased. So did the number of Friends trained to deal professionally with drug and alcohol problems. Although diversity of view is now more common, it remains the case that alcoholic beverages are not served at official Quaker functions. From bodies that recommend that members "practice total abstinence" to those that urge considering "whether you should limit your use or refrain altogether" from alcohol and habit-forming drugs, books of Faith and Practice (*see* DISCIPLINE) still ask each Friend to ponder Quaker experience in making a personal decision. [Sabron Reynolds Newton]

TENDER. This was a word often used in **journals** as Friends described **worship**. When hearts were tender, or people were tender, they had been open to the work of the Spirit among them. In the 17th century, being "tender" meant "susceptible to moral or spiritual influence, impressionable, sympathetic, sensitive to pious emotions" according to the *Oxford English Dictionary.*

TEST ACTS. Laws in **Britain**, beginning in 1673, that only allowed participation in many institutions, including attendance at universities, voting, and office-holding, for adherents of the Church of England. They were repealed in 1828, though a few restrictions remained under other legislation. *See also* BRIGHT, JOHN; FOTHERGILL, JOHN; SCIENCE AND TECHNOLOGY.

TESTIMONY. A term referring to the public witness of actions, beliefs, and behaviors that Friends hold to be consistent with **Truth**. In the 20th century, a number of Friends have summarized the testimonies as integrity, **simplicity**, community, **peace**, and **equality**. The specific actions identified as testimonies vary over time and with the **yearly meeting**. **Robert Barclay**'s *Apology* listed several "things inconsistent with the Christian religion," including **hat honor** and use of flattering titles or bowing (**equality**), vanity in apparel (**simplicity**), swearing oaths (**truth**), and fighting (**peace**). **William Penn** listed 17 witnesses including the form of **worship**, burial (*see* DEATH AND DYING) and **marriage** of Friends, peace, and their understandings of **times and seasons**.

For **evangelical** Friends, the term has taken on the more common meaning of witness to the work of Jesus **Christ** within a person's life. In some yearly meetings, such public testifying is part of the process for recording individuals as **ministers**. [Margery Post Abbott]

TESTIMONY OF THE BRETHREN. An important but controversial disciplinary document affirming the authority of the **business meeting** over individual actions and revelations, dated May 1666, written by **George Whitehead**, **Richard Farnworth**, and others. It was produced in response to long-running problems with followers of **John Perrot**. Some today see it as marking the end of the early Quaker movement by formalizing the central **leadership**. [Rosemary Anne Moore]

THEOLOGY. As a discipline, theology—discourse about **God**—is the "rational wrestling with the mystery" according to Karl Barth. Within Christianity, it is a thoughtful conversation between human experience (individual and corporate), Scripture, and church tradition.

Friends have been ambivalent about theology. **George Fox** regarded theology as "**notions**" or intellectual speculation, a human invention that misled and distracted from **Christ**'s teaching. "And I was to bring people off . . . from men's inventions and windy doctrines, by which they blowed the people about this way and the other way" (Fox, *Journal,* Nickalls, p. 91). **Margaret Fell** considered those who know the words of the scriptures but "know nothing of them in [themselves]" to be "thieves." The first Friends put energy into **preaching** and conversion and appeared to be interested not in theology but in spiritual experience and in social concerns.

Seventeenth-century Friends responded to published accusations of heresy by defending their teachings in light of Scripture. Their replies were undeniably theological. Yet, within their own community they had a strong preference for epistles and **journals**.

During the **Restoration** period, Friends adopted more formal theological positions to justify their beliefs and practices to the world. **Robert Barclay**, trained as a theologian, published a catechism in 1673 and his *Apology for the True Christian Divinity* (first published in Latin in 1676) is clearly a systematic theological treatise. **Elizabeth Bathurst**'s *Truth Vindicated . . .* (1695) examines traditional theological issues such as the nature of Christ, resurrection, original **sin**, **perfection**, and the **sacraments**. **William Penn**'s *No Cross, No Crown* (1682) is, in part, a discussion of the classic "seven deadly sins." In addition to these, three-quarters of Fox's own collected *Works* are epistles and doctrinal writings, including a catechism.

In the 18th century, the ambivalent attitude to the outward nature of theology continued, although Barclay's *Apology* became a household text. A century later, **Joseph John Gurney** was among those who sparked a renewed interest in theology rooted in Scripture. In the 20th century, **liberal Friends**, with their emphasis on faith rooted in experience have returned to an ambivalent attitude toward theology. They see theological books as personal, professional, and political and tend to read the **Bible** as metaphor and story.

Today several theological groups exist, for example, the Quaker Theology Seminar and the Quaker Theological Discussion Group. [David L. Johns]

THOMAS, MARTHA CAREY (1857–1935). American educator and a student of **Emily Howland**, she was the first dean, then president of **Bryn Mawr College**.

THOMPSON, SILVANUS PHILLIPS (1851–1916). English physicist, engineer, and historian of science. He was the author of a standard textbook on calculus, and a leading **liberal** at the **Manchester Conference**. *See also* SCIENCE AND TECHNOLOGY.

THRESHING SESSION. Originally used to refer to **general meetings** for evangelizing. Today, threshing sessions are a form of **business meeting** where only one issue is considered, and, usually, recommendations are brought to the regular business meeting for decision.

TIMBRES, HARRY (1896–1927) and REBECCA JANNEY (LATER CLARK) (1896–2000). American medical **relief** workers who served with the **American Friends Service Committee (AFSC)** in Poland and Russia after World War I and later studied Indian religion with Rabindranath Tagore. *See also* SOUTH ASIA.

TIMES AND SEASONS. For Quakers all times as well as all places are equally sacred; every day is the Lord's Day, a **testimony** expressed in main three ways. First, they refused to name the days of the week or the months of the year by the "world's names," which were based on the names of pagan gods. Thus, the day commonly called Sunday became "First Day" and January became "First Month."

Second, Quakers did not celebrate the festivals and saints' days of the Christian year. They shared the **Puritan** objection that many celebrations were of pagan rather than biblical origin and encouraged licentiousness. Seeing all days as equally sacred and **worship** as directed by the **Holy Spirit**, they celebrated incarnation, redemption, and empowerment when led by the Spirit rather than on fixed days like Christmas or Easter.

Third, they did not hold specific commemorations honoring people or marking a length of time. Since all work is in the service of **God**, and all time is God's time, it is God alone who is to be thanked and honored. Thus, for example, Quakers in **Britain** had no official celebration of the 350th anniversary of the **death** of **George Fox**; nor did they join in with other churches in marking the so-called millennium at the end of the year 1999.

This is a testimony that is slowly slipping into disuse. As Friends are more involved in the **ecumenical** movement and increasingly conform to the surrounding world, they are more inclined to the common names for days and celebrate Christmas. Often the testimony is not taught or is neglected because of consideration for family and custom. [Janet Scott]

TINTAYA, FRANCISCO. Francisco Tintaya was born in the village of Amacari on the shores of Lake Titicaca in the late 1920s or early 1930s (*see* SOUTH AMERICA). He does not know the date, and no documents can be found. His father died when he was a small child, and he ran away from home to escape mistreatment, and then wandered around Bolivia and Peru for several years until he found a home in La Paz as servant to a rich man who treated him well. He had no formal schooling as a child, but through his participation in a **Friends Church** in La Paz, he taught himself to read and write. Tintaya attended Tupac University in La Paz, and although he never graduated, this time prepared him for a career as an electrician. As a young man, he consecrated himself to God for service, and as others recognized his pastoral gifts, he began active church work, serving over the years as **pastor** to four different rural Friends churches.

Tintaya served several years as treasurer of *Iglesia Nacional Evangélica "Los Amigos"* (INELA, also known as Bolivia **Yearly Meeting**), helping to set a standard for responsibility and for honesty in record keeping and reporting (*see* TRUTH). He was one of the first members of INELA to travel to the United States to represent the yearly meeting. During the 1980s he served two three-year terms as president of INELA. Currently, he is retired but remains a sought-out counselor and elder in the Bolivian Friends Church. [Nancy Thomas]

TITHES. Giving one-tenth of the land's produce and profit to **God**, known as tithing, is rooted in Mosaic law. In early England tithes began as freewill offerings that gradually became customary and eventually hardened into law. Over time, the right to collect tithes was no longer solely in the hands of the church. By the 17th century, 40 percent of tithes went to local gentry.

Tithes became a defining issue for early Friends. Their understanding of God's kingdom stood in stark opposition to **Britain**'s ecclesiastical, social, economic, and legal systems (*see* LAMB'S WAR). Compulsory tithes upheld a **church** structure Friends found deceitful and out of God's Life. Tithes were forcibly collected from those at the lower end of the economic scale, while the wealthy often found ways to be exempted. Friends, whose goods were distrained or destroyed, often at many times the value of the tithe due, pictured themselves as innocent, honest tradesmen and husbandmen, despoiled by informers and avaricious clergy. Friends (with their unwillingness to swear) and the poor were at a distinct disadvantage in the expensive, arcane, ecclesiastical, and Exchequer courts of England.

Although Friends witnessed against compulsory tithes for a state-established church, they offered voluntary support for their own **ministers**. Today, books of **discipline** of **yearly meetings** in **Friends General Conference** tend not to mention tithes, except historically. Passages about contributing to the meeting are vague. **Friends United Meeting** yearly meetings in **North America** vary widely, from a fairly clear expectation of tithing 10 percent or more in some to a deep resistance toward any set expectation in others. Yearly meetings in **Evangelical Friends International** expect their members will tithe to their local churches as do most churches in **Africa** and **South America**. The last vestiges of legally enforced tithes were extinguished in England in 1977. [Martha Paxson Grundy]

TOMPION, THOMAS (1648/49–1713). English horologist. Tompion developed many improvements for clocks, including the cylinder escapement that allowed flat watches.

TRINITY. The word "Trinity" has been resisted among Friends because it does not appear in the **Bible** but comes from later developments of Christian **church** tradition. **George Fox** wrote, for example: "And ye professors, who have given new names to the Father, the **Word**, and the Holy Ghost (as Trinity, and three distinct persons), and say the scripture is your rule for your doctrine, but there is no such rule in the scripture, to call them by these new names, which the apostle that gave forth the scripture, doth not give them" (Fox, "A Testimony of what we believe in **Christ**." *Works*, 5:126). **William Penn** also rejected trinitarian language as nonsensical and added to this a distaste for intellectual speculation. Friends' tradition continues to say little about the Trinity.

Quaker belief does not, however, conflict with trinitarian ideas, in the sense that **God** is described in terms of the Father, the Son (**Light**, Word, etc.), and the **Holy Spirit**. Early Friends used biblical terms, and to some extent relied on the Vulgate version of 1 John 5:7 (not found in the most reliable Greek manuscripts) that there are three witnesses in Heaven: Father, Word, and Spirit. The understanding that God-language, **Christ**-language, and Spirit-language are all referring to the same Divine being also enables a tolerance for diversity of expression. [Janet Scott]

TRUEBLOOD, BENJAMIN FRANKLIN (1847–1916). First **North American** missionary to Cuba. *See also* CARIBBEAN; MISSIONS: MODERN MISSIONARY MOVEMENT.

TRUEBLOOD, DAVID ELTON (1900–1994). A native of Iowa, D. Elton Trueblood was one of the most prolific authors of religious publications in his time, producing 36 published volumes, countless articles, and numerous lectures. He was educated at **William Penn College** in Iowa, Brown University, Hartford Theological Seminary, Harvard University, and Johns Hopkins University, where he received his Ph.D. in 1934. In 1935 he began twelve years as editor of *The Friend*. His major teaching appointments included **Guilford**

College (1927–1930), **Haverford College** (1933–1936), Stanford University (1936–1945), where he also taught philosophy of religion and served as chaplain, and **Earlham College** (1945–1965), where he retired as "professor-at- large." In 1939 he taught at **Woodbrooke** in Birmingham, England, where he was a fellow. From 1947 to 1952 he was clerk of **Friends World Committee for Consultation (FWCC)** He also served as director of religious information for the United States Information Agency in Washington, D.C., from 1954 to 1956 and adviser to the Voice of America.

Trueblood and his first wife, Pauline C. Goodenow, married in 1924 and had four children. After her death in 1955, he married Virginia H. Zuttermeister in 1956. They lived on the Earlham College campus until their move to Lansdale, Pennsylvania, in 1989.

In 1949, Elton Trueblood founded the interdenominational Yokefellow Movement, dedicated to the renewal of individuals, the church, and society. He considered himself an "**evangelical** Christian," sharing his faith in his many books including *The Company of the Committed*, *A Place To Stand*, and *The Humor of Christ*. His academic books include *General Philosophy* and *Philosophy of Religion*. [James R. Newby]

TRUTH. A basic article of Quaker faith and practice. In the 17th century, even before they were called Friends, Quakers were known as "**Children of the Light**" and "Publishers of Truth." "Truth" was spelled with a capital "T," which meant they believed it had divine sanction. It could refer to **God** or the will of God. It could refer to the Gospel of Jesus **Christ** as proclaimed in the New Testament and was, at times, used interchangeably with Christ or the **Light** of Christ. This described the theological dimension of Truth.

Early Friends also proclaimed truth on another level. This had to do with truth telling, not telling lies, and honesty and integrity in daily intercourse with other persons. This is truth on the moral and ethical level manifested in human relationships. Quakers sometimes speak of "doing the truth" based on what they discern to be the will of God. The best example was early Friends' refusal to take an oath before a judge or court of law, believing it was hypocritical to swear with one hand on the **Bible** and hold the other hand up to God declaring that now they would tell the truth. In support, they cited

Matthew 5:37 (AV): "Let what you say be simply 'Yes' or 'No'; anything more than this comes from the evil one." Consistency in truth telling was the hallmark of Friends' behavior. They claimed that their word was as good as their bond, to use an old Quaker cliché.

Friends have regarded Truth as fundamentally reflecting ultimate reality and, therefore, integral to their religious profession. This is an article of faith and practice that most Friends attempt to honor and adhere to over the years. But with the increased secularization of life and intellectual forces of postmodern philosophy, Truth has become harder and harder to identify and practice with consistency. *See* CONTINUING REVELATION; FIXED PRICE; TIMES AND SEASONS. [Wilmer A. Cooper]

TUKE, WILLIAM (1732–1822). Founder of the Retreat at York in northern England. (*See* MENTAL HEALTH REFORM.) From 1785, he enjoyed success as an entrepreneur with his son, Henry (1755–1814), setting up the chocolate factory, which was later to become Rowntrees. A **philanthropist**, he donated to the Mount and Bothan Schools in York, and also was involved in the beginnings of Friends Provident Insurance Company.

–U–

UNDERGROUND RAILROAD. Early in the 19th century, efforts to aid fugitives escaping from slavery in the South flourished across the Philadelphia-Baltimore area, in southeast Ohio, New York State, and the area northwest of Cincinnati as well as many other areas (*see* ABOLITION). **African American** churches were central to functioning of the underground railroad and many individual Friends were active participants, despite the reluctance of some **meetings** to be involved.

Many individuals, such as **Laura Haviland**, who were active as railroad agents were also **educators** who opened schools for black students. **Angelina and Sarah Grimké** and **Lucretia Mott** are other Friends well known for their efforts. **Thomas Garrett** helped support two schools in Wilmington, Delaware, provided financial aid to Harriet Tubman (ca.1820–1913), the escaped slave and leader of the underground railroad, and aided over 2,000 slaves to freedom. **Levi Coffin** has been called the "president" of the railroad for his extensive legal work and many risks he took outfoxing slave hunters.

Many Friends were torn between their desire to help fugitives to freedom and the **testimony** of integrity because of the need to break the law secretly in order to protect the lives of the men, women, and children seeking to escape slavery (*see* TROTH). Normally, when Friends felt called to break an unjust law, they had done so in a public manner and with the full understanding they would accept the legal consequences of their actions. [Margery Post Abbott]

UNITARIANISM. In the 17th century, Friends were inaccurately called unitarians—persons who maintain that **God** is one being rather than three persons—because they rejected use of the word **Trinity** as nonbiblical. By the late 18th century, a unitarian strain became visible within Quakerism. In the following century in **North America**, some **Hicksite** Friends, including **Lucretia Mott**, worked with members of the Unitarian Church, which was organized in 1825 on antislavery issues. Mott did not consider herself to be Unitarian, seeing their doctrine as too rationalistic. Today, many **liberal Friends** would consider themselves unitarian. [Margery Post Abbott]

UNITED SOCIETY OF FRIENDS WOMEN INTERNATIONAL (USFWI). The **women**'s organization of **Friends United Meeting**. Its purposes are to enlist and unite all Quaker women in Christian fellowship and service at home and abroad, to stimulate their spiritual development, to cultivate Christian stewardship, to assist in the nurture of the missionary spirit among Friends, and to foster missionary education in the membership of the local **meetings**.

Through the vision and efforts of Eliza (Clark) Armstrong Cox (1850–1885), Western **Yearly Meeting** in 1881 formed the first Woman's Missionary Society. In 1888 women from 10 yearly meetings attended the first assembly in Indianapolis, Indiana. This paved the way for the Glens Falls Conference of 1890, which officially inaugurated the Woman's Foreign Missionary Society of Friends in America, with **Phoebe S. Aydelott** of New England Yearly Meeting as president. Triennial Conferences have continued to be held at various locations to the present. Known in 1917 as the Woman's Missionary Union, the name and focus changed in 1948 to reflect the united witness of American Friends women. "International" was added in 1974 to recognize its global scope.

The *Friends Missionary Advocate*, the official periodical, began in 1885 and continues publication now as *The Advocate*. *Blueprints*, an annual publication of program outlines, has been produced since 1944. **Ecumenical** ties are maintained through Church Women United. Financial support is budgeted to projects of **Friends United Meeting** and other Quaker and Christian organizations. USFWI chapters exist in most yearly meetings outside Europe and Asia. *See also* GREAT COMMISSION; MISSIONS: MODERN MISSIONARY MOVEMENT. [Peggy Hollingsworth]

UNIVERSALISM. In Christian **theology** the term "Universalism" has traditionally referred to the belief that Jesus died for the **salvation** of all people (*see* CHURCH). This, in turn, arose from a belief that a loving **God** would not consign his children to eternal damnation. The first generation of Friends explicitly stated that there is a universal and saving **light** and grace in all people and that individuals who know nothing of Jesus can know salvation if they respond to the Light which reproves **sin** and teaches godliness. This affected the interactions of **Mary Fisher** and others who engaged with non-Christians. **George Fox** is known to have read the Koran, and his correspondence called the king of Algiers to faithfulness to the Koran.

This universal understanding extended to a belief in the full humanity of blacks and **Native Americans**, a position not widely accepted at the time. For instance, **John Woolman** was known for his 1761 visit to meet with, and learn from, Native Americans in western Pennsylvania during a time of hostilities. This position grew eventually to underlie the premise of some Friends that the movement of the Spirit is not confined by any particular **theology** (*see* MYSTICISM). In the 19th century, some **Hicksites** became interested in Buddhism, Hinduism, Theosophy, and **Spiritualism**. Increasing interactions, especially with Asians, through missionary work helped increase this tendency. By the mid-20th century, Friends such as **Marjorie Sykes** and **Horace Alexander**, working in India, were active in bringing together Hindus, Muslims, and Christians to **worship** together in silence through the Fellowship of Friends of Truth.

In the 20th century, **liberal Friends** extended the meaning to indicate that Christianity does not have exclusive possession of **Truth**, nor is it the only path to spiritual enlightenment. John Linton, a British Quaker, popularized this approach at a meeting of the Seekers Association during **London Yearly Meeting** in 1977. Quakerism, he said, had a universalist dimension. This became a label for those Quakers who could not conscientiously regard themselves as Christian in the orthodox sense. These Friends came from Hindu, Buddhist, or Jewish roots or indeed, in some cases, from no religious background of any sort, as well as Christian backgrounds. The universalist position asserted that one did not have to become a Christian before one could be a Quaker, although some universalists see themselves as Christian.

As a result of John Linton's talk, the Quaker Universalist Group was set up within **Britain** Yearly Meeting in 1977. A similar group, the Quaker Universalist Fellowship began in **North America** in 1983. [Ralph Hetherington]

UNPROGRAMMED WORSHIP. Traditional Quaker **worship** service based on expectant (silent) "waiting," during which the worshipping group seeks to become "**gathered**" and to experience a degree of **communion** as they trust the **Holy Spirit** not only to guide the worship through immediately inspired messages and **prayer**, but also to direct each individual worshipper's experience.

UPDEGRAFF, DAVID BRAINERD (1830–1894). Holiness minister. Born into a leading **Gurneyite** Quaker family in Ohio **Yearly Meeting**, Updegraff was educated at **Haverford College**.

Updegraff had a conversion experience in 1860, but the turning point of his life came in 1869 when, under Methodist leadership, he experienced immediate **sanctification**, a state in which he believed that he was cleansed of any propensity or desire to **sin**. Within two years Updegraff had become well known as a Quaker **preacher** and evangelist. He traveled widely, bringing holiness **revivalism** to Gurneyite congregations across the Midwest.

Updegraff was a central figure in transforming American Quakerism after the American Civil War. But while influential, Updegraff also proved controversial. He was a central figure in separations of

Conservative Friends in Western, Iowa, and Kansas Yearly Meetings in the 1870s and in the pressures that led, eventually, to **Joel and Hannah Bean** setting up an independent fellowship at College Park, California. By 1879, he had repudiated the **peace testimony** and teachings on the Inward **Light**, drawing intense criticism from more traditional Friends. He aroused even greater criticism in 1884, when he openly repudiated Quaker teachings on the **spirituality** of the **sacraments** and underwent water **baptism**. Updegraff then persuaded others, such as **Dougan Clark**, to follow suit. Ohio Yearly Meeting decided to tolerate this practice as well as making other changes in their book of **discipline** urged by Updegraff. The actions of Ohio Friends in tolerating the ordinances and revising their discipline to include substantial sections on doctrine, triggered the conference that led to the creation of the **Richmond Declaration of Faith**.

Updegraff was a frequent contributor to non-Quaker holiness periodicals and to the Quaker *Christian Worker* (1871–1894). From 1887 to 1893, he edited his own journal, *The Friends' Expositor*. [Thomas D. Hamm]

URBAN MINISTRIES. In the late 20th century a number of urban ministries have grown up around the United States among all branches of Friends, building on 19th-century **philanthropic** efforts and continuing in the spirit of the **Sunday School movement** and the settlement house work of Friends such as **Emily Greene Balch**. A few examples of modern urban ministries among Friends follow.

Since its inception in Philadelphia in 1879, Friends Neighborhood Guild has provided a full range of social services to all age groups, especially new immigrants; at first Eastern Europeans, then **African Americans**, then Latinos, and more recently, Vietnamese and Cambodians. By the 1950s, it had a self-help housing program, one of the first in the nation and a widely known gang program, headed by **Allen Bacon**. Friends Rehabilitation Program, formed in 1961, currently manages nearly one thousand apartments for low-income **elderly**, **families**, homeless **women**, and persons with special needs.

The Philadelphia Yearly Meeting's weekend work camp program, founded by David Richie (1932–) in the 1950s, continues under the direction of Judy Von Hoy. Jorge Arauz-Cevallos operates a small urban ministry, Fair Hill Friends Ministry. Nearby, the Fair Hill Burial Ground Corporation, a Friends group, is rehabilitating the historic Burial Ground as a means of aiding a blighted community.

In Chicago, Steve and Marlene Morrison Pedigo started work in 1976 with teenagers at Cabrini Green, a three-block-by-six-block public project that in the 1960s housed 26,000 people and had problems of gang violence and drugs. Working through **Bible** studies, recreational and cultural enrichment programs, and camping trips, they reached out to many people in the area. The Chicago Fellowship of Friends, where the Pedigos serve as co-**pastors**, grew out of this work and became a **monthly meeting** under Western **Yearly Meeting** in 1999. It draws its membership from the surrounding community. The Young Friends After School Program has become an all-day program run by interns, and in 1999 the Pedigos developed the "Transforming Community" housing program to assist tenants displaced by the demolition of the Cabrini Green high-rise public housing towers.

In southern California, Fred Newkirk, a graduate of **George Fox College**, has served for over 30 years as director of Inner City Missions in the slums of Long Beach. His Thursday morning and Sunday evening Bible studies are attended by more than 100 people, often homeless or drug addicts. Joe Ginder has served as pastor at Long Beach **Friends Church** since 1996. This Friends church, founded in 1892, has adjusted its focus as the city around it has changed, to become a model multicultural meeting, serving Cambodian, Hispanic, Anglo-, and African American people. The largest ethnic group served is Khmer (Cambodian), and the church translates its sermons and much of its teaching material into Khmer. Long Beach Friends Community Ministries works under the oversight of the Urban Mission Council of Friends Church Southwest. In 1986, the Ginder family was called to a "tent-making" **ministry**, first with youth and later with adults. In the mid-1990s, Ginder cut back to part-time work in the computer software industry to devote more time to this ministry. The church has established a School of Discipleship (in English and Khmer) and is creating a School of Ministry. The church regularly organizes community service projects for youth and sends about 50 youth, including "at-risk" children, to the Quaker Meadows high school camp in the Sequoia National Forest. In 2002 the Summer Youth Leadership Institute opened. [Margery Post Abbott]

–V–

VALIANT SIXTY. An early 20th-century collective name for the Quakers who evangelized central and southern England in 1654. The number originally given by **George Fox** was "seventy," as in Luke 10:1–20, but is "sixty" in the first published edition of the *Journal,* in 1694. About one-fifth of the total were **women**, among them being **Elizabeth Hooten**, **Mary Fisher**, Anne Audland, and Elizabeth Fletcher.

Traveling **ministers** went out in pairs, two men or two women together, generally an older person with a younger, and distributed to cover most of the country. Most of them had joined with Fox during 1652 in the northwest of England, while **James Nayler** and **Richard Farnworth**, two of Fox's earlier colleagues from Yorkshire, provided trouble-shooting support. The strongest teams went to the main cities, **Francis Howgill** and **Edward Burrough** to London, **John Camm** and **John Audland** to Bristol, and **Richard Hubberthorne** with Christopher Atkinson and the teenager **George Whitehead** to Norwich. **Thomas Holmes** went to Wales with his wife **Elizabeth Leavens**.

Traveling **preachers** arriving at a new town would inquire for individuals likely to be helpful, and often found sympathetic local congregations, maybe Baptist or the "**Seeker**" type. Until this practice was made illegal in 1655, the message might be delivered in the parish church after the minister had finished his sermon. If no one would receive the **Quakers**, they preached in the open to anyone who would listen. Their reception was hostile in some places, the women **ministers** being especially vulnerable, for they were defying social convention as well as attacking established religion. They attracted attention out of proportion to their numbers. Overall, the Quaker movement had an explosive success, and by the end of 1654 there were Quaker groups covering much of England and Wales.

Most of these first ministers continued to provide leadership until their deaths, which often came early, as a matter of course, in the 17th century, or as a result of time spent in foul **prisons**, although **John Wilkinson** later opposed Fox on questions of organization. Farnworth was concerned with two seminal disciplinary documents that paved the way for structuring the movement: the ***Epistle of the Elders of***

Balby with **William Dewsbury** in 1656, and the ***Testimony of the Brethren*** with **George Whitehead** in 1666, produced during Fox's incarceration in Scarborough Castle. Whitehead, who had a long life and survived into the 18th century, was a major architect of settled Quakerism. *See also* BRITAIN. [Rosemary Anne Moore]

VALLENTINE, JO (1946–). Teacher, **peace** activist, and politician, Vallentine was raised in a strict Catholic family on a farm near Perth, **Australia**. She was active with People for Nuclear Disarmament and other peace groups, attending the world conference of the **Women's International League for Peace and Freedom** in Sweden in 1983. In 1984 she was elected the independent senator from Western Australia (*see* CIVIL GOVERNMENT; POLITICS), having run on a campaign for nuclear disarmament. After successful campaigns for reelection in 1987 and 1990, she resigned from the Senate in 1992. Since then, Vallentine has continued to be an activist for change, working on a variety of peace, **environmental**, and social justice issues. She is active in her local Quaker community while also exploring a range of earth-based spiritual practices. She helped establish the Alternatives to Violence Project in Australia in 1994 (*see* PENAL REFORM) and continues to be active with various nuclear disarmament groups. Vallentine is married to Peter Fry and mother of Kate and Samantha.

VAN DER MERWE, HENDRICK W. (1929–2001). A **South African** Friend and Afrikaner, Van der Merwe arranged the first meetings between the African National Congress in exile and South African government supporters in 1984 (*see* PEACE TESTIMONY). This became a key step in breaking the deadlock over apartheid. An international peacemaker who maintained strong connections with individuals as diverse as the Mandela family, Steve Biko, and national cabinet ministers, Van der Merwe served as the head of the Centre for Intergroup Studies at the University of Cape Town for 25 years as it evolved into the Centre for Conflict Resolution, which continues to contribute to resolution of conflicts throughout Africa.

VAUX, ROBERTS (1786–1836). American **philanthropist** and promoter of private charity. Vaux played an important role in the creation of Philadelphia's free public school system and in the Prison Reform Society (*see* EDUCATION; PENAL REFORM).

VINELAND. The Society of the Friends of Progress of Vineland, New Jersey, was organized in 1864 and endured until about 1920. Founders included members of **Waterloo** Friends of Human Progress. The public meetings "to promote progress and development" that they held in their own Plum Hall were important for keeping the **women**'s rights movement alive during the chaotic years after the American Civil War. *See* PROGRESSIVE FRIENDS. [Andrea Constantine Hawkes]

VINING, ELIZABETH GRAY (1902–1999). Long active in Philadelphia **Yearly Meeting** and on the Board of **Pendle Hill** study center, she authored over 25 books including biographies, novels, and devotional literature. During **World War II** she joined the staff of the **American Friends Service Committee**. She was selected by the Emperor Hirohito of Japan to serve as tutor to the Crown Prince Akihito of Japan from 1946 to 1950.

–W–

WALTON, J. BARNARD (1884–1963). As executive secretary for **Friends General Conference (FGC)** from 1916 to 1951, Walton visited **monthly** and **quarterly meetings**, isolated Friends, and small worship groups all across **North America**, helping to forge connections among individuals and groups. He was also active in Philadelphia **Yearly Meeting**, the **American Friends Service Committee**, **Friends World Committee for Consultation**, and other Friends organizations. He was especially known for his humor and his ability to work with young Friends. [Martha Paxson Grundy]

WAR TAX RESISTANCE. As an expression of the **peace testimony**, a number of Friends over the centuries have refused either to pay any taxes or else the portions of their taxes which were designated for the propagation of war. All Friends traditionally have supported taxes used to fund **civil government**.

WATERLOO. Separating from the Genesee **Yearly Meeting**, activist **Hicksite** Friends established the independent Yearly Meeting of **Congregational Friends** of Waterloo, New York, in 1848 and met until at least the late 1860s. The Waterloo Congregational, later Friends of Human Progress, wrote the "Basis of Religious Association" that was adopted by most societies of **Progressive Friends**, and they were instrumental in organizing the first **women**'s rights convention at **Seneca Falls**, New York, in 1848. [Andrea Constantine Hawkes]

WATSON, ELIZABETH GRILL (1914–) and GEORGE H. (1916–). Elizabeth was studying for the **ministry** at the Chicago Theological Seminary and University of Chicago Divinity School when she met and married George Watson; both then joined the Religious Society of Friends. Through her writing and speaking, she has become a major voice for feminist **theology** among **liberal Friends** (*see* WOMEN). George, a pacifist and educator, served as president of **Friends World College** from 1972 until 1980. *See* COLLEGES; PEACE TESTIMONY.

WEIGHTY FRIEND. An individual in the **meeting** who is seen by others to have spiritual weight and whose insights are trusted. These individuals are often, but not always, in positions of **leadership**. The term is at times used in a joking or a pejorative manner.

WEST AFRICA. The first **meetings for worship** in West Africa were temporary gatherings of expatriates. In recent decades, however, small indigenous groups of Friends have developed in Ghana and Nigeria. Hillhouse Meeting in Accra, Ghana, meets in a small but permanent thatched-roof building. The Religious Society of Friends in Nigeria, organized in 1995 with the support of the **Friends World Committee for Consultation (FWCC)**, has three worship groups: in Lagos, Port Harcourt, and Enugu. It holds an annual gathering and publishes *The Nigerian Friends Newsletter*. There is also a small **unprogrammed** worship group in Kinshasa, Democratic Republic of Congo. [Mary Ellen Chijioke]

WETHERILL, SAMUEL, JR. (1736–1816). A leader of the **Free Quakers**, **disowned** for taking an affirmation of allegiance (*see*

TRUTH) and publicly criticizing the **Religious Society of Friends**.

WHEELER, DANIEL (1771–1840). British Quaker, most remembered for his work in Russia draining the marshes around St. Petersburg for Czar Alexander I. Wheeler later sailed the South Seas for four years as a missionary. *See* MISSIONS.

WHITE, DOROTHY (ca. 1630–1685). The most prolific Quaker woman writer next to **Margaret Fell**, she published 20 **prophetic** treatises in her lifetime. At least one of these was produced while she was in **prison**. As a "spiritual mother" among first-generation Friends, White wrote in a vivid and ecstatic language, urging readers to hear "The Trumpet of the Lord of Hosts," to seek **God** within themselves, to "Arise in the Power" so that "every Soul may swim in the fulness of Love." [Michele Lise Tarter]

WHITEHEAD, GEORGE (1636?–1723). Minister from Westmoreland in **Britain**, who joined with **George Fox** in 1652 while a teenager. One of the **Valiant Sixty**, his field of activity was at first mainly in eastern England, and later in London, where he kept a grocery store for many years. In 1662, he was one of four men appointed to argue the cause for Quakers before the British House of Commons during consideration of a bill forbidding all Nonconformist **worship** services. Over the years he wrote many books and pamphlets defending Quakerism. The longest survivor of the early converts, he became the main leader with Fox and **William Penn** in the later 17th century. [Rosemary Anne Moore]

WHITTIER COLLEGE. Founded as Whittier Friends Academy in 1887 in Whittier, California, it became Whittier College in 1901. Originally affiliated with California **Yearly Meeting**, which was part of the **Orthodox** branch of Friends, it is now independent.

WHITTIER, JOHN GREENLEAF (1807–1892). North American poet, editor, and abolitionist. Raised in a pious Massachusetts Quaker farm family and self-educated, Whittier was profoundly shaped by images from the **Bible**, the history and legends of New

England, literary classics of the English Reformation, and popular romantic poets, such as Byron and Burns. Following publication of his first poem in 1826 by the non-quaker abolitionist, William Lloyd Garrison (1805–1879), Whittier rapidly established a reputation as a noteworthy regional poet while editing several Whig newspapers. In 1833, following a failed congressional campaign, Whittier endorsed the immediate **abolition** of slavery in a widely distributed tract, *Justice and Expediency*.

Whittier was a charter member of the American Anti-Slavery Society. In 1840, Whittier's support for the Liberty Party caused a temporary break with William Lloyd Garrison and others who opposed abolitionist political activity. In the wake of this crisis, Whittier's faith was greatly intensified. Whittier published a volume of abolitionist poetry, *Voices of Freedom* (1846). In the 1850s, with the publication of poems such as "Skipper Ireson's Ride" and "Telling the Bees," Whittier's celebration of rural New England brought him national recognition. In 1866, *Snowbound* made him financially secure and one of the nation's most prominent literary figures. Following the American Civil War, a virtual Whittier cult developed, complete with a birthday book, busts, special editions of his poetry, a thriving tourist industry, and schools, and an occasional city, named after him. His birthday was made a public holiday throughout New England.

An active member of the Amesbury Weekly **Meeting** in Massachusetts until his **death**, Whittier repeatedly denied charges that he harbored **Unitarian** sympathies. Untroubled by the advent of Darwinian evolutionary theory and even capable of finding virtue in the revivals of Dwight L. Moody (1837–1899), but not in **revivalism** among Friends, Whittier epitomized the ethical idealism and theological flexibility of the late Victorian period. Although later generations would find his poetry sentimental and his **theology** naive, Whittier's contemporaries honored him as a poet, prophet, and folk theologian who urged them to follow their highest aspirations. He was especially influential as a literary critic and mentor of **women** writers. [Bill Kostlevy]

WILBUR, HENRY WATSON (1851–1914). A New York **Hicksite**, Wilbur served as general secretary of **Friends General Conference (FGC)** from 1905 to 1915.

WILBUR, JOHN (1774–1856). John Wilbur began **North American** Friends' "Second Separation" of 1845–1856 between "Wilburite" **Conservative** and "**Gurneyite**" **Orthodox** yearly **meetings** in New England. Followers of **Joseph John Gurney** saw many traditional meetings as barren, with little vocal **ministry**. Wilburites called Gurneyites worldly compromisers regarding music, dress, and luxuries, who loved combining with non-Friends in **Sunday Schools** and service projects. But the deepest issue, a doctrinal dispute about the balance between the **Holy Spirit** and the **Bible**, concerned waiting for divine **leading** as against human initiative (*see* also LIGHT).

At age 28, Wilbur, a farmer and land surveyor from Hopkinton, Rhode Island, was named an **elder** by his Rhode Island **Quarterly Meeting**. He traveled in the ministry throughout New England and New York Yearly Meetings in 1821–1827 and 1833–1837. In 1831–1833, he visited 348 meetings throughout **Britain** in 18 months, warning against the weakening of the **testimonies** and **discipline**. His friend **George Crosfield** published a series of his letters. He stayed in the homes of the **weightiest Friends** everywhere, but not Gurney's.

Wilbur knew from constant correspondence with Crosfield, the Barclays, **Sarah Lynes Grubb**, and others that British Friends had been bitterly divided about granting Gurney a traveling **minute** for his journey to America in 1837–1840. Gurney's trip included a New England circuit. In 1840, Wilbur, with the support of **Moses Brown** and others, revisited Philadelphia and the New York and New England Meetings to witness against Gurney's unsoundness wherever Gurney went. Wilbur attacked all New Englanders who supported Gurney. An angry select quarterly meeting committee later that year visited Wilbur's South Kingston meeting and, when it supported him, persuaded the **yearly meeting** to "lay down" that meeting and merge it with more docile meetings. After four years of wrangling, Wilbur and 500 followers formed their own New England Yearly Meeting, which survived until **reunification** in 1945. Wilbur continued to travel among supporters.

Anger at the Gurneyites' perceived high-handedness, and division over the discipline and doctrines of the primary authority of the Bible or the Spirit, erupted in small Wilburite separations in two New York quarterly meetings in 1847 and 1851, in Baltimore in 1854, and equally divided Ohio Yearly Meeting (Orthodox) in 1854. Division was only avoided in Philadelphia when the Orthodox yearly meeting ended formal recognition of all other yearly meetings. [Hugh Barbour, William P. Taber]

WILKINSON–STORY CONTROVERSY. In the 1670s, John Wilkinson (d. ca. 1683) and John Story, both among the **Valiant Sixty**, led a challenge to George Fox and to the establishment of formal **monthly meetings**. In particular, they objected to the increased structure and centralization of authority. Wilkinson, Story, and several of their followers were **disowned** for causing dissension among Friends. *See* ROGERS, WILLIAM.

WILLCUTS, JACK (1922–1989). Pastor, missionary, author, leader in **Evangelical Friends International (EFI)** and the wider world of Friends. Willcuts and his wife Geraldine raised three children while undertaking **mission** work among the Aymara people of Bolivia (*see* SOUTH AMERICA) and then serving as pastor to **Friends' churches** in the Pacific Northwest of the United States. He was active in **Friends World Committee for Consultation (FWCC)** and Quakers United in Publishing.

WILLIAM PENN COLLEGE. A coeducational **college** founded in Oskaloosa, Iowa, in 1873 by Iowa **Yearly Meeting**. It remains affiliated with the yearly meeting.

WILLIAMS, JOHN P., JR. (1946–). Williams has served as general **superintendent** of **Evangelical** Friends Church–Eastern Region since 1989 and director of **Evangelical Friends International**–North America Region since 1995. While he was senior **pastor** of First Friends Church in Canton, Ohio, from 1979 to 1989 the attendance increased from 423 to 1,200, and a new church was established in 1989 in nearby Jackson Township. By 2001, this new church had an average attendance of approximately 800 people. His innovations include sports ministries in local churches, out of which grew a major in sports ministries at **Malone College**. Williams holds a Ph.D. in higher education from Iowa State University and is a great-grandson of **Emma and J. Walter Malone**. [John Oliver]

WILLIAMS, WALTER ROLLIN (1884–1973). Minister, educator, and missionary. Walter Williams was a leader in Ohio **Yearly Meeting** of Friends, now the Evangelical Friends Church–Eastern Region (EFC-ER). Educated at Ohio Wesleyan University and Ohio State University, he became principal of Damascus Academy.

Appointed to educational work in central China in 1909 (*see* EAST ASIA), he maintained concern and leadership in Asian **missions** for half a century as missionary, board member, **pastor**, **college** teacher, mission **superintendent**, and general superintendent of Ohio Friends.

He authored four books, including *The Rich Heritage of Quakerism*. Four of his grandchildren are recorded ministers, including **John P. Williams Jr.**, who in 1989 became the general **superintendent** of Ohio Friends (EFC-ER) and also serves as director of **Evangelical Friends International**–North American Region. [John P. Williams Sr.]

WILLSON, DAVID (d. 1866). Leader of the Willsonite Children of Peace who broke away from New York Yearly Meeting in 1812 and remained a distinct and separate group until 1879. They reinstituted Old Testament rituals and are best known for the temple they built at Sharon, Ontario, which still stands, and for at one time having the best silver band in Ontario.

WILMINGTON COLLEGE. Founded in 1871 in Wilmington, Ohio, as a coeducational **college** by area **Orthodox** Friends who were then members of Indiana **Yearly Meeting**. When Wilmington Yearly Meeting was set off from Indiana in 1892, the college became affiliated with that yearly meeting and remains so.

WILSON, EDWARD RAYMOND (1896–1987). North American activist for **peace** and internationalism, E. Raymond Wilson was born in Iowa and studied at Columbia University's Teachers College. After a year in Japan and Taiwan in 1926–1927, he worked to limit militarism in schools. In 1932 he married Miriam Davidson and with her, helped found the Bryn Gweled cooperative community in Pennsylvania. Beginning in the 1930s, he developed the International Relations program for the **American Friends Service Committee**, and in 1942 he moved to Washington to lobby for alternative service for

conscientious objectors. Wilson served as executive secretary of the **Friends Committee on National Legislation** from 1943 until 1962. [Margery Post Abbott]

WILSON, LLOYD LEE (1947–). Wilson is a recorded **minister** and member of Rich Square **Monthly Meeting** in North Carolina. Wilson served as executive secretary of **Friends General Conference** from 1982 until 1985 and as **clerk** of North Carolina **Yearly Meeting** (**Conservative**) in 1991 and 1992. In 1992, he published *Essays on the Quaker Vision of* ***Gospel Order*** with the support and permission of his yearly meeting. Wilson and his wife, Susan, founded the Norfolk Quaker House in Virginia, which offered counseling about military service and **conscientious objection** to war (*see* PEACE TESTIMONY). They served on its board of directors and also as counselors until it was laid down in 2001 when he became director of Institutional Research at Chowan College in North Carolina. [Margery Post Abbott]

WINSTANLEY, GERRARD (fl. 1648–1652). English social reformer, leader of the "Digger" movement to turn the village commons into free land to be farmed by the rural poor, later becoming a Friend.

WOMEN. The Quaker **testimony** on gender **equality** began in the 17th century, when **George Fox** preached that through **Christ** men and women could return to the original state of **perfection** and become once more "helps meet" to one another, as they had been in Eden. Women were therefore regarded as equal to men on the spiritual plane, though not necessarily on a social level. Friends recognized the gift of **ministry** in women as well as men (cf. Acts 2:17,18), and encouraged women to travel widely in the ministry, when they felt so led. The traveling women **ministers** endured not only dangers by land and sea, but also the prevalent prejudice against all women preachers. Nevertheless, they persisted and became role models as independent and courageous women wherever they journeyed.

Women's **meetings** dealt with many social issues in the early days of the movement. In the late 1650s and the 1660s, when Fox and other Quaker leaders saw the necessity of setting up small local meetings for business as well as **worship**, they established separate **busi-**

ness meetings for women, despite some initial opposition. **Margaret Fell** and her daughters established a model woman's meeting and nurtured others. These separate women's business meetings became training grounds for Quaker women to learn to speak to a group, write epistles, raise money, run schools, and persuade the men's meeting to agree to a course of action.

Friends offered **education** to girls as well as boys, making Quaker women well prepared to enter the professions and lead the reform movements of the 19th century. In Philadelphia, Quakers established the first medical school for women and trained many pioneer women doctors, as well as the first **African American** doctors and women medical missionaries (*see* MISSIONS). Quakers also educated many of the first women scientists and educators (*see* SCIENCE AND TECHNOLOGY). In **Britain**, women such as **Elizabeth Fry** served as models to women worldwide for concern for women prisoners (*see* PENAL REFORM), and Elizabeth Pease (1807–1897) was an international figure in the **abolition** of slavery.

Working out the realities of the spiritual equality of women and men was never straightforward. In the 19th century, work on behalf of slaves and prisoners led directly to campaigning for women's political equality. First, women experienced discrimination, especially within the antislavery movement, hampering their full participation. Secondly, they learned that action on social issues required more rights and direct political influence for women. Thirdly, they developed **leadership** skills valuable in the fight to gain women the vote.

On both sides of the Atlantic, individual Quaker women were prominent in the leadership of the early "constitutional" phases of the women's suffrage campaign. The history of the American feminist movement generally begins with the 1848 **Seneca Falls Woman's Rights Convention**. Four of the five women organizers and both presiding chairpersons were Quakers. One of them, **Lucretia Mott**, continued for decades to hold the position of "mother" of the movement. Later, **Susan B. Anthony** joined the movement and still later, **Alice Paul**, a New Jersey Quaker, became a leader first in obtaining suffrage, then in working for an Equal Rights Amendment. Anne Knight (1786–1862), who introduced the first manifesto for votes for women in Sheffield in 1851, was one of many British women active in the agitation for suffrage.

In Britain, from 1906 onwards, the campaign became more militant, and many Quakers dissociated themselves from it. However, when Alice Paul encountered militant campaigning in Britain, she took the methods back to the United States in 1911, where they were again controversial. General Quaker opinion on women's suffrage was divided, just as in the surrounding society. Some Quakers even opposed the principle of women's political equality, on the basis that spiritual equality bore no relation to temporal equality. In 1914, Philadelphia **Yearly Meeting (Hicksite)** was the only yearly meeting to approve a **minute** unequivocally in support of women's suffrage. Action for equal political rights in the wider society was paralleled by demands for full decision-making equality within the Religious Society of Friends. In the United States, women achieved this equality in the various yearly meetings, beginning in 1877. In **London Yearly Meeting** this was achieved in 1908. From their arrival in 1902, missionaries in **East Africa** sought to address food prohibitions and **marriage** customs that deprived women of dignity and equal treatment, with mixed results. Girls were educated and separate women's meetings established, including a separate Women's Yearly Meeting approved in 1951. These actions helped develop strong l**eadership** among the women despite the male domination of the East African Yearly Meeting structure.

With the advent of the second wave of feminism in the 1970s in the United States and Britain, various women's groups formed for discussion, study, and action. Newsletters and other publications soon followed. A concern grew for inclusive language in publications and spoken ministry, as well as interest from a small number of women in the developing fields of feminist **theology** and biblical criticism. Among **pastoral** Friends, some women struggled to be recorded as ministers and establish themselves as **pastors**. Awareness of the existence of violence, sexual harassment, and other forms of oppression of women within Quaker **families** and meetings gradually grew among all Friends.

In East Africa, women only slowly gained positions in their meetings. Affiliation with the **United Society of Friends Women**, which came officially in 1967, encouraged the growing work and voice of the women. In the late 20th century, the women sought to maintain connections among Friends throughout Kenya as the number of yearly meetings proliferated, sometimes divisively.

The collectivist ethos of second-wave feminism in Europe and North America meant that individual leaders were not prominent, as had been the case in the previous century. The women's **peace** movement, arising from the Greenham Common women's peace camp in Britain, from 1980 onwards, established a new model, which spread widely, drawing in Quaker women from many parts of the world. In 1990, the First International Theological Conference of Quaker Women, held at **Woodbrooke**, drew together **evangelical**, **Conservative**, and **liberal** women from 21 countries and, in turn, gave rise to similar conferences. [Margaret Hope Bacon, Pam Lunn]

WOMEN'S INTERNATIONAL LEAGUE FOR PEACE AND FREEDOM (WILPF). International **peace** organization founded at the International Women's Congress in The Hague in 1915 with strong Quaker participation. *See also* ADDAMS, JANE; BALCH, EMILY; CAMP, WILLIAM; HULL, HANNAH; LEWIS, LUCY.

WOOD, JAMES E. (1839–1925). A New York Friend, Wood was an innovative farmer and involved in local **politics** opposing campaign spending. Chosen to chair the 1887 **Richmond Conference** despite his disapproval of Quaker **pastors**, he helped the Conference remain prayerfully centered and he worked with **Rufus Jones** to create a unified body for all **Orthodox** Friends. Wood was a leader in the All Friends Conference in 1920, precursor of the **Friends World Committee for Consultation** and helped form the **American Friends Service Committee**. Wood strongly supported **mission** work and served as **clerk** of New York **Yearly Meeting** (**Orthodox**) in 1892 and from 1894 to 1925. He was also president of the American Bible Society. [Margery Post Abbott]

WOODBROOKE QUAKER STUDY CENTRE. The independent **British** settlement founded in 1902 to provide a "wayside inn" for Friends to renew their faith through scholarship and to prepare for responsibilities as part of the priesthood of all believers. The Centre ran a term-time study program for 96 years, but an increasing trend to shorter courses became the mainstay of the program from 2000. Woodbrooke is housed in a former home of **George Cadbury** in Birmingham, England. [Pink Dandelion]

WOODWARD, WALTER CARLETON (1878–1942). Educator, administrator, editor. After growing up in the Quaker community of Newberg, Oregon, Woodward taught history at **Earlham College**. He was then asked to edit the *American Friend* (1917–1942), and to serve as general secretary of Five Years Meeting (later **Friends United Meeting**) from 1917 to 1928. Active in the **ecumenical** Faith and Order Conferences as well as the World Conference of Friends in 1920, he devoted much energy to reuniting the different branches of Friends. [Margery Post Abbott]

WOOLMAN, JOHN (1720–1772). Abolitionist, reformer, writer, and **minister**. Born near Mt. Holly, New Jersey, where he lived most of his life, John Woolman is thought by many to be the central figure of 18th-century Quaker faith and social reform. His antislavery efforts became his primary life's work, and largely due to his efforts, Quakers became the first significant group in America to emancipate their slaves. He was concerned about the rights of **Native Americans**, nonviolence and **war-tax resistance** during the French and Indian War, the destruction of the **environment**, the burden of luxury to the rich as well as the economic plight of the poor. He sought to nurture a renewed **spirituality** for the Religious Society of Friends and to be faithful to Quaker **testimonies** of **equality**, **simplicity**, and **peace**.

Woolman's life exemplified simplicity and 18th-century **Quietism**, which meant not passive withdrawal, but seeking the inward spiritual direction that leads to dynamic outward social action. He focused less on outcomes than on a spiritually centered practice, as he said in his *Journal*, "looking less at the effects of my labour than at the pure **motion** and reality of the concern as it arises from heavenly love." Alfred North Whitehead called Woolman "the apostle of human freedom." Woolman's approaches to issues were much like those of Mohandas K. **Gandhi** (1869–1948) and Martin Luther King Jr. (1929–1968).

In 1761, Woolman visited the Wyoming Valley of Pennsylvania to meet with Native Americans during the French and Indian War. Woolman met peacefully with many bands, often dispensing with interpreters. Paounhung, who knew little if any English, is said to have listened carefully to Woolman's **prayers** and said afterwards, "I love to hear where words come from."

Woolman's *Journal,* his two essays "On Keeping Negroes" (1754, 1762) and his "Plea for the Poor" (composed probably in 1763, published in 1793) have been an inspiration to generations. The *Journal,* published posthumously in 1774, ranks among the world's great spiritual autobiographies and is perhaps the most eloquent example of the genre of the Quaker **journal**. The *Journal* tells the story of his early struggles to follow the "**leadings**" of the Inward **Light**, which he referred to as "the **Truth**," and how, in 1756, when the **North American** Quaker community was in crisis, he gave up his retail business in order to focus on doing God's will. The *Journal* records his gradual life-journey toward the surrender of the self-will to the will of **God**. His concerns for the poor later led him to York, England, where he died of smallpox. [Michael Allen Heller]

WORD. Friends consider the term "word," as used in the prologue to John's Gospel, a basic metaphor for **Christ** outwardly incarnated and inwardly experienced. The oft-used subordinate metaphor "**Light**" connotes both knowledge and energy. This Quaker juxtaposition can be seen by pairing John 1:9 "The true light, which enlightens everyone, was coming into the world" with verse 14, "And the Word became flesh and lived among us, and we have seen his glory."

The perception of having been "spoken to" by Christ historically and inwardly (Hebrews 1:1,2) has nurtured several Quaker **testimonies**, such as a stewardship of the creation as honoring the speech of **God**, prayerfully listening to the Spirit in private and public **worship**, acknowledging that individual lives as well as words "speak," **discerning** with fear and trembling how to be God's "voice" ministerially or prophetically, seeking to use words in speech or in writing with integrity, and denoting the Holy Scriptures as the "words of God," thus preserving for Christ the term "Word of God." *See also* BIBLE; PROPHECY; TRUTH. [Arthur O. Roberts]

WORLD WAR II. During World War II, Quakers were most visible in their advocacy of **conscientious objectors (COs)** to fighting in any form. To this end, in the United States, Friends joined with the Mennonites and Church of the Brethren in advocating for, then administering, **Civilian Public Service** camps for COs. Many COs from **Britain**, the United States, and elsewhere participated in the reconstituted

Friends Ambulance Units, although many Friends, particularly in the United States, chose to fight. Berlin Monthly Meeting established a prohibited youth group in 1935, including the children of Jewish, Socialist, and "Aryan" families, along with other actions in quiet protest of Nazi regulations. Friends aided in the escape of Jews and other refugees from Europe and offered their homes to refugees resettling in other countries. Some Friends suffered German concentration camps for their witness, and some in Asia were caught up in Japanese prison camps. Building on experience gained in the Franco-Prussian War (1870–1871) and World War I (1914–1918), Friends were active in **relief work** during and after the war, as well as in efforts to establish **peace**. In 1947 Friends were awarded the Nobel Peace Prize through the **American Friends Service Committee** and Friends Service Council of London for their work. [Margery Post Abbott]

WORSHIP. Quaker worship now takes many forms and occurs in many languages around the world. All of these forms have evolved since the sometimes dramatic, sometimes profoundly silent worship that was the central experience of early Friends. Abandoning the religious trappings of **church** buildings, rituals, symbols, and stated or ordained clergy, as well as the church calendar, they assembled wherever it was convenient to worship, even out-of-doors.

Robert Barclay describes in Proposition 11 of his ***Apology*** how they began in silence, "watching in holy dependence on the Lord and meeting not only outwardly in one place, but inwardly in the one Spirit and in the one name of Jesus." The beginning of the **meeting** was a time for "turning away from one's own thoughts and for suspending the imagination in order to feel the Lord in the midst and to know a true gathering in his name." When the meeting was **gathered** or **covered** and the Presence could be felt by each person, "it becomes like a flood of refreshment. and extends over the whole meeting. . . . Many of our meetings take place without the utterance of a single word. Yet our hearts are wonderfully overcome with a secret sense of **God**'s power and spirit, which has been ministered without words from one vessel to another." When words or **prayers** were spoken, they arose from "the pure **motions** and of God's spirit."

Then, as now, it was often felt that God spoke to the condition of one person or of the whole meeting through the inspired or **prophetic** words of someone who was moved to speak. Originally, meetings might last for several hours, ending when an **elder** Friend sensed a motion of the **Holy Spirit** to end the meeting. The elder then shook hands with a neighbor, at which point everyone shook hands, with those around them. In the **unprogrammed** tradition, the shaking of hands is still the signal that the meeting has ended.

This form of worship was common to all Quakers for two centuries in their local meetings, as well as in larger assemblies at quarterly and yearly meetings and at funerals (*see* DEATH AND DYING) and **marriages**. **Business meetings** began and ended with such worship and were also expected to continue in a spirit of worship. Worship could also occur spontaneously or by prearrangement at any place or time as an **opportunity** when two people or a small group of people would settle into worship.

By the 18th century, most spoken **ministry** came from **women** or men who had been recorded as having the gift of ministry, although it has always been true that anyone who felt moved to speak was expected to do so. Up through the middle of the 19th century, and in some places, well into the 20th century, the messages of some recorded ministers could be quite long, at least by today's standards for unprogrammed worship. The traditional seating arrangement placed ministers and elders on raised benches facing the meeting.

During the latter half of the 19th century, most North American **Orthodox Gurneyite** meetings became **programmed meetings**. Because of their missionary efforts, a substantial majority of Quakers around the world now practice some form of programmed worship. Usually this resembles Protestant worship led by a **pastor**, although there is a wide range in the amount of programming and in the amount of "open worship" during which anyone may speak, pray, or sing out of the silence.

Unprogrammed meetings have also evolved up through the end of the 20th century. They are now shorter, rarely lasting more than an hour, and only a few meetings still record people who have a "gift" in the ministry. Some meetings have rearranged the seating into a circle or a hollow square, emphasizing equality of each person before God and the circle of spiritual community gathered in God.

Even with all of these changes and Quakerism's acculturation in the lands where it has taken root around the world, many people in both the programmed and unprogrammed traditions can still attest to the continuing power of Quaker worship described by Robert Barclay. [William P. Taber]

–Y–

YANG, STEPHEN (ALSO YANG ZHEN HUA) (1911–2001). Doctor, **educator**, and **peace** activist. In 1922 Yang, a second-generation Quaker, became a student at the Friends Middle School on the campus of the West China Union University (WCUU) in Chengdu, cofounded by Canadian Methodists, American Baptists, and British Quakers (*see* EAST ASIA). Yang graduated from WCUU in 1938 with a medical degree and then taught at the school of medicine there while he continued his medical training. In 1942, he married Ruth Zhang, who was also a doctor. In the 1980s, after being "rehabilitated" following imprisonment (1970–1971) during the Cultural Revolution, Yang participated in the International Physicians for the Prevention of Nuclear War and was allowed by the government to travel to international meetings. [Margery Post Abbott]

YEARLY MEETING. The regional bodies that are responsible to adopt the book of **discipline** and delineate the faith and practice for members of that body. The term also refers to the annual session of that body gathered for **worship**, **business meetings**, and fellowship. Originally, yearly meetings were geographically based and nonoverlapping, but because of the separations among Friends, more than one yearly meeting exists in many regions today.

In all cases each yearly meeting is independent in its doctrinal **covenant** and the transaction of its business and normally adopts its own book of discipline. Recognition of yearly meetings by other Friends is by exchange of epistles written at annual sessions. In the United States, **monthly meetings** normally gather two or three times a year in **quarterly meetings**. Those Friends in two or more "quarters" form the yearly meeting.

In the past, authority rested with the yearly meeting, although business arose from the monthly meetings. Beginning in the 19th century with the **Progressive Friends**, this pattern was challenged. Today, among North American **liberal Friends**, the monthly meeting (local congregation) is considered the primary organizational authority. In Britain, insofar as individuals accept any corporate authority, it ultimately rests with the yearly meeting. **Evangelical Friends International**, in contrast, places organizational responsibility in the yearly meeting. The area (or quarterly) meetings and local **churches** are seen as constituent and subordinate to the parent body. [Margery Post Abbott]

YOUNG FRIENDS MOVEMENT. This 20th-century movement was organized by members in their twenties and thirties and arose independently in the various bodies of Friends in **North America**. During the first half of the century, they became an important site for cross-branch fellowship and a source of support for **reunification**. The latter in fact happened in several **yearly meetings** when the Young Friends of 1915 became the leaders of 1955.

Evangelical Quaker youth had been involved in the interdenominational **Christian Endeavor** Society since the 1860s. Feeling a need to meet with other Friends, the Young Friends of Five Years Meeting (FYM; *see* FRIENDS UNITED MEETING) sponsored an All Young Friends Conference in 1910, which became a regular event until 1935. "Fraternal delegates" from the **Hicksite** Philadelphia Yearly Meeting joined the 1912 conference. Regional groupings were even more inclusive: New England's **Whittier** Fellowship, formed in 1911, drew members from three branches and six yearly meetings. **Canadian** Young Friends followed a similar path. In 1912, FYM established a Young Friends Board, with a paid secretary. Professionalization led to loss of enthusiasm, and the American Young Friends Fellowship was organized in 1934 completely free of FYM control. The present Young Friends of North America was established at a conference at **Guilford College** in 1954. It welcomes members college age and older and especially encourages intervisitation among yearly meetings. Since 1975, regular Youthquake gatherings bring young Friends together, particularly from programmed meetings. **Evangelical Friends International** operates its own youth program.

A similar movement developed in **Britain** after 1902 under the leadership of A. Neave Brayshaw (1861–1920). A distinctive organizing tool was a series of annual "tramps" (visits to **meetings**) beginning in 1905. **Woodbrooke** College in Britain and Woolman School and

Pendle Hill in America served as important centers for cross-branch Young Friends activities. Beginning in the late 20th century, young Friends from both sides of the Atlantic have joined in regular Quaker Youth Pilgrimages. *See* FRIENDS WORLD COMMITTEE FOR CONSULTATION; PICKETT, CLARENCE. [Mary Ellen Chijioke]

YUNGBLUT, JOHN (ca. 1913–1995). North American writer and civil rights activist. Originally an Episcopalian minister, Yungblut joined Friends in 1960. He served as director of the **American Friends Service Committee** program "Mission to Isolated Liberals" in the southern United States and then was director at Quaker House in Atlanta, Georgia, where he worked closely with Martin Luther King Jr. from 1960 to 1968. He is best known for his writings on **mysticism** and **prayer**. [Margery Post Abbott]

–Z–

ZARU, JEAN (1940–). Jean Zaru is the presiding **clerk** of the Ramallah Friends **Meeting** in Palestine (*see* MIDDLE EAST). For many years Zaru taught religion and ethics at the Friends Schools in Ramallah (*see* EDUCATION). Active in leading the YWCA of Jerusalem, YWCA of Jordan, and YWCA of Palestine, she served as the vice president of the World YWCA from 1983 until 1991. Zaru was on the Central Committee of the World Council of Churches (WCC) from 1975 until 1983 and was a member of the Working Group on Interfaith Dialogue of the WCC from 1981 until 1991 (*see* ECUMENISM). She was twice elected to serve as a member of the International Council of the World Conference for Religion and **Peace**. Zaru serves as a volunteer consultant and resource person for many church-related organizations, including the Middle East Council of Churches and particularly on the subjects of Islam and human rights. Zaru is one of the founding members of Sabeel, an ecumenical Palestinian Liberation Theology Center in Jerusalem, and is presently the vice chair of its board. She is also a board member of Wi'am Conflict Resolution Center in Bethlehem. She has been the keynote speaker at numerous conferences around the world and her papers have been published in many books.

Appendix A: Friends Worldwide: Origins of Yearly Meetings

Yearly Meeting	Origins	Founding of YM
Africa		
Central & Southern Africa YM	18th-century whalers	1948
Eglise Evangelique des Amis du Congo	1984 outreach from Burundi YM	1991
Eglise Evangelique des Amis du Burundi (EFI)	1934 Kansas YM mission	1984
Hill House MM, Ghana	Local residents & expatriates	–
Kenya		
Bware YM (FUM)	Formed from Vihiga YM	1994
Central YM (FUM)	Formed from East Africa YM	1992
Chavakali YM (FUM)	Formed from Vihiga YM	1997
East Africa YM (FUM)	1902 U.S. Friends Mission (centered at Kaimosi)	1946
East Africa (N) (FUM)	Formed from East Africa YM	1987
East Africa YM (South) (FUM)	Now Vihiga YM, formed from East Africa YM	1979
Elgon RS of F (W) (FUM)	Formed from East Africa YM	1973
Elgon YM (East) (FUM)	Formed from Elgon RS of F	1993
Kakamega YM (FUM)	Formed from East Africa YM	1993
Lugari YM (FUM)	Formed from East Africa YM	1992
Malava YM (FUM)	Formed from East Africa YM	1992
Nairobi YM (FUM)	Formed from Vihiga YM	1987
Taloi YM (FUM)	Formed from East Africa YM	1994
Vokoli YM (FUM)	Formed from Vihiga YM	1996
Eglise Evangelique des Amis du Rwanda (EFI)	Joint mission work by four EFI YM	1986
Pemba YM (Tanzania)	British Friends Foreign Mission Assn.	1897/1916

YM	Origins	Founding of YM
Africa *(continued)*		
Tanzania YM	1952 movement from Kenya	1984
Uganda YM	1948 outreach from Kenya	1980

Note: Other scattered groups are in Ethiopia (expatriates), Madagascar (British mission), and Nigeria (ca. 1988) (Nigerians who studied abroad).

YM	Origins	Founding of YM
East Asia		
People's Republic of China	1887 American missionaries	–
Hong Kong MM	Expatriates	–
Japan YM	1884 work of Philadelphia YM and AFSC	1917
Seoul MM	1950s AFSC medical social work	1964
Taiwan YM (EFI)	1912 China Mission of evangelical Friends from Ohio	1977
South Asia		
Bhopal MM (India)	1893 Friends Foreign Mission, London	1893
Bundelkhand YM (EFI)	1896 American Friends Mission/ 1897 London Mission	1956
General Conference of India	Fellowship of scattered Friends	1959
Mid-India YM	1866 Fr. Foreign Mission, London	1907
Nepal YM (EFI)	Friends from India	1990s
Southeast Asia		
Cambodia (EFI)	1995, Cambodian converted in California	–
Indonesia YM (EFI)	1987 Southwest Yearly Meeting mission	–
Philippines YM (EFI)	1978 North American EFI missionaries	–

Note: There are other, mainly small, unprogrammed worship groups in Singapore and Sri Lanka.

YM	Origins	Founding of YM
Australia and New Zealand		
Aotearoa–New Zealand YM	1909—first annual Conference	1964
Australia YM	1832, James Backhouse; 1902 General Meeting formed	1964

YM	Origins	Founding of YM
Central and South America		
Bogota MM (Colombia)	1940s—FWCC Membership Committee	1978
Iglesia Nacional Evangélica "Los Amigos" (INELA) (EFI)	1930—Northwest YM mission work in Bolivia	1974
Junta Anual de los Amigos	Union Boliviana (IEUBA)	–
Amigos Central (Boliva)	Indian YM mission	1986
Misión Boliviana de Santidad Amigos	Quaker Center for Ecumencial Education	1986
El Salvador YM	1902 mission—Southwest YM	1991
Iglesia Nacional de Guatemala	1902 mission—Southwest YM	1970
Guatemala-Amigos de Santidad	Holiness YM started 1986	1992
Honduras YM	1903 mission—Southwest YM	1983
Monteverde MM	Post-WWII emigration from U.S.	1952
Iglesia National Evangélica "Los Amigos" del Peru (EFI)	Northwest & Bolivian YM mission work	1961

Note: There are other scattered unprogrammed Friends in Bolivia, Managua, San Jose, etc.

YM	Origins	Founding of YM
Europe and the Middle East		
Austria QM	Part of German YM—Vienna Mtg started 1921	1938
Barcelona MM	Spanish seekers via BBC program	1958
Belgium/Luxembourg MM	Long history, scattered Friends FWCC affiliation	1976
Britain YM	England, Scotland, Wales	1668
Denmark YM	1870 visits by Thomas Shillitoe et al.	1875
Finland YM	Roots in post WWII AFSC/FSC work	1992
France YM	1785 locals contact London, Post WWI relief workers	1933
Germany YM	1700 British and American Visitors; WWI relief work	1925
Ireland YM	1654 first meeting for worship	1669
Middle East YM	1869 work in Syria/Palestine	1929
Moscow MM	British/California/FUM contacts	1996
Netherlands YM	1653 visit by Penn, Fox; 1928 Woodbrooke connections	1931
Norway YM	1814 prisoners in Britain; 1940 renewal	1818
Sweden YM	WWI worship group	1935

YM	Origins	Founding of YM
Europe and the Middle East ***(continued)***		
Switzerland YM	1934 service work camp participants	1944

Note: There are other groups in Egypt, Estonia, Hungary, Italy, Lithuania, and Madrid.

YM	Origins	Founding of YM
Mexico and the Caribbean		
Cuba YM (FUM)	1900 Missionaries	1927
Jamaica YM (FUM)	1881 Iowa YM mission	1941
Reunion General	Joining of Cuidad Victoria and other meetings	1958
Cuidad Victoria (FUM)	Monthly Meeting formed by U.S. Missionaries	1887/88
Asociación Religiosa de Iglesias Evangélicas Amigos (EFI)	Evangelical Friends Mission work	1993
North America		
Alaska YM (EFI)	SW YM mission	1970
Alaska Friends Conference (FGC)	Independent Meetings Movement	1956, 1969
Baltimore YM (FUM/FGC)	English Friends/Consolidation	1672/1968
Canadian YM (FUM/FGC)	Spread from U.S. (Union)	1955
Central YM (Indiana)	Withdrew from 5yrs. Mtg	1926
Evangelical Friends Church Eastern Region (EFI)	Formerly Ohio YM	1812
Evangelical Friends Church Southwest (EFI)	Set up by Iowa YM	1895
Great Plains YM (FUM)	Western migration, formerly Nebraska YM	1908
Illinois YM (FGC)	Set off from Baltimore YM	1875
Indiana YM (FUM)	Strong Carolina roots	1821
Intermountain YM	Set off from Pacific YM	1975
Iowa YM (C)	Separated from Iowa YM	1877
Iowa YM (FUM)	Set off from Indiana YM	1863
Lake Erie YM (FGC)	1939 Association of Friends	1969
Mid-America YM (EFI)	Ex-Kansas YM set off from Indiana	1872
Missouri Valley Friends Conference	Independent Meetings Movement	1955
New England YM (FUM/FGC)	Friends from England/Reunion	1661/1945
New York YM (FUM/FGC)	Friends from England/Reunion	1695/1955
North Carolina YM (C)	British Friends/Separation	1698/1904

YM	Origins	Founding of YM
North America ***(continued)***		
North Carolina YM (FUM)	British Friends/Separation	1698/1904
North Pacific YM	Set off from Pacific YM	1973
Northern YM (FGC)	Set off from Illinois YM	1975
Northwest YM (EFI)	Set off from Iowa YM	1893
Ohio YM (C)	Set off from Baltimore YM	1813
Ohio Valley YM (FGC)	Migration/ former Indiana YM	1821
Pacific YM	1880s College Park Assn.	1947
Philadelphia YM (FGC)	British settlers/Reunion	1681/1955
Piedmont Friends Fellowship (FGC)	Independent Meetings Movement	1971
Rocky Mountain YM (EFI)	Set off by Nebraska YM	1957
South Central YM (FGC)	Independent Meetings Movement	1961
Southeastern YM (FUM/FGC)	Independent Meetings Movement	1962
South Appalachian YM (FGC)	Independent Meetings Movement	1970
Western Association of Friends (FUM)	Separated from Southwest YM	199?
Western YM (FUM)	Set off from Indiana YM	1858
Wilmington YM (FUM)	Set off from Baltimore YM	1892
Wyoming Friends Meeting	Independent Meetings Movement	1990

Abbreviations used:
C—Conservative
EFI—Evangelical Friends International
FGC—Friends General Conference
FUM—Friends United Meeting
MM—Monthly Meeting
RSoF—Religious Society of Friends
YM—Yearly Meeting

Appendix B

Africa	**156,180**
Central and South Africa	200
Eglise Evangelique des Amis du Congo	1,303
Eglise Evangelique des Amis du of Burundi	12,000
Hill House MM, Ghana	18
Kenya	132,825
Bware YM	7,215
Central YM	9,000
Chavakali YM	7,294
East Africa YM Kaimosi	6,153
East Africa YM (N)	13,000
East Africa YM (Vihiga)	14,798
Elgon RS of F (W)	13,000
Elgon East YM	12,000
Kakamega YM	7,000
Lugari YM	14,300
Malava YM	12,000
Nairobi YM	7,500
Toloi YM	4,565
Vokoli YM	5,000
Eglise Evangelique des Amis du Rwanda	3,234
Tanzania YM	3,000
Pemba YM (Tanzania)	100
Uganda YM (FUM)	3,500
Asia	**8,401**
East Asia	
People's Republic of China	?
Hong Kong MM	20

Japan YM	185
Seoul MM	12
Taiwan YM	3,200
South Asia	
Bhopal MM (India)	152
Bundelkhand YM	287
General Conference of India	45
Mid-India YM	250
Nepal YM	400
Southeast Asia	
Cambodia	?
Indonesia YM	3,000
Philippines YM	850
Australia and New Zealand	**1,677**
Aotearoa–New Zealand YM	658
Australia YM	1,019
Central and South America	**58,572**
Bogota MM (Colombia)	20
Iglesia Nacional (INELA) (Bolivia)	7,000
Amigos Central	1,300
Misión Boliviana de Santidad Amigos	22,000
El Salvador YM	550
Iglesia Nacional de Guatemala	20,000
Guatemala Emgajodores	130
Guatemala–Santidad	500
Honduras YM	2,000
Monteverde MM	72
Iglecia Nacional del Peru	5,000
Europe and the Middle East	**19,068**
Austria QM	11
Barcelona MM	10
Belgium/Luxembourg MM	42
Britain YM	16,468
Denmark YM	31
Finland YM	20

France YM	60
Germany YM	298
Ireland YM	1,591
Middle East YM	65
Moscow MM	13
Netherlands YM	105
Norway YM	151
Sweden YM	100
Switzerland YM	103
Mexico and the Caribbean	**1,523**
Cuba YM	373
Jamaica YM	350
Mexico	800
North America	**92,786**
Alaska YM	1,000
Alaska Friends Conference	250
Baltimore	4,638
Canadian YM	1,150
Central YM (Indiana)	287
Evangelical Friends Church Eastern Region	8,775
Friends Church Southwest (EFI)	5,632
Great Plains YM (FUM)	715
Illinois YM (FGC)	1,100
Indiana YM (FUM)	4,754
Intermountain YM	997
Iowa YM (Conservative)	548
Iowa YM (FUM)	3,473
Lake Erie YM (FGC)	884
Mid-America YM (EFI)	4,916
New England YM (FUM/FGC)	4,300
New York YM (FUM/FGC)	3,500
North Carolina (Conservative)	382
North Carolina (FUM)	10,662
North Pacific YM	865
Northern YM (FGC)	1,194
Northwest YM (EFI)	7,012

Ohio YM (Conservative)	531
Ohio Valley YM	812
Pacific YM	1,480
Philadelphia YM	11,800
Rocky Mountain YM	1,154
South Central YM	315
Southeastern YM	561
South Appalachian YM	1,288
Western Association of Friends	530
Western YM	5,304
Wilmington YM	1,977
Total Friends Worldwide	**338,219**

Source: Friends World Committee for Consultation, based on reports received for 2001. Numbers are generally for recorded members of the Religious Society of Friends except in the case of some EFI affiliated meetings, such as Indonesia and the Congo, where numbers reflect participation rather than formal membership. In many yearly meetings the number of active participants are two or three times the membership figures. A few, isolated "international members" are included in the total.

Abbreviations used:
MM = Monthly Meeting
RSoF = Religious Society of Friends
YM = Yearly Meeting

Appendix C: Family Trees of North American and African Yearly Meetings

YEARLY MEETINGS IN NORTH AMERICA

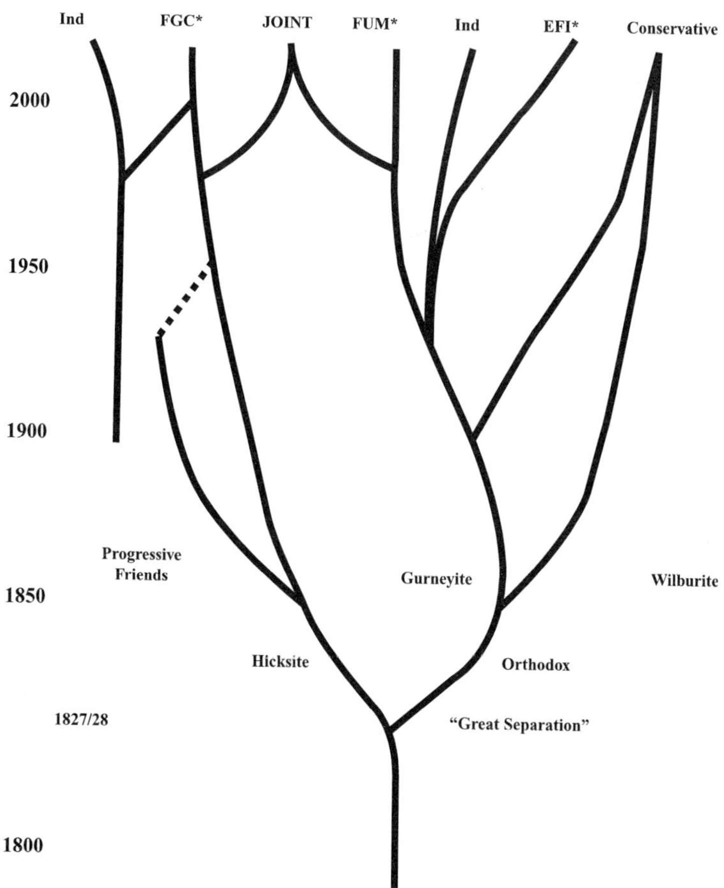

YEARLY MEETINGS IN EAST AFRICA

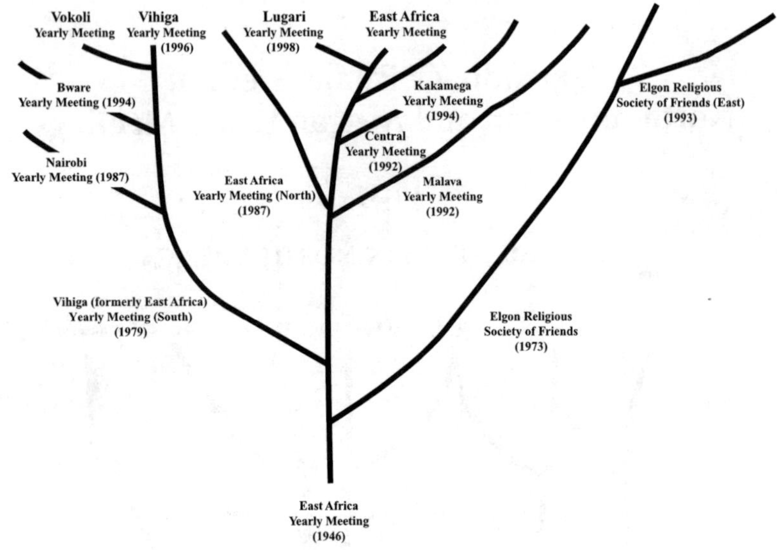

Bibliography

Even in the 17th century, when they ridiculed theological training as the basis for spiritual leadership, Quakers had a higher level of literacy and basic education than prevailed in England and America. They made full use of the printed word to communicate among themselves and with the wider world, a pattern that has persisted ever since. Partly because they were considered distinctive, and partly because their impact on world affairs has far exceeded their numbers, they have also prompted a disproportionate interest among others. The body of literature by and about the Religious Society of Friends and its members is therefore very large indeed.

There have been several distinct periods of Quaker publishing. The prevailing format of the 1650s and 1660s was the pamphlet, often in a counterpoint of Quaker and anti-Quaker argument. Systematic theology, never a Quaker strong point, began appearing in the 1660s, with the most famous being Barclay's *Apology* (1676). Before the end of the 17th century, the memorial and journal, spiritual biography and autobiography respectively, joined historical surveys as the characteristic genres that dominated Quaker publishing into the 19th century. Social thought found expression in essays and addresses to those in power. All of these forms were joined during the late 19th century by a growing body of institutional histories, celebrations of outstanding Quakers and their works, and scholarly works addressed to both Quaker and non-Quaker audiences.

The improved printing technologies of the early 19th century opened the floodgates of mass publication. Among Friends this took the form of repeated reprints of Quaker classics, both individually and in collections, and a spate of periodicals. Both received special impetus from American schisms, so that each branch launched its own selection of authoritative Quaker classics and its weekly or monthly magazine. Today, the major periodical titles include *Quaker Life* (organ of Five Years Meeting), *Friends Journal* (Liberal American), *The Conservative Friend*, *The Friend*

(London), and *Friends Quarterly* (London). *Evangelical Friend* ceased publication in 1994. There are national Quaker publications from Canada, Australia, France, Nigeria, and elsewhere, and magazines for every topic of concern to Friends. Many have been microfilmed, and most are available in the Quaker libraries listed below. Among those of particular interest to students of Quaker history are *Quaker History*, journal of the Friends Historical Association (U.S.), *The Journal of the Friends Historical Society* (Britain), and *Southern Friend*, produced by the North Carolina Friends Historical Society. *Quaker Religious Thought* has been joined recently by *Quaker Theology*, which explores Liberal faith. *Quaker Studies* includes recent scholarship on Quakerism in all disciplines.

This bibliography seeks to present published works most likely to be available to the general reader, particularly in the United States. Exceptions for out-of-print works are made for classics and seminal works widely available in libraries, or when a specific title is the only one available on the subject. Given space limitations, preference has been given to more recent titles, which are not only more likely to be available but will cite the older works in their own bibliographies. The bibliography emphasizes books as the most convenient form of publication for the lay reader. Recent journal articles are included where they represent critical sources for a topic. Inclusion of doctoral dissertations is even more limited. Web links are too unstable to include in a printed work intended to last more than a year or two. While some excellent videos have been produced in recent years, these are often very difficult to identify, locate, and acquire and are therefore omitted from this listing. To include the maximum number of works, each title is listed only once, and individual essays are listed separately from collections only under exceptional circumstances.

This bibliography is mainly limited to works about Quakers only. The exceptions are a few works that are so central to our understanding of the origins of the movement that they are mandatory reading for anyone seeking to understand the subject. The bibliographies of the works listed will indicate many other works dealing with subjects—from evangelical mission movements to women abolitionists—that have significant Quaker content and/or set the context for the distinctive experience of Friends.

Anyone wanting to read about Quakerism would do best to start with a selection of the titles listed under *General Works*. It is worth reading a sample to understand the varying points of view taken by Quaker authors. There are also some good, more local, general introductions for Britain and North America. The 17th century stands as the reference point for all later Friends, making it the logical first narrower topic. The Rowntree series (*The Beginnings of Quakerism*, *The Second Period of Quakerism*, *The Later Periods of Quakerism; and Quakerism in the American Colonies*) has never been replaced as the primary narrative for the 17th and 18th centuries. All later works refer to and build upon these works, even when correcting them. From there, the reader is encouraged to expand to later periods, particular geographic regions, and the special topics listed in the outline. Once started, there is enough material to keep a reader engaged for a lifetime.

Those seeking further works are urged to investigate the holdings of the major Quaker research libraries in the U.S. and Britain. Their parent institutions also maintain a reasonably stable presence on the Web, which is now the best source for up-to-date contact information, their catalogs, and links to other Web resources.

Library of the Religious Society of Friends in Britain, Friends House, Euston Road, London (www.quaker.org.uk)
Woodbrooke Quaker Study Centre, Birmingham, England (www.woodbrooke.org.uk)
Quaker Collection, Magill Library, Haverford College, Haverford, Pennsylvania (www.haverford.edu)
Friends Historical Library of Swarthmore College, Swarthmore, Pennsylvania (www.swarthmore.edu)
Friends Historical Collection, Hege Library, Guilford College, Greensboro, North Carolina (www.guilford.edu)
Friends Archives, Cattell Library, Malone College, Canton, Ohio (www.malone.edu)
Quaker Collection, Wilmington College Library, Wilmington, Ohio (www.wilmington.edu)
Friends Collection, Lilly Library, Earlham College, Richmond, Indiana (www.earlham.edu)
Quaker Room, Friends University, Wichita, Kansas (www.library.friends.edu)
Quaker Collection, Wilcox Library, William Penn University, Oskaloosa, Iowa (www.wmpenn.edu)
Murdock Learning Resource Center, George Fox University, Newberg, Oregon (www.georgefox.edu)
Whittier College, Whittier, California (www.whittier.edu)
The Library of Philadelphia Yearly Meeting (www.pym.org)

These libraries are also the major repositories for Quaker records and archives. The *Guide to the Records of Philadelphia Yearly Meeting*, compiled by Jack Eckert (Haverford, Pa.: Haverford College; Philadelphia: Records Committee of Philadelphia Yearly Meeting; Swarthmore, Pa.: Swarthmore College, 1989) includes a list of North American yearly meetings and the repositories for their records. (Since publication of the *Guide*, New York Yearly Meeting has transferred its archives to Friends Historical Library of Swarthmore College.) Thomas C. Hill's comprehensive *Monthly Meetings in North America: An Index* (4th ed., Cincinnati, Ohio: the author, 1997, with supplements) includes detailed listing of monthly meeting records and their locations. Most early British records are in local public records offices, but the Friends House Library is always the first place to start a search. Besides official Quaker records, the repositories generally hold significant collections of personal papers and the records of Quaker-related organizations. The distribution of such manuscript materials among the Quaker repositories is a function of both geography and the sectarian history of the parent institutions. Similarly, research libraries and historical societies hold a great deal of manuscript material emanating from localities. Much of this unpublished material has been microfilmed and is widely held in Quaker collections. Many early publications have also been microfilmed; the most important collection being *Early Quaker Writings: Microfilms of Printed Works, 1650–1750; from the Library of the Society of Friends* (London: World Microfilms, 1974–1977), 25 reels.

Because Quaker books do not have wide exposure in general bookstores, those seeking to purchase in-print works and to discover new titles are advised to consult one of the excellent Quaker outlets. In the United States these include the Friends General Conference Bookstore, the Pendle Hill Book Store, Friends United Press, and Barclay Press. All have a presence on the Web. [Mary Ellen Chijioke]

BIBLIOGRAPHIES

Friends Historical Library of Swarthmore College. *Catalog of the Book and Serials Collections of the Friends Historical Library*. 6 vol. Boston : G. Hall, 1982.

Smith, Joseph. *A Descriptive Catalogue of Friends' Books; or, Books Written by Members of the Society of Friends*. 2 vol. London: Joseph Smith, 1867. Reprint, New York: Kraus Reprint, 1970.

——. *Supplement*. . . . London: E. Hicks, jun., 1893. Reprint, New York: Kraus Reprint, 1970.

——. *Bibliotheca Anti-Quakeriana; or, A Catalogue of Books Adverse to the Society of Friends*. . . . London: Joseph Smith, 1873. Reprint, New York: Kraus Reprint, 1968.

——. *Bibliotheca Quakeristica: A Bibliography of Miscellaneous Literature Relating to the Friends (Quakers)*. London: Joseph Smith, 1883. Reprint, New York: Kraus Reprint, 1968.

Wing, Donald. *Short-title Catalogue of Books Printed in England, Scotland, Ireland, Wales, and British America, and of English Books Printed in Other Countries, 1641–1700*. 3 vol. New York: The Index Society, 1945–1951. 2nd ed., rev. and enlarged. New York: Index Committee of the Modern Language Association of America, 1972–1988.

DIRECTORIES

Friends World Committee for Consultation. *Quakers around the World: A Handbook of the Religious Society of Friends Quakers*. London: FWCC, 1994–. (Irregular)

Friends World Committee for Consultation. Section of the Americas. 1996 *Friends Directory of Meetings, Churches and Worship Groups in the Section of the Americas; and Resource Guide*. Philadelphia: FWCC Section of the Americas, 1995.

GENERAL WORKS

Brinton, Howard H, ed. *Friends for 300 Years: The History and Beliefs of the Society of Friends Since George Fox Started the Quaker Movement*. New York: Harper and Bros., 1952. Revised ed., *Friends for 350 Years*, ed. Margaret Hope Bacon. Wallingford, Pa.: Pendle Hill Publications, 2002.

Cooper, Wilmer A. *A Living Faith: An Historical Survey of Quaker Beliefs*. Richmond, Ind.: Friends United Press, 1990. 2nd ed. with subtitle, *A Historical and Comparative Survey of Quaker Beliefs*, 2001.

Frost, J. William, and John M. Moore, eds. *Seeking the Light: Essays in Quaker History in Honor of Edwin B. Bronner*. Wallingford, Pa.: Pendle Hill Publications and Friends Historical Association, 1986.

Gillman, Harvey. *A Light That Is Shining: An Introduction to the Quakers*. 2nd ed. London: Quaker Home Service, 1997.

Jones, Rufus. *Later Periods of Quakerism*. 2 vol. London: Macmillan, 1921. Reprint, Westport, Conn.: Greenwood, 1971.

Punshon, John. *Portrait in Grey: A Short History of the Quakers*. London: Quaker Home Service, 1984; Reprint with revisions, 1986.

Trueblood, D. Elton. *The People Called Quakers*. New York: Harper and Row, 1966. Reprint, Richmond, Ind.: Friends United Press, 1971.

Williams, Walter R. *The Rich Heritage of Quakerism*. Grand Rapids, Mich.: Eerdmans Publishing, 1962. Reprint, Newberg, Ore.: Barclay Press, 1987.

ORIGINS

Barbour, Hugh. *The Quakers in Puritan England*. Yale Publications in Religion, 7 [*i.e.* 8]. New Haven: Yale University Press, 1964. Reprint, Richmond, Ind.: Friends United Press, 1985.

Barbour, Hugh, and Arthur O. Roberts, eds. *Early Quaker Writings, 1650–1700*. Grand Rapids, Mich.: William B. Eerdmans, 1973. Reprinted, Wallingford, Pa.: Pendle Hill Publications, 2003.

Besse, Joseph. *A Collection of the Sufferings of the People Called Quakers for the Testimony of a Good Conscience. . . .* London: Luke Hinde, 1753. 2 v. *Index* by Lorand V. Johnson, ed. Audrey Sullivan. Fort Lauderdale, Fla.: Genealogical Society of Broward Co., Fla., c.1991. [Regional segments, newly indexed, are being published in facsimile, by Sessions Book Trust of York, England.]

Braithwaite, William C. *The Beginnings of Quakerism*. London: Macmillan, 1912. 2nd ed., rev. by Henry J. Cadbury. Cambridge: The University Press, 1955. Reprints, York, England: William Sessions in association with the Rowntree Book Trust, 1981. Bowie, Md.: Heritage Press, 1998.

——. *The Second Period of Quakerism*. London: Macmillan, 1919. 2nd ed., rev. by Henry J. Cadbury. Cambridge: The University Press, 1961. Reprint, York, England: William Sessions in association with the Rowntree Book Trust, 1979.

Corns, Thomas N., and David Loewenstein, eds. *The Emergence of Quaker Writing: Dissenting Literature in Seventeenth Century England*. London: Frank Cass, 1995.

Gwyn, Douglas. *Seekers Found: Atonement in Early Quaker Experience*. Wallingford, Pa.: Pendle Hill Publications, 2000.

Hill, Christopher. *The World Turned Upside-Down: Radical Ideas during the English Revolution*. London: Temple Smith; New York: Viking, 1972. Reprint, New York: Viking Penguin, 1984.

Moore, Rosemary. *The Light in Their Consciences: Early Quakers in Britain, 1646 –1666*. University Park, Pa.: Pennsylvania State University Press, 2000.

Nuttall, Geoffrey F., comp. *Early Quaker Letters, from Swarthmore Mss. to 1660*, calendered, indexed, and annotated by Geoffrey F. Nuttal. London: The Library, Friends House, 1952.

——. *The Holy Spirit in Puritan Faith and Experience*. 2nd ed. Oxford: Blackwell, 1947. Reprint, Chicago: University of Chicago Press, 1992.

Penn, William. *A Brief Account of the Rise and Progress of the People Called Quakers*. London: printed and sold by T. Sowle, 1694. Reprint, Richmond, Ind.: Friends United Press, 1976.

Reay, Barry. *The Quakers and the English Revolution*. London: Temple Smith; New York: St. Martin's Press, 1985.

Taylor, Ernest E. *The Valiant Sixty*. London: Bannisdale, 1947. 3rd ed. York, England: William Sessions, 1999.

Underwood, T. L. *Primitivism, Radicalism, and the Lamb's War: The Baptist-Quaker Conflict in Seventeenth-Century England*, Oxford Studies in Historical Theology. New York: Oxford University Press, 1997.

BY GEOGRAPHICAL REGION

Africa

Amugune, Japheth. *A Christian Pioneer*. Tiriki, Kenya: East Africa Yearly Meeting of Friends, 1971.

Kimball, Herbert, and Beatrice Kimball, eds. *Go into All the World: A Centennial Celebration of Friends in East Africa*. Richmond, Ind.: Friends United Press, 2002.

Mombo, Esther. *A Historical and Cultural Analysis of the Position of Abaluyia Women in Kenyan Quaker Christianity, 1902–1979, Mellen Quaker Studies Series*. Lewiston, N.Y.: Edwin Mellen Press, forthcoming 2003.

Rasmussen, Ane Marie Bak. *A History of the Quaker Movement in Africa*. London: British Academic Press. 1995.

Smuck, Harold. *Friends in East Africa*. Richmond, Ind.: Friends United Press, 1987.

Asia and Oceania

Brodie, Audrey and James Brodie. *Keeping Track: Quakers in Nineteenth Century New Zealand,*, Quaker Historical Manuscripts, no. 5. Wellington, N.Z.: Beechtree Press for New Zealand Yearly Meeting of the Society of Friends, 1999.

Cooley, James C. "The American Quaker Presence in Late Nineteenth Century China." In *The Influence of Quaker Women on American History: Biographical Studies*, ed. Carol and John Stoneburner, *Studies in Women and Religion*, vol. 21. Lewiston, N.Y.: Edwin Mellen Press, 1986, pp. 311–328.

DeVol, Charles E. *Fruit That Remains: The Story of the Friends Mission in China and Taiwan Sponsored by The Evangelical Friends Church—Eastern Region (Formerly Ohio Yearly Meeting of Friends)*. Canton, Ohio: Evangelical Friends Church—Eastern Region, 1988.

Nicholson, Herbert Victor. *Treasure in Earthen Vessels: The Story of Searching for, Finding and Sharing the Overflowing Love of God*. Upland, Calif.: the author, 1972. Reprint with subtitle, *God's Love Overflows in Peace and War*. Whittier, Calif., 1972.

Sykes, Marjorie. *An Indian Tapestry: Quaker Threads in the History of India, Pakistan and Bangladesh, from the Seventeenth Century to Independence,* completed and ed. by Geoffrey Carnall. York, England: Sessions Book Trust, 1997.

——. *Quakers in India: A Forgotten Century*. London: George Allen and Unwin, 1980.

Toda, Tetsuko Kawahara. *From Pastoral to Non-Pastoral: Quaker Experience in Japan*. Yamanashi, Japan: Yamanashi Women's Junior College, 1999.

West, Margaret and Audrey Brodie. *Remembrance of Friends Past: Testimonies and Memorials to the Lives and Works of New Zealand Quakers Who Died from 1843–1998*. Quaker Historical Manuscripts, no. 6. Wellington, N.Z.: Beechtree Press, 1999.

Wood, Patrick. *Time Will Make Things Clear: The Story of Stephen Yang, Chinese Quaker in the 20th Century*. Reading, England: Sowle Pess, 2000.

Britain and Europe

Dandelion, Pink. *A Sociological Analysis of the Theology of Quakers: The Silent Revolution*. Studies in Religion and Society, vol. 4. Lewiston, N.Y.: Edwin Mellen Press, 1996.

Davie, Martin. *British Quaker Theology since 1895*, Lewiston, N.Y.: Edwin Mellen Press 1997.

Davies, Adrian. *The Quakers in English Society, 1650–1725*, Oxford Historical Monographs. Oxford: Clarendon Press, 2000.

Friends Meeting in Geneva: History, Insights, Practice. [Geneva, Switzerland 1982].

Gilman, Harvey and Alastair Heron, eds. *Searching the Depth: Essays on Being a Quaker Today*. 2nd ed. London: Quaker Home Service, 1998.

Greaves, Richard L. *Dublin's Merchant-Quaker: Anthony Sharp and the Community of Friends, 1643–1707*. Stanford: Stanford University Press, 1998.

Hall, David J. "The Study of Eighteenth-Century English Quakerism: From Rufus Jones to Larry Ingle." *Quaker Studies* 5(2): 105–119 (March 2001).

Heron, Alastair. *Quakers in Britain: A Century of Change, 1895–1955*. Kelso, Scotland: Curlew Graphics, 1995.

Hodgken, Alice Mary. *Friends in Ireland*. London: Friends Tract Association, 1910. Reprint. Cookstown, Northern Ireland: Booktree Publications, 1996.

Kennedy, Thomas. *British Quakers, 1860–1920: The Transformation of a Religious Community*. Oxford: Oxford University Press, 2001.

Lloyd, Arnold. *Quaker Social History, 1669–1738*. London: Longmans, Green, 1950. Reprint, Westport, Conn.: Greenwood Press, 1979.

Morgan, Nicholas. *Lancashire Quakers and the Establishment, 1660–1730.* Halifax, England: Ryburn Academic Publishing, 1993.

Schmitt, Hans A. *Quakers and Nazis: Inner Light in Outer Darkness.* Columbia: University of Missouri Press, 1997.

Spielhofer, Sheila. *Stemming the Dark Tide: Quakers in Vienna, 1919–1942*. York, England: William Sessions, 2001.

Tjossem, Wilmer L. *Quaker Sloopers: From the Fjords to the Prairies*. Richmond, Ind.: Friends United Press, 1984.

Vann, Richard T. *The Social Development of English Quakerism, 1655–1755*. Cambridge, Mass.: Harvard University Press, 1969.

——, and David Eversley. *Friends in Life and Death: The British and Irish Quakers in the Demographic Transition, 1650–1900*, Cambridge Studies in Population, Economy and Society in Past Time. Cambridge, England: Cambridge University, 1992.

Wigham, Maurice J. *The Irish Quakers: A Short History of the Religious Society of Friends in Ireland*. Dublin: Historical Committee of the Religious Society of Friends in Ireland, 1992.

Central and South America and the Caribbean

Chapman, Ralf. *Bolivian Friends from Mission to Yearly Meeting*. Newberg, Ore.: Friends Missionary Literature, 1980.

Durham, Harriet Frorer. *Cuban Quakers*. Hollywood, Fla.: Dukane Press, 1972.

Enyart, Paul. *Friends in Central America*. South Pasadena, Calif.: William Carey Library, 1970.

Hilty, Hiram. *Friends in Cuba*. Richmond, Ind.: Friends United Press, 1977.

North America

Bacon, Margaret Hope. *The Quiet Rebels: The Story of the Quakers in America*. New York: Basic Books, 1969. Rev. ed. Wallingford, Pa.: Pendle Hill Publications, 1999.

Barbour, Hugh, et al. *Quaker Crosscurrents: Three Hundred Years of Friends in the New York Yearly Meetings*. Syracuse: Syracuse University Press, 1995.

Barbour, Hugh, and J. William Frost. *The Quakers*, Denominations in America, no. 3. Westport, Conn.: Greenwood Press, 1988. Paperback ed. Richmond, Ind.: Friends United Press, 1994.

Bauman, Richard. *For the Reputation of Truth: Politics, Religion, and Conflict among the Pennsylvania Quakers, 1750–1800*. Baltimore, Md: Johns Hopkins Press, 1971.

Beebe, Ralph K. *A Garden of the Lord: A History of Oregon Yearly Meeting of Friends Church*. Newberg, Ore.: Barclay Press, 1968. Reprint, 1991.

Benjamin, Philip S. *The Philadelphia Quakers in the Industrial Age,* 1865–1920. Philadelphia: Temple University Press, 1976.

Bronner, Edwin B. *William Penn's "Holy Experiment": The Founding of Pennsylvania, 1681–1701*. New York: Columbia University Press, 1962. Reprint, Westport, Conn.: Greenwood Press, 1978.

Carroll, Kenneth L. *Quakerism on the Eastern Shore*. Baltimore: Maryland Historical Society, 1970.

Chu, Jonathan. *Neighbors, Friends, or Madmen: The Puritan Adjustment to Quakerism in Seventeenth-Century Massachusetts Bay*, Contributions to the Study of Religion, no. 14. Westport, Conn.: Greenwood Press, 1985.

Dorland, Arthur Garratt. *The Quakers in Canada: A History*. Toronto: Ryerson Press, 1968.

Earlham School of Religion. *Among Friends: A Consultation with Friends about the Condition of Quakers in the U.S. Today*, An Earlham School of Religion Report. Richmond, Ind.: Earlham, 1999.

Elliott, Errol T. *Quakers on the American Frontier: A History of the Westward Migrations, Settlements and Developments of Friends on the American Continent*. Richmond, Ind.: Friends United Press, 1969.

Ferris, David. *Memoirs of the Life of David Ferris, an Approved Minister of God. . . .* Philadelphia: J. Simmons, 1825. Reprinted from the 1855 ed., with new material, as *Resistance and Obedience to God: Memoirs of David Ferris (1707–1779)*, ed. Martha Paxson Grundy. Philadelphia: Friends General Conference, 2001.

Fischer, David Hackett. *Albion's Seed: Four British Folkways in America*, America: A Cultural History, vol. 1. New York: Oxford University Press, 1989.

Forbush, Bliss. *History of Baltimore Yearly Meeting of Friends: Three Hundred Years of Quakerism in Maryland, Virginia, the District of Columbia, and Central Pennsylvania.* Sandy Spring, Md.: Baltimore Yearly Meeting of Friends, 1972.

Haines, Deborah L. "Friends General Conference: A Brief Historical Overview." *Quaker History* 89(2): 1–16 (Fall 2000).

Hamm, Thomas D. "The Problem of the Inner Light in Nineteenth-Century Quakerism." In *The Lamb's War: Quaker Essays to Honor Hugh Barbour*, ed. Michael L. Birkel and John W. Newman. Richmond, Ind.: Earlham College Press, 1992, pp. 101–117.

Hickey, Damon D. *Sojourners No More: The Quakers in the New South, 1865–1920*. Greensboro, N.C.: North Carolina Friends Historical Society and North Carolina Yearly Meeting of Friends, 1997.

Hinshaw, Gregory P. *Indiana Friends Heritage, 1821–1996: The 175 Anniversary History of Indiana Yearly Meeting of Friends (Quakers)*. Richmond, Ind.: Indiana Yearly Meeting, [1996].

Hinshaw, Seth B. *The Carolina Quaker Experience, 1665–1985: An Interpretation*. Greensboro, N.C.: North Carolina Yearly Meeting and North Carolina Friends Historical Society, 1984.

Holden, David E. W. *Friends Divided: Conflict and Division in the Society of Friends*. Richmond, Ind.: Friends United Press, 1988.

Jones, Rufus M., with Isaac Sharpless and Amelia M. Gumere. *The Quakers in the American Colonies*. London: Macmillan, 1911. Reprint, New York: W.W. Norton, 1966.

Kaiser, Geoffrey D. *The Society of Friends in North America, 1661–1997*. 18th ed. Sumneytown, Pa.: the author, 1997 [Graphic chart of the genealogy of yearly meetings.]

Kashatus, William C. *Conflict of Conviction: A Reappraisal of Quaker Involvement in the American Revolution*. Lanham, Md.: University Press of America, 1990.

Leach, Robert J., and Peter Gow. *Quaker Nantucket: The Religious Community Behind the Whaling Empire*. Nantucket: Mill Hill Press, 1997. Reprint, 1999.

Le Shana, David C. *Quakers in California: The Effects of 19th Century Revivalism on Western Quakerism*. Newberg, Ore.: Barclay Press, 1969.

Marietta, Jack D. *The Reformation of American Quakerism, 1748–1783*. Philadelphia: University of Pennsylvania Press, 1984.

Mekeel, Arthur J. *The Relation of the Quakers to the American Revolution*. Washington, D.C.: University Press of America, 1979. Rev. ed., *The Quakers and the American Revolution*. York, England: Sessions Book Trust, 1996.

Moore, J. Floyd. *Friends in the Carolinas* (High Point Annual Lecture, 1963). High Point, N.C.: High Point Monthly Meeting of Friends, 1963. Rev. ed., Kathleen Coe, et al., Greensboro, N.C.: Tercenternary Celebration Steering Committee, North Carolina Friends Historical Society and North Carolina Yearly Meeting of Friends, 1997.

Moore, John M., ed. *Friends in the Delaware Valley: Philadelphia Yearly Meeting, 1681– 1981*. Haverford, Pa.: Friends Historical Society, 1981.

Nelson, Jacquelyn S. *Indiana Quakers Confront the Civil War*. Indianapolis, Ind.: Indiana Historical Society, 1991.

Pestana, Carla Gardina. *Quaker and Baptists in Colonial Massachusetts*. Cambridge: Cambridge University Press, 1991.

Realignment: Nine Views among Friends, Pendle Hill Monday Evening Lecture Series, Autumn, 1991. Wallingford, Pa.: Pendle Hill, 1992.

Roberts, Arthur O. *Tomorrow Is Growing Old: Stories of the Quakers in Alaska*. Newberg, Ore.: Barclay Press, 1978.

Schrauwers, Albert, ed. *Faith, Friends and Fragmentation : Essays on Nineteenth Century Quakerism in Canada*, Canadian Friends Historical Assocation, no. 1. Toronto: Canadian Friends Historical Association, 1995.

Specht, Neva Jean. "Mixed Blessing: Trans-Appalachian Settlement and the Society of Friends, 1780–1813." Ph.D. dissertation, University of Delaware, 1998.

Spencer, Carole. "The American Holiness Movement: Why Did It Captivate Nineteenth-Century Quakers?" *Quaker Religious Thought* 28(4), no. 90: 19–30 (January 1998).

Tolles, Frederick B. *Quakers and the Atlantic Culture*. New York: Macmillan, 1960.

Wilson, Robert H. *Philadelphia Quakers, 1681–1981: A Tercentenary Family Album*. Philadelphia: Philadelphia Yearly Meeting of the Religious Society of Friends, 1981.

Worrall, Arthur. *Quakers in the Colonial Northeast*. Hanover, N.H.: University Press of New England, 1980.

Worrall, Jay. *The Friendly Virginians: America's First Quakers*. Athens, Ga.: Iberian, 1994.

BY BRANCH

Conservative Friends

Brady, John. *A Short History of Conservative Friends*. Richmond, Ind., 1992.

Lowndes, Walter. *The Quakers of Fritchley*. Fritchley, England: Friends Meeting House, 1980. Rev. reprint, Fritchley: Preparative Meeting of the Religious Society of Friends, 1986.

Taber, William. *The Eye of Faith: A History of Ohio Yearly Meeting, Conservative*. Barnesville, Ohio: Representative Meeting of Ohio Yearly Meeting, Religious Society of Friends, 1985.

Evangelical Friends

Cazden, Elizabeth. "Rhode Island Monthly Meeting: An Evangelical Secession from New England Yearly Meeting." *Quaker History* 87(2): 1–16 (Fall 1998).

DeVol, Charles E., ed. *Focus on Friends*. Canton, Ohio: Missionary Board of Evangelical Friends Church Eastern Region, 1982.

Fendall, Lon. "Evangelical Quakers and Public Policy." In *Truth's Bright Embrace: Essays and Poems in Honor of Arthur O. Roberts*, ed. Paul N. Anderson and Howard R. Macy, 323–333. Newberg, Ore.: George Fox University Press, 1996.

Roberts, Arthur O. *The Association of Evangelical Friends: A Story of Quaker Renewal in the Twentieth Century*. Newberg, Ore.: The Barclay Press, 1975.

Hicksite and Progressive Friends

Bronner, Edwin B. *"The Other Branch": London Yearly Meeting and the Hicksites, 1827–1912*. London: Friends Historical Society, 1975.

Fager, Charles E. "FGC's 'Uniform Discipline' Rediscovered." *Quaker History* 89(2): 51–59 (Fall 2000).

Hamm, Thomas D. *God's Government Begun: The Society for Universal Inquiry and Reform, 1842–1846*. Bloomington: Indiana University, 1995.

Hamm, Thomas D. "The Hicksite Quaker World, 1876–1900." *Quaker History* 89(2): 17–41 (Fall 2000).

Ingle, H. Larry. *Quakers in Conflict: The Hicksite Reformation*. Knoxville: University of Tennessee Press, 1986. Reprint, Wallingford, Pa.: Pendle Hill Publications, 1998.

Thomas, Allen C. "Congregational or Progressive Friends: A Forgotten Episode in Quaker History." *Bulletin of the Friends Historical Society* 10 (1): 21–32 (November 1920).

Liberal and Independent Friends

Abbott, Margery Post. "Transformation of the Light: Jungian Thought and 20th-Century Friends." *Quaker History* 89(1): 47–59 (Spring 2000).

Cazden, Elizabeth. "'Wicked Hard to Herd Up': Independent Meetings and the Friends Fellowship Council." *Quaker History* 90(2): 1–14 (Fall 2001).

Deep Roots, New Growth: One Hundred Years of Friends General Conference, 1900–2000. Philadelphia: Friends General Conference, 2000.

Fager, Chuck. "Beyond the Age of Amnesia: Charting the Course of 20th Century Liberal Quaker Theology." *Quaker Theology* 2(2): 131–158 (Autumn 2000).

——. *Without Apology: The Heroes, the Heritage and the Hope of Liberal Quakerism*. Media, Pa.: Kimo Press, 1996.

Frost, J. William. "A Century of Liberalism." *Friends Journal* 46(10): 8–14 (October 2000).

Harris, Howell John. "War in the Social Order: The Great War and the Liberalization of American Quakerism." In *Religious and Secular Reform in*

America: Ideas, Beliefs and Social Change, ed. David K Adams and Cornelis A. van Minnen, 179–203. New York: New York University Press, 1999.

Manousos, Anthony, ed. *A Western Quaker Reader: Writings by and about Independent Quakers in the Western United States, 1929–1999.* Whittier, Calif.: Friends Bulletin, 2000.

Orthodox and Gurneyite Friends

Gurney, Joseph John. *Observations on the Religious Peculiarities of the Society of Friends*. London: J. and A. Arch, 1824. 7th ed. *Observations on the Distinguishing Views and Practices of the Society of Friends*, 1834. Reprinted as *A Peculiar People*, ed. Don Green. Richmond, Ind: Friends United Press, 1979.

Hamm, Thomas D. *The Transformation of American Quakerism: Orthodox Friends, 1800– 1907*, Religion in North America Series. Bloomington: Indiana University Press, 1988. Reprint, 1992.

Minear, Mark. *Richmond, 1887: A Quaker Drama Unfolds*. Richmond, Ind.: Friends United Press, 1987.

Punshon, John. *Reasons for Hope: The Faith and Future of the Friends Church*. Richmond, Ind.: Friends United Press, 2001.

THEOLOGY AND CHURCH GOVERNMENT

Faith and Theology

Abbott, Margery Post, ed. *A Certain Kind of Perfection: An Anthology of Evangelical and Liberal Quaker Writers*. Wallingford, Pa.: Pendle Hill Publications, 1997.

——. *An Experiment in Faith: Quaker Women Transcending Differences*. Pendle Hill Pamphlet, 232. Wallingford, Pa.: Pendle Hill Publications, 1995.

Allen, Richard. *Yours in Friendship: An Open Letter to Enquirers*, ed. Alison Leonard. London: Quaker Home Service, 1995.

Barclay, Robert. *Apology for the True Christian Divinity: As the Same is Held Forth and Preached by the People, Called, in Scorn, Quakers. . . .* London, 1678. Reprinted, Glenside, Pa.: Quaker Heritage Press, 2002.

——. *Barclay's Apology in Modern English*, ed. Dean Freiday. Newberg, Ore.: Barclay Press, 1991.

Bauman, Richard. *Let Your Words Be Few: Symbolism of Speaking and Silence among Seventeenth-Century Quakers*, Cambridge Studies in Oral and Literate Culture, 8. Cambridge: Cambridge University Press, 1983.

Benson, Lewis. *Catholic Quakerism*. Gloucester, England: the author, 1966. Reprint, Philadelphia: Book Services Committee, Philadelphia Yearly Meeting, Religious Society of Friends, 1968, 1983.

Birchard, Bruce. *The Burning One-ness Binding Everything: A Spiritual Journey.* Pendle Hill Pamphlet, 332. Wallingford, Pa.: Pendle Hill Publications, 1997.

Brinton, Howard H. *The Religious Philosophy of Quakerism: The Beliefs of Fox, Barclay, and Penn as Based on the Gospel of John.* Wallingford, Pa.: Pendle Hill Publications, sponsored by the Monthly Meeting of Friends of Philadelphia, 1973.

———. *Quaker Journals: Varieties of Religious Experience among Friends*. Wallingford, Pa.: Pendle Hill Publications, 1972.

Cadbury, Henry J. *Behind the Gospels*. Pendle Hill Pamphlet, 160. Wallingford, Pa.: Pendle Hill Publications, 1968.

———. *The Eclipse of the Historical Jesus*. Pendle Hill Pamphlet, 133. Wallingford, Pa: Pendle Hill Publications, 1964.

Caldwell, Samuel. *That Blessed Principle: Reflections on the Uniqueness of Quaker Universalism. . . .* Ladenberg, Pa.: Quaker Universalist Fellowship, 1988. Reprinted as *Inward Light: How Quakerism Unites Universalism and Christianity*, Philadelphia: Religious Education Committee, Philadelphia Yearly Meeting, Religious Society of Friends, 1997.

Cattell, Everett L. *The Spirit of Holiness*. Grand Rapids, Mich.: William B. Eerdmans, 1963. Reprint, Kansas City, Mo.: Beacon Hill, 1977.

Damiano, Kathryn A. "On Earth as It Is in Heaven: Eighteenth Century Quakerism as Realized Eschatology." Ph.D. dissertation, Union of Experimenting Colleges and Universities, Cincinnati, Ohio, 1988.

Dandelion, Ben Pink, Douglas Gwyn, and Timothy Peat. *Heaven on Earth: Quakers and the Second Coming*. Kelso, Scotland: Curlew Books; Birmingham, England: Woodbrooke College, 1998.

God the Trickster: Eleven Essays by Friends. ed. Ben Pink Dandelion. London: Quaker Books, 2001.

Gwyn, Douglas. *The Covenant Crucified: Quakers and the Rise of Capitalism*. Wallingford, Pa.: Pendle Hill Publications, 1995.

———. *Seekers Found: Atonement in Early Quaker Experience.* Wallingford, Pa.: Pendle Hill Publications, 2000.

———. *Unmasking the Idols: A Journey among Friends*. Richmond, Ind.: Friends United Press, 1989.

Fager, Chuck, ed. *Reclaiming a Resource: Papers from the Friends Bible Conference, Arch Street Meetinghouse, Philadelphia, Pennsylvania, Eleventh Month 10–12, 1989*. Falls Church, Va.: Kimo Press, 1990.

Hoffman, Jan. *Called to Be a People*. Sunderland P. Gardner Lecture, 1998; Canadian Quaker Pamphlet Series, no. 48. Argenta, B.C.: Argenta Friends Press, 1998.

Loring, Patricia. *Listening Spirituality.* Vol. 1, *Personal Spiritual Practices among Friends*. Washington, D.C.: Openings Press, 1997.

Macy, Howard R. "Ordinary Prophets, Extraordinary Lives." In *Truth's Bright Embrace: Essays and Poems in Honor of Arthur O. Roberts*, ed. Paul N. Anderson and Howard R. Macy, 3–13. Newberg: George Fox University Press, 1996.

Penn, William. *No Cross, No Crown; or, Several Sober Reasons Against Hat-Honour, Titular- Respects, You to a Single Person, with the Apparel and Recreations of the Times.* 1669. 2nd ed., much enlarged, with subtitle: *A Discourse Shewing the Nature and Discipline of the Holy Cross of Christ. . . .* London: printed for Mark Swaner, and sold by A. Sowl, B. Clark and J. Bringhurst, 1682. Reprint, York, England: William Sessions, 1999.

PNW Quaker Women's Theology Conference, 1995. Newberg, Ore., 1995.

The Quaker Universalist Reader, No. 1: A Collection of Essays, Addresses and Lectures; Originally Published Individually in Great Britain by the Quaker Universalist Group. Ladenberg, Pa.: Quaker Universalist Fellowship, 1986. [with Study Guide]

Quaker Women's Conference on Faith and Spirituality, December 2–5, 1999, Canyon Camp, Hinton, Oklahoma. *Proceedings:* n.p., 2000.

Scott, Janet. *What Canst Thou Say?: Towards a Quaker Theology*. London: Quaker Home Service, 1980.

Seeger, Daniel. *The Place of Universalism in the Society of Friends*, The Classics of Western Spirituality: A Library of the Great Spiritual Masters. Leicester, England: Quaker Universalist Group, 1984. Reprint, 1990.

Steere, Douglas V., ed. *Quaker Spirituality: Selected Writings*. New York: Paulist Press, 1984. *Introduction.* . . Reprint, separately, Philadelphia: Philadelphia Yearly Meeting of the Religious Society of Friends, 1988. *Introduction* published separately, Philadelphia: Philadelphia Yearly Meeting of the Religious Society of Friends, 1988.

Steven, Caroline. *Quaker Strongholds*. London: K. Paul, Trench, Trübner, 1890. Reprint, Chula Vista, Calif.: Wind and Rock Press, 1995.

Taber, William. *The Prophetic Stream*. Pendle Hill Pamphlet, 256. Wallingford, Pa: Pendle Hill Publications, 1984.

Trevett, Christine. *Previous Convictions and End-of-the-Millenium Quakerism*, Swarthmore Lecture, 1997. London: Quaker Home Service, 1997.

Trueblood, D. Elton. *Basic Christianity: Addresses of D. Elton Trueblood*, ed. James R. Newby. Richmond, Ind.: Friends United Press, 1977.

Wallis, Jack H., ed. *Findings: An Inquiry into Quaker Religious Experience*. London: Quaker Home Service, 1993.

Watson, Elizabeth. *Daughters of Zion: Stories of Old Testament Women*. Richmond, Ind.: Friends United Press, 1982.

——. *Wisdom's Daughters: Stories of Women around Jesus*. Cleveland: Pilgrim Press, 1997.

West, Jessamyn, ed. *The Quaker Reader*. New York: Viking Press, 1962. Reprint, Wallingford, Pa.: Pendle Hill Publications, 1992.

Willcutts, Jack L. *Why Friends Are Friends: Some Core Quaker Convictions*. Newberg, Ore.: Barclay Press, 1984.

Wildwood, Alex. *A Faith to Call Our Own: Quaker Tradition in the Light of Contemporary Movements of the Spirit*, Swarthmore Lecture, 1999. London: Quaker Home Service, 1999.

Worship and Ministry

Bauman, Richard. "Speaking in the Light: The Role of the Quaker Minister." In *Explorations in the Ethnography of Speaking*, ed. Richard Bauman and Joel Sherzer. London and New York: Cambridge University Press, 1974, 149–160.

——. *Let Your Words Be Sew—Symbolism of Speaking and Silence Among 17th Century Quakers*. Cambridge Studies in Oral and Literate Culture, No. 6. Cambridge: Cambridge University Press, 1983.

Bownas, Samuel. *A Description of the Qualifications Necessary to a Gospel Minister: Containing Advice to Ministers and Elders among the People Called Quakers. . .* London: Luke Hinde, 1750. 1767 ed. reprint, Philadelphia: Pendle Hill Publications and Tract Association of Friends, 1989.

Gorman, George. *The Amazing Fact of Quaker Worship*, Swarthmore Lecture, 1973. London: Quaker Home Service, 1973 .

Grundy, Martha Paxson. *Tall Poppies: Supporting the Gifts of Ministry and Eldering in the Monthly Meeting*. Pendle Hill Pamphlet, 347. Wallingford, Pa.: Pendle Hill Publications, 1999.

Hinshaw, Seth B. *The Spoken Ministry Among Friends: Three Centuries of Progress and Development*. Davidson, N.C.: North Carolina Yearly Meeting and North Carolina Friends Historical Society, 1987.

Kingrey, David W., and Jack L.. Willcuts. *Team Ministry: A Model for Today's Church*. Newberg, Ore.: Barclay Press, 1980.

Maddock, Keith R. *Spiritual Guidance among Friends*. Canadian Quaker Pamphlet Series, no. 50. Argenta, B.C.: Argenta Friends Press, 1999.

Opening Doors to Quaker Worship. Philadelphia: Religious Education Committee, Friends General Conference, 1994.

Punshon, John. *Encounter With Silence: Reflections from the Quaker Tradition*. Richmond, Ind.: Friends United Press; London. Quaker Home Service, 1987.

Roberts, Trish. *More than Equals: Spiritual Friendships*. Pendle Hill Pamphlet, 345. Wallingford, Pa.: Pendle Hill Publications, 1999.

Steere, Douglas V. *On Speaking Out of the Silence: Vocal Ministry in the Unprogrammed Meeting for Worship*. Pendle Hill Pamphlet, 182. Wallingford, Pa.: Pendle Hill, 1972.

Taber, William. *Four Doors to Meeting for Worship*. Pendle Hill Pamphlet, 306. Wallingford, Pa.: Pendle Hill Publications, 1992.

Devotional Reading

Boulding, Kenneth. *The Practice of the Love of God*, William Penn Lecture, 1942. Philadelphia: Book Committee, Religious Society of Friends, Philadelphia and Vicinity, 1942. Reprint, Wallingford, Pa.: Pendle Hill Publications, 2000.

———. *There Is a Spirit: The Nayler Sonnets*. New York: Fellowship Publications, 1945. Reprint, Pendle Hill Pamphlet, 337. Wallingford, Pa.: Pendle Hill Publications, 1998.

Burnell, S. Jocelyn. *Broken for Life*. Swarthmore Lecture, 1989. London: Quaker Home Service, 1989.

Cronk, Sandra. *Dark Night Journey: Inward Repatterning Toward a Life Centered in God*. Wallingford, Pa.: Pendle Hill Publications, 1991.

Foster, Richard J. *The Celebration of Discipline: The Path to Spiritual Growth*. San Francisco: Harper and Row, 1978. Reprinted 1988. [with Study Guide, 1983]

Kelly, Thomas R. *The Eternal Promise*. New York: Harper and Row, 1966. Reprint, Richmond, Ind.: Friends United Press, 1977; 2nd ed. with subtitle *A Sequel to A Testament of Devotion,* 1991.

———. *Sanctuary of the Soul: Selected Writings of Thomas Kelly*, ed. Keith Beasley-Topliffe. Nashville, Tenn.: Upper Room Books, 1997.

———. *A Testament of Devotion*. New York: Harper and Brothers, 1941. Reprint: San Francisco: HarperSanFrancisco, 1992.

Macy, Howard R. *Rhythms of the Inner Life*. Old Tappan, N.J.: Fleming H. Revell, 1988.

Morrison, Mary. *Without Nightfall upon the Spirit*. Pendle Hill Pamphlet, 311. Wallingford, Pa.: Pendle Hill Publications, 1994.

Penn, William. *Some Fruits of Solitude: in Reflections and Maxims Related to the Conduct of Human Life*. London: printed for Thomas Northcott, 1693. Reprinted as *Fruits of Solitude*. Bedford, Mass.: Applewood Books, 1996.

Renfer, Linda Hill, ed. *Daily Reading from Quaker Writings, Ancient and Modern*. 2 vol. Grants Pass, Ore.: Serenity Press, 1988–1995.

Roberts, Arthur O., with Robin Roberts. *Messengers of God: the Sensuous Side of Spirituality*. Newberg, Ore.: Barclay Press, 1996.

Smith, Hannah Whitall. *The Christian's Secret of a Happy Life*. New York: Willard Tract Society, 1875. Reprint, New York: Ballantine Books, 1986.

Trueblood, D. Elton. *The Meditations of Elton Trueblood*, ed. Stephen R. Sebert and W. Gordon Ross. New York: Harper and Row, 1975.

Wilson, Louise. *Inner Tenderings*. Richmond, Ind.: Friends United Press, 1996.

Yount, David. *Be Strong and Courageous: Letters to My Children about Being a Christian*. Franklin, Wisc.: Sheed and Ward, 2000.

Church Government

Cronk, Sandra L. *Gospel Order: A Quaker Understanding of Faithful Church Community*. Pendle Hill Pamphlet, 297. Wallingford, Pa.: Pendle Hill Publications, 1991.

Hadley, Herbert M. *Quakers World Wide: A History of Friends World Committee for Consultation.* London: FWCC, in association with William Sessions, 1991.

Lacey, Paul. *Leading and Being Led*. Pendle Hill Pamphlet, 264. Wallingford., Pa.: Pendle Hill Publications, 1985.

Loring, Patricia. *Listening Spirituality,* v. 2, *Corporate Spiritual Practice among Friends.* Washington, D.C.: Openings Press, 1997.

——. *Spiritual Discernment: The Context and Goals of Clearness Committees*. Pendle Hill Pamphlet, 305. Wallingford, Pa.: Pendle Hill Publications, 1992.

Morley, Barry. *Beyond Consensus: Salvaging Sense of the Meeting*. Pendle Hill Pamphlet, 307. Wallingford, Pa.: Pendle Hill Publications, 1993.

Sheeran, M. *Beyond Majority Rule: Voteless Decisions in the Society of Friends*. Philadelphia, Pa.: Philadelphia Yearly Meeting of the Religious Society of Friends, 1983.

Wilson, Lloyd Lee. *Essays on the Quaker Vision of Gospel Order*. Burnsville, N.C.: Celo Valley Books, 1993. Reprint, Wallingford, Pa: Pendle Hill Publications, 1996.

Wood, Jan. "Spiritual Discernment: The Personal Dimension." In *Friends Consultation on Discernment, Quaker Hill Conference Center, Richmond, Indiana*, 7–16. Richmond, Ind.: Quaker Hill, 1985.

Woodrow, Peter. *Clearness: Processes for Supporting Individuals and Groups in Decision- Making*. Philadelphia: New Society Publishers, 1976.

Ecumenism and Interfaith Relations

Ambler, Rex. *Creeds and the Search for Unity: A Quaker View*. London: Quaker Home Service for the Committee on Christian Relationships, London Yearly Meeting of the Religious Society of Friends (Quakers), 1989.

Dart, Martha. *To Meet at the Source: Hindus and Quakers*. Pendle Hill Pamphlet, 289. Wallingford, Pa.: Pendle Hill Publications, 1989.

Haslam, Fred. *A Record of Experience with and on Behalf of the Religious Society of Friends in Canada and with the Canadian Ecumenical Movement, 1921–1967; With Some Thoughts for the Future*. Toronto: the author, 1968.

London Yearly Meeting. Committee on Christian Relationships. *Unity in the Spirit: Quakers and the Ecumenical Pilgrimage*. London: Quaker Home Service for the Committee, 1979.

Nuhn, Ferner. *Friends and the Ecumenical Movement*. Philadelphia: Friends General Conference, 1970.

O'Reilly, Mary Rose. *The Barn at the End of the World: The Apprenticeship of a Quaker, Buddhist Shepherd.* Minneapolis: Milkweed Editions, 2000.

Pym, Jim. *The Pure Principle: Quakers and Other Faiths*. York, England: William Sessions, 2000.

Steere, Douglas V. *Mutual Irradiation: A Quaker View of Ecumenism.* Pendle Hill Pamphlet, 175. Wallingford, Pa.: Pendle Hill Publications, 1971.

Tennyson, Margaret. *Friends and Other Faiths*. London: Quaker Home Service, 1972.

To Lima with Love: The Response of the Religious Society of Friends in Great Britain to the World Council of Churches Document, Baptism, Eucharist and Ministry. London : Quaker Home Service for London Yearly Meeting of the Religious Society of Friends (Quakers), 1987.

Missions and Outreach

Angell, Stephen. "Rufus Jones and the Laymen's Foreign Missions Inquiry: How a Quaker Helped Shaped Modern Ecumenical Christianity." *Quaker Theology* 2(2): 167–209 (Autumn 2000).

Cattell, Everett L. *Christian Mission: A Matter of Life*. Richmond, Ind.: Friends United Press, 1981.

Gilman, Harvey. *Spiritual Hospitality: A Quaker's Understanding of Outreach*. Pendle Hill Pamphlet, 314. Wallingford, Pa.: Pendle Hill Publications, 1994.

Greenwood, John Ormerod. *Quaker Encounters*. Vol. 2, *Vines on the Mountains,* and vol. 3, *Whispers of Truth*. York, England: William Sessions Ltd., 1977–1978.

Grundy, Martha Paxson. "The Bethany Mission for Colored People: Philadelphia Friends and a Sunday School Mission." *Quaker History* 90(1): 50–82 (Spring 2001).

Hinshaw, Vicki, ed. *Evangelical Friends Mission Prayer Directory*. 11th ed. Arvada, Colo.: 1998.

Jones, Christina H. *American Friends in World Missions*. Richmond, Ind.: Brethren Publishing House for the American Friends Board of Missions, 1946.

McCutchen, Retha. "Expanding Ministries Around the World." *Quaker Life* 39(10): 16–17 (December 1998).

Nixon, E. Anna. *A Century of Planting: A History of the American Friends Mission in India*. Newberg, Ore.: The Barclay Press, 1985.

Thomas, Samuel S. "Gender and Religion on the Mission Station: Roxie Reeve and the Friends African Mission." *Quaker History* 88(2): 24–46 (Fall 1999).

Religious Education and Young Friends

Jolliffe, Kyle. *Seeking the Blessed Community: A History of Canadian Young Friends, 1875– 1996*. Guelph, Ont.: Ampersand Printing, 1997.

Kline, Florence Ruth, with Martha Paxson Grundy, eds. *Companions along the Way: Spiritual Formation with the Quaker Tradition; A Resource for Adult Religious Education*. Philadelphia: Philadelphia Yearly Meeting of the Religious Society of Friends, 2000.

Mather, Eleanore Price. *Pendle Hill: A Quaker Experiment in Education and Community*. Wallingford, Pa.: Pendle Hill, 1980.

Robertson, Rosamond. *Growing Friends: Worship, Prayer and Spiritual Experience with Children*. London: Quaker Home Service, 1990.

Snyder, Mary. *Opening Doors to Quaker Religious Education*. Philadelphia: Religious Education Committee of Friends General Conference, 1999.

QUAKER COMMUNITY AND CULTURE

Arts and Architecture

Butler, David. *Quaker Meeting Houses of Britain: An Account of Some of the 1,300 Meeting Houses and 900 Burial Grounds in England, Wales and Scotland, from the Start of the Movement in 1652 to the Present Time; and Research Guide to Sources*. 2 vol. London: Friends Historical Society, 1999.

Caulfield, Anna Breiner. *Quakers in Fiction: An Annotated Bibliography*. Northampton, Mass.: Pittenbruach Press, 1993.

Eichenberg, Fritz. *Art and Faith*. Pendle Hill Pamphlet, 68. Wallingford, Pa.: Pendle Hill Publications, 1952. Rev. 1962. Reprint, 1984.

Greenwood, John Ormerod. *Signs of Life: Art and Religious Experience*. Swarthmore Lecture, 1978. London: Friends Home Service Committee, 1978.

Mürer, Esther Greenleaf, comp. *Beyond Uneasy Truce: The Saga of Quaker and the Arts in 100 Quotations*. n.p.: Fellowship of Quakers in the Arts, 2000.

Nicholson, Frederick J. *Quakers and the Arts: A Survey of Attitudes of British Friends to the Creative Arts from the Seventeenth to the Twentieth Century*. London: Friends Home Service Committee, 1968.

Pointon, Marcia. "Quakerism and Visual Culture, 1650–1800." *Art History* 20 (3): 397–431 (September, 1997).

Sox, David. *Quakers and the Arts*: *"Plain and Fancy"; An Anglo-American Perspective*. York, England: Sessions Book Trust; Richmond, Ind.: Friends United Press, 2000.

Weeks, Silas B. *New England Quaker Meetinghouses, Past and Present*. Richmond, Ind.: Friends United Press, 2001.

Williamson, Jane. *Stephen Foster Stevens: Quaker Cabinetmaker*. Boston, Mass.: Society for the Preservation of New England Antiquities, 1998.

Business and Economics

Cherry, Gordon E. "Bournville, England, 1895–1995." *Journal of Urban History* 22(4): 493– 508 (May 1996). [Cadbury chocolates]

Forster, Margaret. *Rich Desserts and Captain's Thin: A Family and Their Times, 1831–1931*. London: Chatto and Windus, 1997. [Carr biscuit family]

Hansell, Norris. *Josiah White, Quaker Entrepreneur*. Easton, Pa.: Canal History and Technology Press, 1992.

Harrison, Richard S. "Some Eighteenth-Century Cork Quaker Families: A Key to Cork City Development." *Journal of the Cork Historical and Archaeological Society* 104: 131– 136 (1999).

Holland, Stanley A. "Augustus Cover and the Grand Junction Canal Company." *Journal of the Friends Historical Society* 58(1): 37–43 (1997).

Milligan, Edward. *Quakers and Railways*. York, England: Sessions Book Trust, 1992.

Quaker Peace and Service. Committee on Sharing World Resources. *Quaker Approaches to Development* by Rex Ambler, et al. 2nd ed. London: Quaker Peace Service, 1988.

Quakers and Business Group. *Good Business: Ethics at Work; Advices and Queries on Personal Standards of Conduct at Work*. London: The Group, 2000.

Spears, Larry C, ed. *Reflections on Leadership: How Robert K. Greenleaf's Theory of Servant-Leadership Influenced Today's Top Management Thinkers*. New York: John Wiley and Sons, 1995.

Walvin, James. *The Quakers: Money and Morals*. London: John Murray, 1997.

Windsor, David Burns. *The Quaker Enterprise: Friends in Business*. London: Frederick Muller, 1980.

Yates, W. Ross. *Joseph Wharton: Quaker Industrial Pioneer*. Bethlehem, Pa.: Lehigh University Press, 1987.

Education

Hole, Helen. *Things Civil and Useful: A Personal View of Quaker Education*. Richmond, Ind.: Friends United Press, 1978.

Kashatus, William C. *A Virtuous Education: Penn's Vision for Philadelphia Schools*. Wallingford, Pa.: Pendle Hill Publications, 1997.

Lacey, Paul A. *Education and the Inward Teacher*. Pendle Hill Pamphlet, 278. Wallingford, Pa.: Pendle Hill Publications, 1988.

——. *Growing into Goodness: Essays on Quaker Education*. Wallingford, Pa.: Pendle Hill Publications in cooperation with Friends Council on Education, 1998.

O'Reilley, Mary Rose. *The Peaceable Classroom*. Portsmouth, N.H.: Boynton/Cook, 1993.

Reader, John. *Schools and Schoolmasters: Some Thoughts aon the Quaker Contribution to Education*. Swarthmore Lecture, 1979. London: Quaker Home Service, 1979.

Woody, Thomas. *Early Quaker Education in Pennsylvania.* Contributions to Education, no. 105. New York: Teachers College, Columbia University, 1920. Reprint, New York: AMS Press, 1972.

Family and Relationships

Boulding, Elise. *One Small Plot of Heaven: Reflections on Family Life by a Quaker Sociologist*. Wallingford, Pa.: Pendle Hill Publications, 1989.

Calderone, Mary S. *Human Sexuality and the Quaker Conscience*. Rufus Jones Lecture, 1973. Philadelphia: Friends General Conference, 1973.

Frost, J. William. *The Quaker Family in Colonial America: A Portrait of the Society of Friends*. New York: St. Martin's Press, 1973.

Heath, Harriet. *Answering That of God in Our Children*. Pendle Hill Pamphlet, 315. Wallingford, Pa.: Pendle Hill Publications, 1994.

——. *Using Your Values to Raise Your Child To Be an Adult You Admire*. Seattle, Wash.: Parenting Press, 2000.

Heron, Alastair, ed. *Towards a Quaker View of Sex: An Essay by a Group of Friends*. London: Friends Home Service Committee, 1964.

Hill, Leslie. *Marriage: A Spiritual Leading for Lesbian, Gay, and Straight Couples*. Pendle Hill Pamphlet, 208. Wallingford, Pa.: Pendle Hill Publications, 1993.

Levy, Barry. *Quakers and the American Family: British Settlement in the Delaware Valley*. New York: Oxford University Press, 1988.

MacKinnon, Alison. "'My Dearest Friend': Courtship and Conjugality in Some Mid and Late Nineteenth-Century Quaker Families." *Journal of the Friends Historical Society* 58(1): 44–58 (1997).

New England Yearly Meeting. Committee on Ministry and Counsel. Family Life Sub-Committee. *Living with Oneself and Other: Working Papers on Aspects of Family Life, Containing Queries and Advices for Friends Meetings and Individual*. Freeport, Maine: The Yearly Meeting, 1978. 3rd draft, 1985.

Redfern, Keith, and Sue Collins, eds. *Relative Experience: A Contemporary Anthology of Quaker Family Life*. London: Quaker Home Service, 1994.

Quaker Lesbian and Gay Fellowship. *Speaking our Truth: A Plain Quaker's Guide to Lesbian and Gay Lives*. Swindon, Wilts; England: The Fellowship, 1993.

This We Can Say: Talking Honestly About Sex. Reading, England: Nine Friends Press, 1995.

Watson, Elizabeth G. *Clearness for Marriage*. Philadelphia, Family Relations Committee, Philadelphia Yearly Meeting, 1980. Rev. ed., *Marriage in the Light: Reflections on the Commitment and Clearness Process*, 1993.

——. *Sexuality, a Part of Wholeness*. Philadelphia: Family Relations Committee, Philadelphia Yearly Meeting, [1982].

Politics

Mullen, Tom, ed. *Witness in Washington: Fifty Years of Friendly Persuasion*. Richmond, Ind.: Friends United Press, 1994. Reprint, 1995.

Nash, Gary B. *Quakers and Politics: Pennsylvania, 1681–1726*. Boston: Northeastern University Press, 1993.

Tolles, Frederick B. *Quakerism and Politics*, Ward Lecture, 1956. Greensboro, N.C.: Guilford College, 1956.

Science and Technology

Clark, Robert A., and J. Russell Elkinton. *The Quaker Heritage in Medicine*. Pacific Grove, Calif.: Boxwood Press, 1978.

Eddington, Arthur. *Science and the Unseen World*. Swarthmore Lecture, 1929. London: Quaker Home Service, 1929. Reprint, 1969.

Raistrick, Arthur. *Quakers in Science and Industry*. London: Philosophical Library, 1950. Reprint, York, England: Sessions Book Trust, 1993.

Rombeau, John L., and Donna Muldoon. *Jonathan E. Rhoads: Quaker Sense and Sensibility in the World of Surgery*. Philadelphia: Hanley and Belfus, 1997.

Schwabe, Calvin W. *Quakerism and Science*. Pendle Hill Pamphlet, 343. Wallingford, Pa.: Pendle Hill Publications, 1999.

SOCIAL TESTIMONIES AND CONCERNS

General

Boulding, Elise. *Building a Global Civic Culture*. John Dewey Lecture. New York : Teachers College, Columbia University, 1988. Reprint, Syracuse, N.Y.: Syracuse University Press, 1990.

Cave, Elizabeth, and Ross Morley, eds. *Faith in Action: Quaker Social Testimony; Writings from Friends in Britain Yearly Meeting, Including Jonathan Dale*. London: Quaker Home Service, 2000.

Dale, Jonathan. *Beyond the Spirit of the Age: Quaker Social Responsibility at the End of the Twentieth Century*. Swarthmore Lecture, 1996. London: Quaker Home Service, 1996.

Kenworthy, Leonard S., ed. *Friends Face the World: Some Continuing and Current Quaker Concerns.* Philadelphia: Friends General Conference; Richmond, Ind.: Friends United Press; Kennett Square, Pa.: Quaker Press, 1987.

Powelson, Jack, with Gusten Lutter and Jane Kashnig. *Seeking Truth Together: Enabling the Poor and Saving the Planet in the Manner of Friends*. Boulder, Colo.: Horizon Society Publications, 2000.

Punshon, John. *Testimony and Tradition: Some Aspects of Quaker Spirituality*. Swarthmore Lecture, 1990. London: Quaker Home Service, 1990.

Sein, Heberto, M. *Search for Revolution: Social Structural Change*. Paullina, Iowa: Paullina Monthly Meeting of Friends, 1972.

Environment

Adams, Anne, ed. *The Creation Was Open to Me: An Anthology of Friends' Writings on That of God in All Creation*. Wilmslow, England: Quaker Green Concern, 1996.

Brown, Judith Reynolds. *God's Spirit in Nature.* Pendle Hill Pamphlet, 336. Wallingford, Pa.: Pendle Hill Publications, 1998.

Finch, Suzanne, ed. *A Quaker Testimony to the Earth?: Is There a New Quaker Testimony Evolving, to Creation and All Life?; A Book of Quaker Witness, Questions, and Materials for Meetings*. Brideport, England: the editor, 2000.

Gould, Lisa Lofland. *Caring for Creation: Reflections on the Biblical Basis of Earthcare*. Burlington, Vt.: Friends Committee on Unity with Nature, 1999.

Watson, Elizabeth G. *Healing Ourselves and Our Earth*. Burlington, Vt.: Friends Committee on Unity with Nature, 1991.

White, Gilbert F. *Geography, Resources and Environment: Themes from the Work of Gilbert F. White*, ed. Robert W. Kates and Ian Burton. 2 vol. Chicago: University of Chicago Press, 1986.

Yungblut, John. *Walking Gently on the Earth*. J. Bernard Walton Memorial Lecture, 27. Brooksville, Fla.: Southeastern Yearly Meeting of the Religious Society of Friends, 1991.

Equality, Race Relations, and the Rights of First Nations

Barbour, Hugh, ed. *Slavery and Theology: Writings of Seven Quaker Reformers, 1800–1870; Elias Hicks, Joseph John Gurney, Elizabeth Gurney Fry, Lucretia Coffin Mott, Levi Coffin, John Greenleaf Whittier, John Bright*. Dublin, Ind.: Prinit Press, 1985.

Barton, Lois. *A Quaker Promise Kept: Philadelphia Friends' Work with the Allegany Senecas, 1795–1960*. Eugene, Ore.: Spencer Butte Press, 1990.

Beard, Elkanah. *To Spend Some Time among the Colored People: The Civil War Writings of an Indiana Quaker*, ed. Daniel J. Salemson. Southern Friend 20(1): 5–75 (spring 1998).

Cadbury, Henry Joel. "Negro Membership in the Society of Friends: An Historical Study Resulting from a Course on the Social Testimonies of the Society of Friends. . . . " *Journal of Negro History* 21(2): 151–213 (1936). Reprint, Philadelphia : Friends Book Store, 1936.

Day, Lynda Rose. "Friends in the Spirit: African Americans and the Challenge to Quaker Liberalism, 1776–1915." *Long Island Historical Journal* 10(1): 1–16 (Fall 1997).

Drake, Thomas E. *Quakers and Slavery in America*. Yale Historical Publications: Miscellany, 51. New Haven, Conn.: Yale University Press, 1950. Reprint, Gloucester, Mass.: P. Smith, 1965.

Frost, J. William, ed. *Quaker Origins of Antislavery*. Norwood, Pa.: Norwood Editions, 1980.

Hamm, Thomas D., et al. "Moral Choices: Two Indiana Quaker Communities and the Abolitionist Movement." *Indiana Magazine of History* 87(2): [117]–154 (June 1991).

Harrison, Eliza Cope, ed. *For Emancipation and Education: Some Black and Quaker Efforts, 1680–1900*. Philadelphia: Aubury Arboretum Association, 1997.

Hilty, Hiram. *Toward Freedom for All: North Carolina Quakers and Slavery*. Richmond, Ind.: Friends United Press, 1984. Rev. ed., *By Land and by Sea: Quakers Confront Slavery and its Aftermath in North Carolina*. Greensboro, N.C.: North Carolina Friends Historical Society, 1993.

Ives, Kenneth, et al. *Black Quakers: Brief Biographies*. 2nd. ed. Chicago: ProgresivPublishr, 1991.

Jennings, Judith. *The Business of Abolishing the British Slave Trade,* 1783–1807. London: Frank Cass, 1997.

Jordan, Ryan. "The Indiana Separation of 1842 and the limits of Quaker Anti-Slavery." *Quaker History* 89(1): 1–27 (Spring 2000).

Kelsey, Rayner Wickersham. *Friends and the Indians, 1655–1917*. Philadelphia: Associated Executive Committee of Friends on Indian Affairs, 1917.

Kennedy, Thomas C. "Southland College: The Society of Friends and Black Education in Arkansas." *Southern Friend* 7(1): 39–69 (Spring, 1985).

Knockwood, Noel. *"Where Words Come From": On Natives and Quakers*. Canadian Quaker Pamphlet , no. 28. Argenta, B.C.: Argenta Friends Press, 1988.

Lapsansky, Emma J. "New Eyes for the 'Invisibles' in Quaker-Minority Relations." *Quaker History* 90(1): [1]–7 (Spring 2001).

Lay, Benjamin. *All Slave-Keepers That Keep the Innocent in Bondage*. Philadelphia: [Benjamin Franklin], 1737. Reprint, New York: Arno Press and The New York Times, 1969.

Milner, Clyde A., II. "Albert K. Smiley: Friend to Friends of the Indians." In *Churchmen and the Western Indians, 1820–1920*, ed. by Clyde A. Milner, II and Floyd A. O'Neil. Norman.: University of Oklahoma Press, 1985, 143–175.

——. *With Good Intentions: Quaker Work among the Pawnees, Otos, and Omahas in the 1870s*. Lincoln.: University of Nebraska Press, 1982.

Richter, Daniel K. "'Believing That Many of the 'Red People Suffer Much for the Want of Food': Hunting, Agriculture and a Quaker Construction of Indianness in the Early Republic." *Journal of the Early Republic* 19(4); 601–628 (Winter 1999).

Selleck, Linda B. *Gentle Invaders: Quaker Women Educators and Racial Issues during the Civil War and Reconstruction*. Richmond, Ind.: Friends United Press, 1995.

Soderlund, Jean R. *Quakers and Slavery: A Divided Spirit*. Princeton: Princeton University Press, 1985.

Sterling, Dorothy. *Ahead of Her Time: Abby Kelley and the Politics of Anti-Slavery*. New York: W.W. Norton, 1991.

Swatzler, David. *A Friend among the Senecas: The Quaker Mission to Cornplanter's People*. Mechanicsburg, Pa.: Stackpole Books, 2000.

Weeks, Stephen B. *Southern Quakers and Slavery: An Institutional History*. Baltimore, Md.: Johns Hopkins Press, 1896. Reprint, New York: Bergman, 1968.

Mental Health

Brown, Judith Reynolds. *A Glove on My Heart: Encounters with the Mentally Ill*. East Olympia, Wash.: PeaceWorks, 2001.

Cherry, Charles L. *A Quiet Haven: Quakers, Moral Treatment, and Asylum Reform*. Rutherford, N.J.: Fairleigh Dickinson University Press, 1989.

Elam, Jennifer. *Dancing with God through the Storm: Mysticism and Mental Illness*. Pendle Hill Pamphlet, 344. Wallingford, Pa.: Pendle Hill Publications, 1999.

Glover, Mary R. *The Retreat, York: An Early Quaker Experiment in the Treatment of Mental Illness*, ed. by Janet R. Glover. York, England: William Sessions, 1984.

Stewart, Kathleen Anne. *The York Retreat in the Light of the Quaker Way: Moral Treatment Theory; Human Therapy of Mind Control?* York, England: William Sessions, 1992.

Peace

Alexander, Horace G. *The Growth of the Peace Testimony of the Society of Friends*. London : Friends Peace Committee; Leeds: Northern Friends Peace Board, 1939. 3rd ed., with additions by Erick Tucker. London: Quaker Peace Service, 1982.

Apsey, Lawrence A. *Following the Light for Peace*. Katonah, N.Y.: Kim Pathays, 1991.

——. *The Transforming Power for Peace*. Philadelphia: Friends General Conference, Committee on Religious Education, 1960. Reprint, ed. Karen Eppler. Plainfield, Vt.: Alternatives to Violence Project; Philadelphia: Friends General Conference, 2001.

Beer, Jennifer E. *Peacemaking in Your Neighborhood: Reflections on an Experiment in Community Mediation*. Philadelphia: New Society Publishers, 1986.

——, et al. *Peacemaking in Your Neighborhood: The Mediator's Handbook.* Philadelphia: Friends Conflict Resolution Program, 1993; 3rd ed., under title, *The Mediator's Handbook*, with Eileen Stief. Gabriola Island, B.C.: New Society Publishers, 1997.

Boulding, Elise. *Cultures of Peace: The Hidden Side of History*. Syracuse Studies on Peace and Conflict Resolution. Syracuse, N.Y.: Syracuse University Press, 2000.

Brock, Peter. *Pioneers of the Peaceable Kingdom*. Princeton: Princeton University Press, 1968.

——. *The Quaker Peace Testimony: 1660 to 1914*. York, England: Sessions Book Trust, 1990.

Cadbury, Henry J. "Quakers and Peace." In *Nobel Lectures: Peace*, ed. Frederick W. Haberman. Vol. 2 (1926–1950): 391–398. Amsterdam: Elsevier for the Nobel Foundation, 1972.

Cary, Stephen. *Partners for Peace: Quaker International Service and Peacemaking*. Philadelphia: American Friends Service Committee, 1993.

Clark, Bronson. *Not By Might: A Vietnam Memoir*. Glastonbury, Conn.: Chapel Rock Publishers, 1997.

Cronk, Sandra. *Peace Be with You: A Study of the Spiritual Basis of the Friends Peace Testimony*. Philadelphia: Tract Association of Friends, 1984.

Curle, Adam. *The Basis of Quaker Work for Peace and Service*. London: Quaker Peace and Service, 1980.

Douglas, Glynn. *Friends and 1798: Quaker Witness to Non-violence in 18th Century Ireland.* Dublin: Historical Committee of the Religious Society of Friends in Ireland, 1998.

Fager, Chuck, ed. *A Continuing Journey: Papers from the Quaker Peace Roundtable, Eleventh Month, 10–12, 1995.* Wallingford, Pa.: The Issues Program, Pendle Hill, 1996.

——, ed. *Friends and the Vietnam War: Papers and Presentations from a Pendle Hill Conference, Bryn Mawr College, Pennsylvania, July 16–20, 1998*. Wallingford, Pa.: Pendle Hill, 1998.

——, ed. *Sustaining Peace Witness in the Twenty-First Century: Papers from the 1997 Quaker Peace Round Table*. Wallingford, Pa.: The Issues Program, Pendle Hill, 1997.

Friends in Civilian Public Service: Quaker Conscientious Objectors in World War II Look Back and Look Ahead; a Conference November 4–7, 1996. Wallingford, Pa.: Pendle Hill, 1998.

Frost, J. William. "Our Deeds Carry Our Message: The Early History of the American Friends Service Committee." *Quaker History* 81(1) (Spring 1992).

Hamm, Thomas D. "Hicksite Quakers and the Antebellum Nonresistance Movement." *Church History* 63 (December, 1994): 557–569.

——, et al. "The Decline of Quaker Pacifism in the Twentieth Century: Indiana Yearly Meeting of Friends as a Case Study." *Indiana Magazine of History* 96(1): 44–71 (2000).

Ingle, H. Larry. "The American Friends Service Committee, 1947–1949: The Cold War's Effect." *Peace and Change* 23(1): 27–48 (Jan. 1998).

Jones, T. Canby. *George Fox's Attitude toward War: A Documentary Study*. Annapolis, Md.: Academic Fellowship, 1972. Reprint, Richmond, Ind: Friends United Press, 1984.

Kuennig, Licia, ed. *Historical Writings of Quakers against War.* Glenside, Pa.: Quaker Heritage Press, 2002.

Lampen, John, ed. *No Alternatives?: Nonviolent Responses to Repressive Regimes*. York, England: William Sessions, 2000.

Mendl, Wolf. *Prophets and Reconcilers: Reflections on the Quaker Peace Testimony*. Swarthmore Lecture, 1974. London: Friends Home Service Committee, 1974.

Ohio Yearly Meeting of Friends (Conservative). *Statements Opposing War*, comp. by the Peace Committee. Columbiana, Ohio: The Committee, 1981. Reprint, with additions, 1988.

Orr, Edgar W. *The Quakers in Peace and War, 1920–1967*. Eastbourne, Sussex: W.J. Offord and Son, 1974.

Penn, William. *Essai d'un Projet pour render la Paix de l'Europe solide et durable. . . .* 1693. Facsimile reprint, York, England: William Sessions, 1986.

Rubinstein, David. *York Friends and the Great War*. York, England: Borthwick Institute, 1999.

Standing, Arthur C. *One Man's Story: A Conscientious Objector in World War I*, ed. Reva Griffith. Kansas City, Mo.: John and Riva Griffith, 1997.

Stieren, Carl, ed. *Crossing Borders: Canadian Friends and International Affairs, 1931–1997.* Argenta, B.C.: Argenta Friends Press, 1998.

Van der Merwe, Hendrik W. *Reconciling Opposites: Reflections on Peacemaking in South Africa*. Backhouse Lecture, 2001. Armadale North, Victoria: Australia Yearly Meeting of the Religious Society of Friends (Quakers), 2001.

Weddle, Meredith Baldwin. *Walking in the Way of Peace: Quaker Pacifism in the Seventeenth Century*. Oxford: Oxford University Press, 2001.

Williams, Sue, and Steve Williams. *Being in the Middle by Being on the Edge: Quaker Experience of Non-official Political Mediation*. London: Quaker Peace and Service, in association with Sessions Book Trust, 1994.

Yarrow, C. H. Mike. *Quaker Experiences in International Conciliation*. New Haven, Conn. : Yale University Press, 1978.

Zuber, Richard L. "Conscientious Objectors in the Confederacy: The Quakers in North Carolina." *Southern Friend* 9(1): 42–60 (1987).

Penal Reform

Adamson, Christopher. "Evangelical Quakerism and the Early American Penitentiary Revisited: The Contributions of Thomas Eddy, Roberts Vaux, John Griscom, Stephen Grellet, Elisha Bates, and Isaac Hopper." *Quaker History* 90(2): 35–58 (Fall 2001).

Bacon, Margaret Hope. *Abby Hopper Gibbons: Prison Reformer and Social Activist*. Albany: State University of New York Press, 2000.

Maddock, Keith R. *Beyond the Bars: A Quaker Primer for Prison Visitors*. Pendle Hill Pamphlet, 342. Wallingford, Pa.: Pendle Hill Publications, 1999.

Newell, Tim. *Forgiving Justice: A Quaker Vision for Criminal Justice.* Swarthmore Lecture, 2000. London: Quaker Home Service, 2000.

Philanthropy

Dorsey, Bruce. "Friends Becoming Enemies: Philadelphia Benevolence and the Neglected Era of American Quaker History." *Journal of the Early Republic* 18: 395–428 (Fall 1998).

Haviland, Margaret Morris. "In the World but Not of the World: The Humanitarian Activities of Philadelphia Quakers, 1790–1820." Ph.D. dissertation, University of Pennsylvania, 1992.

James, Sydney V. *A People among Peoples: Quaker Benevolence in Eighteenth-Century America*. Cambridge, Mass.: Harvard University Press, 1963.

Life of Elisha Tyson, the Philanthropist, by a citizen of Baltimore. Baltimore: B. Lundy, 1825. Reprint, Baltimore: Baltimore Monthly Meeting of Friends, Stony Run, 1994.

Waddilove, Lewis E. *One Man's Vision: The Story of the Joseph Rowntree Village Trust*. London: George Allen and Unwin, 1954. Reprint, York, England: William Sessions, 1982.

Relief and Reconstruction

Borries, Achim von. *Quiet Helpers: Quaker Service in Postwar Germany*, ed. Peter Daniels. London: Quaker Home Service; Philadelphia: American Friends Service Committee, 2000.

Borton, Lady. *After Sorrow: An American among the Vietnamese*. New York: Viking, 1995.

Bush, Roger. *FAU: The Third Generation: Friends Ambulance Unit Post-War Service and International Service, 1946–1959*. York, England: William Sessions, 1998.

Forbes, John. *The Quaker Star under Seven Flags, 1917–1927*. Philadelphia: University of Pennsylvania Press, 1962.

Frost, J. William. "Our Deeds Carry Our Message: The Early History of the American Friends Service Committee." *Quaker History* 81(1) (Spring 1992).

Greenwood, John Ormerod. *Quaker Encounters*. Vol. 1, *Friends and Relief: A Study of Two Centuries of Quaker Activity in the Relief of Suffering Caused by War or Natural Calamity*. York, England: William Sessions, 1975.

Hatton, Helen. *The Greatest Amount of Good: Quaker Relief in Ireland, 1654–1921*. Kingston-Montreal: McGill-Queens University Press, 1993.

Hostetter, Doug. *The Bosnian Student Project: A Response to Genocide*. Pendle Hill Pamphlet, 334. Wallingford, Pa.: Pendle Hill Publications, 1997.

McClelland, Grigor. *Embers of War: Letters from a Quaker Relief Worker in War-Torn Germany*. London: British Academic Press; New York: St. Martin's Press, 1997.

Mendlesohn, Farah. *Quaker Relief Work in the Spanish Civil War*, Quaker Studies, vol. 1. Lewiston, N.Y.: Edwin Mellen Press, 2002.

Nyonzima, David, and Lon Fendall. *Unlocking Horns: Forgiveness and Reconciliation in Burundi*. Newberg, Ore.: Barclay Press, 2001.

Sessions, William K. *They Chose the Star: Quaker Relief Work in France, 1870–1875*. York, England: Sessions Book Trust, 1991.

Smith, Lyn. *Pacifists in Action: The Experience of the Friends Ambulance Unit in the Second World War.* York, England: Sessions Book Trust, 1998.

Stephenson, Madeleine Yaude, and Edwin "Red" Stephnson [*sic*]. *Journey of the Wild Geese: A Quaker Romance in War-Torn Europe*. Pasadena, Calif.: International Productions, 1999.

Weissman, Benjamin M. *Herbert Hoover and Famine Relief to Soviet Russia, 1921–1923*. Stanford: Hoover Institution Press, Stanford University, 1974.

Simplicity and Quaker Distinctives

Foster, Richard J. *Freedom of Simplicity*. San Francisco: Harper and Row, 1981.

Kraak, Deborah E. "Variations on Plainness: Quaker Dress in Eighteenth Century Philadelphia." *Costume* 34 (2000): 51–63.

Levering, Frank, and Wanda Urbanska. *Simple Living; One Couple's Search for a Better Life*. New York: Viking, 1992.

Major, Val. "Times and Seasons: The Quaker View." *Friends Quarterly* 32[i.e., 31](1): 20–25 (January 1998).

Pym, Jim. *Listening to the Light: How to Bring Quaker Simplicity and Integrity into Our Lives*. London: Rider, 1999.

Ryberg, Sven. *Return to Simple Living*. Edinburgh: Friends World Committee on Consultation, European and Near East Section, 1973.

Taber, Fran. "Finding the Taproot of Simplicity: The Movement between Inner Knowledge and Outer Action." In Leonard S. Kenworthy, ed. *Friends Face the World.* Philadelphia: Friends General Conference; Richmond, Ind.: Friends United Press; Kennett Square, Pa: Quaker Press, 1987, 59–72.

Whitmire, Catherine. *Plain Living: A Quaker Path to Simplicity*. Notre Dame, Ind.: Sorin Books, 2001.

Temperance

Levering, Robert. *Friends and Alcohol: Recovering a Forgotten Testimony*. Pendle Hill Pamphlet, 31. Wallingford, Pa.: Pendle Hill Publications, 1994.

Truth/Integrity

Cooper, Wilmer A. *The Testimony of Integrity in the Society of Friends*. Pendle Hill Pamphlet, 296. Wallingford, Pa.: Pendle Hill Publications, 1991.

London Yearly Meeting. Committee for Integrity and Truth in Public Affairs. *Questions of Integrity*. London: The Yearly Meeting, 1993.

Women

Allen, Kerri, and Mackinnon, Alison. "Allowed and Expected To Be Educated and Intelligent: The Education of Quaker Girls in Nineteenth Century England." *History of Education* 27, no. 4 (1998): 391–402.

Bacon, Margaret Hope. *Mothers of Feminism; The Story of Quaker Women in America.* San Francisco: Harper & Row, 1986. Reprint, Philadelphia: Friends General Conference, 1995.

——, ed. *Wilt Thou Go on My Errand: Journals of Three Eighteenth Century Quaker Women Ministers. . . .* Wallingford, Pa.: Pendle Hill Publications, 1994.

Brown, Elisabeth Potts, and Susan Mosher Stuard, eds. *Witnesses for Change: Quaker Women over Three Centuries*. New Brunswick, N.J.: Rutgers University Press, 1989.

Chace, Elizabeth Buffum, et al. *Virtuous Lives: Four Quaker Sisters Remember Family Life, Abolitionism, and Women's Suffrage*, ed. Lucille Salitan and Eve Lewis Perera. New York: Continuum, 1994.

Densmore, Christopher. "The Quaker Origins of the First Woman's Rights Convention." *Friends Journal* 44(7): 26–28 (July 1998).

Fell, Margaret. *Womens Speaking Justified, Proved, and Allowed of by the Scriptures*. London: 1666. Reprint, Amherst, Mass.: Mosher Book and Tract Committee, New England Yearly Meeting, 1980; also in many anthologies of women's religious writings, including Trevett, below.

Garman, Mary, Judith Applegate, Margaret Benefiel, and Dortha Meredith, eds. *Hidden in Plain Sight: Quaker Women's Writings, 1650–1700*. Wallingford, Pa: Pendle Hill Publications, 1996. Reprint 2003. Published in Italian as *Nascoste in piena vista.* Florence: L. S. Olschki, 1999.

Graham, Maureen. *Women of Power and Presence: The Spiritual Formation of Four Quaker Women Ministers*. Pendle Hill Pamphlet, 294. Wallingford, Pa.: Pendle Hill Publications, 1990.

Kenworthy, Leonard S., ed. *Nine Contemporary Quaker Women Speak*. Kennett Square, Pa.: Quaker Publications, 1989.

Larson, Rebecca. *Daughters of Light: Quaker Women Preaching and Prophesying in the Colonies and Abroad, 1700–1775*. New York: Alfred A. Knopf, 1999.

Leach, Robert. *Women Ministers: A Quaker Contribution*. Pendle Hill Pamphlet, no 227. Wallingford, Pa.: Pendle Hill Publications, 1990.

Mack, Phyllis. *Visionary Women: Ecstatic Prophecy in Seventeenth-Century England.* Berkeley : University of California Press, 1992.

Scheffler, Judith. "There Was Difficulty and Danger on Every Side': The Family and Business Leadership of Rebecca Lukens" *Pennsylvania History* 66, no. 3 (Summer, 1999): 276– 310.

Sklar, Kathryn Kish. *Women Rights Emerges within the Antislavery Movement: A Brief History with Documents, 1830–1870.* Boston, Bedford/St. Martins Press, 2000.

Spencer, Carole D. "Evangelism, Feminism and Social Reform: The Quaker Woman Minister and the Holiness Revival." *Quaker History* 80(1): 24–46 (Spring 1991).

Stoneburner, Carol, and John Stoneburner, eds. *The Influence of Quaker Women on American History: Biographical Studies*. Studies in Women and Religion, vol. 21. Lewiston, N.Y.: Edwin Mellen Press, 1986.

Tarter, Michele Lise. Quaking in the Light: The Politics of Quaker Womens Corporeal Prophecy in the Seventeenth-Century Transatlantic World. In *A Centre of Wonders: the Body in Early America*, ed. Janet Moore Lindemann and Michele Lise Tarter. Ithaca, N.Y.: Cornell University Press, 2001. pp. 145–162.

Trevett Christine. *Quaker Women Prophets in England and Wales, 1650–1700.* Lewiston, N.Y.: Edwin Mellen Press, 2001.

——. *Women and Quakerism in the Seventeenth Century.* York, England: Sessions Book Trust, 1991.

——, ed. *Womens Speaking Justified: And Other Seventeenth-Century Quaker Writings about Women*. London: Quaker Home Service, 1989.

Wilcox, Catherine M. *Theology and Women's Ministry in Seventeenth-Century English Quakerism*, Studies in Women and Religion, v. 35. Lewiston, N.Y.: Edwin Mellen Press, 1995.

BIOGRAPHY

Collective Works

"A Biographical Dictionary of Former Quaker Leaders in America." In Hugh Barbour and J. William Frost, *The Quakers*. Westport, Conn.: Greenwood Press, Inc., 1988; paperback ed., Richmond, Ind.: Friends United Press, 1994, pp. 281–380.

Elliott, Errol. *Quaker Profiles from the American West*. Richmond, Ind.: Friends United Press, 1972.

Dictionary of Australian Quaker Biography, comp. by Marjorie and William Oats for Australia Yearly Meeting. Hobart, Tasmania: The Yearly Meeting, 1989– . v.

Harrison, Richard S. *A Biographical Dictionary of Irish Quakers*. Dublin: Four Courts Press; Portland, Ore.: ISBS, 1997.

Kenworthy, Leonard, ed. *Living in the Light: Some Quaker Pioneers of the 20th Century*. 2 vol. (Vol. 1, *In the U.S.A.*; vol. 2, *In the Wider World*) Kennett

Square, Pa.: Friends General Conference and Quaker Publications, 1984–1985.

Kohler, Charles. *A Quartet of Quakers: Isaac and Mary Penington, John Bellers, John Woolman*. London: Friends Home Service Committee, 1978.

Skidmore, Gil. *Dear Friends and Brethren: 25 Short Biographies of Quaker Men*. Reading, England: Sowle Press, 2000.

——. *Dear Friends and Sisters: 25 Short Biographies of Quaker Women*. Reading, England: Sowle Press, 1998.

Individual Biographies

ADDAMS, JANE

Addams, Jane. *Twenty Years at Hull House: With Autobiographical Notes*. New York: Macmillan, 1910; Boston: Bedford/St. Martin's, 1999; New York: Signet Classic, 1999.

——. *Jane Addams on Peace, War, and International Understanding*, ed. by Allen F. Davis. New York: Garland, 1976.

——. *The Social Thought of Jane Addams*, ed. by Christopher Lasch. Indianapolis: Bobbs Merrill, 1965. 2nd ed., New York, 1997.

Davis, Allen F. *American Heroine: The Life and Legend of Jane Addams*. London: Oxford University Press, 1973. Rev. ed., Chicago: Ivan Dee, 2000.

Linn, James W. *Jane Addams: A Biography*. New York: Appleton-Century, 1935. Reprint, Urbana: University of Illinois Press, 2000.

Polikoff, Barbara Garland. *With One Bold Act: The Story of Jane Addams*. Chicago: Boswell Books, 1999.

ALLEN, WILLIAM

Sox, David. "William Allen and the Waldensians." *The Friend* (London) 158(23): 4–6 (9 June 2000).

ANTHONY, SUSAN BROWNELL

Anthony, Susan B. *The Ghost in my Life*. New York: Chosen Books, 1971. Reprint, Waco, Tex.: Word Books, 1979.

Barry, Kathleen. *Susan B. Anthony: A Biography of a Singular Feminist*. New York : New York University Press, 1988.

Sherr, Lynn. *Failure Is Impossible: Susan B. Anthony in Her Own Words*. New York: Times Books, 1995.

ASHBRIDGE, ELIZABETH (SAMPSON SULLIVAN)

Ashbridge, Elizabeth. *Some Account of the Fore Part of the Life of Elizabeth Ashbridge . . . , Written by Herself*. Liverpool: James Smith, 1806. Published in America as *Some Account of the Early Part of the Life of Elizabeth Ashbridge* . . . Reprint in American Women's Narratives, ed. by William L. Andrews, Madison, Wisc.: University of Wisconsin Press, 1990, pp. 117–146.

Levenduski, Christine M. *A Peculiar Power: A Quaker Woman Preacher in Eighteenth-Century America*. Washington, D.C.: Smithsonian Institution Press, 1996.

AYDELOTTE, FRANK

Blanshard, Frances, ed. *Frank Aydelotte of Swarthmore*. Middleton, Conn.: Wesleyan University Press, 1970.

BACON, MARGARET HOPE

Bacon, Margaret Hope. *Love Is the Hardest Lesson: A Memoir*. Wallingford, Pa.: Pendle Hill Publications, 1999.

BALCH, EMILY GREENE

Balch, Emily Greene. *Beyond Nationalism: The Social Thought of Emily Green Balch*, ed. by Mercedes M. Randall. New York: Twayne Publishers, 1974.

Solomon, Barbara Miller. "Emily Greene Balch and the Tradition of Peace: New England Brahmin and Convinced Quaker." In Carol Stoneburner and John Stoneburner, eds., *The Influence of Quaker Women on American History: Biographical Studie,* pp. 359–378. Studies in Women and Religion, vol. 21, Lewiston, N.Y.: Edwin Mellen Press, 1986.

BARBOUR, HUGH

Birkel, Michael and John W. Newman. *The Lamb's War: Quaker Essays to Honor Hugh Barbour*. Richmond, Ind.: Earlham College Press, 1992.

BARCLAY, ROBERT

Graves, Michael P. "Robert Barclay and the Rhetoric of the Inward Light," *Quaker Religious Thought* 26: 17–32 (March 1993).

Trueblood, D. Elton. *Robert Barclay*. New York: Harper & Row, 1968.

BARNARD, HANNAH JENKINS

Bassett, T.D. Seymour. "Barnard, Hannah Jenkins," in James, E.T., James, J.W., and Boyer, P.S., eds, *Notable American Women, 1607–1950*. Cambridge, Mass.: Harvard Belknap Press of Harvard University Press, 1971, 88–90.

Maxey, David W. "New Light on Hannah Barnard, a Quaker Heretic,'" *Quaker History* 78(1): [1]–86 (1989).

BARTRAM, JOHN

Bartram, John. *The Correspondence of John Bartram, 1734–1777*, ed. Edmund Berkeley and Dorothy Smith Berkeley. Gainesville: University Presses of Florida, 1992.

Berkeley, Edmund and Dorothy Smith Berkeley. *The Life and Travels of John Bartram: From Lake Ontario to the River St. John*. Tallahassee: University Presses of Florida, 1982.

Slaughter, Thomas P. *The Natures of John and William Bartram*. New York: Alfred A. Knopf, 1996. Repr. New York: Vintage Books, 1997.

BEAN, HANNAH (ELLIOTT) SHIPLEY and JOEL

Hamm, Thomas D. "Joel Bean and the Revival in Iowa." *Quaker History* 76(1): 33–49 (Spring 1987).

BELLERS, JOHN

Clarke, George, ed. *John Bellers: His Life, Times and* Writings. London: Routledge and Kegan Paul, 1987. Reprint as *John Bellers, 1654 to 1725, Quaker Visionary: His Life, Times and Writings.* York, England: Sessions Book Trust, 1993.

BENEZET, ANTHONY

Jackson, Maurice. "The Social and Intellectual Origins of Anthony Benezet's Antislavery Radicalism." In *Explorations in Early American Culture: A Supplemental Issue of Pennsylvania History* 66 (1999): 86–112.

Kashatus, William C. "A Reappraisal of Anthony Benezet's Activities in Educational Reform, 1754–1784." *Quaker History* 78(1): 24–36 (Spring 1989).

BENSON, LEWIS

Wallace, T.H.S., ed. *None Were So Clear: Prophetic Quaker Faith and the Ministry of Lewis Benson.* Camp Hill, Pa.: New Foundation Publications, 1996.

BISHOP, GEORGE

Feola, Maryann S. *George Bishop, Seventeenth-Century Soldier Turned Quaker*. York, England: William Sessions, Ebor Press, 1996.

BOULDING, ELISE and KENNETH EWART

Boulding, Elise. *Born Remembering*. Pendle Hill Pamphlet, 200. Wallingford, Pa.: Pendle Hill Publications, 1975.

BRIGHT, JOHN

Byrd, Robert O. *John Bright: Faithful Friend and Fruitful Politics.* Canadian Quaker Pamphlet, no. 35. Argenta, B.C.: Argenta Friends Press, 1991.

BRINTON, ANNA (SHIPLEY) COX and HOWARD HAINES

Mather, Eleanore Price. *Anna Brinton: a Study in Quaker Character*, Pendle Hill Pamphlet. 176. Wallingford, Pa.: Pendle Hill Publications, 1971.

BROWN, MOSES

James Blaine. *The Browns of Providence Plantations*. Vol. 1, *Colonial Years*. Cambridge, Mass.: Harvard University Press, 1952; vol. 2, *The Nineteenth Century* (and reprint of vol. 1). Providence, R.I.: Brown University Press, 1968.

CADBURY, HENRY JOEL

Bacon, Margaret Hope. *Let This Life Speak: The Legacy of Henry Joel Cadbury*. Philadelphia: University of Pennsylvania Press, 1987.

CALDERONE, MARY

Mace, David. "Mary Steichen Calderone: Interpreter of Human Sexuality." In Leonard S. Kenworthy, ed., *Living in the Light: Some Quaker Pioneers of the 20th Century*. Vol. 1, *In the U.S.A*. Kennett Square, Pa.: Friends General Conference and Quaker Publications, 1984–1985.

CATCHPOOL, THOMAS CORDER PETTIFOR

Catchpool, Corder. *On Two Fronts: Letters of a Conscientious Objector*. London: Headley Bros. 3rd ed. London: George Allen and Unwin. Reprint, New York: Garland, 1972.

Bryan, Alex. *Corder Catchpool: A Hero Who Never Made Heroic Gestures; Corder Catchpool, 1883–1952*. London: Quaker Home Service, 1982.

CATTELL, CATHERINE ISABELLA DeVOL and EVERETT LEWIS

Cattell, Catherine De Vol. *Over the Teacup*. Newberg, Ore.: Barclay Press, 1983.

Murray, Donald R. "Everett L. Cattell: Man of Wisdom and Integrity." In Leonard S. Kenworthy, ed. *Living in the Light: Some Quaker Pioneers of the 20th Century*. Vol. 1, *In the U.S.A*. Kennett Square, Pa.: Friends General Conference and Quaker Publications, 1984–1985.

CÉRÉSOLE, PIERRE

Kenworthy, Leonard S. "Pierre Ceresole: Pick and Shovel Peacemaker." In Kenworthy, ed., *Living in the Light: Some Quaker Pioneers of the 20th Century*. Vol. 2, *In the Wider World*. Kennett Square, Pa.: Friends General Conference and Quaker Publications, 1984–1985.

CHURCHMAN, JOHN

Hall, Edna M. *A Quiet Habitation: The Life and Work of John Churchman, 1705–1775; with Extracts from His Journal*. Somerset, England: the author, 1983.

CLARKSON, THOMAS

Gifford, Zerbanoo. *Thomas Clarkson and the Campaign Against Slavery*. London: Anti-Slavery International, 1996.

Wilson, Ellen Gibson. *Thomas Clarkson: A Biography*. New York: St. Martin's Press, 1990.

COFFIN, CATHERINE WHITE and LEVI COFFIN

Coffin, Levi. *Reminiscences of Levi Coffin, the Reputed President of the Underground Railroad*. London: S. Low, Marston, Searle, and Rivington; Cincinnati: Western Tract Society, 1876. Reprint, New York: A. M. Kelley, 1968. Abridged ed. Richmond, Ind.: Friends United Press, 1991. Reprint, 2000.

Yanessa, Mary Ann. *Levi Coffin, Quaker: Breaking the Bonds of Slavery in Ohio and Indiana*. Richmond, Ind.: Friends United Press, 2001.

COOPER, WILMER ALBERT

Cooper, Wilmer A. *Growing Up Plain among Conservative Wilburite Quakers: The Journey of a Public Friend*. Richmond, Ind.: Friends United Press; Wallingford, Pa.: Pendle Hill Publications, 1999.

COPPIN, FANNY MARION JACKSON

Drinkard-Hawkeshaw, Dorothy. "Coppin, Fanny Murial Jackson (1837–1913)." In *Dictionary of American Negro Biography*, ed. Rayford W. Logan and Michael R. Winston, 130–132. New York: W. W. Norton, 1982.

Fishel, Leslie H. "Coppin, Fanny Marion Jackson." In *Notable American Women, 1607–1950: A Biographical Dictionary*, ed. Edward T. James, 1: 383–385. Cambridge, Mass.: Belknap Press of Harvard University Press, 1971.

CUFFE, PAUL (also CUFFEE)

Cuffe, Paul. *Captain Paul Cuffe's Logs and Letters, 1808–1817: A Black Quaker's "Voice from within the Veil,"* ed. Rosalind Cobb Wiggins. Washington, D.C.: Howard University Press, 1996.

Thomas, Lamont D. *Rise to be a People: A Biography of Paul Cuffe*. Urbana: University of Illinois Press, 1986. Reprint as *Paul Cuffe: Black Entrepreneur and Pan-Africanist*, 1988.

Westgate, Michael. *Captain Paul Cuffe (1759–1817): A One-Man Civil Rights Movement*. 3 vol. Boston: Museum of the National Center of Afro-American Artists and Education and Resources Group (ERG), 1989.

Wiggins, Rosalind C. "Paul and Stephen: Unlikely Friends." *Quaker History* 20(1): 8–27 (Spring 2001).

DALTON, JOHN

Smyth, A. L. *John Dalton, 1766–1844: A Bibliography of Works by and about Him*. Manchester, England: Manchester University Press, 1966. 2nd ed. with subtitle, *With an Annotated List of His Surviving Apparatus and personal Effects*. Manchester, England: Manchester Literary and Philosophical Society, 1998.

Thackray, Arnold. *John Dalton: Critical Assessments of His Life and Science*. Cambridge, Mass.: Harvard University Press, 1972.

DARBY, ABRAHAM

Raistrick, Arthur. *Dynasty of Iron Founders: The Darbys and Coalbrookdale*. York, England: Sessions Book Trust in association with Iron Bridge Gorge Museum Trust, 1989.

Trinder, Barrie. *The Darbys of Coalbrookdale*. Chichester, England: Phillimore, 1974; Chichester, England: Phillimore in association with the Ironbridge Gorge Museum Trust, 1991.

DAVIDSON, MARY JANE and ROBERT JOHN

Tyzack, Charles. *Friends to China: The Davidson Brothers and the Friends Mission to China, 1887 to 1939*. York, England: William Sessions, 1988.

DeVOL FAMILY

Cattell, Catherine D. *From Bamboo to Mango*. Newberg, Ore.: Barclay Press, 1976.

Nixon, Eva Anna. *On the Cutting Edge: the Story of a Surgeon and His Family Who Served Country Folk to Kings in Four Nations*. Newberg, Ore.: Barclay Press, 1987.

DEWSBURY, WILLIAM

Smith, Edward. *Willilam Dewsbury, ca. 1621–1688: One of the First Valiant Sixty Quakers*. London: Darton and Harvey, 1836. Reprint, York: Sessions Book Trust. 2nd facsimile ed. 1997.

DORLAND, ARTHUR GARRATT

Dorland, Arthur Garratt. *Along the Trail of Life: A Quaker Retrospect*. Belleville, Canada: Mika, 1979.

DOUGLASS, SARAH MAPPS

Bacon, Margaret Hop. "New Light on Sarah Mapps Douglass and Her Reconciliation with Friends." *Quaker History* 90(1): 28–49 (Spring 2001).

Ives, Kenneth. "Sarah Mapps Douglass, 1806–1882." In Kenneth Ives, Rosalind Cobb Wiggins, Ann Bustill Smith, Cynthia Kerman ,Carleton Mabee, and William Powers, *Black Quakers: Brief Biographies*. 2nd. ed., 49–62. Chicago: ProgresivPublishr, 1995.

DuBOIS, RACHEL MIRIAM DAVIS

Dubois, Rachel Davis, with Corann Okorodudu. *All This and Something More: Pioneering in Intercultural Education*. Bryn Mawr, Pa.: Dorrance, 1984.

Cattell, Elizabeth. "Rachel Davis DuBois: Pioneer in Intergroup Relations." In Leonard S. Kenworthy, ed., *Living in the Light, : Some Quaker Pioneers of the 20th Century*. Vol. 1, *In the U.S.A*. Kennett Square, Pa.: Friends General Conference and Quaker Publications, 1984–1985

DYER, MARY BARRET

Burgess, Robert S. *To Try the Bloody Law: The Story of Mary Dyer*. Burnsville, N.C.: Celo Valley Books, 2000.

Johns, David L. "'Hanging as a Flag: Mary Dyer and Quaker Hagiography." *Quaker Religious Thought* 30(1), no. 95: 7–23 (Aug. 2000).

EDDINGTON, ARTHUR

Burnell, S. Jocelyn. "Arthur S. Eddington: 'Our Most Distinguished Astrophysicist.'" In Leonard S. Kenworthy, ed., *Living in the Light: Some Quaker Pioneers of the 20th Century*. Vol. 2, *In the Wider World*. Kennett Square, Pa.: Friends General Conference and Quaker Publications, 1984–1985.

EDMUNDSON, WILLIAM

Edmondson, William. *A Journal of the Life, Travels Sufferings, and Labour of Love in the Work of the Ministry, of That Worthy Elder, and Faithful Servant of Jesus Christ, William Edmundson*. London: J. Sowle, 1715. Abridged as *The Journal of William Edmondson, 1627–1712*, ed. William D. Deutsch. Richmond, Ind.: Friends United Press, 1974.

EICHENBERG, FRITZ

Eichenberg, Fritz. *Artist on the Witness Stand*, Pendle Hill Pamphlet. 257. Wallingford, Pa.: Pendle Hill Publications, 1984.

——. *The Wood and the Graver: The Work of Fritz Eichenberg*. Barre, Mass.: Imprint Society; New York: C.N. Potter. 1977.

Harnden, Philip. *Letting That Go, Keeping This: The Spiritual Pilgrimage of Fritz Eichenberg*. Pendle Hill Pamphlet, 353. Wallingford, Pa.: Pendle Hill Publications, 2001.

FELL, MARGARET ASKEW (later FOX)

Fell, Margaret. *A Sincere and Constant Love: An Introduction to the Work of Margaret Fell*, ed. T. H. S. Wallace. Richmond, Ind.: Friends United Press, 1992.

Barbour, Hugh. *Margaret Fell Speaking*. Pendle Hill Pamphlet, 206. Wallingford, Pa.: Pendle Hill Publications, 1976.

Kunze, Bonnelyn Young. *Margaret Fell and the Rise of Quakerism*. Stanford, Calif.: Stanford University Press, 1994.

Ross, Isabel. *Margaret Fell, Mother of Quakerism*. London: Longmans, Green, 1949. 2nd ed., York, England: William Sessions Book Trust, Ebor Press, 1984.

FISHER, MARY (later BAYLY later CROSS)

Stewart, Mary Althea. "Public Justice and Personal Liberty: Variety and Linguistic Skill in the Letters of Mary Fisher." *Quaker Studies* 3(2): 133–159 (Winter 1998).

FOGELKLOU, EMILIA (later NORLIND)

Fogelklou, Emilia. *Reality and Radiance: Selected Autobiographical Works of Emilia Fogelklou*. Richmond, Ind.: Friends United Press, 1985.

Lutz, Harold T. "Emilia Fogelklou: Swedish Mystic and Friend." In Leonard S. Kenworthy, ed., *Living in the Light: Some Quaker Pioneers of the 20th Century*. Vol. 2, *In the Wider World*. Kennett Square, Pa.: Friends General Conference and Quaker Publications, 1984–1985.

FOX, CAROLINE

Fox, Caroline. *The Journals of Caroline Fox, 1835–1871: A Selection*, ed. Wendy Monk. London: Elek, 1972.

Tod, Robert J. N. *Caroline Fox: Quaker Blue-Stocking, 1819–1871: Friend of John Stuart Mill, Thomas and Jane Carlyle and Frederick Denison Maurice and Helper of Sailors in Distress*. York, England: William Sessions, 1980.

FOX, GEORGE

Fox, George. *Works of George Fox*. Philadelphia: Marcus T.C. Gould, 1831. 8 vol. Reprint, State College, Pa.: New Foundation Publications, George Fox Fund, 1990.

——. *Truth of the Heart: An Anthology of George Fox*, ed. Rex Ambler. London: Quaker Books, 2001.

——. *The Journal of George Fox*, ed. Norman Penney. Cambridge: The University Press; Philadelphia: J. C. Winston, 1911. 2 vol. Reprint, New York: Octagon Books, 1973.

——. *Journal of George Fox*, ed., J. L. Nickalls. Cambridge: Cambridge University Press, 1952. Reprint 1975. Rev. reprint, Philadelphia: Religious Society of Friends, 1985.

——. *Book of Miracles*, ed. Henry J. Cadbury. Cambridge: The University Press, 1948. Reprint with new forewords, Philadelphia: Friends General Conference; London: Quaker Home Service, 2000.

——. *Narrative Papers of George Fox, Unpublished or Uncollected*, ed. Henry J. Cadbury. Richmond, Ind.: Friends United Press, 1972.

——. *The Power of the Lord is Over All; The Pastoral Letters of George Fox*, ed. T. Canby Jones. Richmond, Ind.: Friends United Press, 1989.

——. *The Short Journal and Itinerary Journals of George Fox* …, ed. Norman Penney. Cambridge: Cambridge University Press; Philadelphia: Friends' Book Store, for the Friends Historical Association, 1925.

Cadbury, Henry J., ed.. *Annual Catalogue of George Fox's Papers: Compiled in 1694–1697*. Philadelphia: Friends Book Store; London: Friends Book Centre, 1939.

Gwyn, Douglas. *Apocalypse of the Word: The Life and Message of George Fox (1624–1691)*. Richmond, Ind.: Friends United Press, 1986. [with Study Guide, 1987]

Ingle, H. Larry. *First Among Friends: George Fox and the Creation of Quakerism*. New York: Oxford University Press, 1994. Reprint, 1996.

Mullet, Michael, ed. *New Light on George Fox, 1624–1691: A Collection of Essays*. York, England: William Sessions, Ebor Press, 1994.

Pickvance, Joseph. *A Reader's Companion to George Fox's Journal*. London: Quaker Home Service, 1989.

Windsor, Arthur, comp. *George Fox Epistles: An Analytical Phrase Index*. Gloucester, England: George Fox Fund, 1992.

FRY, ELIZABETH GURNEY

Drenth, Annemieke van, and Francisca de Haan. *The Rise of Caring Power: Elizabeth Fry and Josephine Butler in Britain and the Netherlands*. Amsterdam: Amsterdam University Press, 1999.

Rose, June. *Elizabeth Fry*. London: Macmillan; New York: St. Martin's Press, 1980. Reprint, London: Quaker Home Service, 1994.

GANDHI, MOHANDES KARAMCHAND "MAHATMA"

Alexander, Horace. *Ghandi through Western Eyes*. New York: Asia Publishing House, 1969. 2nd ed. Philadelphia: New Society Publishers, 1989.

Chadha, Yogesh. *Rediscovering Gandhi*. London: Century Books, 1997. Published in the U.S. under title, *Gandhi: A Life*. New York: Wiley, 1997.

Maxwell, David. "Quaker Testimonies and Gandhian Parallels." *Friends Quarterly* 31(3): 107– 111 (July 1998).

GARRETT, THOMAS

Garrett, Thomas. *Letters of Thomas Garrett*, comp. and ed. James A. McGowan. Princeton, N.J.: Ken-Ray Press, 1982.

McGowan, James A. *Station Master on the Underground Railroad: The Life and Letters of Thomas Garrett*. Moylan, Pa.: Whimsie Press, 1977.

GRELLET, STEPHEN

Comfort, William Wistar. *Stephen Grellet, 1773–1855*. New York: Macmillan, 1942.

GRIMKÉ, ANGELINA EMILY (later WELD) and SARAH MOORE

Grimké, Angelina E., and Grimké, Sarah. *The Public Years of Sarah and Angelina Grimké: Selected Writings, 1835–1839*, ed. Larry Ceplair. New York: Columbia University Press, 1989.

Lerner, Gerda. *The Grimké Sisters from South Carolina: Rebels against Slavery.* Boston: Houghton, Mifflin, 1867. Reprint with subtitle *Pioneers for Woman's Rights and Abolition*. New York, Schocken Books, 1971; New York: Oxford University Press, 1998.

——. *The Feminist Thought of Sarah Grimké*. New York: Oxford University Press, 1998.

Todras, Ellen H. *Angelina Grimké: Voice of Abolition.* North Haven, Conn.: Shoe String Press, 1999.

GURNEY, JOSEPH JOHN

Gurney, Joseph John. *A Journey in North America: Described in Familiar Letters to Amelia Opie*. Norwich, England: printed for private circulation by J. Fletcher, 1841. Reprint, New York: Da Capo Press, 1973.

Swift, David E. *Joseph John Gurney: Banker, Reformer, and Quaker*. Middletown, Conn.: Wesleyan University Press, 1962.

HAM SOK HON

Ham Sok Han. "*Kicked by God*," trans. David E. Ross. Philadelphia: Wider Quaker Fellowship, 1969. Reprint, in Korean and English, 2000.

Lee, Yoon-Gu. "Sok-Hon Ham: 'A Wandering Albatross.'" Leonard S. Kenworthy, ed., *Living in the Light: Some Quaker Pioneers of the 20th Century*. Vol. 2, *In the Wider World*. Kennett Square, Pa.: Friends General Conference and Quaker Publications, 1984–1985.

Soo Kim Sung. *Ham Sok Han: Voice of the People and Pioneer of Religious Pluralism in Twentieth Century Korea*. Seoul: Samin Books, 2001.

HANCOCK, CORNELIA

Hancock, Cornelia. *South after Gettysburg: Letters of Cornelia Hancock, 1863–1868*, ed. Henrietta Stratton Jaquette. Philadelphia: University of Pennsylvania Press, 1937. Reprint as *Letters of a Civil War Nurse: Cornelia Hancock, 1863–1865*, Lincoln: University of Nebraska Press, 1998.

HASLAM, FRED

Muma, Dorothy. "Fred Haslam: 'Mr. Canadian Friend.'" ed. *Living in the Light: Some Quaker Pioneers of the 20th Century*. 2 vol. (Vol. 1, *In the U.S.A.*; vol. 2, *In the Wider World*), 2: 70–84. Kennett Square, Pa.: Friends General Conference and Quaker Publications, 1984–1985.

HAVILAND, LAURA SMITH

Haviland, Laura Smith. *A Woman's Life-Work: Labors and Experiences*. Chicago: Walden and Stowe, 1881. Reprint, Salem, N.H.: Ayer, 1984.

HICKS, EDWARD

Ford, Alice. *Edward Hicks: His Life and Art*. New York: Abbeville Press, 1985.

———. *Edward Hicks, Painter of the Peaceable Kingdom*. Philadelphia: University of Pennsylvania Press, 1952. Reprint, 1998.

Mather, Eleanore Price, and Dorothy Canning Miller. *Edward Hicks: His Peaceable Kingdoms and Other Paintings*. Newark: University of Delaware Press; New York: Cornwall Books, 1983.

Weekley, Carolyn J., with Laura Pass Barry. *The Kingdoms of Edward Hicks*. Williamsburg, Va.: Colonial Williamsburg Foundation, in association with Harry N. Abrams, 1999.

HICKS, ELIAS

Hicks, Elias. *Journal of the Life and Religious Labors of Elias Hicks: Written by Himself*. New York: Isaac T. Hopper, 1832. Reprint of the 5th ed., New York: Arno Press and The New York Times, 1969.

Forbush, Bliss. *Elias Hicks: Quaker Liberal*. New York: Columbia University Press, 1956. Condensed by Norma Jacob as *Introducing Elias Hicks*. Philadelphia: Friends General Conference, 1984.

Kerman, Cynthia Earl. "Elias Hicks and Thomas Shillitoe: Two Paths Diverge." *Quaker Studies* 5(1): 19–47 (October 2000).

HODGKIN, HENRY T.

Greenwood, John Ormerod. *Henry Hodgkin: The Road to Pendle Hill*. Pendle Hill Pamphlet, 229. Wallingford, Pa.: Pendle Hill Publications, 1980.

HOOVER, HERBERT CLARK

Hoover, Herbert C. *The Memoirs of Herbert Hoover*. 3 vol. New York: Macmillan, 1951–1952. Reprinted, in 2 vol., 1965.

Allen, Anne Beiser. *An Independent Woman: The Life of Lou Henry Hoover*. Westport, Conn.: Greenwood Press, 2000.

Clements, Kendrick A. *Hoover, Conservation, and Consumerism: Engineering the Good Life*. Lawrence: University Press of Kansas, 2000.

Fausold, Martin L. *The Presidency of Herbert C. Hoover*. Lawrence: University Press of Kansas, 1985.

Nash, George H. *The Life of Herbert Hoover*. 3 vol. New York: W. W. Norton, 1983–1996.

Nash, Lee, ed. *Understanding Herbert Hoover: Ten Perspectives*. Stanford, Calif: Hoover Institution Press, 1987– . v.

Walch, Timothy M., and Dwight Miller. *Herbert Hoover and Franklin D. Roosevelt: A Documentary History*. Westport, Conn.: Greenwood Press, 1998.

Wilson, Joan Hoff. *Herbert Hoover: Forgotten Progressive*, ed. Oscar Handlin. Boston: Little Brown, 1975.

HOPPER, ISAAC TATEM

Hopper, Isaac T. *Kidnappers in Philadelphia: Isaac Hopper's Tales of Oppression, 1780– 1843*, comp. Daniel E. Meaders. New York: Garland, 1994.

Bacon, Margaret Hope. *Lamb's Warrior: The Life of Isaac T. Hopper*. New York: Thomas Y. Crowell Co., 1970.

HOWLAND, EMILY

Breault, Judith Colucci. *The World of Emily Howland: Odyssey of a Humanitarian*. Millbrae, Calif.: Les Femmes, 1976.

HULL, HANNAH CLOTHIER and WILLIAM ISAAC

Frost, J. William. "William I. Hull and the Quaker Search for Peace, 1908–1920." In Michael L Birkel and John Newman, eds. *The Lamb's War: Quaker Essays to Honor Hugh Barbour,* 95–210. Richmond, Ind.: Earlham College Press, 1992.

JONES, RUFUS MATTHEW

Jones, Rufus. *Rufus Jones: Essential Writings,* ed. Kerry Walters. Maryknoll, N.Y.: Orbis, 2001.

Endy, Melvin B. "The Interpretation of Quakerism: Rufus Jones and His Critics." *Quaker History* 70(1): 3–21 (Spring 1981).

Kent, Stephen A. "Psychological and Mystical Interpretations of Early Quakerism: William James and Rufus Jones." *Religion*. 17: 251–274 (1987).

A Rufus Jones Companion. Wellesley, Mass.: Wellesley Monthly Meeting of the Religious Society of Friends, 2001.

Vining, Elizabeth Gray. *Friend of Life: The Biography of Rufus M. Jones*. Philadelphia: Lippincott, 1958. Reprint, Philadelphia: Philadelphia Yearly Meeting of the Religious Society of Friends, 1981.

JONES, THOMAS ELSA

Jones, Thomas Elsa. *Light on the Horizon: The Quaker Pilgrimage of Tom Jones*. Richmond, Ind.: Friends United Press, 1973.

Lacey, Paul A. "Thomas E. Jones: The Dreamer and the Builder." In Leonard S. Kenworthy, ed., *Living in the Light, Some Quaker Pioneers of the 20th Century*. Vol. 1, *In the U.S.A*. Kennett Square, Pa.: Friends General Conference and Quaker Publications, 1984–1985.

KEITH, GEORGE

Frost, J.William, ed., *The Keithian Controversy in Early Pennsylvania*. Norwood, Pa.: Norwood, 1980.

KELLY, THOMAS RAYMOND

Jones, T. Canby. *Thomas R. Kelly as I Remember Him.* Pendle Hill Pamphlet, 284. Wallingford, Pa.: Pendle Hill Publications, 1989.

Steere, Douglas V. "Thomas Kelly: A Brother Lawrence for Our Time." In *The Lamb's War: Quaker Essays to Honor Hugh Barbour*, ed. Michael L. Birkel and John W. Newman. Richmond, Ind.: Earlham College Press, 1992, pp. 211–222.

KING, FRANCIS T.

Hickey, Damon D. "Godfather of Southern Quaker Revivalism?: Francis T. King of Baltimore and Post-Civil War North Carolina Friends." *Southern Friend* 20(2): 11–22 (Autumn 1998).

KIRKBRIDE, THOMAS S.

Tomes, Nancy. *A Generous Confidence: Thomas Story Kirkbridge and the Art of Asylum-Keeping*. Cambridge: Cambridge University Press, 1984.

KNIGHT, ANNE

Malmgreen, Gail. "Anne Knight and the Radical Subculture." *Quaker History* 71(2): 100–113 (Fall 1982).

LAY, BENJAMIN

Kashatus, William C. "Abington's Fiery Little Abolitionist." *Old York Road Historical Society Bulletin* 45: 35–39 (1985).

LITU, JOEL

Adede, R. K. *Joel Litu, Pioneer African Quaker.* Pendle Hill Pamphlet, 243. Wallingford, Pa.: Pendle Hill Publications. 1982.

LLOYD, DAVID

Lokken, Roy N. *David Lloyd, Colonial Lawmaker*. Seattle, Wash.: University of Washington Press, 1959.

LOGAN, JAMES

Tolles, Frederick B. *James Logan and the Culture of Provincial America*. Boston: Little, Brown, 1957.

LONSDALE, KATHLEEN

Lonsdale, Kathleen. *The Christian Life— Lived Experimentally: An Anthology of the Writings of Kathleen Lonsdale*, selected by James Hough. London: Friends Home Service Committee, 1976.

Kenworthy, Leonard S. "Kathleen Lonsdale: Eminent Scientist and Concerned Quaker." In Leonard S. Kenworthy, ed. *Living in the Light,* Vol. 2*, In the Wider World*. Kennett Square, Pa.: Friends General Conference and Quaker Publications, 1984–1985.

LUND, SIGRID HELLIESEN

Lund, Sigrid Helliesen. *Always on the Way: The Autobiography of Sigrid Helliesen Lund (1892–1987)*, trans. and ed. Kathryn Parke. Tempe, Ariz.: Beverly-Merriam, 2000. Originally published in Norwegian by Tiden Norsk Forlag, 1982.

Gibbins, Margaret S. *Sigrid Helliesen Lund: Portrait of a Friend*. London: Friends World Committee for Consultation, European and Near East Section, and Quaker Home service, 1980. Reprint in Kenworthy, ed. *Living in the Light,* op. cit., 2: 145–159.

LUNDY, BENJAMIN

Lundy, Benjamin. *The Life, Travels and Opinions of Benjamin Lundy: Including His Journeys to Texas and Mexico*, comp. Thomas Earle. Philadelphia:

William D. Parish, 1847. Reprints, New York: Arno Press, 1969; New York: Augustus M. Kelley, 1971.

———. "The Diary of Benjamin Lundy, Written During His Trip through Upper Canada in January, 1832," ed. Fred Landon. *Papers and Records of the Ontario Historical Society*. Vol. 19 (1922). Reprint, Baltimore, Md.: Baltimore Monthly Meeting of Friends, Stony Run, 1999.

Dillon, Merton L. *Benjamin Lundy and the Struggle for Negro Freedom*. Urbana: University of Illinois Press, 1966.

LUNG'AHO, DAUDI

Ganira, L.T. *Daudi Lung'aho, an African Missionary: A Biography.* Tiriki, Kenya: East Africa Yearly Meeting of Friends, 1970.

LUNG'AHO, THOMAS GANIRA

Smuck, Harold V. "Thomas G. Lung'aho: East Africa Quaker, Educator and Administrator." In Leonard S. Kenworthy, ed. *Living in the Light.,* Vol. 2, *In the Wider World.* Kennett Square, Pa.: Friends General Conference and Quaker Publications, 1984–1985.

MALONE, EMMA ISABEL BROWN and JOHN WALTER

Malone, J. Walter. *J. Walter Malone: The Autobiography of an Evangelical Quaker*, ed. John W. Oliver. Lanham, Md.: University Press of America, 1993.

Oliver, John. "Emma Brown Malone: Background and Implanting Quakerism in Kenya." *Canadian Quaker Historical Journal* no. 61: 17–26 (Spring 1997).

———. "J. Walter Malone: *The American Friend* and an Evangelical Quaker's Social Agenda." *Quaker History* 80(2): [63]–84 (1991).

———. Oliver, John. "Walter and Emma Malone: Friends of Sinners and the Poor," *Quaker Studies 6* (2) (March 2002): 195–210.

MOTT, LUCRETIA COFFIN

Mott, Lucretia C. *Lucretia Mott: Her Complete Speeches and Sermons*, ed. Dana Greene. New York: Edwin Mellen Press, 1980.

———. *Lucretia Mott Speaking: Excerpts from the Sermons and Speeches of a Famous Nineteenth Century Quaker Minister and Reformer,* comp. Margaret Hope Bacon. Pendle Hill Pamphlet, 234. Wallingford, Pa.: Pendle Hill Publications, 1980.

———. *Selected Correspondence of Lucretia Mott*, ed. Beverley Palmer, with Holly Byers Ochoa and Carol Faulkner. Urbana, Ill.: University of Illinois Press, 2002.

Bacon, Margaret Hope. *Valiant Friend: The Life of Lucretia Mott*. New York: Walker. 1980. 2nd ed., Philadelphia: Friends General Conference, 1999.

MURRAY, LINDLEY

Allott, Stephen. *Lindley Murray, 1745–1826 : Quaker Grammarian of New York and Old York*. York, England: Sessions Book Trust, 1991.

Monaghan, Charles. *The Murrays of Murray Hill*. Brooklyn, N.Y.: Urban History Press, 1998.

Van Ostade, Ingrid Tieken-Boon. *Two Hundred Years of Lindley Murray*, The Henry Sweet Society Studies in the History of Linguistics, vol. 2. Munster: Nodus Pulikationen, 1996.

NAYLER, JAMES

Nayler, James. *A Collection of Sundry Books, Epistles and Papers Written by James Nayler, Some of Which Were Never Before Printed: with an Impartial Relation of the Most Remarkable Transactions Relating to His Life*. London: J. Sowle, 1716. Reprint Cincinnati: B. C. Stanton, 1829; and as *Works*, ed. Emlyn Warren. 13 vol. in 5, with 4 suppl. in 3. Oxford, 1995–1996.

——. *Selections from the Writings of James Nayler*, ed. Brian Drayton. Worcester, Mass.: Mosher Book and Tract, New England Yearly Meeting, 1994. 2nd ed. 2001.

Bittle, William. *James Nayler, the Quaker Indicted by Parliament*. York, England: William Sessions; Richmond, Ind.: Friends United Press, 1986.

Damrosch, Leo. *The Sorrows of the Quaker Jesus: James Nayler and the Puritan Crackdown on the Free Spirit*. Cambridge, Mass.: Harvard University Press, 1996.

Massey, Vera. *The Clouded Quaker Star: James Nayler, 1618–1660*. York, England: Sessions Book Trust; Richmond, Ind.: Friends United Press, 1999.

Spencer, Carole. "James Nayler: Antinomina or Perfectionist?" *Quaker Studies* 6(1): 106–117 (October 2001)

NITOBE, INAZO OTA

Nitobe, Inazo Ota. *The Works of Inazo Nitobe*. 5 vols. [In English]. Tokyo: University of Tokyo Press, 1969–1972.

Oshiro, George M. "Mary P. E. Nitobe and Japan." *Quaker History* 86(2): 1–15 (Fall 1997).

Suzuki, Tadanobu. *Bridge across the Pacific: The Life of Inazo Nitobe, Friend of Justice and Peace*, Canadian Quaker Pamphlet, no. 41. Argenta, B.C.: Argenta Friends Press, 1994.

NIXON, RICHARD MILHOUS

Nixon, Richard. *The Memoirs of Richard Nixon*. New York: Grosset and Dunlap, 1978.

Aitken, Jonathan. *Nixon: A Life*. Washington, D.C.: Regnery, 1993.

Ambrose, Stephen E. *Nixon*. 3 vol. New York: Simon and Schuster, 1988–1992.

Hoff, Joan. *Nixon Reconsidered*. New York: Basic Books, 1994.

Kutler, Stanley I. *The Abuse of Power: The New Nixon Tapes*. New York: Simon and Schuster, 1997.

Morris, Roger. *Richard Milhous Nixon: The Rise of an American Politician*. New York: Holt, 1990.

Parmet, Herbert. *Richard Nixon and His America*. Boston: Little, Brown, 1990.

Strober, Gerald S., and Deborah H. Strober. *Nixon: An Oral History of His Presidency*. New York: HarperCollins, 1994.

Wicker, Tom. *One of Us: Richard Nixon and the American Dream*. New York: Random House, 1991.

NOEL-BAKER, PHILIP JOHN

Whittaker, D.J.. *Fighter for Peace: Philip Noel-Baker, 1889–1982*. York, England: William Sessions, 1989.

PAUL, ALICE

Gilmore, Inez Haynes. *The Story of the Woman's Party*. New York: Harcourt Brace, 1924. 2nd ed. as *Uphill with Banners Flying*, Penobscott, Maine: University of Maine Press, 1964. Reprinted as *The Story of Alice Paul and the National Woman's Party*, Fairfax, Va.: Denlinger's Publishers, 1977.

Lunardini, Christine A. *From Equal Suffrage to Equal Rights: Alice Paul and the National Woman's Party*. New York: New York University Press, 1986.

Fry, Amelia R. "Alice Paul." In Carol Stoneburner and John Stoneburner, eds., *The Influence of Quaker Women on American History: Biographical Studies in Women and Religion*. Vol 21. Lewiston, N.Y.: Edwin Mellen Press, 1986.

PENINGTON, ISAAC and MARY PROUDE SPRINGETT

Penington, Isaac. *The Works of the Long-Mournful and Sorely-Distressed Isaac Penington*. London: B. Clark, 1681. 4th ed. under title, *The Works of Isaac Penington, a Minister of the Gospel in the Society of Friends: Including His Letters.* 4 vol. Sherwoods, N.Y.: D. Heston, 1861–1863; Philadelphia: Friends' Book-Store, 1863. Reprint, Glenside, Pa.: Quaker Heritage Press, 1994–97.

——. *The Light Within, and Selected Writings*. Philadelphia: Tract Association of Friends of Philadelphia, 1983. Reprint, 1998.

Penington, Mary. *Some Account of Circumstances in the Life of Mary Penington: from Her Manuscript Left for Her Family*. London: printed for Harvey and Darton, 1821. Reprinted as *Experiences in the Life of Mary Pennington*, ed. Norman Penney. Philadelphia: Biddle Press, 1911; reprint London: Friends Historical Society, 1992.

Kohler, Charles. *Meet We Must: A Life of Mary Penington, 1623–1682*. London: Quaker Home Service, 1986.

PENN, WILLIAM

Penn, William. *The Papers of William Penn*, ed. Mary Maples Dunn, Richard S. Dunn, et al. 5 vol. Philadelphia: University of Pennsylvania Press, 1981–1987.

——. *The Peace of Europe; The Fruits of Solitude, and Other Writings*, ed. Edwin B. Bronner, Everyman Library. London: J.M. Dent; Rutland, Vt.: C.E. Tuttle, 1993.

——. *The Political Writings of William Penn,* ed. Andrew R. Murphy. Indianapolis: Liberty Fund, 2002.

——. *William Penn on Religion and Ethics: The Emergence of Quaker Liberalism*, ed. Hugh Barbour, Studies in American Religion, vol. 53. Lewiston, N.Y.: Edwin Mellen Press, 1991.

Dunn, Richard, and Mary Maples Dunn, eds. *The World of William Penn*. Philadelphia: University of Pennsylvania Press, 1986.

Endy, Melvin B. *William Penn and Early Quakerism*. Princeton: Princeton University Press, 1973.

Frost, J. William. "'Wear the Sword as Long as Thou Canst': William Penn in Myth and History." *Explorations in Early American Culture* 4: 13–45 (2000).

Geiter, Mary K. *William Penn, Profiles in Power*. Harlow, England: Longman, 2000.

PENNINGTON, LEVI TALBOTT

McNichols, Donald. *Portrait of a Quaker: Levi T. Pennington (1875–1975), A Critical Biography*. Newberg, Ore.: Barclay Press, 1980.

PERROT, JOHN

Carroll, Kenneth L. *John Perrot, Early Quaker Schismatic*, Journal of the Friends Historical Society, Suppl. 33. London: Friends Historical Society, 1971.

PICKETT, CLARENCE EVAN

Miller, Lawrence McK. *Witness for Humanity: A Biography of Clarence E. Pickett*. Wallingford, Pa.: Pendle Hill Publications, 1999.

PITMAN, DOROTHY

Pitman, Dorothy. *Four Score and Ten Years: Memoirs of Dorothy Pitman*. Hagerstown, Ind.: Exponent Publishers, 1992.

ROBERTS, ARTHUR O.

Roberts, Arthur O. *Drawn by the Light: Autobiographical Reflections of Arthur O. Roberts.* Newberg, Ore.: Barclay Press, 1993.

ROSS, ELIZABETH GRISCOM ("BETSY")

Morris, Robert. *The Truth about the Betsy Ross Story*. Beach Haven, N.J.: Wynnehaven, 1982.

ROWNTREE, JOHN WILHELM

Allott, Stephen. *John Wilhelm Rowntree, 1868–1905, and the Beginnings of Modern Quakerism*. York, England: Sessions Book Trust, 1994.

ROWNTREE, JOSEPH

Vernon, Anne. *A Quaker Business Man: The Life of Joseph Rowntree, 1836–1925.* London: George Allen and Unwin, 1958. Reprint, York, England: Sessions Book Trust, 1982.

RUSHMORE, JANE PALEN

Johnson, Emily Cooper. *Under Appointment: The Life of Jane P. Rushmore*. Philadelphia: University of Pennsylvania Press, 1953.

RUSTIN, BAYARD TAYLOR

Rustin, Bayard. *Down the Line*: *The Collected Writings of Bayard Rustin*. Chicago: Quadrangle Books, 1971.

Anderson, Jervis. *Bayard Rustin: Troubles I've Seen; a Biography*. New York: HarperCollins, 1997.

Haughton, Buzz. "Bayard Rustin: An Annotated Bibliography of Materials Relating to Rustin as a Quaker and Peace Activist." *Quaker Studies* 4(1): 56–67 (Summer 1999).

Levine, Daniel. *Bayard Rustin and the Civil Rights Movement*. New Brunswick, N.J. : Rutgers University Press, 2000.

SCHOFIELD, MARTHA

Smedley, Katherine. *Martha Schofield and the Re-education of the South, 1839–1916*. Studies in Women in Religion, vol. 24. Lewiston, N.Y.: Edwin Mellen Press, 1987.

SCOTT, JOB

Scott, Job. *Essays on Salvation by Christ: and the Debate That Followed Their Publication.* Glenside, Pa.: Quaker Heritage Press, 1993.

SEEGER, DANIEL A.

Bien, Peter and Chuck Fager, eds. *In Stillness There Is Fullness: A Peacemaker's Harvest; Essays and Reflections in Honour of Daniel A. Seeger's Found Decades of Quaker Service*. Bellefonte, Pa.: Kimo Press, [2000].

Irons, Peter. *The Courage of Their Convictions*. New York: Free Press; London: Collier Macmillan, 1988. 2nd ed. with subtitle, *Sixteen Americans Who Fought Their Way to the Supreme Court*. New York: Penguin, 1990, 155–178.

SEIN, HEBERTO M.

Sein, Suzanne Fehr. "Heberto Sein: International Interpreter." In Leonard S. Kenworthy, ed. *Living in the Light, Some Pioneers of the 20th Century.* Vol. 2, *In the Wider World*. Kennett Square, Pa.: Friends General Conference and Quaker Publications, 1984–1985.

SMITH, HANNAH WHITALL

Smith, Hannah Whitall. *The Unselfishness of God and How I Discovered It: A Spiritual Autobiography*. New York: Fleming H. Revell, 1903. Reprint, Ulrichsville, Ohio: Barbour, 1993.

Henry, Marie. *The Secret Life of Hannah Whitall Smith*. Grand Rapids, Mich: Chosen Books, 1984.

Strachey, Barbara. *Remarkable Relations: The Story of the Pearsall Smith Family*. London: Gollanscz, 1980. U.S. ed. subtitled *The Story of the Pearsall Smith Women*. New York: Universe Books, 1982.

STANTON, ELIZABETH CADY

Banner, Lois. *Elizabeth Cady Stanton: A Radical for Women's Rights*. Boston: Little Brown, 1980.

Griffith, Elisabeth. *In Her Own Right: The Life of Elizabeth Cady Stanton*. New York : Oxford University Press, 1984.

Pellauer, Mary D. *Towards a Tradition of Feminist Theology: The Religious Social Thought of Elizabeth Cady Stanton, Susan B. Anthony, and Anna Howard*

Shaw. Chicago Studies in the History of American Religion, vol. 15. Brooklyn, N.Y.: Carlson, 1991.

STEERE, DOUGLAS VAN

Hinson, E. Glenn. *Love at the Heart of Things: A Biography of Douglas V. Steere*. Wallingford, Pa.: Pendle Hill Publications; Nashville: Upper Room Books, 1998.

STEPHEN, CAROLINE

Tod, Robert J. N. *Caroline Stephen, Quaker Mystic, 1834–1909*. Birmingham, England: 1978.

STURGE, JOSEPH

Tyrrell, Alex. *Joseph Sturge and the Moral Radical Party in Early Victorian Britain.* London: Christopher Helm, 1987.

SYKES, MARJORIE

Sykes, Marjorie. *In Quaker Friendship: Letters from Marjorie Sykes to Martha Dart, 1967 to 1994*, comp. and ed. Martha Dart. London: William Sessions, 1999.

——. *Transcending Tradition: Excerpts from the Writings and Talks of*. . . . York, England: William Sessions, in association with Woodbrooke College, 1995.

Dart, Martha. *Marjorie Sykes, a Quaker–Ghandian*. York, England: Sessions Book Trust, in Association with Woodbrooke College, 1993.

THOMAS, MARTHA CAREY

Thomas, M. Carey. *The Making of a Feminist: Early Journals and Letters of M. Carey Thomas*, ed. Marjorie Housepian Dobkin. Kent, Ohio: Kent State University Press, 1979.

Lefkowitz, Helen. *The Power and Passion of M. Carey Thomas*. New York: Alfred A. Knopf, 1994.

TRUEBLOOD, DAVID ELTON

Trueblood, D. Elton. *A Life of Search*. Richmond, Ind.: Friends United Press, 1996. Newby, James R. *Elton Trueblood, Believer, Teacher, and Friend*. San Francisco: Harper and Row, 1990.

TUKE, SAMUEL and WILLIAM and SARAH

Sessions, William K. *The Tukes of York in the Seventeenth, Eighteenth and Nineteenth Centuries*. London: Friends Historical Society, 1971.

UPDEGRAFF, DAVID BRAINERD

Bill, J. Brent. *David B. Updegraff: Quaker Holiness Preacher.* Richmond, Ind.: Friends United Press, 1983.

VAN DER MERWE, HENDRIK W.: Van der Merwe, H. W. *Peacemaking in South Africa: A Life in Conflict Resolution*. Cape Town: Tafelberg, 2000.

VINING, ELIZABETH GRAY: Jones, Mary Hoxie. "Elizabeth Gray Vining: The Measure of a Life." In Leonard S. Kenworthy, ed. *Living in the Light: Some Quaker Pioneers of the 20th Century*. Vol. 1, *In the U.S.A*. Kennett Square, Pa.: Friends General Conference and Quaker Publications, 1984–1985.

WATSON, ELIZABETH and GEORGE

Watson, Elizabeth. *Guests of My Life*. Burnsville, N.C.: Celo Press, 1979.

——. *This I Know Experimentally*, Rufus Jones lecture, 1977. Philadelphia: Religious Education Committee, Friends General Conference, 1977.

WHITTIER, JOHN GREENLEAF

Whittier, John Greenleaf. *Letters of John Greenleaf Whittier*, ed. John B. Pickard. 3 vol. Cambridge, Mass.: Belknap Press of Harvard University Press, 1975.

——. *The Poetry of John Greenleaf Whittier: A Readers' Edition*, ed. William Jolliff. Richmond, Ind: Friends United Press, 2000.

Von Frank, Albert J. *Whittier: A Comprehensive Annotated Bibliography*. New York: Garland, 1976.

Warren, Robert Penn. *John Greenleaf Whittier's Poetry: An Appraisal and a Selection*. Minneapolis: University of Minnesota Press, 1971. Reprint, 1992.Woodwell, Roland H. *John Greenleaf Whittier: A Biography*. Haverhill, Mass.: John Greenleaf Whittier Homestead, 1985.

WILLCUTS, JACK L.

Willcuts, Jack L. *The Sense of the Meeting: Editorial Writings of Jack L. Willcuts,* ed. Susan Willcuts Kendall. Newberg, Ore.: Barclay Press, 1992.

WILSON, EDWARD RAYMOND

Wilson, E. Raymond. *Thus Far on My Journey*. Richmond, Ind.: Friends United Press, 1976.

Levering, Samuel R. "E. Raymond Wilson: Practical Quaker Dreamer." In Leonard S. Kenworthy, ed., *Living in the Light: Some Quaker Pioneers of the 20th Century*. Vol. 1, *In the U.S.A*. Kennett Square, Pa.: Friends General Conference and Quaker Publications, 1984–1985.

WINSTANLEY, GERRARD

Boulton, David. *Gerrard Winstanley and the Republic of Heaven*. Dent, England: Dales Historical Monographs, 1999.

Bradstock, Andrew, ed. *Winstanley and the Diggers, 1649–1999*. Portland, Ore.: Frank Cass, 2000.

WOOLMAN, JOHN

Woolman, John. *The Works of John Woolman: in Two Parts*. Philadelphia: printed by Joseph Crukshank, 1774. 2 vol. (vol. 1: The *Journal*; vol. 2: Major essays). Reprint as *The Journal and Major Essays of John Woolman*, ed. by Phillips P. Moulton, A Library of Protestant Thought. New York: Oxford University Press, 1971. Reprint, Richmond, Ind.: Friends United Press, 1989.

Birkel, Michael L. "John Woolman on the Cross." In *The Lamb's War: Quaker Essays to Honor Hugh Barbour*, ed. Michael L. Birkel and John W. Newman. Richmond, Ind.: Earlham College Press, 1992, pp. 91–100.

Dodson, Shirley, ed. *John Woolman's Spirituality and Our Contemporary Witness: A Study Guide Based on the Autumn, 1994, Pendle Hill Monday*

Evening Lecture Series. Philadelphia: Philadelphia Yearly Meeting Religious Education Committee; Wallingford, Pa.: Pendle Hill, 1995.

Heller, Mike, ed. *The Tendering Presence: Essays on John Woolman.* Wallingford, Pa.: Pendle Hill Publications, 2003.

Olmsted, Sterling. *Motions of Love: Woolman as Mystic and Activist*. Pendle Hill Pamphlet, 312. Wallingford, Pa.: Pendle Hill Publications, 1993.

——. and Mike Heller, eds. *John Woolman: A Nonviolence and Social Change Source Book*. Wilmington, Ohio: Wilmington College Peace Resource Center, 1997.

Sox, David. *John Woolman, Quintessential Quaker, 1720 to 1772*. York, England: Sessions Book Trust; Richmond, Ind.: Friends United Press, 1999.

Index

Note: Bold page numbers refer to main entries in the dictionary.

The Contributors

Margery Post Abbott
Rose Adede
Paul N. Anderson
Margaret Hope Bacon
Jacalynn Stuckey Baker
Hugh Barbour
Larry Barker
Gayle D. Beebe
Claus Bernet
Elise Boulding
Irv Brendlinger
Dan Cammack
Max L. Carter
Elizabeth Cazden
Mary Ellen Chijioke
Diego Chuyma
Andrew Clark
Wilmer A. Cooper
Karen Cromley
Peter Curtis
Kathryn A. Damiano
Pink Dandelion
Martha Dart
Martin Davie
Christopher Densmore
David Edinger
Lon Fendall
Dean Freiday
J. William Frost
Loida Eunice Fernandez Gonzales
Michael P. Graves
Martha Paxson Grundy
Douglas Gwyn
Deborah Haines
Thomas D. Hamm
Buzz Haughton
Andrea Constantine Hawkes
Thomas Head
Michael Allen Heller
Ralph Hetherington
Damon D. Hickey
Jan Hoffman
Peggy Hollingsworth
Larry Ingle
David L. Johns
T. Canby Jones
Louisa M. Kaufman
Cynthia Earl Kerman
Jennifer Kinghorn
Alan Kolp
Bill Kostlevy
Paul Lacey
Emma Jones Lapsansky
James Le Shana
Rose Lewis
Karna Linden
Patricia Loring
Pam Lunn

Howard R. Macy
Édgar Amílcar Madrid
Jack D. Marietta
Johan Maurer
David W. Maxey
David McFadden
William F. Medlin
Lawrence McK. Miller
Esther Mombo
Howard W. Moore
Rosemary Anne Moore
Geoffrey Morries
James Morris
Esther Greenleaf Mürer
Michi Nakamura
Mike Nellis
James R. Newby
Sabron Reynolds Newton
Eva Anna Nixon
John W. Oliver
T. Vail Palmer Jr.
Frank Parkinson
Franco Perna
David Purnell
Hugh S. Pyper
Ron Rembert
Arthur O. Roberts
June Rose
Virginia Schurman
Janet Scott
Edward F. Snyder
Carole Spencer
Ron Stansell
Jack Sutter
Frances Irene Taber
William P. Taber
Michele Lise Tarter
Konrad Temple
Nancy Thomas
Carole B. Treadway
Lonnie Valentine
T. H. S. Wallace
David Williams
John P. Williams Sr.
Lloyd Lee Wilson
Warren Witte

Members of the Advisory Committee

Paul N. Anderson (1956–) is professor of Biblical and Quaker Studies at George Fox University in Oregon, where he has taught since 1989. Prior to his service at George Fox he served in pastoral and educational ministries among Friends in Northwest Yearly Meeting, Indiana Yearly Meeting, and Evangelical Friends Church–Eastern Region. Anderson received his undergraduate and graduate degrees from Malone College and Earlham School of Religion, and his Ph.D. in New Testament from the University of Glasgow in Scotland. His book, *The Christology of the Fourth Gospel*, was published in Germany and the United States in 1996 and 1997, and his "Meet the Friends" series has received a wide distribution. Anderson compiled the report of the 1985 World Gathering of Young Friends and edited the *Evangelical Friend* from 1990 to1994. He is currently editor of *Quaker Religious Thought* and an organizer of Quaker Theological Discussion Group.

Hugh Barbour (1921–) was born in Beijing, educated in England, and obtained degrees from Harvard and Yale Universities. He taught for 38 years at Earlham College and Earlham School of Religion (after teaching at Syracuse and Wellesley). He wrote *The Quakers* (with Jerry Frost), *Early Quaker Writings* (with Arthur Roberts), and *The Quakers in Puritan England*. He and his wife, Sirkka, served as Resident Friends at Cambridge.

Gayle Beebe (1959–) was born in Eugene, Oregon, to Quaker parents. A recorded minister in the Friends Church, he has served as pastor at churches in Oregon and California. He received his bachelor's degree from George Fox University, a master's in strategic management from Claremont Graduate University in California in 1997, and a doctorate in religion and theology from Claremont in 1997. Beebe was the director of the Friends Center at Azusa Pacific University in California from 1998 to 2000 before becoming president and professor of theology and religion at Spring Arbor College in Michigan.

Diego Chuyma (1963–) became a lay pastor in 1984 after completing high school in Pucarani, Bolivia, and taught at the Friends School in La Paz and in other Bolivian schools until 1987. Elected first as youth superintendent of Cordillera District for the Friends Church, in 1987 he became youth superintendent of the *Iglesia Nacional Evangélica "Los Amigos" Boliviana* (National Evangelical Friends Church of Bolivia). Following study at Pendle Hill, Pennsylvania, in 1987–1988, he earned a bachelor's degree in Pastoral Ministries with a minor in Missions at Barclay College in Haviland, Kansas, in 1992, and then in 1995 was awarded a master's in divinity from Azusa Pacific University in California. In 1995, he returned to Santa Cruz, Bolivia, and established "Nueva Esperanza" Friends Church where he is currently the pastor. Chuyma established, and now is director of, the Centro Teologico los Amigos (Friends Theological Center), composed of Quaker theology students in the Universidad Evangélica Boliviana where he has taught since 1995.

Loida Eunice Fernandez Gonzales (1950–) is a member of Ciudad Victoria Monthly Meeting in Mexico and studied theology in Mexico City before joining the staff of Friends World Committee for Consultation (FWCC) in 1978. She was the first executive secretary for the COAL, an organization of Latin American Friends formed in 1978 under the auspices of FWCC. Her mother, Albertina, was a clerk of the Reunión General Iglesia de los Amigos (General Gathering of Mexican Friends) in the 1960s. Currently, Fernandez is actively involved in facilitating the translation and production of Quaker literature in Spanish as the staff person for FWCC in Latin America.

William J. Frost (1940–) received his undergraduate education at DePauw University in Indiana and his graduate degrees at the University of Wisconsin. He has been on the religion faculty and director of the Friends Historical Library at Swarthmore College since 1973 and is currently the Jenkens Professor of Quaker History. He has written extensively about Friends including *The Quaker Family in Colonial America*, and coauthored *The Quakers* with Hugh Barbour.

Corilda Grover (1950–) has been active in the work of Friends World Committee for Consultation (FWCC) since attending the 1985 World Conference of Young Friends in North Carolina. A member of Northwest Yearly Meeting of Friends Church, she served as executive secretary of FWCC, Section of the Americas, from 1998 to 2002.

Martha Paxson Grundy (1939–) is a member of the Cleveland Monthly Meeting of Lake Erie and was the first clerk of the oversight committee for the Travelling Ministries Program of Friends General Conference (FGC). She obtained her Ph.D. in American history from Case Western Reserve University in Cleveland, Ohio, in 1990. She is married to Kenneth Grundy and the mother of three children. Grundy has served in various roles with FGC, including recording clerk of their Central Committee from 1987 to 1993. She was clerk of Lake Erie Yearly Meeting from 1990 to 1992 and on the board of *Friends Journal* from 1993 to 1996. Her book, *Resistance and Obedience to God: Memoirs of David Ferris (1707–1779),* was published in 2001.

Thomas Hamm (1957–) was born in New Castle, Indiana. He was educated at Butler University in Indiana and received his Ph.D. in history from Indiana University in 1985. Since 1987 he has served as archivist and professor of history at Earlham College. He is a lifelong member of Indiana Yearly Meeting and author of numerous articles on Quaker history as well as several books including *The Transformation of American Quakerism* (1988) and *God's Government Begun* (1995).

Emma Jones Lapsansky (1945–) is a member of the Philadelphia Yearly Meeting and has been professor of history and curator of special collections at Haverford College since 1995. In the 1960s, she worked with the National Council of Churches Delta Ministry on civil rights in Mississippi. She obtained her bachelor's and master's degrees as well as a doctorate in American civilization in 1975 from the University of Pennsylvania. She has also taught at Temple University in Pennsylvania, the University of Pennsylvania, and Princeton University in New Jersey. Her book, *Neighborhoods in Transition: William Penn's Dream and Urban Reality*, was published in 1994. She has served on the boards of Friends Central School and Lansdowne Friends School in Pennsylvania, was on the Advisory Committee for Friends Council on Education from

1992 to 1995 and coordinates a care circle for PWA. She is also active as a lecturer and consultant on family and community life, architecture and community planning, religion and popular culture in 19th-century America as well as Quaker history, and she leads workshops on fighting racism, sexism, and homophobia.

Esther Mombo (1957–) was born in Kisii District, Kenya, and is a member of the Getembe Monthly Meeting of Bware Yearly Meeting. After high school, she studied theology at St. Paul's United Theological College, Limuru, and did an M.Phil at Trinity College, Dublin, and a Ph.D. at Edinburgh University. She has taught high school and later at theological colleges. Currently she is the academic dean of St. Paul's United Theological College, doing administration as well as teaching in History and Women Studies.

John Punshon (1935–) became a convinced Friend while a student at Oxford University. With a view to a political career, he served as a city councilman, stood for Parliament twice, and worked for some time in the field of trade union law. In 1979, he became Quaker studies tutor at Woodbrooke Quaker Study Centre in Birmingham, England, and was professor of Quaker studies at Earlham College and Earlham School of Religion in Indiana from 1991 until his retirement in 2001. Widely appreciated as a speaker at Quaker events worldwide, he also preached regularly while living in the United States and is a recorded minister in Indiana Yearly Meeting. His books include *Portrait in Grey: A Short History of the Quakers* (1984), *Encounter With Silence* (1987), *Testimony and Tradition* (the 1990 Swarthmore Lecture) and *Reasons for Hope: The Faith and Future of the Friends Church* (2001).

Arthur Roberts (1923–) was raised in the Quaker community of Greenleaf, Idaho, and studied at Pacific College (now George Fox University), Nazarene Theological Seminary, and received his Ph.D. from Boston University. He is a recorded minister in Northwest Yearly Meeting and taught religion at the then George Fox College from 1953 to 1988. More recently he was the mayor of Yachats, Oregon, for two terms. A prolific writer and poet, Roberts edited *Concern* magazine for the Association of Evangelical Friends (now Evangelical Friends International) from 1947 to 1970, and then edited *Quaker Religious Thought* from 1990 through 2000. His numerous books on theology, history, and inspirational topics include *Through the Flaming Sword* (1959) on George Fox, *Early Quaker Writings* (1973, with Hugh Barbour), *Tomorrow Is Growing Old: Stories of Quakers in Alaska* (1978), *Messengers of God: The Sensuous Side of Spirituality* (1996), and his spiritual autobiography, *Drawn by the Light* (1993).

Janet Scott (1941–) holds degrees from the University of Cambridge, the Open University, and the University of London and is currently working at the University of Cambridge teaching Religious Studies and Religious Education in the Faculty of Education. She gave a Swarthmore lecture in 1980 published as *What Canst Thou Say*, and served as clerk of Meeting for Sufferings from 1992 until 1995. Scott was one of the team of clerks at the World Conference of Friends in 1991 and represents Friends on the World Council of Churches Faith and Order Commission.

Nancy J. Thomas (1945–) was born in Iowa and holds a B.A. in Spanish from George Fox College (1968), a master's degree in secondary education from the University of Oregon (1969), and a Ph.D. in Intercultural Studies from Fuller Theological Seminary (1998). She and her husband, Harold, have served as missionaries to Bolivia under Northwest Yearly Meeting of Friends from 1972 to 1989 and from 1999 to the present. Since 1999, Hal and Nancy have co-directed the Center for Intercultural Studies at the Universidad Evangélica Boliviana in Santa Cruz, Bolivia.

Carol Treadway (1938–) is a birthright Friend raised in Ohio Yearly Meeting-Conservative. She later joined North Carolina Yearly Meeting (Conservative) while serving as librarian of the Friends Historical Collection, Guilford College in Greensboro, North Carolina. She is editor of *The Southern Friend: Journal of the North Carolina Friends Historical Society* and other publications of the society.

About the Authors

Margery Post Abbott lives in Portland, Oregon, and is a "Released Friend" who writes about Quakerism and travels in the ministry with the support of her Monthly Meeting. Her book *A Certain Kind of Perfection* (1996) brings together the writings of evangelical and liberal Quakers from North America, Europe, and Australia. She is working on *Public Friends: A Ministry for the 21st Century*, a book that explores modern experience of travel in the ministry among Friends worldwide. She has also published numerous articles and pamphlets about Friends and lectured at numerous venues including Earlham School of Religion in Richmond, Indiana, Woodbrooke Quaker Study Centre in Birmingham, England, and the 1997 International Quaker Consultation on Identity, Authority, and Community. Abbott has been deeply involved in various Quaker organizations and served as presiding clerk of the independent North Pacific Yearly Meeting, co-clerked the first Pacific Northwest Quaker Women's Theology Conference bringing together women from the liberal and evangelical branches of Friends, and participated in the Fifth World Conference of Friends in Chavakali, Kenya.

Mary Ellen Chijioke is director of the Hege Library at Guilford College in North Carolina after having served as curator of the Friends Historical Library of Swarthmore College in Pennsylvania, the academic center of "Hicksite" Quakerism. She has an academic background in both African and Quaker studies and has had professional responsibility for one of the world's premier research libraries on Quaker history. Her more than 15 years in Africa, including three in Kenya where she was active in Quaker affairs, has given her an international perspective and a firsthand knowledge of the results of Quaker evangelism. For many years she wrote the biennial review of recent literature for the journal *Quaker History* and is currently coediting Willis R. Hotchkiss's diary.

Pink Dandelion is programmes leader for the Centre for Postgraduate Quaker Studies, which is a collaboration between Woodbrooke Quaker Study Centre and the University of Birmingham, England. He is also director of the Centre for Quaker Studies at the University of Sunderland, and an honorary lecturer in the Department of Theology at the University of Birmingham, England. His books include *The Sociological Analysis of The Theology of Quakers* (1996), *Heaven on Earth: Quakers and the Second Coming* (1998), and *God the Trickster?* (2001). He is convener of the Quaker Studies Research Association and editor of the fully refereed journal *Quaker Studies*.

John William Oliver Jr. is professor emeritus of the history department at Malone College in Ohio. He is clerk/convener of the Quaker Historians and Archivists biennial conferences and has served on the executive committee of the Ohio Academy of History. Oliver has written extensively on Walter and Emma Malone, issues of race and gender among Quakers in Kenya, and Quakers in Cleveland, Ohio, in the late 19th century. He is currently writing a biography of the Malones and coediting the diary of Willis R. Hotchkiss, a Quaker missionary to Kenya. He edited the book *J. Walter Malone: The Autobiography of an Evangelical Quaker* (1993). In addition to his work in Quaker history, he serves as coordinator for the North American Chapter of the Orthodox Peace Fellowship and is coeditor of *Cradles of Conscience: Ohio's Independent Colleges and Universities* (2003) and also coeditor with Charles and Carolyn Cherry of a forthcoming history of Quaker colleges in the United States.